Charles Wilson

The recovery of Jerusalem

A narrative of exploration and discovery in the city and the Holy Land

Charles Wilson

The recovery of Jerusalem
A narrative of exploration and discovery in the city and the Holy Land

ISBN/EAN: 9783337282677

Printed in Europe, USA, Canada, Australia, Japan

Cover: Foto ©ninafisch / pixelio.de

More available books at **www.hansebooks.com**

THE
RECOVERY OF JERUSALEM.

A NARRATIVE OF

EXPLORATION AND DISCOVERY IN THE CITY
AND THE HOLY LAND.

By CAPT. WILSON, R. E., CAPT. WARREN, R. E.,

ETC., ETC., ETC.

With an Introduction

BY

ARTHUR PENRHYN STANLEY, D. D.,

DEAN OF WESTMINSTER.

EDITED BY

WALTER MORRISON, M. P.,

HONORARY TREASURER TO THE PALESTINE EXPLORATION FUND.

NEW YORK:
D. APPLETON & COMPANY,
549 & 551 BROADWAY.
1871.

EDITOR'S PREFACE.

The following pages are put forth in the hope that they will be found to contribute in no small measure to our knowledge of the Holy City and the sacred localities about it; that they will help to show not only what is known, but what is unknown; and that they will serve as a further aid to real students of the Book which gives this volume all its interest.

The Editor thinks it desirable to give a few words of explanation by way of preface. The work of the Fund had grown so much upon the hands of the Committee, had assumed dimensions so much larger than was originally contemplated, that it became important to devise some means, besides the medium of the "Quarterly Statement" issued by the Fund, of summing up and popularizing the main results obtained. This has been done in the following pages. In this volume will be found, besides other papers, an account of Captain Wilson's Survey, for which the necessary funds were supplied by Miss Burdett Coutts; and of the excavations in Jerusalem itself by Captain Warren, illustrated by plans and wood-cuts. It is due to Captain Warren to state that his interesting and valuable narrative has been drawn up under heavy pressure, owing to shortness of time and ill-health. Returning to England in May, suffering from fever and exhaustion caused by work more arduous and anxious than can be here explained, he found himself called upon not only to prepare a complete account of his excavations, but also to give at several meetings an oral statement.*

The limits of this volume have compelled the Editor, most unwillingly, to make considerable reductions in Captain Warren's original paper. Care has been taken to preserve all that relates to the actual work, while his conclusions are given in full. The revised paper has been submitted to Captain Warren.

Ill-health has prevented Mr. Deutsch from contributing an essay on the Moabite Stone, as had been originally contemplated. There will be found, however, an accurate history of the finding and the steps taken for the recovery of the stone, with two of the latest translations.

The Editor has to record his thanks to Mr. Greville

---

* There are five illustrations for which the thanks of the Editor are due to the manager of the " Illustrated London News." These are, the two full-page engravings of Wilson's Arch and Robinson's Arch, and the three small ones of the shafts at the Southeast Angle, the Golden Gateway, and the chamber at the Northeast Angle. All of these, except the last, which is from a sketch by Captain Warren, were taken in Jerusalem, by Mr. Simpson, who examined all the works in company with him. They subsequently appeared in the " Illustrated London News;" and permission has been very kindly given to reproduce them here with some slight alterations made by Captain Warren himself.

Chester and Mr. Phené Spiers for their valuable contributions, prepared at very short notice.

He must, also, express his gratitude to the Count de Vogüé for the fulfilment of his promise to contribute his paper on the Hauran. He was already at the front with the French army, occupied in his noble work with the ambulance corps, when a letter from the Secretary reached him, reminding him of the promised contribution. He hastened back to Paris, sent off the MS., which wanted only the last paragraphs, and returned to his post. The translation has been made with great care, and, though it has not had the author's personal revision, it will be found as interesting as it is important.

With regard to the title: more than two-thirds of the volume are concerned with the Holy City itself, while the remaining pages describe explorations in that range of country which, in a wide sense, may be considered the Holy Land. It is hoped, therefore, that the adoption for its title of the old Crusading watchword, the "Recovery of Jerusalem," will be thought germane to the general object of the Society under whose auspices it was put forth. That old cry pointed to the Land as well as to the City, and may fairly be used for the purpose of the new Crusade. The materials for the book, with the exception of those on the surveys of Jerusalem and Sinai, carried out under the direction of Colonel Sir Henry James, R. E., and that by the Count de Vogüé, have been entirely furnished by the expeditions organized by the Palestine Exploration Fund.

It had been originally intended that it should be edited by the Honorary Officers of the Fund; but the pressure of other labors threw this duty on one of the Treasurers.

9, PALL MALL EAST,
  November, 1870.

TABLE OF CONTENTS.

	PAGE
PREFACE	v
INTRODUCTION BY THE DEAN OF WESTMINSTER	xiii

PART I.

ORDNANCE SURVEY OF JERUSALEM BY CAPTAIN WILSON, R. E. . . 3
EXCAVATIONS AT JERUSALEM BY CAPTAIN WARREN, R. E. :
   CHAP. I. Commencement of Operations 26
      II. Method of Mining adopted 42
      III. West Wall of Noble Sanctuary . . . 58
          Wilson's Arch 58
          Robinson's Arch 72
          Suburban Gates of Second Temple . . . 86
      IV. Southern Wall 91
      V. Eastern Wall and Southeast Angle . . . 105
          Northeast Angle . . . 124
      VI. North Side 147
          Bethesda, according to Early Tradition . 152
          Souterrain No. 1. Convent of Sisters of Sion 154
          Souterrain No. 2. Convent of Sisters of Sion . 157
      VII. Tanks and Souterrains of the Sanctuary . . 159
      VIII. Important Discovery north of the Platform of the Dome of the
          Rock 170
          Important Discovery on the Sakhra . 172
          Solomon's Stables . . . 176
      IX. The Waters of Jerusalem . 182
          Aqueducts from Solomon's Pools . 182
          Virgin's Fount and Pools of Siloam 186
          Rock-cut Aqueducts in Kedron Valley . 199
          Chasm in Rock at Lifta . . . 206

		PAGE
Chap. X. The Holy City	. .	209
Muristan	.	210
Gate Gennath	.	213
Damascus Gate	. .	215
Excavation at British Cemetery	. .	218
Shaft in Valley Street	.	218
XI. Ophel . . .	. .	222
Ophel Wall .	. .	224
Extra Tower , , , , ,	. .	228
Cavern in Front of Triple Gate	. .	230
Sculptured Slab .	. .	235
Khalat al Jaluid .	. .	235
The Holy City .	. .	236
Sarcophagus . . .	.	237
XII. The Temple of Herod .	.	241
The Temple of Solomon . .		243
Solomon's Palace .	. .	249
Appendices		255

PART II.

Sea of Galilee. By Captain Wilson, R. E. . . .	263
The Architectural Remains of Palestine. By R. Phené Spiers, Esq.	302
The Hauran. By the Count de Vogüé	319
The Survey of Palestine. By Lieutenant Anderson, R. E. .	341
On the Pottery and Glass found in the Excavations. By the Rev. Greville J. Chester	368
Moabite Stone	383
Sinai. By the Rev. F. W. Holland	403

LIST OF ILLUSTRATIONS.

	PAGE
ROBINSON'S ARCH	*Frontispiece*
HARAM AREA, OR NOBLE SANCTUARY	7
SHAFT AT SOUTHEAST ANGLE	26
HESBAN	33
WILSON'S ARCH	58
Do. do. (*from tracing*)	62
CAPITAL OF PILASTER	68
EASTERN END OF VAULT	71
VOUSSOIR OF FALLEN ARCH	81
BASE OF COLUMN	82
LAMP	83
SOUTH AND EAST WALL	92
ANCIENT JAR	109, 371
INCISED CHARACTERS	111
STONE C OF EASTERN WALL	112
GALLERY AT SOUTHEAST ANGLE	115
ANCIENT MARKS ON HANDLES OF VASES	118, 369
GALLERY AT GOLDEN GATE	121
NEWLY-DISCOVERED PASSAGE IN OLD WALL	129
SECTION THROUGH BIRKET ISRAIL	147
TRIPLE GATE	179
ROCK-CUT PASSAGE ABOVE VIRGIN'S FOUNT	195
ROCK-CUT TOMB	200
DORIC CAPITAL, SILOAM	207
GENNATH GATE	214
ROCK IN MOUNT MORIAH	222
MONUMENTAL SLAB	225
JERUSALEM AT TIME OF KING HEROD	236
FORD OVER THE JORDAN	261
THE LAKE OF GALILEE	263
TEL HUM	266

LIST OF ILLUSTRATIONS.

Temple of Hibbariyeh
Temple of Theltha
Architecture of the Hauran
Upper Valley of the Jordan
Valley of the Jordan
Valley of Shechem
Four-lipped Lamp
Ancient Dish
Portion of Large Jar
Portion of Large Jar
Vase found at Birket Israil
Potter's Mark
Potter's Mark
Lamps
Inscribed Lamp
Lamp—Pool of Bethesda
Glass Vase from Sepulchral Cave
Glass Lamp
Stone Weight
Seal of Haggai
Sarcophagus
Copper Lamp-stand
Sinai
Map of Peninsula of Sinai

INTRODUCTION.

BY THE DEAN OF WESTMINSTER.

The Committee of the Palestine Exploration Fund having done me the honor of asking me to write a Preface to the collected papers of the Society, I gladly comply, though not without a misgiving lest I should do injustice to a subject on which, full of absorbing interest as it once was to me, and dear as it must now be for its own sake, as well as for the memories of past years, I have been prevented by the pressure of other occupations from bestowing the continuous attention that it deserves.

It has seemed to me that the simplest and most useful mode of introducing this volume to the public would be, to point out in each essay what are the most important additions to our knowledge—especially in the light of such hopes or anticipations as I, in common with others, some fourteen years ago ventured faintly to express.

I. The first and most important of all the sites of Palestine, and that which occupies the largest portion and furnishes the title of the following pages, is the ancient city of Jerusalem.

When I first visited Palestine in 1852, I felt constrained

to express what has doubtless occurred to many others, that, when we pass from the comparatively secure knowledge of what may be called the external situation * of the city to its internal relations, we exchange a sphere of perfect certainty for a mass of topographical controversy, unequalled for its extent, for its confusion, and for its bitterness. If the materials, however slight, on which our judgment was to be formed were all before us, it might be worth while to attempt to unravel the entanglement. But the reverse is the case. The data exist, perhaps in abundance, but they are inaccessible. When Jerusalem can be excavated we shall be able to agree; till then the dispute is for the most part as hopeless as was that concerning the Roman Forum before the discovery of the pedestal of the column of Phocas." †

This hope has been fulfilled. At last the excavations of Jerusalem have been begun, slowly and gradually indeed, but, when these pages are read, it will probably be thought, as rapidly as the circumstances would permit. In the plain and unadorned narrative of Captain Warren, the difficulties and dangers of the undertaking might almost escape notice. Yet the perils will appear sufficiently great to any one who draws out from the good-humored story the fact that these

---

* There is one point, in the external topography of Jerusalem, in which Captain Warren has corrected an erroneous conclusion, which I shared in company with most others who have written on the subject. He has called attention to what I confess seems to me so incontrovertible, that I wonder how it should so long have escaped notice—that the valley or ravine of Hinnom, instead of being confined, as it has been usually in modern times confined, to the valley *south* of Jerusalem, includes, if it is not identical with, the glen of the Kedron *east* of the city. This appears to follow beyond question from Jer. xix. 11; and it agrees, not only with the Mussulman nomenclature, but with almost all the Biblical indications on the subject, and especially with the word Ge-hinnom.

† "Sinai and Palestine," Chap. III.

excavations were carried on at the constant risk of life and limb to the bold explorers. The whole series of their progress was a succession of "lucky escapes" (p. 42). Huge stones were day after day ready to fall, and sometimes did fall, on their heads (p. 193). One of the explorers was "injured so severely that he could barely crawl out into the open air" (p. 66); another extricated himself with difficulty, torn and bleeding; while another was actually buried under the ruins (p. 217). Sometimes they were almost suffocated by the stifling heat; at other times they were plunged for hours up to their necks in the freezing waters of some subterranean torrent (p. 188); sometimes blocked up by a falling mass, without light or escape (p. 102). And these labors had to be carried on not with the assistance of those on the spot, but in spite of the absurd obstacles thrown in the way of work by that singular union of craft, ignorance, and stupidity, which can only be found in Orientals—workmen who in "winter could never get the idea drummed into their heads that working would make them warm" (p. 53). Turkish dignitaries believing that the sacred rock lies on the top leaves of a palm-tree, from the roots of which spring all the rivers of earth, and with a ready pretence for evading every request * (pp. 28, 31).

The readers of these pages will be compensated by being thus enabled to form the acquaintance of such good and tried friends as Captain Warren and his faithful Achates, Sergeant Birtles. We trust that they are compensated by the results of their labors.

To these I briefly turn.

---

* It is gratifying to find that the French archæologists seem generously to have given their aid to the work (pp. 62, 157).

1. The original stimulus to the whole undertaking was supplied by the benevolent wish of Miss Burdett Coutts to ascertain the best means of bringing water to the thirsty city. The answer to this is given in the excellent Ordnance Survey, accomplished under the auspices of Captain Wilson, and the elaborate description of the ancient water supplies given by Captain Warren (p. 182). It may be added that in this investigation the interesting question of the supposed spring inside the walls of Jerusalem and under the Temple Courts has been for the first time followed to the bottom; and the result appears to be that, while there is no actual spring within the walls, the whole mount is so honey-combed with cisterns (pp. 14, 17) as to give ample materials for the conjecture of Tacitus, and for the imagery of Scripture, while at the same time it takes away from them the foundation of exact and literal truth.

2. The course of the ancient walls, on which hangs the much-disputed question of the possible authenticity of the Holy Sepulchre, still remains unsolved; or rather so much additional progress has been made toward its solution that, as far as the excavations have as yet gone, they disparage, rather than confirm, the alleged proof that the walls excluded the site from their compass, and therefore admitted of its genuineness (p. 9).

3. The controversy respecting the Temple Area is still *sub judice;* but whatever materials can be furnished are set forth by Captain Warren in the most impartial and unostentatious form (pp. 84, 134, 170, 241).

4. The external aspect of the ancient Jerusalem is in two or three points brought out with new force.

There are some proofs discovered of the form of the ancient houses (p. 82).

There is also the astounding revelation of the immense height of the Temple wall above the Kedron Valley (p. 146).

5. Some approximation to the date of the walls of the Temple has been made by the discovery of the supposed Phœnician characters marked in red paint on their surface (p. 107).

6. The interesting discovery by Dr. Robinson of what he supposed to be the arch of the bridge, which later travellers much contested, has now been definitely confirmed by the disclosure of its remaining fragments (pp. 73-78).

7. The whole history of the cartography of Jerusalem is for the first time clearly set forth, while it has reached its best illustrations in the maps and contours now for the first time published (pp. 22, 25).

It is impossible to conclude this brief statement of the results of this part of the subject, without noting the kindly and just appreciation of the three chief explorers of the internal topography of Jerusalem, Mr. Williams, Dr. Robinson, and Mr. Fergusson (p. 223). There still remains much to be done; the Tombs of the Kings have yet to be found, as they must be found, somewhere within the walls; the area of the "Noble Sanctuary" has yet to be explored thoroughly; the exact course of the walls still to be traced. But this must form the next act of the Society's operations.

II. In turning from the Holy City to the Holy Land, the first region which attracts our attention is the Lake of Gennesareth. It might have seemed that nothing new remained to be told as to the general aspect of the lake.

Yet it may, I think, be truly said, that there has been no account given at once so accurate and so vivid as that with which Captain Wilson prefaces his narrative (p. 263). Nor, as far as I am aware, has there ever been published by an eye-witness a complete description of a storm on the lake in illustration of the Gospel narrative (p. 265).

In speaking of the localities on the lake, I was obliged, fourteen years ago, to say that "There is nothing which enables us to fix with certainty the precise spots of the history of our Saviour's residence, Capernaum, Bethsaida, Chorazin." *

It is too much perhaps to maintain that these points have been fixed with certainty. But it may be affirmed now positively that a far nearer approach has been made than ever before:

1. As regards Capernaum, what may be called the intrinsic arguments in favor of Tel Hum had been often urged; and in recent years the recognition of the remains of a Jewish Synagogue in the great ruin on that spot gave much additional interest to the question. But what is new and, it seems to me, almost decisive is the identification of the fountain at Tabigah with the fountain of Capernaum, by the discovery that the track round the rock of Khan Minyeh is an aqueduct carrying the waters of the fountain into the plain of Gennesareth (p. 272). This at once elevates the claims of Tel Hum to be the ancient Capernaum to the very highest rank.

2. As regards Chorazin, the identification of it with the ruins of Kerazeh had been slightly indicated by others, but here again it is substantiated more firmly than heretofore.

* "Sinai and Palestine," Chap. X.

3. The determination of these two sites naturally leaves Khan Minyeh for the *Western* Bethsaida. It may be doubted, as Captain Wilson properly reminds us, whether the MSS. allow of two places of that name. But, if there be a Western, as well as an Eastern, Khan Minyeh offers a site.

4. There is another point on which it has been extremely difficult to arrive at any fixed conclusion—the scene of the demoniacs and the swine.

The difficulty is to find any spot with "a precipice" and "tombs" near the lake on the eastern side. Mr. Elliott and Lord Lindsay differ in their printed accounts from each other. Two separate parties of British travellers, in 1861 and in 1863, in their private accounts communicated to me, also differ from each other, and from the two published accounts.* After this entanglement it would be rash to say that Captain Wilson's identification of the site with the entrance of Wady Semakh (in which he agrees with Dr. Thomson and Mr. Macgregor) is likely to stand. But it must be taken as the most careful that has been made (pp. 286, 287).

III. The comparative absence of architectural remains in Palestine is doubtless one reason why it is difficult to regard the exploration of the Holy Land with the same archæological interest which is excited in respect to Greece, Rome, Asia Minor, and the cities on the Tigris and Euphrates. Still there is enough in the temples of "the holy mountain" of Hermon, in the tombs of the valley of the Kedron, in the recently-discovered synagogues at Meiron and Tel Hum, and in the masonry of the walls of the sanc-

---

* "Sinai and Palestine," Chap. X.

tuaries of Jerusalem and Hebron, to deserve a complete investigation; and toward this an excellent step is made in Mr. Spiers's paper (p. 302).

IV. Count de Vogüé's essay on the Hauran is the most scientific account we possess in English of that mysterious district. Its unfinished state and abrupt conclusion give it a peculiar interest. There can have been few concerned in the exploration of Palestine who did not feel a thrill of sympathy, when, amid the horrors of the carnage after the battle of Wörth, they came on the affecting narrative of the scene in which the chivalrous Prussian Prince tenderly announced to the Count de Vogüé the sad tidings that, among the killed and wounded whom he came to tend, the first body that he would find would be that of his brother.

V. The Ordnance Survey of Palestine was so obvious a duty for the English nation to undertake, that it is needless to dwell on its importance. It is therefore only right that this volume should contain a narrative of the mode in which the work was conducted by Lieutenant Anderson, "and some geometricians who could not easily fail of knowing the truth when they were sent to measure the country" (to use the happy quotation from Josephus prefixed to the chapter). Besides the interest of the general narrative (pp. 341-367), it may be worth while to call special attention to the remarks on Dothan and Jacob's Well (pp. 360-362).

VI. The objects of pottery—described by Mr. Chester—open a new sphere of sacred archæology hitherto almost untouched; the peculiarity of those in the early Christian era seems well worth noticing.

VII. Of all the discoveries connected with the Palestine Exploration Fund, that of the Moabite Stone, if not the most important, is undoubtedly that which has excited the keenest and most general interest, and deservedly so.

1. It is the only inscription which has hitherto been found reaching back to the age of the Jewish monarchy.

2. It indicates the possibility—one might almost say the certainty—that more such inscriptions might be discovered, if only we had the means of searching for them. It removes the disagreeable impression that, as no written record on stone had ever been found, no such record had ever existed. Strange, almost incredible as this seemed, when compared with the acres of inscriptions (many of a much earlier date) in Egypt—yet it was a not unnatural conclusion, until this unexpected discovery broke the silence and dispelled the illusion.

3. Whether or not the King of Moab who is mentioned is the same "Mesha" as the monarch of whom we read in 2 Kings iii., he evidently belongs to the same dynasty. The few indications that the inscription contains of the state of Moab agree with those contained in the Sacred Books.

4. Whatever may be the variations of readings in other parts of the inscription, there is an entire agreement as to some of the most interesting parts. The name of Mesha, the names of Chemosh and Moloch, the name of Omri, the names of the various Moabite towns, above all, the name of Jahveh or Jehovah for the God of Israel—appear in both the versions here presented to us.[*]

---

[*] The essay on the Moabite Stone has the peculiar merit of giving not only the various versions of the inscription, but an exact account of the much disputed and much misunderstood details of the discovery.

VIII. Among the chapters in this volume, the one to which I feel individually called to bear the strongest testimony of interest and satisfaction is that on the explorations in the Peninsula of Sinai, by Mr. Holland. "Is it possible," I ventured to ask in 1856, " to ascertain the route by which the Israelites passed through the Desert? . . . Can we be guided by tradition? . . . Such a question can only be authoritatively answered by a traveller, who, with complete knowledge of Arabic, has sifted and compared the various legends and stories of the Peninsula."* " Hitherto no one traveller has traversed more than one or at most two roads of the Desert; and thus the determination of the route of the Israelites has been obscured, first, by the tendency of every one to make the Israelites follow his own track, and secondly, by his inability to institute a just comparison between the facilities or the difficulties which attend the routes that he has not seen. This obscurity will always exist till some competent traveller has explored the whole Peninsula of Sinai." Such a traveller has happily been found—or rather two such travellers have been found—one, the Rev. F. W. Holland, writer of this essay, the other Mr. E. H. Palmer, to whose rare knowledge of Arabic Mr. Holland bears full witness; and the general results are contained in the closing pages of this volume.

It is with, I trust, the pardonable gratification of an old Sinaitic traveller, that I observe how this elaborate investigation in almost every instance confirms the conclusions at which I had arrived after my hasty survey—always under the reserve suggested by the probability that they might be modified by a more complete research. The spot of the

---

* "Sinai and Palestine," Chap. I., pp. 27, 33.

passage of the Red Sea (p. 413)—the course of the Israelites by the Wady Useit and the Wady Tayibeh (p. 416)—the identification of the Wilderness of Sin with the plain of El Murkhah (p. 418)—the identification of Rephidim with Feiran, and of the sacred hill of Aaron and Hur[*] with the eminence crowned by the ruins of Paran (pp. 420-422)—the identification of the Ras Sufsáfeh and the plain of Ráhah with the scene of the giving of the Law and the Israelite encampment (pp. 408-412)—the general failure of the ancient names—the probable change in the resources of the wilderness (p. 424)—the comparatively modern date of the Sinaitic inscriptions—all these points, which I had laid down as the nearest approximations which I could make to the truth, have now all been established, as far as they are likely to be, by explorers who can speak with authority, as the first who have traversed not one route only, but every possible route in the Desert, and have seen not one or two only, but every possible scene of the great acts of the Exodus. Such a ratification of what could at the time have been treated only as conjecture, is the best reward that any traveller can have; and I beg to tender my sincere thanks to the adventurous investigators who, at so much risk to themselves, and with so much advantage to Biblical lore, have been the first to penetrate into every nook and corner of those secluded fastnesses; and, having qualified themselves to say positively where the sacred events could not have taken place, have been the first to be able to say with authority where they probably did take place.

With these words of gratitude I commend this volume

---

[*] In this instance Mr. Holland rather inclines against the identification; but I am glad to find that my view—in the first instance suggested by the lamented Ritter—is adopted by Captain Wilson, Captain Palmer, and Mr. Palmer.

to the serious attention of all who care for the additional light which sincere desire for truth and patient investigation can throw on the most sacred of all books, on the most interesting of all geographies. Much has been done, but much remains to be done; and it is in order to stimulate and insure the completion that this instalment is given to the world. May that completion be worthy of the beginning, worthy of the indefatigable zeal and labor which first set on foot this new Crusade, worthy of the Holy Land and the Holy History which it is intended to illustrate and elucidate!

PART I.

JERUSALEM.

THE ORDNANCE SURVEY OF JERUSALEM.

1864-'65.

BY CAPTAIN WILSON, R.E.

EARLY in the year 1864 the sanitary state of Jerusalem attracted considerable attention; that city, which the Psalmist had described as "beautiful for situation, the joy of the whole earth," had become one of the most unhealthy places in the world, and the chief reasons assigned for this melancholy change were, the inferior quality of the water and the presence of an enormous mass of rubbish which had been accumulating for centuries. With the rubbish it was hardly possible to deal, but the water-supply seemed an easier matter, and several schemes were proposed for improving it, either by repairing the ancient system, or by making new pools, cisterns, and aqueducts. Before, however, any scheme could be carried out, it was necessary to obtain an accurate plan of the city, and with this view Miss Burdett Coutts, a lady ever ready to promote good works, placed a sum of £500 in the hands of a committee of gentlemen interested in Jerusalem.

The committee requested Lord de Grey, then Secretary of State for War, to allow a survey to be made by a party of Royal Engineers from the Ordnance Survey under the direction of Sir Henry James, and obtained a favorable answer. It was, however, stipulated that an officer should accompany the party, and that Government should be put to no expense.

I had always had a strong wish to visit Jerusalem and Palestine, and when Sir Henry James was kind enough to offer me the command of the small party, I gladly availed myself of an opportunity which might never occur again, and accepted the conditions on which the appointment was made. These were, that I was not to receive any remuneration for my services, and was to bear the cost of my own travelling and personal expenses, which amounted eventually to between £300 and £400.

On our return to England, the cost of publication was defrayed by a grant of £500 from the Treasury, a sum which has since been more than repaid by the large sale of plans, photographs, etc.

On the 12th of September, 1864, we * left Southampton amid the cheers and good wishes of the numerous friends who had come to wish us "good-by," and after a pleasant voyage reached Jaffa on the 30th of September, and Jerusalem on the 3d of October.

On first catching sight of Jerusalem, I must confess to having experienced a keen feeling of disappointment, which did not pass away for some days. We had travelled up from Ramleh during the night, and on our way had been looking forward to the moment when we should see the gray walls, the mosques and minarets of the Holy City; but, instead of these, the first object that met our eyes was the unsightly pile of buildings which the Russians had recently erected outside the northwest angle of the walls.

Before leaving England many doubted the success of any attempt to make a close, contoured survey of a city in which there was such a large Moslem population. We found, however, that the difficulties had been exaggerated, and though, at first, the inhabitants looked upon us with suspicion, think-

---

* The party consisted of myself, Sergeant (now Sergeant-Major) McDonald, and Corporals Frerie, McKeith, Davidson, and Wishart, of the Royal Engineers, from the Ordnance Survey.

ing we had some ulterior design, they soon became accustomed to our presence, and we were able to say, on leaving Jerusalem after a residence of ten months, that we had accomplished our object without having had a difficulty or dispute with any one. This happy result was due in great measure to our confining ourselves entirely to the work of the survey, to the prompt weekly payments made to those we employed, and to the active support received on all occasions from Mr. Moore, the British Consul, and from the Pacha of Jerusalem. I must not forget to mention also the assistance so kindly given by the learned Prussian Consul, Dr. Rosen; by Dr. Chaplin, and Mr. Schick, who frequently accompanied me in my subterranean explorations; by Dr. Sandreczki, to whom I owe the nomenclature of the city; and lastly, by two kind friends in England, who supplied me with the funds necessary to make those tentative excavations which were attended with so much success.

Before entering into any details, it will be necessary to lay before those of our readers who are not familiar with the subject a slight sketch of the topography of the Holy City.

Jerusalem is emphatically a mountain city. The Bible teems with allusions to this peculiarity in its situation. Built on the very backbone of the country, the summit of that long ridge which traverses Palestine from north to south, and only approached by wild mountain-roads, the position of the city was one of great natural strength, and this gave the inhabitants that feeling of security from hostile attack which seems to be implied by the Psalmist in the well-known verse, "As the mountains are round about Jerusalem, so is the Lord round about his people." The modern city stands, as the ancient one did before it, on the southern extremity of a spur or plateau enclosed by two ravines, which bear the familiar names of Kedron and Hinnom. The ravines rise at the water-shed within a short distance of each other, at an altitude of 2,650 feet above the Mediterranean; the easternmost, the valley of Kedron or Jehoshaphat, runs eastward for $1\frac{1}{2}$ miles, and then makes a sharp bend to the south; the westernmost, the valley of Hinnom, after following a direction nearly south for 1¼ miles, turns to the east, and passing through a deep gorge joins the Kedron at Bir Eyûb, a deep well south of the city. Both ravines are at first mere depressions of the ground, but after the change in their respective courses they fall more rapidly, and at Bir Eyûb are 670 feet below the original starting-point. A third ravine, the Tyropœon—valley of the Cheesemongers, or perhaps Tyrians—rises well up in the plateau, and after passing through the city and dividing it into two unequal halves, joins the Kedron at Siloam. On the eastern spur, Mount Moriah, once stood the temples of Solomon, Zerubbabel, and Herod, and on the western, which is 120 feet higher than Moriah, were situated the palace of Herod, the three great towers Hippicus, Phasaelus, and Mariamne, and the Upper City of Josephus.

The sides of the valleys of Kedron and Hinnom are now encumbered with rubbish, but they are still sufficiently steep to be difficult of access, and every here and there places are found where the rock has been scarped or cut perpendicularly downward to give additional security. It was probably in these natural defences which protect the city on the south, east, and west, that the Jebusites trusted when they boasted to David, "Thou wilt not come in hither; the blind and lame shall drive thee back."* The only side on which the city could be attacked with any chance of success was on the north; and here, as Josephus tells us, it was defended by three walls of great strength, able, before the introduction of gunpowder, to offer a stubborn resistance to any force brought against them.

The modern city is entirely surrounded by a massive well-built wall, provided with numerous flanking towers, and is protected on the north by a ditch partly cut in the rock. There are five gates now open, and five closed; of the former the Jaffa Gate is on the west, the Damascus Gate

---

* I have here followed the rendering in the German version, which appears to give the force of the original better than our own.

on the north, St. Stephen's on the east, and the Sion and
Dung Gates on the south. Of the latter the Bab az-Zahiré
is on the north, the Golden Gate on the east, and the Single,
Double, and Triple gates on the south. The plateau on
which the city stands slopes uniformly to the southeast, and
contains about 1,000 acres; it is of tertiary limestone, and
the upper beds provide an extremely hard compact stone,
called by the Arabs "mezzeh," while the lower, in which
most of the ancient tombs and cisterns have been cut, consist of a soft white stone, called "melekeh."

On Mount Moriah there is now a large open space, called
Haram esh-Sherif, a place of peculiar sanctity in the eyes
of all true Moslems. Its surface is studded with cypress
and olive, and its sides are surrounded in part by the finest
mural masonry in the world. At the southern end is the
Mosque El Aksa, and a pile of buildings formerly used by the
Knights Templar; nearly in the centre is a raised platform
paved with stone, and rising from this is the well-known
Mosque, Kubbet es-Sakhra, with its beautifully-proportioned
dome. Within this sacred enclosure, the Sanctuary, as we
may well call it, stood the Temple of the Jews; all traces
of it have long since disappeared, not one stone has been left
upon another, and its exact position has for years been one
of the most fiercely-contested points in Jerusalem topography. The two theories which have obtained the largest
number of supporters are, 1st, that which makes the Temple
enclosure coextensive with the Sanctuary; and 2d, that
which confines it to a square of 600 feet at the southwestern
corner of the same place. It is still uncertain which of
these two views is correct, and the question can hardly be
definitely settled till excavations are made within the Haram walls. On one point all are agreed, that the magnificent triple cloister, the Stoa Basilica, built by Herod, stood
on the top of the southern wall, and the appearance of this
when perfect must have been grander than any thing we
know of elsewhere. It is almost impossible to realize the
effect which would be produced by a building longer and

higher than York Cathedral, standing on a solid mass of masonry almost equal in height to the tallest of our church-spires; and to this we must add the dazzling whiteness of stone fresh from the mason's hands.

The western hill is thickly covered with houses, except on the west, where there is an open space occupied by the gardens of the Armenian Convent. At the northwest corner is the citadel with its three towers, representing probably those built by Herod the Great, and adjoining them on the south are the barracks of the Turkish garrison. One of the towers, that known as the Tower of David, stands on a mass of solid masonry, decidedly Herodian in character, and its dimensions agree well with those of the tower Phasaelus, as given by Josephus; another, which now protects the Jaffa Gate, is smaller, and may perhaps be identified with the tower Hippicus, as, on an examination of an ancient cistern beneath, the remains of an aqueduct were found which formerly brought water into the city at that point.

Along the northern side of the hill a street runs from the Jaffa Gate on the west to the Sanctuary on the east, following apparently the course of a small lateral branch of the Tyropœon Valley. North of this line stretches the Christian quarter of the town, rising gradually to the northwest, till it reaches the corner of the modern wall at Kalat Jalûd, a ruined castle, supposed by some writers to be the tower Psephinus of Josephus. Nearly in the centre of this quarter lies the Church of the Holy Sepulchre, which is said to contain within its walls the Tomb of our Lord. At the time of the Crucifixion the Sepulchre was without the walls, now it is well within them. Some writers explain this by saying that after Constantine built his Church of the Resurrection, the town spread out and surrounded it, while others are equally certain that the present site must have been within the limits of the ancient city, and that we must look elsewhere for the Sepulchre and even for the church built by Constantine. The solution of this difficult question depends on the course of the second wall which surrounded the city; if it ran to the east of the church, there is no reason why the present tradition should not be correct; if it ran to the west, the tradition must be wrong. Up to the present time no one has seen any portion of this wall; the point from which it started and that at which it ended are alike unknown. It was, however, ascertained during the progress of the survey, that the old arch near the south end of the bazaars, called the Gate Gennath, was a comparatively recent building, and that the ruins near the Church of the Holy Sepulchre, which had been pointed out as fragments of the second wall, were really portions of a church.

There is in addition a fourth hill north of the Sanctuary, and rising 100 feet above it, which apparently corresponds to the Bezetha of Josephus. It is now principally occupied by Moslem houses, but the Sœurs de Sion have built a convent on its northern slope, and on its western face are the British and Austrian Consulates. Immediately to the east of this hill is a small valley, which falls into the Kedron about 100 yards south of St. Stephen's Gate; on its left bank stands the church of St. Anne, and in its bed has been formed the traditional pool of Bethesda, called in the most ancient MSS. of the New Testament Bethzatha, a name not unlike that of the fourth hill, Bezetha.

It is hardly possible, in a short paper like the present, to give any detailed description of the ancient buildings and traditional localities within and around Jerusalem. The two places of greatest interest are the Church of the Holy Sepulchre and the Sanctuary, and, as most of Captain Warren's excavations have been made in the immediate vicinity of the latter, I propose confining myself to a few remarks on its natural and artificial topographical features.*

---

* In the notes which accompany the Ordnance Survey of Jerusalem are notices of most of the public buildings, including the Church of the Holy Sepulchre. I have not touched on the subject here, as the church has often been described, and the only additional information obtained during the survey was that the court-yard in front of the south door is supported by vaults.

The Sanctuary, or Haram Area, has a general elevation of 2,419 feet above the Mediterranean, and its surface is almost level, if we except the raised platform in the centre, a deep hollow in front of the Golden Gate, and a slight rise toward the northwest corner. It has been formed by cutting the rock away in some places, by building supporting vaults in others, and by filling in hollows with large stones and rubbish.

The Northeast Corner appears to be formed by filling up a portion of the valley which has been described above, as running down between the church of St. Anne, and the fourth hill Bezetha, and much of this has been done since the erection of the Golden Gate, for the northern side of that building is covered by a mass of rubbish 26 feet high. Until the survey was made this valley had attracted little attention, though it was always a well-marked natural feature, and the pool of Bethesda and the pools which formerly existed to the west and south of the church of St. Anne were made in its bed. The accumulation of rubbish was, however, so great that the exact point at which it joined the Kedron could not then be ascertained. I was under the impression that its mouth lay between St. Stephen's Gate and the northeast tower of the Haram, believing that this portion of the wall stood on a dam made to retain the waters of the pool, but Captain Warren's excavations have shown that it was some distance to the south, and that the pool of Bethesda was made across the valley, and not in the direction of its length. This makes the depth of rubbish in the northeast angle of the Haram over 100 feet, and it would be exceedingly interesting to discover of what it is composed, or whether the ravine is not partly arched over by a series of vaults.

In the Northwest Corner the natural rock is either visible or slightly covered with earth over some extent of ground, and the surface has been artificially formed by cutting down the rock under the Turkish Barracks to a depth of, at one point, 23 feet, and then entirely removing the upper strata as far as the northwest angle of the raised platform, where the rock is scarped and rises nearly to the level of the pavement. Between the corner and the platform the ridge of Moriah must have been in one place very narrow; and here, as Captain Warren points out, the rock gives place to turf, and there are other indications which would lead us to believe that there was at one time a ditch cut in the solid rock.

A little northwest of the barracks, on ground belonging to the Convent of the Sœurs de Sion, is an escarpment in the rock facing south, and from this a subterranean passage, discovered by Signor Pierotti, runs under the so-called Via Dolorosa, and abuts on an escarpment facing north. The passage appears to have been made to protect or conceal the transit of troops across a broad ditch cut through the narrow neck of land which separates the small eastern valley from the Tyropœon which runs through the city. It may also have protected an aqueduct entering the Sanctuary, as at its southern end a curious rock-hewn passage was found. The actual course of this ditch, which isolated the spur of Mount Moriah, has not yet been traced, and is one of the points to which the attention of future explorers should be directed.

On the raised platform in the centre of the area stands the beautiful Dome of the Rock, Kubbet es-Sakhra, built over the sacred rock from which Mohammed is said to have ascended into heaven. Much has been written on the isolated position of this rock, and its elevation above the general level of the Sanctuary, as if there were something extraordinary in it, but if the pavement of the platform were removed and the ground restored to its original form, it would have no remarkable prominence. The cave beneath the rock is similar to others in the neighborhood of the city; it may have been enlarged, but any marks of chiselling on the sides are now concealed by a thick coat of plaster. The circular opening in the roof of the cave looks like the mouth of a cistern, but it has not the usual marks left by the draw ropes; it is somewhat similar in character to the openings often found in the vestibules of tombs. No trace could be found of any drains connecting the Bir el Arwah beneath the cave with the fountain of the Virgin and Siloam; the system of drainage given by De Vogüé in his "Temple de Jérusalem," on the authority of Pierotti, is purely imaginary, and has no existence on the ground.

At the *Southeast Corner* the level surface is formed by the vaults known as Solomon's Stables, the age of which has been the subject of much dispute. In their present state they are certainly a reconstruction, one of the piers being formed of an old lintel, and others of weather-worn stones taken from the walls, and this is also shown by the manner in which the vaulting joins an immense mass of rubble masonry at the southeast angle. The vaults vary in width and splay outward toward the north, so as to cover the increased space caused by the direction of the eastern wall of the Sanctuary, which leaves the southern one at an angle of 92° 50'.

Near the *Southwest Corner* of the enclosure I was fortunate enough to make an important discovery in connection with the Gate of Mahomet (Barclay's Gate) and the Mosque of El Burak, beneath the Bab el Maghâribe. Barclay's Gate and the western portion of the Mosque of Burak, to which it formerly gave access, have generally been considered fragments of one of those approaches which Josephus describes as leading from the western side of the Temple to the suburbs of the city. The eastern portion of the mosque is, however, comparatively modern, and it was always a question how the ascent to the level of the area above was managed; this has now been settled by my finding a continuation of the ancient passage in a cistern to the east of the Bab el Maghâribe. From Barclay's Gate it ran for 60 feet in a direction perpendicular to the western wall of the Sanctuary to a chamber covered by a well-built dome, and at this point turned at right angles to the south. The first section of the passage from the wall to the domed chamber had a level floor, the ascent to the Sanctuary being in the southern branch. Whether this was by a ramp or flight of steps cannot be known without excavation, as the floor is covered by over 20 feet of rubbish. The arch which covers this last section has a raking springing, which rises to the south at about one in twenty; a slope which would bring the passage to the surface in the Stoa Basilica, Herod's grand cloister, opposite Robinson's Arch. This arrangement of the passage, which is so different from the long straight ramp leading from the Double Gate to the Sanctuary, was rendered necessary either by an abrupt rise in the rock to the east, or by the presence of buildings above, which it was necessary to avoid.

While the survey was going on, I was very much struck with an account given by Dr. Tobler of a visit which he had paid to a large pool, called El Burak, north of the Wailing Place, and outside the wall of the area. It seemed to offer great facilities for an examination of the wall, and I determined to try and trace it as far north as possible. On visiting the pool and lighting it up with magnesium wire, I found that it was partly covered by an arch, built with stones of great size, but without mortar, and having a span of 42 feet. The arch, which Sir Henry James has called after my name, is one of the most perfect and magnificent remains in Jerusalem, and its age is probably the same as that of the Sanctuary Wall at the Wailing Place. I was at the time under the impression that the arch connected the Sanctuary with a causeway across the Tyropœon Valley, but Captain Warren's excavations have since shown that there were a series of arches forming a viaduct which led up toward the palace of Herod on the western hill. We tried to break through a wall at the north end of the pool, hoping to follow the great wall of the Sanctuary beyond it; but not having a supply of mining-tools, failed to penetrate more than a few feet.

Near the Bab el Mathara of the Sanctuary a cistern was visited, which, like that east of Barclay's Gate, appears to have been an ancient approach to the area, as it pierces the great wall and is perpendicular to it. The covering arch, though not built with such large stones as Wilson's Arch, has every appearance of being Roman masonry.

One of the peculiar features of the Sanctuary is that the ground is perfectly honeycombed with a series of remarkable rock-hewn cisterns, in which the water, brought by an aqueduct from Solomon's Pools, near Bethlehem, was stored. Some of the cisterns are formed by, as it were, mining out the soft rock (melekeh), and leaving a roof of the hard rock (mezzeh) which lies above it; while others are made by making an open excavation like a tank, and then arching it over with masonry. The former are certainly the most ancient, apparently having been made before the arch came into common use for covering large openings; and it is a curious fact that no large cisterns of this kind are found in the Sanctuary north of the Dome of the Rock. The cisterns appear to have been connected by a system of channels cut out of the rock; so that when one was full the surplus water ran into the next, and so on till the final overflow was carried off by a channel into the Kedron. One of the cisterns, that known as the Great Sea, would contain two million gallons; and the total number of gallons which could be stored probably exceeded ten millions. Some of the excavations are from 25 to 50 feet in height, and their form is in certain cases so peculiar that we can scarcely doubt they were originally made for some other purpose. I would especially call attention to a long cruciform cistern at the southeast angle of the raised platform, and to one a few yards south of it, which has a large chamber raised 4 or 5 feet above the general level of the bottom. Whether these were connected with the Temple service, and if so, in what manner, it is hardly possible to say, without removing the plaster with which they are now thickly covered.

The age of that portion of the wall of the Sanctuary which is visible above-ground varies at different points;

and, for a full description of it, I must refer my readers to the notes on the Ordnance Survey.

Along the western wall of the Sanctuary runs the depression of the Tyropœon Valley—a ravine of great depth, now filled with rubbish. A descent of a well near the Sanctuary, the Hammam esh-Shefa, in which we found the natural rock 80 feet below the present surface, enabled us to form some idea of the depth of the valley, and the height of the wall of the Sanctuary at that point; and in an excavation made in search of the pier of Robinson's Arch, near the southwest angle, we found no rock at a depth of more than 40 feet. In this excavation we came down directly on the top of the pier; but, having no means of keeping the loose rubbish back, the Arab workmen became frightened, and refused to go on; and, to our great regret, we had to fill up the excavation. Captain Warren was afterward more successful; and, with the aid of mining-frames, was able to get to the bottom of the pier, and thence push on to the wall, and make those remarkable discoveries which have attracted so much attention.

As the survey originated in a desire to provide Jerusalem with a better and more ample supply of water than it has at present, a sketch of the ancient and modern systems may be interesting.

The ancient supply appears to have been obtained from springs, wells, the collection of rain in pools and cisterns, and water brought from a distance by aqueducts. The extensive remains of cisterns, pools, and aqueducts show that little dependence was placed on any natural springs existing in or near the city; and, indeed, from the formation of the ground it is doubtful whether any existed besides the Fountain of the Virgin in the Kedron Valley. There may have been a source in the Tyropœon Valley; but it could only have been a small and not very lasting one.

The only well known at present is Bir Eyûb, a little below the junction of the Kedron and Hinnom Valleys; but others may possibly exist in the city and neighborhood, which have been accidentally closed by rubbish, or purposely stopped during some siege, and never reopened. This well, which has a depth of 125 feet, is still, in summer, one of the principal sources of supply. The water is collected in a large rock-hewn chamber, and is derived from the drainage of the two valleys and their offshoots. The supply is directly dependent on the rainfall; and in winter, after from three to five consecutive days' rain, the water rises above the shaft, and flows down the valley in a stream. The well has been deepened at some period, as at a depth of 113 feet there is a large chamber, from the bottom of which a shaft, 12 feet deep, leads to the present collector. There is a great quantity of rubbish in the valley; and in constructing the well the idea seems to have been to stop out the surface-drainage which might be charged with impurities from the city, and depend entirely on the water running in between the lower layers of limestone. The well might be greatly improved by enlarging and freshly cementing the collecting-chamber, as at present a large quantity of water is lost, and some arrangement of a public nature might be made for raising the water and conveying it to the city. This is now in the hands of the fellahin of Silwan (Siloam), who charge from one penny to sixpence per goat-skin for water delivered in the city, and are much addicted to cheating by partly filling the skins with air. The water of Bir Eyûb has that peculiar taste which arises from the surface-drainage of the city being imperfectly stopped out.

There are a number of cisterns in the city which may almost be called wells, as, besides receiving the drainage from the houses, there is a constant infiltration of water going on between the limestone strata. They are not a very fertile source of supply, but, even in the driest summer, give three or four bucketsful between sunset and sunrise. These cisterns appear to be of very great antiquity, and have been formed by sinking deep shafts through the rock, and then making a bottle or retort-shaped excavation at the bottom to act as collector

The pools of which remains exist are the Birket Mamilla, Birket es-Sultan, two pools of Siloam, Birket Sitti Miriam, and a pool near the Tombs of the Kings outside the city; and the so-called pools of Hezekiah and Bethesda within, besides three, of the existence of which there is an undoubted tradition, one near the Jaffa Gate, one near the Gate of the Chain of the Sanctuary, and a third near the church of St. Anne.

The Birket Mamilla is still in use; it collects the surface-drainage of the upper part of the valley of Hinnom, and transmits its water to the pool of Hezekiah by a conduit which passes under the city wall a little north of the Jaffa Gate, and has a branch running down to supply the cisterns of the citadel. The average depth of the pool is 19 feet; but there is a large accumulation of rubbish at the bottom, and it now holds water imperfectly. It is closely surrounded on all sides by the tombs of a large Moslem cemetery; and, as all the water collected passes through these, it is hardly fit for drinking. About 38 feet below the lower end of the pool there is an ingenious arrangement for regulating the flow of water to the city.

The Birket es-Sultan lies in the valley of Hinnom, and at so low a level that its waters could only have been used for the irrigation of any gardens which may have existed lower down the valley. The pool does not now hold water; it is of considerable size, and has been formed by building a solid dam across the valley; the upper end is closed by a small embankment. The two pools of Siloam are at the bottom of the Tyropœon Valley, and were probably made for the irrigation of the gardens below. They derive their supply partly from surface-drainage, and partly from the Fountain of the Virgin, the water of which is brought to them by a subterranean channel.

The Birket Sitti Miriam, near St. Stephen's Gate, is of no great size. It is, however, peculiar from its position, which is such that it can receive little or no surface-water, and its supply must therefore have been brought by an aqueduct. It appears to be more modern than the others, and still holds a little water.

The pool to the left of the north road, a little beyond the Tombs of the Kings, is now nearly filled with soil, washed down by the winter rains; but there is still at one end a shallow excavation which holds water after heavy rains. This must have been the largest pool in the neighborhood of the city, and is admirably situated for collecting the surface-water of the upper branches of the Kedron. It is yet uncertain how its water was brought into Jerusalem.

The pool of Bethesda (Birket Israel) lies in the valley which runs past St. Anne's Church; but the drainage of this is not sufficient to supply such a large tank, and it must have been fed from some other source. Though partly filled with rubbish, it still has a depth of 40 feet; it is out of repair, and does not now hold water.

The pool of Hezekiah receives its supply from the Birket Mamilla. It is in bad repair, but holds a certain amount of water. The bottom is covered with a thick deposit of vegetable mould, the accumulation of several years; and in one corner there is a large open cess-pit of so foul a description that it could not be approached.

Little information could be gained regarding the other pools, which are now completely filled with rubbish.

The cisterns of Jerusalem may be divided into four classes, of which the oldest are the small retort-shaped ones described above; the second are those excavations with roofs of natural rock, of which the "Great Sea," in front of the Mosque El Aksa, is a good specimen. The third class are those in which the rock has been cut down perpendicularly and an arch thrown over the excavation, as in those near the Golden Gateway. The fourth class are the modern ones, built in the rubbish, and supplied entirely by rain collected on the roofs and terraces of the houses.

Water was brought into the city by two aqueducts, the "low level" and the "high level," but the course of the former can alone be traced within the walls of the city. It crosses the valley of Hinnom a little above the Birket es-Sultan, and winding round the southern slope of the modern Sion, enters the city near the Jewish almshouses; it then passes along the eastern side of the same hill, and runs over the causeway and Wilson's Arch to the Sanctuary. The numerous Saracenic fountains in the lower part of the city appear to have been supplied by pipes branching off from the main, but the pipes are now destroyed, and the fountains themselves are used as receptacles for the refuse of the town. This aqueduct derived its supply from the pools of Solomon, Ain Etan, and a reservoir in Wady Arûb, and still carries water as far as Bethlehem; its total length is over 40 miles, not far short of the length of the aqueduct which Josephus tells us was made by Pontius Pilate.

The pools of Solomon near the head of Wady Urtas are three in number; they receive the surface-drainage of the ground above them and the water of a fine spring known as the Sealed Fountain. The pools have been made by building solid dams of masonry across the valley, and are so arranged that the water from each of the upper ones can be run off into the one immediately below it. The lower pool is constructed in a peculiar manner, which appears to indicate that it was sometimes used as an amphitheatre for naval displays; there are several tiers of seats with steps leading down to them, and the lower portion of the pool, which is much deeper than the upper, could be filled with water by a conduit from one of the other reservoirs.

The "high level aqueduct," called by the Arabs that of the Unbelievers, is one of the most remarkable works in Palestine. The water was collected in a rock-hewn tunnel four miles long, beneath the bed of Wady Byar, a valley on the road to Hebron, and thence carried by an aqueduct above the head of the upper pool of Solomon, where it tapped the waters of the Sealed Fountain. From this point it wound along the hills above the valley of Urtas to the vicinity of Bethlehem, where it crossed the water-shed, and then passed over the valley at Rachel's Tomb by an inverted stone siphon, which was first brought to notice by Mr. Macneill, who made an examination of the water supply for the Syria Improvement Committee. The tubular portion is formed by large perforated blocks of stone set in a mass of rubble masonry; the tube is 15 inches in diameter, and the joints, which appear to have been ground, are put together with an extremely hard cement. The last trace of this aqueduct is seen on the plain of Rephaim, at which point its elevation is sufficient to deliver water at the Jaffa Gate, and so supply the upper portion of the city; but the point at which it entered has never been discovered, unless it is connected in some way with an aqueduct which was found between the Russian convent and the northwest corner of the city wall.

The present supply of water is almost entirely dependent on the collection of the winter rainfall, which is much less than has generally been supposed, as, by a strange mistake, the rain-gauge was formerly read four times higher than it should have been. According to Dr. Chaplin's observations, the average rainfall during the years 1860-'64 was 19.86 inches, the maximum being 22.975 inches and minimum 15.0 inches.

In addition to Bir Eyúb, which has been described above, the inhabitants draw water from the Fountain of the Virgin and the Hammam esh-Shefa. The former gives a constant though small supply at all times, and at intervals the water rises with some force and runs down through a rock-hewn passage to Siloam. These intermittent flows appear to be dependent on the rainfall; in winter there are from three to five flows per diem, in summer two, later on in the autumn only one, and, after a failure of the early rains, but once in three or four days. The taste of the water is decidedly unpleasant and slightly salt, arising from its having filtered down through the mass of rubbish and filth on which the city stands. The well Hammam esh-Shefa is in the old cotton-market close to the Sanctuary; its supply is not very large, and the quality of its water is inferior.

There is said to be a spring in the passage beneath the Convent of the Sœurs de Sion, but the water has a most unpleasant taste, owing to the presence of a large body of sewage, which is only separated from it by a heap of loose rubbish.

There are several good springs at some little distance from Jerusalem, but the cost of transport is so great that the water can only be used by the rich, and it lies at too low a level to be brought in by pipes or aqueducts.

The principal dependence of the inhabitants is on the cisterns, which receive the rain collected on the roofs and terraces of their houses. Those cisterns which have lately been built by Europeans in convents and dwelling-houses are good, and, being carefully cleaned out once a year, always keep the water sweet, but it is far otherwise in the native houses. When rain commences to fall, every effort is made to collect as much as possible; all the channels are thrown open, and through these the summer's accumulation of rubbish is carried into the cisterns below; water is even collected from the streets, and the state they are in at the end of the dry season is almost too filthy for description. During early summer little evil arises from using the water of these cisterns, the heavier particles settling to the bottom; toward autumn, however, the water gets low, the buckets in descending stir up the deposit, and the mixture which thousands then have to use as their daily beverage is too horrible to think of. It is at this time that a miasma appears to rise from the refuse, and that the fever season commences. It is difficult to obtain statistical information in Jerusalem, but one fact alone will show the unhealthy nature of the city: the Jewish population is estimated at about 9,000, yet in twelve months more than 13,000 cases of sickness were attended to in their own hospital and that of the Protestant Mission. Much relief might be obtained by the adoption of a few simple sanitary precautions; every cistern should be well cleaned once a year and the refuse removed to a distance, instead of being thrown in front of the door to be carried back to the cistern by the first shower. The roofs and terraces of the houses should be well swept, and the water from them made to pass through wire-gauze or some simple filtering apparatus before entering the cistern.

Intimately connected with the water supply is the drainage of the city, of which it is hardly too much to say that there is none. Those drains which exist are little more than cess-pits, and, except after heavy rain, there is no discharge from the mouth of the present main. Few cities have more facilities for good drainage than Jerusalem, and it seems formerly to have been as well managed as the water supply, the mouth of the main drain being in the valley of the Kedron, where the sewage was probably used as manure for the gardens. This old drain is still perfect for more than seven hundred feet, and might be made use of in any new system of drainage. The great difficulty in the way of any improvement is the enormous quantity of sewage which is now collected in the rubbish beneath the town, and which, if opened or disturbed, would probably give rise to an epidemic.

Captain Warren will give a full description of the recent discoveries in the city, and I will only add in conclusion a brief sketch of the progress of Jerusalem cartography to the present date. The earliest plan known is that made by Arculf toward the end of the seventh century; it gives the city in both plan and elevation, and shows six gates, two on the west side, three on the east, and one (St. Stephen's Gate) on the north. In the next plan, dating from the twelfth century, the city wall is represented by a circle, and the interior is divided into four equal parts by two streets running from north to south and east to west. The buildings in each quarter are given in relief, and we easily recognize the Dome of the Rock, Mosque of El Aksa, church of St. Anne, Church of the Sepulchre, and Tower of David. There are five gates, one apparently leading from the Haram Area to the Kedron Valley; the

Gate of St. Stephen is on the north side, and just outside it is a fine basilica dedicated to the first martyr.

Early in the fourteenth century Marinus Sanutus published his map, which is a great improvement on the earlier ones. An attempt is made to give the outline of the walls and the direction of the streets correctly, and it has not been altogether unsuccessful.

The most interesting feature in this plan is a certain Fons Sion, outside the walls and close to the Tower of David, said to be one of the springs which King Hezekiah closed, after leading the water to the Tower of David, and thence to the pool north of the church of St. Anne. It appears to me that in this tradition we have a hint of the point at which the "high-level aqueduct" from Bethlehem entered the city; this aqueduct has never been seen nearer than the plain of Rephaim (so called); but, supposing it to enter at the Tower of David, it would pass thence through the passage beneath the English Mission premises, and over Wilson's Arch to the Haram, and so on to the pool north of St. Anne's Church.

Between the fourteenth and nineteenth centuries a vast number of plans were made, but the authors appeared to have paid more attention to an enumeration of the traditional sites than to a correct representation of the ground and net-work of streets. In 1818, however, Sieber visited Jerusalem, and his plan, though exceedingly incorrect, is the turning-point in Jerusalem cartography. Henceforward, we find a steady progress in the ground plans of the city and delineation of the hill features.

In 1833 Mr. Catherwood visited Jerusalem, and was able to make a correct plan of the Haram Area and the buildings within it; unfortunately, his plans were made in detached pieces, and in joining them together afterward an error was made at the northwest angle of the area, which is much to be regretted, as otherwise his plan is minutely accurate. In 1838 Dr. Robinson published a plan compiled from the surveys of Sieber and Catherwood, which is decidedly in advance of those which preceded it, and this was shortly followed by the plans of Schultz and Williams. In 1849 appeared the plans of Aldrich and Symons, of Dr. Tobler and Gadow; the first of these, made by Lieutenants Aldrich and Symons, R. E., in 1841, after the conclusion of the Syrian war, is extremely correct as far as regards the direction of the walls and the delineation of the ground outside the city, but in the interior there are many errors, especially in the neighborhood of the sacred area.

Dr. Tobler makes many additions to and corrections in previous plans, and his work and that of Symons enabled Thrupp, in 1855, and Robinson, in 1856, to bring out plans of still greater accuracy. In 1856 also appeared Barclay's Plan, which gives many additional details; but all previous plans were eclipsed by the excellent one constructed by Van de Velde from the measurements of Symons and Tobler, and published, with a valuable memoir,* by Dr. Tobler in 1858. This, on which great care and labor were bestowed, was, up to the date of the publication of the Ordnance Survey in 1866, the most faithful plan of the Holy City. It only remains to notice two works which appeared in 1864, those of Pierotti and De Vogüé. Of the former it is impossible to speak in too severe terms, for he has introduced into his plan of the Haram Area a system of cisterns and subterranean channels which have no existence in reality, and has thus misled many students of Jerusalem topography, among others De Vogüé, who has copied the errors on to his own plan.

It is quite certain that Pierotti never visited the cisterns he professes to describe, as in one place, at the southeast angle of the Mosque Platform he represents as a small circular excavation the large cruciform cistern, which is one of the curiosities of the Haram, and in another he shows in a similar manner the interesting cistern near Barclay's Gateway, which is in reality one of the approaches to the Temple

* To this memoir I owe the details given above; it is an admirable *résumé* of the progress of Jerusalem cartography.

of Herod. Even the subterranean passage under the convent of the Sœurs de Sion, discovered by himself, is so incorrectly drawn that it is quite certain he never went to the end of it, for two enormous sewers are shown which have no existence; a chamber is added on to the south, where there is nothing but solid rock, and the curious rock-hewn passage at the southern end, discovered by myself, and afterward explored to its end by Captain Warren, is not noticed, though 7 or 8 feet high. I have entered into Pierotti's case rather fully, as there are many in England who still believe in his statements. De Vogüé's beautiful work is confined to the Haram Area, and is chiefly architectural. He adopts Catherwood's ground plan of the whole area, but gives in addition plans of some of the vaults and passages on a larger scale, and more correctly than previous authors. The Ordnance Survey Plans of Jerusalem were surveyed and drawn on the same scale and with the same accuracy as the cadastral or parish plans of England, which are probably known to most of our readers; and special plans on a still larger scale were made of the Haram Area, and the principal churches and public buildings. The following is a list of them:

1. Plan of Jerusalem and vicinity, with the hills shaded:
    Scale $\frac{1}{10000}$, or 6.33 inches to a mile.
2. Plan of Jerusalem, with streets, buildings, and contours:
    Scale $\frac{1}{2500}$, or 25.34 inches to a mile.
3. Plan of Haram esh-Sherif, with cisterns, vaults, and contours:
    Scale $\frac{1}{500}$, or 10.56 feet to a mile.
4. Plans of the Church of the Holy Sepulchre and Dome of the Rock.
    Scale $\frac{1}{250}$.
5. Plans of the Citadel, David's Tomb, churches of St. Anne, St. James, the Ascension, the Tomb of the Virgin, the Flagellation, etc.:
    Scale $\frac{1}{500}$.

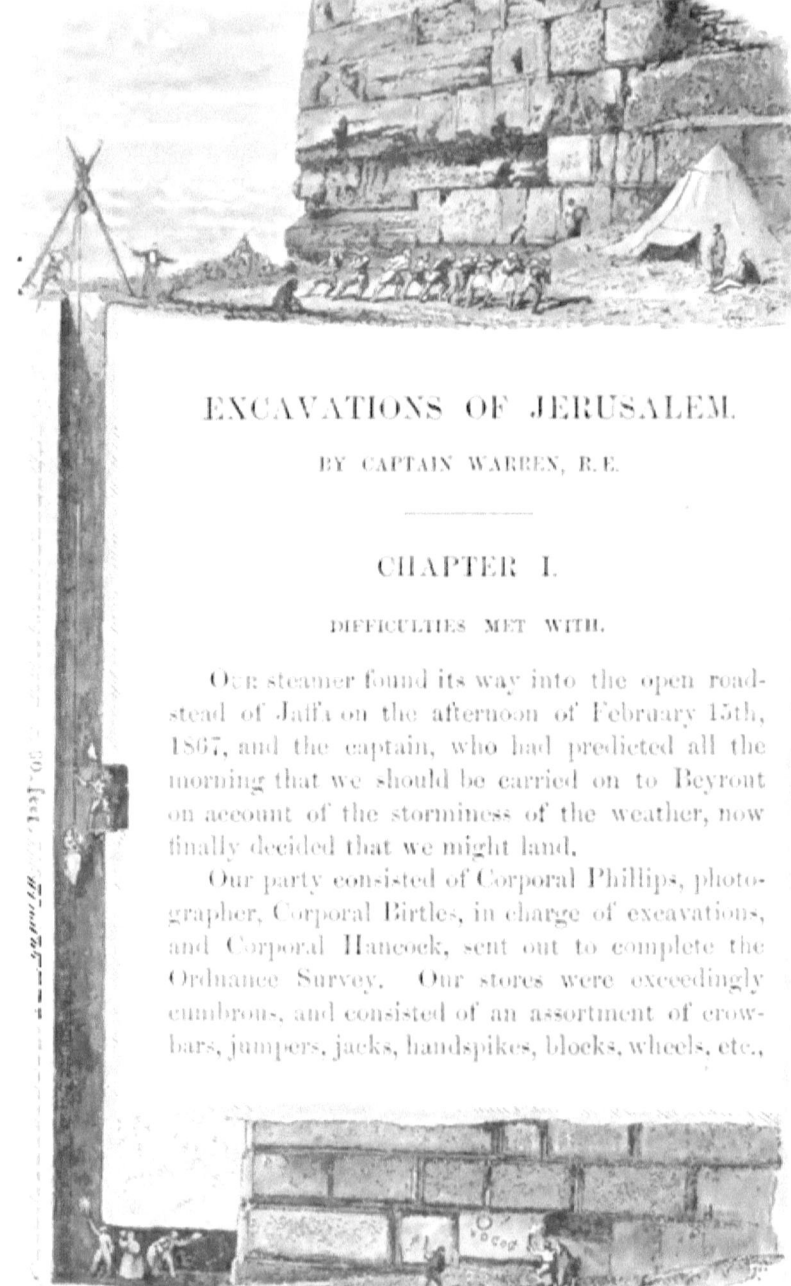

EXCAVATIONS OF JERUSALEM.

BY CAPTAIN WARREN, R.E.

CHAPTER I.

DIFFICULTIES MET WITH.

Our steamer found its way into the open roadstead of Jaffa on the afternoon of February 15th, 1867, and the captain, who had predicted all the morning that we should be carried on to Beyrout on account of the storminess of the weather, now finally decided that we might land.

Our party consisted of Corporal Phillips, photographer, Corporal Birtles, in charge of excavations, and Corporal Hancock, sent out to complete the Ordnance Survey. Our stores were exceedingly cumbrous, and consisted of an assortment of crowbars, jumpers, jacks, handspikes, blocks, wheels, etc., packed in small boxes for mule or camel load. One large box, however, there was which proved the greatest nuisance, for it had nearly overturned our shore-boat at Alexandria, and finally it had to be opened and its contents distributed, for no camel could carry it. It having come with us at all was through the good-natured interference of the man from whom the stores were bought; for he had proper sizes of the boxes sent down to him for packing the tools in, but he came somehow to the conclusion that a large box would suit us better, and when his mistake was discovered it was too late to be remedied. We had also boxes containing theodolites, sextants, etc., and the custom-house authorities pronounced they were *warlike stores*, until Mr. Habib Kayat, the Vice-Consul, undertook to vouch for their being of a peaceful nature and not liable to go off.

We left Mr. Kayat's hospitable abode on 16th February, passing the night at Ramleh, and started next morning at 4 A.M. A most furious piercing cold wind was blowing, the strongest wind I have met with, and we crept along like snails; our mules on several occasions were blown over, and on the road behind us a little later was a mournful spectacle—a party of our American friends, a gentleman and his daughter, both blown off their horses and unable to mount again until they rolled along to the lee-side of a guard-house out of the wind. We were thirteen hours getting up to Jerusalem, over a distance of about twenty-four miles, which can now be ridden easily in four hours; but at that time the road was not commenced, and we were delayed a good deal in picking up our fallen animals.

On arrival at Jerusalem, I lost no time in presenting myself to the British Consul, Mr. Moore, with whom I went to call upon his Excellency Izzet Pacha, the Governor of Jerusalem, who said that no vizierial letter had come, but that pending its arrival he would give me authority for digging anywhere except actually in the interior of the Sanctuary.

We immediately commenced work alongside the Sanctuary wall to south; but in four days the work was stopped on the representation of the military Pacha, who asserted that if we dug near the wall we should bring it down. (This wall we afterward examined in all its parts.)

I asked the Consul if he would call again with me, and show to the Pacha that we were not likely to do any damage; but he explained that it would be far better if I took all these arrangements upon myself, as the Pacha might acquiesce if asked in a private manner, when he would take umbrage at being asked by the Consul. I accordingly called on the Pacha, who said we had better wait for the vizierial letter, which arrived at the end of the week. Unfortunately, by the confusion between Hebron and Jerusalem, it expressly excluded the Noble Sanctuary, and I was advised not to present it.

I next paid a visit to the military Pacha, and spoke about the security of the walls where we had been excavating; but it was evident that he had only made use of that as a means of stopping us, and he assured me it was perfectly absurd for us to come and dig about Jerusalem, when the Moslem traditions gave every information. He then proceeded to explain to me the whole structure of the Noble Sanctuary, winding up with the information that the sacred rock, the Sakhra, lies on the top leaves of a palm-tree, from the roots of which spring all the rivers of the earth, and that the attempt of a Frank to pry into such matters could only be attended by some dire calamity befalling the country. The old gentleman was extremely civil, and asked me to come some day and see him inspect the troops; but whenever I wanted him to fix a day, he would always pitch upon Sunday, though there were other days when they were brought out. He did not return my visit for some months, but was always apologizing for not doing so; and at last a friend who knew him told me that that was his way of proceeding, and that he did not intend to call, unless obliged to do so. A few days after this, I saw him in one of the narrow streets, standing and admiring his horse,

with some of his people about, and it appeared to be a good
opportunity for passing between them without recognizing
him. The next morning I received a message from him,
asking me if I would be at home that day, and he paid me
his long-deferred visit in the afternoon, and was most agreeable. We were very good friends after this, but he could
not influence affairs much now either way.

In March, I went into the Jordan Valley for a month,
and on my return I found Nazif Pacha had replaced Izzet
as Governor, and that he had already attempted to stop the
works twice during my absence. The first time he sent for
Sergeant Birtles, and said that he had no business to work
at all; but he was shown that Izzet Pacha had given me
leave. He next tried to stop the work on the pretext that
we were digging in a cemetery, but found that he had been
too ready to give ear to false reports. He stopped our work
near the Damascus Gate before we had finished, and gave
an order that we were not to dig nearer than 40 feet to any
of the city walls or the Sanctuary. I had a long list of
places for excavating in, and as fast as he stopped us at one
point we went off to another, in hopes of wearing off his
excessive zeal in time; but it soon became evident that he
was a very different stamp of man to the previous Governor, and that our work appeared to offend him.

It is true that I was furnished with a vizierial letter, instructing the authorities to afford to me "the necessary facilities in respect of the object of the mission, and permission and all possible facilities to dig and inspect places after
satisfying the owners," but then the letter went on to add,
"with the exception of the Noble Sanctuary and the various Moslem and Christian shrines." So wide an exception afforded an excuse for constant interference with our
work afterward; and a confusion, real or assumed, between the Sanctuary at Jerusalem, and the far more jealously guarded Sanctuary at Hebron, led to further annoyances.

I was anxious to make an examination of the latter

mosque, and after some little demur his Excellency promised to write a letter giving me authority to enter every part of the mosque, and accordingly we set out on the 24th of May, 1867, accompanied by a Lieutenant and four Zaptis. On arrival at Hebron I sent word to the Modir of our object, and he at once asked me to join him at a dinner out in a vineyard, where some friends were to be present. The feast consisted chiefly of a sheep roasted whole, and would have been pleasant enough had not I been in the seat of honor, and plagued by the Modir and Judge wishing to stuff little titbits of fat, plucked out with their fingers, down my unwilling throat. Although we were, with three exceptions, all Moslems, yet I found, to my astonishment, that I was expected to bring wine, and, still more so, that one of the Moslems intended to drink it. It seemed rather a strong measure in a city considered to be one of the most fanatical; but then the man, I suppose, made the matter easy by singing a little hymn before each gulp, thus turning the wine into water, or otherwise altering its condition by acting as a charm. This occurred at noon, and in the evening the Modir coming to dine with me, I felt somewhat averse to offering him any thing but water. He, however, very soon asked if I had any peppermint-water, as his stomach was sick. I had none, so he wanted something strong, and brandy would just suit him; he shortly made a large hole in the bottle, and talked continuously about what he would show me in the mosque, asked how many days we would require to be in it photographing, and whether we would give him copies of the tombs, etc. Every thing appeared to be most easy. I was very anxious to get rid of him, as I had an attack of fever on me, and did not enjoy his company. At last I felt sure he would have to be carried off if he remained much longer, and told his Zaptis to lead him away, and he was eased along between two, with a third behind to help if necessary. Next day in the morning, I went with my zaptis to the serai to present the letter. I found the streets lined with soldiers, and every thing got ready for our visit to the mosque, but, on reading the letter, the Modir's assurance at once appeared to leave him, and he became very serious. We went off in state to the mosque, and, entering at the southwest gate, went up as far as visitors are allowed to go, and then the Modir began to linger, and on turning the corner I saw before us a closed door. He now began to make apologies that it could not be opened to-day, etc., but, finding they were not taken in, he said we must go round by the other door; so we entered at the northwest entrance, and on our right I saw an iron door on the level of the street, which I believe would lead into the cave of Machpelah; this, they said, had not been opened for six hundred years. On getting to the top of the steps we were again stopped by a closed door, and the key was not forthcoming. I refused to go away, and eventually the Judge was sent for, who read the letter attentively, and said that it was so written as to put all the responsibility of showing the mosque upon the Modir, so that if the people made any row about it the Modir would be in fault. This I afterward found to be the case, and after considerable delay it was arranged that I should be taken round the mosque, and be allowed to look in at the tombs of Abraham, etc., but not to go in. I had therefore but the small satisfaction of looking in through a hole in the door, and could go no farther. My impression is, that the bakshish offered would have prevailed had I then had Jerius for a dragoman; but at this time I had a very inferior style of man, having only arrived in Jerusalem after the season had commenced. Had I also been free from fever, I might have gained entrance by sitting down at the door for several hours, and refusing to go unless I was allowed inside, or was dragged away by violence, but I was unable to continue at the work more than five hours.

On leaving Hebron I wrote to tell the acting Consul of the manner in which I had been served; but the Pacha denied it, and said that I had not only visited the tombs, but had tried to get into the cave of Machpelah itself. I returned to Jerusalem on the 29th of June, after a month in the plain of Philistia, and at once called upon the Pacha with reference to the Hebron difficulty. The Lieutenant of Zaptis was called in, and the Pacha warned him he must speak the truth, on which he fell down on his knees and swore he would say exactly what occurred, and immediately began an account of what ought to have occurred—how we were taken all over the mosque, and how I had been perfectly satisfied. I felt rather indignant, and, having brought Mr. Fergusson's plan of the mosque in my pocket, showed the Pacha where I had been; but the officer, who stated he had been with Mr. Fergusson, said that I had been into every place he had been in. "But," I said, "Mr. Fergusson was in here and saw the monuments." "And you were there too," replied the Lieutenant. "But I was not there, and only could look in through a hole in the door," I replied. "Ah, then, Mr. Fergusson was not there;" and so we went on, until I saw the Pacha had made up his mind that I had seen every thing which Mr. Fergusson had seen, and that the officer's statement was perfectly satisfactory. I wished very much to get the matter sifted before witnesses; but I could get no action taken at the Consulate, and the Lieutenant of Zaptis was moved immediately from Jerusalem. I cannot help feeling that the manner in which the Pacha was allowed to bring this man's evidence to weigh against mine was very detrimental to our future operations; at the same time I could do nothing more than protest against it, for I could not bring evidence to show that I had not been taken into every place Mr. Fergusson had, except the book and plan. A few weeks after, I met my friend the Modir in the Sanctuary, and again wanted to bring the matter forward with him as a witness, but could get no action taken. The Pacha only said he was quite sure I had seen the mosque, and that, if I wanted to see it a *second* time, I must get a special letter from the Porte. A special letter, however, would have been of no use with this Pacha, for they nearly

always end up with "provided you see no objection," and he always did manage to see an objection.

I have omitted to say that the Modir of Hebron, after drinking so much brandy in my tent, sent to me a message the morning I left his city to ask me if I would let him have a bottle of the *vinegar* he had found so good the other evening. I thought it might have been called by some more pleasant name, and sent back word that I was sorry I had not a full bottle, and enclosed half a bottle of real vinegar.

On my return to Jerusalem at the end of June, 1867, I found the Pacha still putting difficulties in our way; but we were fast approaching the close of the first scene in the drama, and after that I expected we should be able to get on better. My idea was as follows: the Pacha strictly prohibited our working nearer to the walls than 40 feet; but he was quite unaware of our powers of mining, and felt quite safe so long as we were not near the wall aboveground. My object then was to commence at the required distance and mine up to the wall, obtain the necessary information, publish it, and then, when it was known at Constantinople, to commence again on the surface about 20 feet off, and, if stopped, to protest on the plea that we had already been up to the wall, that it was known at the Porte, and that the custom was established. At the same time I was urging on the authorities at home the necessity of getting a more favorable vizierial letter, if we were to work without hinderance.

In July we got up to the Sanctuary wall at the southeast angle, and, having examined it, the account was sent home; pending its publication I went down along the western shores of the Dead Sea, and afterward, crossing over the Jordan, I examined the country of Gilead, during which time photographs were taken of subjects which were hitherto almost unknown, among others the spring head of the Waters of Hesban, which may perhaps be taken as a representation of the head of the brook which ran through the midst of the land in the early days of Jerusalem.

On 10th September, 1867, an opportunity presented itself for bringing his Excellency to book; and the result of the interview was, that I was enabled to continue our work until early in the following year without molestation.

When our men were working at the newly-discovered aqueduct near the Cœnaculum, some **soldiers came and** told them **to leave off** work; and when they refused, they threatened **to whip** them, and abused the Frank who directed them, calling me a "pig." When I heard of this I went with the consular **cavass (the acting Consul being** ill in bed) to the Pacha, **and told him about it. He** said I must produce **the soldiers; but I said I had no power to detain them, and I considered that all that was necessary for** me to **do was to relate the facts, so that he might find out the** culprits. After a good deal of beating about the bush, I pressed **the matter on him, and he sent a cavass with my** interpreter **to look for the soldiers. In the afternoon I** heard that **Sergeant Birtles had been made prisoner, and** was being marched **to the serai. I immediately went, and** obtained **the dragoman and cavass of the Consulate, and** went **up to the Pacha. I asked him if it was by his orders that Sergeant Birtles had been made prisoner; he** replied **that he had released him. I asked him if it had been** done **with his orders; and then commenced an excited** conversation **for an hour; but it always returned to the same** point: **either it was done with his authority, and in** that case **I should report the matter home, or else it was without his authority, and if so, he must say so in writing, so that I might give a copy to Sergeant Birtles to show to anybody he wished. His Excellency tried all manner of means of getting out of this; when I first entered he had treated me** extremely coldly, **and had not offered me a chair, but I sat** down in that next **to him; then he got a man to talk Arabic to** one of my witnesses, **to try and confuse his evidence; but I** refused to allow him **to speak except through the proper in**terpreter, **and then he got up and said he had an engagement;** but **I kept in** my seat, and **said I would wait until** he returned. Finding I would not give way, he offered me the first civility I had experienced at his hands since his arrival—he sent for chibouks and comfits, and we smoked away for half an hour, talking on indifferent subjects. I must remark here that he had never before offered me any thing but a cigarette; and I was not aware of the difference until I had been in Jerusalem some months, when I saw that the foreign Consuls were given chibouks. I then inquired, and found that the practice of giving a cigarette is a sign of entertaining an inferior. I complained to the Acting Consul, but he gave a very good reason for his preferring a cigarette himself, viz., that they were cleaner.

The Pacha had now given me the chibouk, and I was careful in all my after-visits to refuse the cigarette, and look uneasy until the chibouk arrived. After having smoked for some time, his Excellency again asked me if I were not satisfied; but I returned to the charge, and said I must have a written paper of explanation. He then summoned up the cavass who had imprisoned Sergeant Birtles, and sentencing him to imprisonment in my presence, asked if I were satisfied. I said that was his affair; all I wanted was a paper written by him saying that a mistake had been made which I might give to Sergeant Birtles. It took another two hours before he would give in; but finally he said he would write one that afternoon. I wanted him very much to write it on the spot, but saw he would not go so far, and eventually had to content myself with a promise that it should be sent to me that evening. It was, however, several days before the letter was written, and not until I had sent several times to the Consulate on the subject, and at last had written to say that I was sorry to find the Pacha could not keep to his word, and that I should take other steps.

Sergeant Birtles acted admirably in the matter; he understood what I wished to a nicety. He was on the works when the cavass came to imprison the workmen; but he said that the workmen were under him, and he could not let them be interfered with. The cavass said then he should imprison Sergeant Birtles, and did so, though he was warned that he was a British subject. Sergeant Birtles walked with him through the streets when my dragoman met them, and again the cavass was told he was doing wrong, but he said he knew what he was about. On arriving at the serai, one of the officers took him up in triumph to the Town Major, who at once saw what an error had been committed, and said Sergeant Birtles might go; but Sergeant Birtles very properly said he had been imprisoned, and would not be released until I arrived. The Pacha then sent for him twice, first told him, and then begged him to go away; but he declined very respectfully to do so until I had come to release him myself.

It was of the utmost consequence to our progress that this matter should have been settled as it was; for had the Pacha once established his right to send and take our men off the work without first applying to me, we should have had them continually in a state of alarm; as it was, I guaranteed their safety for any thing I ordered them to do, as I considered I could safely do so.

After this affair we had very little trouble for some months; and we gradually approached the Sanctuary wall, and finally worked alongside it, and the Pacha made no open opposition, for he was somewhat taken aback by the result of his last exploit, and he also was trying to open negotiations with me with regard to the road then being constructed from Jerusalem to Jaffa.

In January I found that an intrigue was going on. I must premise that our system of excavating was to employ the tenants of the ground, and to pay them for any damage done to their crops, and also to give the landlords presents for the privilege of digging in their soil. A certain class, however, officials of the Turkish Government, endeavored to extort backshish by bringing pressure to bear against us, with a view to being bought off. Had I given way, it would have been as well to have closed the works at once; it would have been necessary to fee all the officials employed, who would again, after the custom of the country, have expected money from the land-owners, and these again would have recouped themselves at our expense. When they found that I would not give way, all kinds of difficulties were thrown in our path; Effendis were sent without notice to inspect our work, our workmen were tampered with, a message from the Pacha was communicated to me through the Consulate to the effect that I must get his permission before commencing any shaft, a step which led to a long and unsatisfactory correspondence. However, firmness carried the day, and having protested, on behalf of the Committee, against any change in the manner of conducting the works, I commenced them again on April 2, 1868. Corporals Duncan and Hanson having arrived for service at Jerusalem, Sergeant Birtles was sent home for the recovery of his health, it having suffered from the effects of the trying circumstances under which we were placed, when endeavoring to keep up supplies and medicine at our camp, to the east of Jordan, ninety miles from Jerusalem by the nearest road, where one of our party was ill with fever.

In April I found it would be necessary to explain personally to the Committee the real difficulties which attended our work at Jerusalem; and, active opposition having again ceased for a season, I made arrangements for work to be carried on at Ophel during my absence—where there could not possibly be any objection—and Dr. Chaplin having very kindly undertaken to superintend the work. I left Jaffa on May 15, 1868, arriving in England on 26th, and met the Committee; when I learned that the British Ambassador had already been written to for a more favorable vizierial letter. I then stated that an expenditure of £350 per month would be the least sum which I considered would be sufficient for carrying on the work; and it was settled that that sum should be paid to me, and that a draughtsman and more overseers should follow me, together with Sergeant Birtles. I left England on June 13th with my family, and arrived at Jerusalem on 30th, having been away just six weeks.

Shortly before my departure from Jerusalem the Commander-in-Chief of the Mediterranean Fleet, Lord Clarence Paget, had been there, and having seen our works, and explained to the Pacha the necessity of his helping us, he also very kindly promised to ask the Governor-General of Syria to write to the Pacha on the subject. On my return I learned that he had not been able to see the Governor-General, in consequence of some alteration in his plans. Nevertheless, the presence of our fleet along the coast, the influx of our sailors and marines into Jerusalem, and the opinion of the British Admiral, not only had their effect upon the people, but to a certain extent influenced the Pacha himself; and I now continued our work as formerly without any active opposition.

In July another vizierial letter was received, but it only enforced the former one; and at the same time the Consul wrote to tell me that the Ambassador regretted to find it was not possible to obtain any thing more liberal in its bearing. However, I was then working alongside the Sanctuary wall, with the tacit sanction of the Pacha, and had as much work as I could get through. Fever now began to attack us; and on the 10th of August Corporal Duncan succumbed, and was buried in the British Cemetery. He was an excellent fellow, exactly suited to the work we had in hand, and his loss was doubly to be regretted.

Sergeant Birtles arrived in August, and four non-commissioned officers as overseers on the 10th of September; and toward the end of the month Corporal Hanson, who had also suffered somewhat from fever, was sent home.

Corporal Turner was very quickly attacked with inflammatory fever, and the works were stopped, for the other three corporals had to attend him. Sergeant Birtles also had a very severe attack; and at times, during the months of September and October, we were all ill except the three non-commissioned officers. After a very narrow escape, Corporal Turner was invalided home in November, and our works were resumed; and I became on very friendly terms with the Pacha, who sent deputies now and then to examine our works, and he appeared quite content to let us dig along the Sanctuary wall.

In November, I received intimation that, on account of the lack of funds, the expenditure must be reduced to £200 per month all told.

A certain Effendi now began to intrigue and put difficulties in our way, on the pretence that our mining operations were interfering with Mahometan tombs, and that our shafts were dangerous to wayfarers. A long correspondence ensued, but in spite of this and other difficulties the work progressed.

I also wrote to the Pacha, and requested he would pay me a visit, as he had never been to see me. After a good deal of opposition, he agreed to do so. He saw a sewing-machine, for the first time, in my house, and was intensely delighted with it, and took a piece of cloth I sewed for him off to his hareem.

In May, on account of the various difficulties, I wrote to the Ambassador, asking for a more liberal vizierial letter; but he replied (July 12, 1869) that the Porte had declined to give one, and had refused to entertain the request made for me to pursue my investigations in the Noble Sanctuary.

In June, 1869, a royal firmaun (appendix) signed by the Sultan, arrived, which altogether dashed our hopes, for it still further restricted my liberty, and after this I did not consider it right to attempt to dig in the Sanctuary.

In March, 1869, a demand was made by the Local Government on account of alleged damages to a house of the Wacouf, or custodian of mosque property, near the Gennath Gate.

I found it was of no use endeavoring to show to the Government that the rents were all of ancient date, and proposed that an architect should be sent on each side to decide the matter. M. Cæsar Daly, the eminent French architect, happened to be at Jerusalem at the time, and I asked him if he would go on my part. He said he had only two days to spare, which he intended to devote to a journey to the Dead Sea; but, on learning the circumstances of the case, he most generously insisted on giving up this visit, and going through with the matter. The Government sent on their behalf the town architect and some members of the Mejelis.

I cannot resist availing myself of this opportunity of expressing my gratitude to M. Daly for his generous self-denial in giving up his own pursuits in order to render me assistance; his intervention saved the Society from an iniquitous attempt at extortion, for he demonstrated clearly that the damage was not attributable to our excavations.

I was under the impression that now the demand would be withdrawn; but no; the Government said that the opinion of one architect was as good as another; and so the matter was left.

I then pressed the Consul to ask that it should be decided by arbitration between the reports of the two; but he said that, as we had the last word, it was better to leave the matter at rest. I was very strongly averse to such an arrangement, and declined to dig any more near houses, until it should be settled.

In a few weeks there was another demand, now reduced to £30; but I refused to give any thing, as the damage was not our doing. An Effendi was then sent to me from the Pacha, to ask what I would give. I replied that if the Pacha wrote to acknowledge that the damage was not done by us, a present would be given to the mosque of £5, in order to cement our friendship.

Corporal Ellis was now attacked with inflammatory fever, and was invalided.

June, 1869.—On leaving for the Lebanon, the Consul desired me to leave £30 to his credit, for the purpose of paying the Pacha, should the matter be decided against us; and I asked him to take charge of the affair altogether, as I was sure the Committee would willingly acquiesce in any arrangement he should make. To my great mortification,

I found, on my return in November, that nothing had been done. I now pressed again for a settlement, and in February, 1870, the Turkish Government at last proposed M. Schick as umpire. I agreed to this, provided that M. Schick arbitrated between the reports of the two architects. He inspected the house (April 6th) and decided that cracks in the wall had not been caused by our operations.

I now thought that every thing would be settled; but just before finally leaving Jerusalem, the Consul advised me to pay £15 to the Government, the half of the demand. I requested a letter embodying this advice, but he did not think it was necessary; and so I left an order on the banker for £15, and left the matter entirely in the Consul's hands.

Meanwhile, Corporal Cock had a severe attack of fever, and he was at once invalided home for fear of a relapse.

Corporal McKenzie had a violent attack of fever while I was down at Jaffa, arranging for our departure. This was a matter of some alarm; but Dr. Chaplin was on the spot in time to relieve it. To Dr. Chaplin's care and attention we owe the lives of the whole party; nor was this the only service rendered by him to our party. From first to last he attended them when ill, and this work was no sinecure, without fee; and he was ever ready to give a helping hand to our operations, either by superintending them during my own temporary absence, or by using his influence with the people of the place. Nor should I omit to acknowledge the assistance and countenance afforded to me by others of influence and position in the country, such as Mr. G. Jackson Eldridge, our Consul-General at Beyrout, the foreign Consuls generally, the leading members of the Greek and Latin Churches, the Chief Rabbis, and many of the leading Moslems, and the English and German residents in Jerusalem. I have to thank them not only for the moral support afforded by their manifest interest in our work, but for many services from time to time rendered to us.

We left Jaffa April 13th, arriving in England April 30th, 1870.

5

CHAPTER II.

METHOD OF MINING ADOPTED.

The system adopted in excavating at Jerusalem was that ordinarily used in military mining; therefore it is unnecessary to describe the details, as these can be obtained in any book of reference.

The work was one of considerable danger, for we were frequently subject to being blown up by the loose shingle which in an instant would destroy our galleries; to being smashed by the large pieces of masonry which lay huddled together above us, loosely lying one over the other, and ready to collapse at the slightest movement beneath them; or else to having our skulls stove in by the stones and iron bars which the fellahin, in their anxiety to be smart, occasionally allowed to fall back on us from the mouth of the shafts.

Although great precautions were taken to provide against accidents, especially during the last year, when one seemed almost due, yet it does appear that our extraordinary immunity from loss of life was owing in a great measure to what would be generally called a chapter of lucky escapes; for on several occasions the time of accidents happened to coincide with moments when the men were drawn away from those portions of the works where they occurred, and thus in some cases the result was simply a loss of time and money, in others the places had to be abandoned.

It was during the first fifteen months that we ran the greatest risks, for then Sergeant Birtles and I were alone;

we were very inadequately supplied with stores from England, and at the same time were being urged to the utmost of our powers. During that time we sunk partially-unsheeted shafts through soils whose treacherous nature only by degrees became known to us; and I have considerable reluctance in looking back upon those few months, when by necessity we were obliged to overstep the bounds of caution, and appeared to be courting destruction.

At that time so little was known of the ground about the Noble Sanctuary that each step we took was expected to yield some wonderful information, and the enthusiasm among the Frank residents and visitors was unbounded. The chances also of our being stopped at any moment by the Pacha were so great that we had no time to wait and think. I think it very fortunate that it was Sergeant Birtles I had with me at that time; we had served together since the year in which we both entered the army; we perfectly understood each other, and I knew that all my instructions would be carried out implicitly, and that every thing left to him would be done well. When I asked him if he were willing to come with me to Palestine, he said he would go with me anywhere; and I think it due to his merit to say that, if my ten years' experience of his worth had not enabled me to be certain of his acting exactly as I required, I should have felt it necessary on more than one occasion to pack up hastily and retire from the field; for there were times when a little divergence from the instructions would have enabled Nazif Pacha to have got the upper hand, and to have stopped our work entirely at Jerusalem.

I have so often been asked by visitors at Jerusalem whether they could not *walk down* our shafts without giving us the trouble of going with them, that I think some explanation is required.

They were simply square pits sunk in the ground, from 50 to 100 feet in depth, and sheeted round with wood, to keep the earth from falling in. Had the soil been firm and natural, there would have been no great difficulty about this; but we were working in the *débris* of ancient cities, where the shingle is found to run like water, and the great masses of cut stone will crunch up a mining case in a trice.

This *débris* is difficult to describe. On the rock, pretty nearly all over the city, there is found from 2 to 4 feet of a very firm rich mould, filled with potsherds and the remains of lamps for burning fat. These are the oldest lamps found; but yet, strange to say, they are very nearly similar to the fat-lamps used in the present day about the country among the natives. So much for Eastern custom.

Above this clay mould are successive layers of stone chippings, not long chips, but cubical or nearly hemispherical, and we have generally termed it shingle. Between these are broken stones of 2 to 6 inches cube, or great lumps of broken cut stone, and sometimes, by good luck, a layer of fat earth, about 1 to 3 feet thick. In the city, and along the Tyropœon Valley within the walls, the water percolating through has deposited enough mud to prevent the shingle being altogether without cohesion, and it would generally stand while we put in our frames; but outside, and especially on the east side of the Kedron Valley, it is found altogether without a particle of earth, in layers, sometimes 20 feet deep; and here work was most dangerous, and if it were not for the rare presence here and there of a layer of fat earth, under whose protection we ventured to burrow, we could never have reached the wall of the northeast angle.

Both within and without, but more particularly in the Tyropœon Valley within, the soil is impregnated with some poisonous matter, probably very ancient sewage; and whenever we scraped skin off our hands, instead of healing up at once, the wound would sicken, and in a few days fester up; so that when we were first working at Robinson's Arch, above the pavement, our hands were continually sore; but below the pavement the earth appeared to be sound. It was generally in the aqueducts that we found the lamps and beautiful glass vases, which got unfortunately broken for the most part in coming home; and in the soil itself the pottery was nearly all broken, so that nothing was distinguishable except the handles; but such solid things as stone weights, etc., were found. Persons have often wondered at our not finding old hoards; but I think that is not to be wondered at, when we consider the accumulation of rubbish, and that in olden times the rock caves would probably have been used for concealing treasure. But there is a further consideration, for during the last twenty years a great portion of the city has been turned up in the building of the Austrian and Prussian Hospices, the English Church, the Latin Patriarch's House, the Synagogues, and other public and private buildings; in executing these works, ten times the money has been expended, and ten times the area has been examined, as in the course of our operations: and yet what has been found? At the Convent of the Sisters of Sion, where a strict watch has been kept by the French archæologists during the excavations for the foundations, hardly an article of interest has been found, only a lamp or two, and a stone weight; and yet near here the Jews and Romans must have had many a sturdy tussle during the great siege.

That in places there may be objects of the greatest interest hidden, I think there can be no doubt; but the opening of them up will probably be due to some lucky chance, and the searching for them appears to be altogether out of the question at present; though there can be little doubt that the finding of a few rare articles of Jewish workmanship of a by-gone age would create an interest in those who care very little for the settlement of disputed points of topography.

The mining cases were called "boxes" by the fellahin, and they are boxes with neither top nor bottom; they are made of 2 or 3 inch planks, 12 inches wide; each case consists of four pieces, the two side-pieces have tenons at each end, the two end-pieces have corresponding mortices.

In the ground outside the city cases 4 feet in the clear

were generally used; but in the city they were only 3 feet in the clear, and sometimes only 2 feet for the first four or five, so as to take up as little of the roadway as possible.

In commencing a shaft, we generally found good mould for the first 4 feet, and through this we cut, and put in the four cases, commencing from the bottom; but below this we had to put in each case as we got down, first cutting away for one end and then for the other end; then for one side; and finally the other side keyed them together; the soil was then jammed in behind the side last fixed; but it was a difficult matter, as we could not afford to cut any portion of the wood away from the cases, so as to let the hand through, for fear of weakening them.

When we were in very loose soil, shingle, etc., we had to drive in wooden forks, and stuff in brushwood, to prevent the mass slipping; but this did not always prove successful, especially if the men were left an hour or two by themselves, for on coming back a hole large enough to bury an ox would be found. As we had many of these shafts going on together, it was impossible to watch them all at once, and cases occurred where a hole of this kind formed somewhat away from the shaft, and would go on enlarging as we went down, until we had close beside us a long funnel-shaped void—perhaps 30 feet high, 5 feet in diameter at the bottom, and going up to nothing at the top. Suddenly some large stone in the side of it would lose its equilibrium, and descend with a crash, dragging tons of stones with it, and dashing one side of our shaft flat against the other; the men would scramble up the rope and boards like mice at the first alarm, just escaping; and on looking down would be seen a dislocated shaft of 20 feet depth or so, the remaining 10 or 20 feet being all filled in. A case of this kind did not often happen to the extent here described, and then only quite outside the city in the open ground; but it was impossible to mine through the shingle outside without having voids of more or less extent forming around us, and it became very dangerous work. Of course battens were used, so as to unite all the cases together, and sometimes planks were screwed upright all along the inside, so that we had 4 or 5 inches of timber; but that is very little to resist the thrust of a descending block of several tons' weight, or the explosive force of a mass of falling shingle.

One of the most ticklish pieces of work we had, was in sinking a shaft down alongside the corner of an old wall; when, after passing its foundation, we sunk 30 feet, and, coming on rock, drove galleries in two directions. We then commenced a third, which appeared to get on all right, and the workmen were allowed to go on with an occasional inspection. I was summoned down urgently one morning to the place, and on descending found that our shaft had no earth on two of its sides, from the rock upward to the foundations of the corner, which were sticking out over a great void quite as large as the shaft itself. The soil we were working through had been very wet on this side (there had been some old shaft, I suppose), and the stuff had gradually all come down in the shape of mud into the gallery the men were working in, without being observed by them, and had been carried up. It was of vital importance to our work that there should be no subsidence of any old wall, and so the only thing to be done was to fill this place up as fast as we could. Accordingly the fellahin were bundled out, and Sergeant Birtles and I proceeded to tamp up the branch galleries, while every thud of earth let down to us shook small pieces from the foundations, which rattled over our heads with an ominous noise. But as long as we were in these galleries we were comparatively safe, for had the smash come we should probably have only been shut in, and might have starved on until we were dug out; but when they were tamped up, and we were in the shaft itself, it was a very ugly job, for we had to break open the side of the shaft and throw earth and stones into the cavity, while each basketful thrown in, though helping to fill it up, made the trembling foundations more and more unsafe; and all the time, through the opening we had made, stones and rubbish kept flying in upon us from above, taking away our breath, blowing out the light, and giving us an idea how something larger would come down. We were battling against time; gradually we found ourselves mounting up the 30 feet, until after five hours of it we were able safely to underpin the old wall, and feel that we had once more stolen a march upon accidents.

Our galleries were somewhat more unsafe to leave for a short time to the care of the workmen even than our shafts, for if a start of soil commenced they would run away until it closed up the gallery, then, coming back, they would clear away, and allow another fall to take place, and then perhaps another, for experience taught them very little. Then when they were visited it would be found that they had not advanced at all, but had got a great hole above them perhaps 15 feet in height. This trick was most awkward, and the only remedy was to make them strike work and send for a corporal directly any thing out of the common happened; and if they did not do so to dismiss them on the spot, with no pay for the week. But it is needless to say this did not always secure us, for even with our own non-commissioned officers it was not possible at times to stop a fall when the shingle was very loose. To show how difficult it was to work in, I may state that we tapped an old tank at Robinson's Arch with a hole not 12 inches square, and yet the shingle flowed out of this for several days until the tank was nearly empty (we were of course carrying it off from below the fall), and as it was flowing it came so fast that it resembled more a cataract of water than of stone.

It was sometimes, therefore, useless to attempt to continue a gallery after we had come upon a very loose layer of stuff, and our only course was to try back, in hopes of meeting with the rare layers of black earth which here and there occurred; and under this we would work until it would suddenly run out, when there would be an explosion, the men would be sent flying, and the first 6 feet or so of our gallery would be found full of shingle. On one or two occasions,

GALLERIES.

when there was nothing of any consequence above us, we continued the gallery in spite of its caving in all round us, and then as we went along we had to fill in huge spaces with brushwood; the only danger at this time was lest there should be a large stone lying about which might smash through every thing. When under the cemetery and places of consequence, we were always on the lookout to prevent any fall of shingle, and at the slightest sign of it we were obliged to tamp up.

The galleries were originally either 3 feet square, or 4 feet 6 inches in height and 3 feet wide. We found, however, by experience, that the best height for our workmen was from 3 feet four inches to 3 feet 8 inches, and the width from 2 feet 8 inches to 2 feet 10 inches.

The rapid alternations of humidity and dryness acted very injuriously upon the wood; and it was found after three to four months to have too far decayed to be capable of supporting any thing. The renewing of these cases in places where shingle was, presented some difficulties.

Foul air was seldom met with, but the atmosphere very often became so completely vitiated by the number of men who breathed it that candles would not burn. On these occasions we rigged up our forge-bellows and zinc piping, and pumped down a current of fresh air; but at Robinson's Arch we were not able to do this in some of the small passages, and the work at the head of the gallery had to go on in the dark. Some of the passages here were so small that they could only be cleared out by the men crawling on their knees, and then there was barely room for passage. On one occasion, when taking some visitors down this shaft, one of them behind took the wrong turning, and got into one of these passages; after getting to the end of it, and finding no outlet, he returned and went up another, and finally in his struggles his light went out. After we had got up to the surface he was missed, and was eventually dragged out in a fainting state, and was with difficulty hauled up. He insisted he had been more than a mile underground, though he had been little over one hundred yards; but it is wonderful how deceptive distances are when you are crawling on your knees and stomach. One of the least agreeable associations connected with our work was the effluvia from the number of Arabs employed; it was sometimes necessary to keep them out on mornings when visitors were coming down.

Our tools consisted of a small pickaxe, mattock, and basket, and a spalling-hammer; but we had also levers, handspikes, etc., but these the men could not be taught to use with safety; indeed, a lever or handspike is not an article that every Frank can wield effectively unless he is practised or has knowledge. We used mining-trucks for the soil in the galleries, and wheelbarrows outside; but it was only the young men who could be taught to wheel a barrow in a decent manner, for there are some muscles wanting development in the arms of the fellahin, and after the few runs of a barrow they would come and say they were done up; and next morning they complained of feeling as if they had been well thrashed with the *corbatch*, and gave up work altogether.

Gunpowder could not be used, except when we were away from all buildings, and then only for breaking up large stones which lay in our way, and were too hard to be broken up with the hammer; we used it in blasting through the fallen voussoirs of Robinson's Arch. It was at that time, I think, that an odd rumor was got up among the Moslems; they said we were going to deposit little lumps of gunpowder all around the walls of the Noble Sanctuary, and that these would grow and grow until they became barrels, and that then in about twenty years we would come back with some machine and blow the whole place up.

Our workmen came for the most part from Siloam and Lifta (Niphtoa), villages near Jerusalem, and we also employed Nubians and men from the city; and to secure ourselves from theft, they were all mixed up in each excavation, for these several people quarrelled very much; but this we did not mind, so long as they did not fight. They were so jealous of each other that they never could agree, and one side always split on the other. The men were also searched when they left work.

I offered to take Jews upon the works; but though several came to try it, one day was always quite sufficient for them, they were quite unused to the hard work. I had, however, a Jewish overseer, that is, a man who kept above-ground and beat the men with his *corbatch* when they were idling. He was a first-rate fellow, and was called by the fellahin "the devil"—the only Jew I met in the country who was not afraid of the natives. We had also now and then a tall Nubian for the same purpose; these men are very much respected in Jerusalem for their honesty and trustworthiness, and are employed in guarding the vineyards, etc. I have also noticed that other Moslems from Egypt and Abyssinia are equally respected; and I cannot help thinking that it is not so much due to their being any better than the natives, but because they have no family ties in the country, and feel that their employers are their only friends. Probably a Syrian Moslem in Egypt or Nubia would develop into an honest man. One very remarkable trait among these Moslems is, the absence of any feeling about *color*; you see the children of the black slaves made quite as much of as those more white; and the sheikhs of tribes and villages often have a good deal more black blood than the lower classes, on account of there having been slaves in the family.

Our men at first insisted on being paid the same as those in the city, and all at one rate. They also took to praying while they were at work; but this was soon put a stop to, and a deduction of pay made for each prayer. We observed that they never prayed either before or after work; in fact, the village fellah in his younger days appears to be rather a free-thinker. One good old soul, however, we had on the works, who asked leave regularly every Friday to go into the mosque and pray for us all; and as he took the sins of the whole party with him, he received working pay for the time he was away—he was of the family of the Prophet. A little deference of this sort paid to the feelings of the old heads of families allowed us to be much stricter with the younger branches.

After our work had been going on a short time, the pay of the best workmen was raised, but this caused a general strike. Allah made men one stronger than another, and therefore they must all be paid the same. Next week the extra pay was given in form of an allowance for superior work, and in a few weeks the different classes of pay were recognized: they ranged from six to seven piastres, about 1s. 3d. to 1s. 5d., a most exorbitant rate of pay; but they could not be got to work for less, it being the rate paid in the city. As soon as the rates of pay were established, we were able to keep a tight hand over them, for idleness could be checked by a reduction, flagrant misconduct being punished by dismissal on the spot.

Sergeant Birtles always carried about in his pocket enough to settle with a man straight off. When the offence was gross idleness, the man had the option of a licking with the *corbatch* and a deduction of pay instead of dismissal, and he generally chose the former. After a time we had very little trouble with the men on the score of wages, especially when they found they received the full amount instead of having a percentage deducted by middle-men.

The fellahin well understand the meaning of justice, but not of kindness; and we found after a short time that we had an immense influence over them. For instance, in February, 1868, we took about three hundred down to Jericho for excavating, and they would have gone across the Jordan with us. As it was, some twenty men were marched up one day to the ford of Damieh, some twenty-five miles off, to build a causeway for getting a palanquin across the river, and others accompanied us on the other side; and they were quite satisfied with what they were paid. Again, in 1869, on return from the Lebanon, I wanted to carry a sick lady up from Jaffa to Jerusalem, and telegraphed to Sergeant Birtles in the evening to send twelve men down. He went to Lifta, about 9 P. M., turned out the village, picked out twelve men who had been on the works at some previous time, and sent them off. They only waited for their bits of bread, and trudging off met us at Ramleh, and carried the lady up to Jerusalem. No bargain was made with them of any kind, and they were paid what I thought enough, without a murmur. Had the men been wanted from a village where the men had not been drilled into order, it would probably have taken a day and a half before the twelve men could have been got off, and then the sum charged would have been enormous.

The best working-time for the fellahin is the summer, for then, working from sunrise to sunset, a really good day is got out of them, and they do not suffer from the heat much. Unfortunately, this is the worst time for Franks, who with hard manual labor are nearly certain to get severe attacks of fever. In the winter-time the fellahin are very miserable, and have no idea of working to get warm—that could never be drummed into their heads. In the winter also, there, the soil gets so wet that excavating is very much more expensive and laborious.

One of the strangest things is the manner in which the Easterns can get round and blind an unsuspecting Frank. It is so very hard at first to think that they are always trying to hide the truth from you—to tell you something they think you will believe. As an instance: when the late Corporal Duncan came out to relieve Sergeant Birtles, a fellah refused to allow him to open a shaft on his land, on the pretext that we had always promised to pay him for a shaft previously sunk, and had never done so. I saw the man, his wife, and his mother, had quite worked upon the corporal by their tears and lamentations; and I found it necessary to take him up to my office, and show him the fellah's receipt for the money, before he could credit that they were seeing how far they could go. The fellah had calculated on Sergeant Birtles having taken the receipts with him, and seemed highly amused at being caught.

The difficulty of obtaining stores was considerable, for we could not get a thing in Jerusalem except picks and mattocks. We were eventually supplied with stores from Malta, which were excellent, except the mining cases, which decayed in a few weeks, and became so rotten that you might almost poke your finger through them—they could not be used a second time, while those from England were used over and over again.

There were a few planks to be bought in Jerusalem; but the dealer when he first heard we were in want of wood put a double price on, so that it was cheaper to send to England. It was not until he heard that our cases had landed that he came down to fair prices, when he found we were not in want of them.

The baskets we obtained by sending down an order to Lydd for them, with a written pass to preserve them on their way up, lest the soldiers on the road should take them by force; and we had to have a man on the lookout when they were coming into town, lest some Frank should tempt the man by a higher price to swear the soldiers had taken them.

During the three years our works were open, about four to five hundred visitors went over them, and during Easter time for several days we could do little work in consequence of the great number of people always about. At the beginning I thought that too many could not go down, for so little was known of what we were doing in England, that it was very desirable that as many as possible should be able to go home and describe what was going on. During the last year, however, I did not offer the same facilities for going down, for we had no great vaults to show at the southeast and northwest angle, and so much had been said about those we found on the western side of the Sanctuary, that the visitors generally seemed to expect to be able to walk about in "houses and streets underground," as they expressed it, and were evidently disappointed at having to crawl for several hundred feet along a 3 feet 6 inches gallery merely to see "an old wall."

There were many, however, who really took an interest in every thing, and understood Jerusalem, and to go with them and hear their shrewd remarks was a great relief after taking a party down whose only remark at the end might be, "Now, tell me, what's it all about?" or some other such vague question, which I generally answered by conveying an intimation that for me to tell them all about it would require a knowledge on their parts of most of the standard works on Jerusalem, and of the results of our researches besides. A lady who noticed my embarrassment on one of these occasions, proposed that no visitors should be allowed down who could not answer certain questions on the topography of Jerusalem, which seemed rather a good idea.

It was most satisfactory, however, to find that in many instances our labors were not wasted, for many people who went down the shafts perfectly innocent on the subject appeared to be suddenly inoculated with unlimited enthusiasm, and rapidly got the matter up and pressed it forward when they went home.

It was extraordinary to notice how the ladies would find their way into nearly all the places where the gentlemen could go; in the vaults under the causeway there were rope ladders they had to go down, and holes they were pushed through, and they were never satisfied till they had seen the "Masonic Hall" and the "Secret Passage."

At Robinson's Arch they went as far as the pier of the bridge and saw the fallen voussoirs, and at the southeast angle they went along the upper and lower galleries, and were shown the Phœnician characters on the wall close to the rock. Above the Virgin's Fount, also, they were taken into the rock-cut passage, and shown the shaft leading down to the water of the pool.

One of the first lessons the Arabs on the works had to learn was that they were to receive no backshish from visitors; and it was a somewhat difficult task, for many, with very kind intention, I have no doubt, tried their best to make the men take money, although I told them that any man discovered taking any thing would be immediately dismissed. All backshish was to go into my pocket as donations to the Fund; and by dint of making one or two examples of offenders the fellahin began to understand it to be their interest not to be discovered in receiving any thing.

A good deal of time was lost and candles wasted in conducting visitors round; but as a general rule those who were not already subscribers to the Fund gave sums in Jerusalem, either through our banker or to me, or one of the non-commissioned officers, or else promised to subscribe on arrival in England.

In this way the total sum of £398 9s. 6d. was received by me from all nations, including one gift of £250, two of £10, five of £5; the remainder were principally donations of £1, or 2 napoleons; the total number of donors were eighty-three, a great number of whom were Americans.

A very few of the visitors appeared to think they had a right to give their donations to the fellahin on the works in spite of the prohibition to the contrary, and several attempts were made to induce Sergeant Birtles or the other non-commissioned officers to take money; one gentleman, the head of a large party, vainly endeavored to seduce Sergeant Birtles into receiving a subscription they had got up of £4, and suddenly it appeared to him that he had offered it in too ostentatious a manner; so he asked him in privately to the sitting-room of the hotel under some pretext, and again tried to induce him to take the money, and on being again refused, got up angrily and said, "Then how much will you take?" Sergeant Birtles replied that he would take any sum as a donation to the Fund, but would give a proper receipt for it, upon which the gentleman buttoned up his pockets, declaring that he would give nothing at all.

Some of these little episodes are extremely disagreeable, but many of the more reasonable visitors commented to me in the most flattering terms on the conduct of the non-commissioned officers in this and other respects.

It was very amusing when my dragoman first discovered that presents were really refused. He had gone round with a party, and came up with a gratified look on his stolid mahogany face, saying that a lady he had conducted to her hotel had offered a sovereign, which he had said he could could not receive. I commended him highly upon his conduct, and at the same time I feel bound to say that I felt grieved to think he would make up for the loss in some much more unworthy manner.

CHAPTER III.

WEST WALL.

On 20th November, 1867, a shaft was commenced alongside the west wall of the Noble Sanctuary, immediately under the southern end of Wilson's Arch. The bottom of this pool is $3\frac{1}{2}$ feet below the springing of the arch,* and is composed to a depth of 3 feet 6 inches of a very hard concrete, formed of stones about 3 inches cube, set in a dark cement. Below this we found black soil, and at 24 feet came in contact with a mass of masonry, apparently the voussoirs and drafted stones of a fallen arch and wall. Here we were delayed some days, as the stones, being of hard "mezzeh," could not be broken up with the hammer. Eventually a hole about two feet square was broken through, and we were able to continue our shaft. The stones passed through appeared to be similar to those in the Sanctuary wall, and the mass of them together is about 8 feet deep.

Continuing down, at 44 feet below the spring of the arch we came on water, tasting like that of the Hammam esh Shefa, or of the Virgin's Fount; and on observing it for four days, it was found to bubble in at the northern end of the shaft and run out to the south. The influx of water was so great, when we attempted to empty it out, that we were only able to get down 2 feet below its level, and had then to stop.

* 2391.5 above mean level of the sea at Jaffa. Cf. Ordnance Survey of Jerusalem, published by the Government.

WILSON'S ARCH.

A heavy rain came on, and next morning the water had disappeared from the bottom of the shaft, and we were able to get down 7 feet lower, when we came on water again and soft rock at 51 feet 9 inches below the springing of the arch. The bottom course of the Sanctuary wall is here let into the rock, and we sunk down 2 feet 10 inches, until we could see it resting upon the hard mezzeh, which seems generally to have 3 or 4 feet of solid rock overlying it. We had to keep buckets going, ladling out the water, as we concluded this work; and when we left off the water rose to a height of about one foot above the rock. Periodical observations have been made during the last two years, and there is always more or less water found here; sometimes it rises 3 or 4 feet above the rock, and then again subsides; it has a gentle motion to the south. The lower 8 or 10 feet of earth is full of limestone crystals.

It would appear then that there is still a stream of water, whether from rainfall or from springs, percolating through the Tyropœon Valley.

An attempt was now made to drive a gallery from the bottom of this shaft, on the surface of the rock, across the valley to the west; but the pick would make no impression, and gunpowder could not be used so near to the Sanctuary wall.

We now made a landing in the shaft at 25 feet below the springing of the arch, somewhat above the large stones we had met with, and drove a gallery along the Sanctuary wall to the south, in search of any signs of the second suburban gate, as given in Fergusson's restoration of the Temple. At 23 feet we came upon a wall of well-dressed stones lying east and west, and abutting on to the Sanctuary wall; we were close to the top of it, and, passing over, found a pavement extending 11 feet, and then a wall in front of us, which proved to be immediately below the southern wall of the Pool el Burak. No signs of any gateway could be found, and the gallery was abandoned. We now sunk a shaft about 18 feet south of the southern end of the Pool el

Burak, along the Sanctuary wall, to a depth of 17 feet, in search of a gateway, with no results.

If a second suburban gateway* existed to the south of Wilson's Arch and similar to Barclay's Gate, it would have been visible in the shafts or gallery, or in some part of the Sanctuary wall exposed in the chambers underneath the Hall of Justice.

The whole of the Sanctuary wall exposed in this excavation is evidently *in situ*. There are twenty-one courses of drafted stones averaging 3 feet 8 inches to 4 feet in height, and making in all a height of about 75 feet 6 inches above the rock. The courses are similar to, but in a much better state of preservation, than the courses at the Wailing Place; the wall, when first built, appears to have been exposed to view from the very bottom, and it is probably one of the oldest portions of the Sanctuary now existing, and may have formed part of the original enclosure wall of the Temple in accordance with Jewish tradition.

It was now desirable to ascertain whether the pier on which the western haunch of Wilson's Arch rested, was of the same style of masonry as the Sanctuary wall (as at Robinson's Arch), and to find the lay of the rock underneath the arch.

Accordingly, a shaft was commenced under the arch along the east side of the pier at about 7 feet from the southern end, through the hard concrete of the pool. Down to 25 feet below the springing of arch the pier was found to be built of large squared stones (not drafted) similar to those *above* the drafted stones at the Wailing Place; below this, to a depth of 19 feet 3 inches, the pier is built of large rough bowlders resting on the rock, which is here 44 feet 3 inches below the springing of arch.

There are seven courses of the squared stones, averaging 3 feet 2 inches to 4 feet 2 inches in height, and in the three lowest courses a recess is cut (somewhat similar to those at Robinson's Arch), the lintel over it being 4 feet 2

---

* Cf. Josephus, Ant., B. xv., ch. 11, § 5.

inches high. This recess is cut 5 feet into the pier; it is about 6 feet wide and 9 feet 5 inches in height. Apparently it had once been used as a gateway or chamber, as there are grooves cut in the stone as though for a metal gate.

This recess we found very convenient, as in front of it we came across a similar mass of fallen stones to what we had encountered on the opposite side, and we were thus enabled to get nearly clear of them by going in under the lintel; the *débris* of these fallen stones terminates near the bottom of this recess, 4 feet below where the rough stones of the pier commenced, and somewhat above the level on the other side; this is a significant fact; it points to this having been the level of the surface when this pier was built, and therefore to the pier and the original arch having been constructed long after the erection of the Sanctuary wall: it opens up also several questions with regard to the building of the bridge and causeway, which must be deferred until the whole of the details of the excavations have been described.

The rock from which the pier springs, was found to be 10 feet above the point where we had struck it alongside the Sanctuary wall, and to shelve down to the east; a gallery was therefore driven along its surface to the east under the arch, until we arrived close to our first shaft; this was very dangerous work, as the soil passed through was red mud and rough stones, and we were continually being flooded with water, which it was difficult to keep under; eventually we were nearly swamped out, and had to leave many of our gallery-frames behind us. The lowest point in the valley appeared to be about 6 feet to the west of the Sanctuary wall, but the rock is very nearly level just here.

There were now so many points of consideration connected with the appearance of this arch, both above and under ground, that it became a matter of very great moment, that we should find out the construction of the remainder of the causeway. The shaft alongside the pier was now filled up to a level with the bottom of the recess, and a hole driven through the pier for the purpose of ascertaining its thickness, and the nature of the space on the other side. We had already the record of Captain Wilson (Notes O. S., page 75) having attempted to break through the wall to the north of the pool, and having discovered that he was breaking into a tank of water; and we were here more than 20 feet below that level. After breaking through 5 feet we found the pier to be only 10 feet thick; but there was another wall in front of us of different material, giving another 4 feet, so that, with the space between, the pier is 14 feet 6 inches thick. Beyond this we broke into an aqueduct filled up with silt running from north to south; it was only just large enough for a man to creep through, and a few feet farther to the south, it was so small that some of the smallest fellah boys were employed in it.

I had now more work than Sergeant Birtles could manage, and was looking out for some assistant, when a countryman appeared in Jerusalem who had wandered there with the intention of carrying out some eccentric ideas he had, with regard to the immediate improvement of the fellahin, etc. I was very glad to secure his assistance, and at the same time give him an idea of the people when showing to the best advantage, that is, under control. He worked with us very well for a few days, but a little more knowledge of the Arabs rapidly dispelled his dreams; he found he was somewhat in advance of his time, and shortly after left for home. I paid him the wages I thought he had earned, and he departed, glad to have had an opportunity of so quickly learning something of the people. A few days after, an anonymous donation to the Palestine Exploration Fund was put into my hands, being the exact amount of wages I had paid to him for his labor.

Our work here now began to cause much interest in the city, and many visitors there were to see the foundation of the Sanctuary wall, among others the Consul-General for France, M. de Barrére, who was most enthusiastic about our

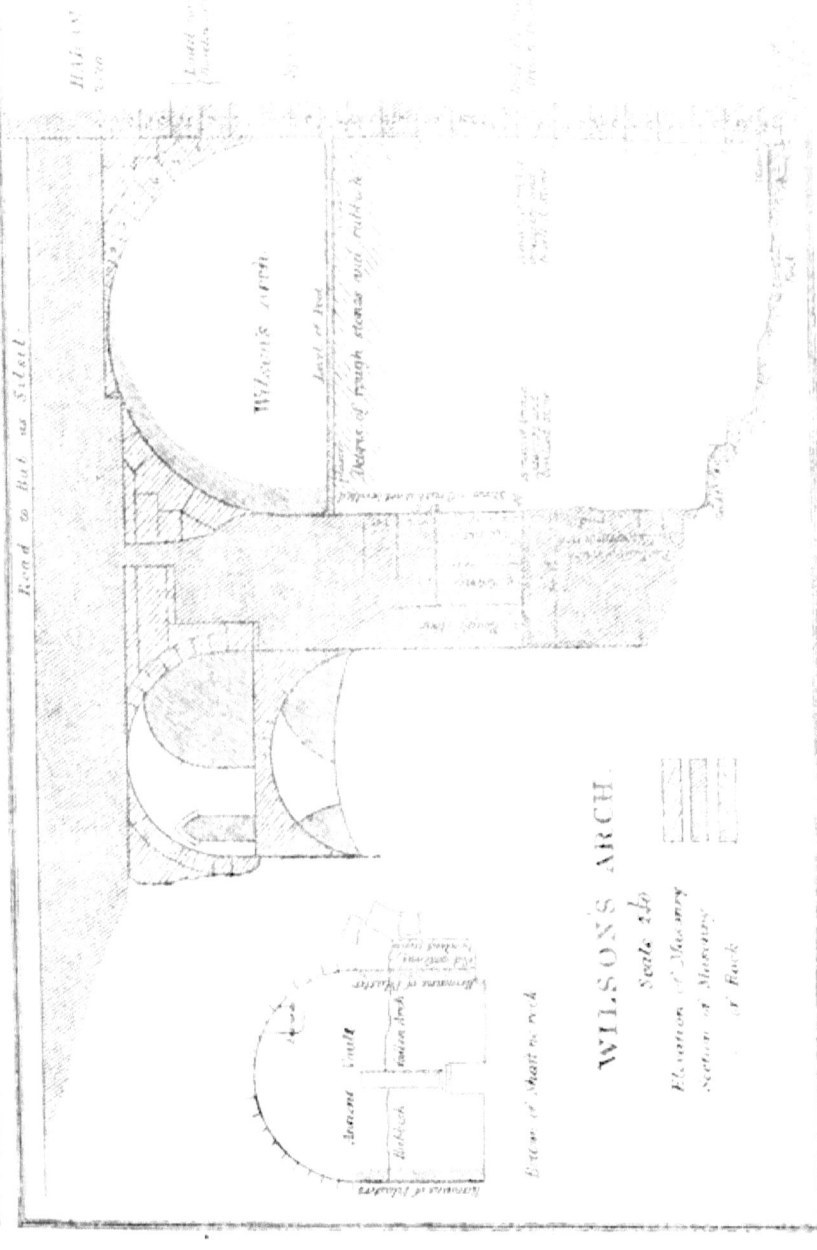

discoveries, and whom I have to thank for many acts of courtesy when in difficulties.

We now excavated in a chamber to the southwest of the pier of Wilson's Arch, and made our fortunate discovery of the vaults which form the causeway. This chamber has a window blocked up to the north, and a door to the south; we first tried the door, but found it only to open into another chamber full of earth; then at the window, and in doing so a stone rolled outward from us, making a resounding noise, as though it fell into a great vault. I allowed some few hours to elapse in case of foul air, and then set to work exploring; but before giving you any account of it, I must try and describe how these vaults exist. The road over the causeway is about 25 feet above the present level of the ground in the Tyropœon Valley, about 53 feet above the level of the ground when the pier of Wilson's Arch was built, and about 84 feet above the rock. The present Street of David runs immediately above the secret passage shortly to be described; and the arches of the causeway and Wilson's Arch lie all to the north of this passage.

Wilson's Arch is immediately in front of the Double Gate of the Chain and of Peace. To its south there is a vacant space 8 feet wide covered by a trimmer arch, and farther southward a very old arch and a lot of vaults of various dates, on which the present Hall of Justice is built; the entrance to the hall being from the causeway near to the Gate of the Chain. The outer walls of the Hall of Justice measure about 95 feet from north to south, and about 80 feet east to west, and would, if the trimmer arch were thrown down, be separated from the causeway by a void of 8 feet. To enter the vaults, you go down to the Jews' Wailing Place, enter a little garden, to the north, surrounding the Hall of Justice, and see an arch in front of you supporting the floor of the Hall; you enter at a level 25 feet below the causeway, and clambering over a little Moslem dwelling, find yourself under a confusing succession of pointed ragwork arches of Moslem style, with the Sanctuary wall to your right; the drafted stones well preserved and very black and glazed, apparently from the smoke of fires; advancing to north, you see a small entrance to your left, and, continuing on, you again see the Sanctuary wall to the right, and a little entrance down into the Pool el Burak. This pool is at south covered over by an arch of 17 feet 6 inches' span, apparently of Roman construction, and on it the north wall of the Hall of Justice is built, and beyond you see the trimmer arch; then, farther on, the Arch of Wilson. The shape of the voussoirs in Wilson's Arch must be particularly noticed, as they appear to be of a date not earlier than the fifth or sixth century. The corbels on the haunches of the north side of the arch must be noticed because they appear to have supported a balcony, the continuation of the secret passage, which seems to have entered the Sanctuary wall immediately south of Wilson's Arch about 10 feet below the roadway.

We will now return a little, and go in at the small passage we saw to our left on entering the vaults; we find this turns round at once into vaults running north, with pointed arches apparently Saracenic, and here and there are words scratched on the stones in modern Hebrew characters.

We pass through two of these vaults, and then scramble on the stomach under a low arch, and find ourselves in another similar vault; and these last two are in continuation of the arch mentioned above which carries the front or northern side of the Hall of Justice.

These vaults were already known, and a sketch of them is given in the Ordnance Survey plans. The passages through them, however, had to be cleared out, and, after a surreptitious visit from some meddling Effendis, a mousetrap had to be constructed between the last two vaults just under the arched communication; it consisted simply of a pit sunk about 6 feet, and 6 feet long, and width of doorway, with a plank to cross over on; and when we left off work we drew our drawbridge up and carried it off; the pit was not, of course, to catch any of the Effendis in, only to scare them. They naturally got a very exaggerated account of the pit we had dug for them, and never ventured in again while we were at work here without permission.

It was in this last vault, beyond the mouse-trap, that we found the way into the causeway. At the southern end there was a doorway, already spoken of; then we tried the window blocked up to north of the vault, and after taking out a course the backing fell through away from us, and we found we had got upon more vaults—on January 18, 1870.

On getting through the hole made in the blocked-up window, we found ourselves in a system of vaults, with semicircular and segmental arches, totally different to those we had previously been working in. We were just outside the north or front wall of the Hall of Justice, and we found the same trimmer arch covering a space of 8 feet, and uniting this wall to the arches of the causeway or viaduct. The street above lies immediately on the trimmer arch, so that the houses on the opposite side of the street to the Hall of Justice rest on the viaduct, and therefore I presume they are comparatively modern. It has already been stated that the span of Wilson's Arch is 42 feet, and its width 43 feet; but these vaults in continuation are not only of less span, but they are in duplicate, that is to say, there are two sets of them, the southern one 23 feet 6 inches wide, the northern 21 feet wide, making in all a width of 44 feet 6 inches, just a little more than that of Wilson's Arch. It is then apparent that one of these sets is older than the other, and the southern seems by its appearance to claim the priority; and if so, the original viaduct arch over the Pool el Burak was only 23 feet 6 inches wide; this must at some time or other have been broken down; then a restoration took place, the causeway was widened by a fresh set of arches to the north, and the void space over the Pool el Burak was spanned by the present Wilson's Arch, and made the width of the double causeway.

It does not appear probable that these arches were ever exposed to view (except Wilson's Arch); they appear to have been used as secret chambers for stores and for water. One striking peculiarity about them is that they have other sets of chambers below; that is to say, between each set of piers there are at least two sets of arches, thus dividing up the space so that it could be used to advantage.

A learned rabbi came one evening to show me how these vaults might be referred to in a passage in the Talmud, where it is mentioned that for some ceremonial purpose a chamber was kept near the Temple, built arch upon arch; but as far as could be made out in that case the springing of the upper arch should rest on the crown of the lower, which was not the case here.

Some portions of these arches are in ruins and have fallen, and the walls are much decayed. Sergeant Birtles had a narrow escape when we were examining the place: he clambered up a piece of wall where the stones where sticking out like teeth; at about 8 feet from the ground one of these gave way, and he fell back with it in his arms; luckily, it was so heavy that they turned in falling, and fell together sideways; it then rolled over on to him, and injured him severely, so that he could barely crawl out into the open air. He suffered from this injury for some months.

The southern of these twin viaducts is broken in its continuity to the west by a large chamber of very ancient masonry which intervenes and has been arched over; and the northern viaduct has, in two of its arches, been filled up with small passages with Saracenic arches, apparently for some system of water supply. In them there are draw-wells opening from overhead, and there is the mark where the bucket appears to have rubbed the sides; they terminate on all sides in open spaces quite choked full of rubbish. Above could be seen, here and there, the form of the vaults of the northern viaduct. In one of the passages leading west is an opening leading down into the ancient vault referred to above, which has luckily been used as a tank, and thus the plaster has preserved some of the original outline of the carved stones. This chamber acquired the name of the Masonic Hall from some circumstances connected with its discovery, and by that name I shall term it when referring to it again. It forms a portion of the southern viaduct; but its semicircular arch is much less ancient than its walls; it lies nearly north and south, but considerably skewed to the general line of the viaduct. The entrance opens down to it from the north, the floor of the little passage leading to it being about 3 feet above the crown of the arch, so that there is a steep shelving passage into it. I was lowered down by means of a rope, and was considerably surprised to find myself in a large rectangular vaulted chamber of ancient construction, with a column or pedestal sticking up from the centre.

On examining further, the chamber was found to have originally been 23 feet from east to west, and 20 feet 4 inches from north to south, but 10 feet 4 inches has been added on at the south, so that it is now 30 feet 8 inches in length; but the arch over the southern portion is not of the same date as that of the northern, and, to conceal this, the column was raised in the centre under the break, and two pointed arches thrown over from the column to the sides, the span of each being about 10 feet. The column has since fallen in part, and much of the ribbed arch; the silt has closed up over it, and thus the stump of the column is found projecting through. It is to be remarked, that the 10 feet added on to this chamber occupies the position which the secret passage would have held, and is under the street. Passing through a small hole in the wall to the south, we again find ourselves in one of the Saracenic vaults supporting the Hall of Justice; this has again a door leading to the south; but the chamber there, if existing still, is filled with earth and roots of trees.

To return to the Masonic Hall; the walls are built of square stones extremely well jointed, and looking as if laid without mortar. At each corner there were pilasters with capitals (see sketch), but that at the northeast angle alone is in a moderate state of preservation. At the southeast

angle is a double entrance with lintels over it, and there
have been ornaments on them and on the jambs, but they
cannot be traced exactly. We worked through this gate-
way, which was blocked up, and found the old wall to have
been of bevelled stone on the outside; beyond was a lot of
rough masonry, put in probably when the causeway was
built. This chamber has every appearance of being the
oldest piece of masonry visible in Jerusalem, with the ex-

CAPITAL OF PILASTER.

ception of the Sanctuary walls, and perhaps as old as they.
To proceed onward, we get up out of this chamber by a ladder placed for the accommodation of the many ladies who
visited it, and go through the northern entrance into the
Saracenic water-chambers, and turn to the west. After
passing through this little passage to its end we are at the
western extremity of the third arch of the northern viaduct;
and we now duck down under a little doorway, and find

ourselves under a fourth, and then under a fifth arch of the
northern viaduct, while opening into them are the smaller
arches (with thicker piers) of the southern viaduct. Here
we have to turn south, and passing under a small gate with
a lintel we find ourselves in a secret passage leading under
the Street of David: it is greatly filled with rubbish and
sewage, but the arch is white and clean; this passage is 12
feet wide, and the vault is semicircular; its crown is about
9 feet below the level of the roadway, and in between must
run the aqueduct from the Pools of Solomon. Walking up
this passage, and looking to the right, we see the entrances
to the vaults of the southern and northern viaducts; one is
nearly choked up with rubbish, another is used as a tank,
etc. Having traced the passage to a distance of 220 feet
from the Sanctuary wall, we found a thin wall blocking up
the passage; we broke through it, and dropped down about
6 feet into a continuation of it stopped up by a wall to the
west, but opening with a door to the south; through this
we crept and then saw light, and, getting through into another chamber to the south, we found ourselves in a donkey-
stable, the owner of which happened to be there, and he, on
seeing us grimed with dirt, rushed out swearing he was followed by Gins. Subsequently we found a further portion
of this secret passage used as a tank (at 250 feet from the
Sanctuary wall), and there can be little doubt but that it
can be traced for several yards farther up the street, if indeed it does not still exist right up to the Jaffa Gate.

Mejir ed-Din mentions "the Street of David, so named
from a subterranean gallery which David caused to be made
from the Gate of the Chain to the citadel called the Mihrab
of David. It still exists, and parts of it are occasionally
discovered. It is all solidly vaulted." *

There cannot be a doubt but that the secret passage we
have found, is that referred to by Mejir ed-Din; but it
does not appear to me that its construction is of so ancient
a date as the time of David, or even of Herod; and one ar-

---

* Williams, Appendix, 156.

gument against the passage and the causeway being ancient is our discovery of a vaulted passage immediately to the south of, and 40 feet below, the present street, in connection with a postern opening out of the city into the valley; it is difficult to understand how this old postern could have been used if the causeway existed at the same time. I will now try and describe it. The farthest point to the west that we have traced the secret passage is 250 feet from the Sanctuary wall; and it here is used as a tank under one of the houses of Joseph Effendi; the roadway above (2,422 feet) is nearly on a level with the general level of the Sanctuary, and the crown of the arch of the secret passage is about 8 or 10 feet below the street, the springing of the arch being 2,410 feet.

The portion of the secret passage used as a tank opens from a vaulted chamber on the southern side of the causeway, and a little to the east of the production of the street called *The Valley*. In this chamber Joseph Effendi told me he had found the mouth of a cistern some years ago, and had covered it up with refuse from the house; the present floor of the chamber is on a level with the springing of the arch of secret passage. After some searching we found the mouth of the cistern at 6 feet below the present surface; but when found it became a question whether a man could descend it, and if down whether he could be got up again. It consists of a narrow shaft reaching down for 25 feet below the present floor of the chamber, so narrow that we could not bend our legs to get up from one step to another of the rope-ladder; and it was found at last that the only method of managing it was to get hauled up by the rope about a foot at a time; but then the strain on the rope from the friction of the body against the sides was very great.

Having arranged for our ascent, we descended, and found the shaft to open through the crown of an arch into a chamber running east and west, and about 4 feet to the south of the secret passage above.

The crown of the arch of this chamber is 40 feet 6 inches below the level of the street above, and 13 feet 6 inches below the bottom of the secret passage, where it is turned into a tank in which there is water. This chamber is 14 feet 6 inches in length, 8 feet broad at the western, and 10 feet 6 inches at the eastern end. It is plastered. Its roof is peculiar; it is a straight-sided, pointed arch; the rise at the widest point is only 2 feet. At the western end a hole was made in the masonry, but after going in 4 feet damp earth was met with, and no signs of the continuation of the chamber. We had to be very careful, as in case of our breaking into a tank there would have been a difficulty in getting up our working-party in safety. The *débris* was next cleared from side to side, and a hole punched in the middle of the wall to the east, when we found a door-way built up; this led into another vaulted chamber, also lying east and west, 18 feet long, and, like the first chamber, wider at its eastern extremity, being 12 feet wide to the west and 13 feet 9 inches to the east. There was no plaster about this chamber. The arch is nearly semicircular, of nineteen courses of nearly equal size. At the eastern end is a semicircular

EASTERN END OF VAULT C (CAUSEWAY).

arch of 5 feet span, resting on a lintel 12 feet long and 2 feet high, forming the top of a door-way, whose height was not ascertained. This door-way, 5 feet wide, leads to a passage only 2 feet 6 inches wide, and covered over with blocks of stone laid horizontally. At 10 feet up this passage to the east there is appearance of some building having given way and blocked up the passage; and I considered it prudent not to meddle with it, as there were houses overhead.

It will be seen, on reference to the woodcut, that the gate-way at the eastern end is of a description likely to have been used as the entrance to a passage or postern.

In this chamber a volute of an Ionic capital was found. It would appear as though these vaults had been the vestibule to a postern leading from the Upper City into the Tyropœon Valley.

There is a report in Jerusalem that there are other vaults somewhat to the north of the causeway reaching up toward the Jaffa Gate. I went down to visit them shortly before leaving Jerusalem; but the filth was too great to allow of one getting up into them, as they were used for the refuse and sewage of the houses round about.

I should have mentioned that in the northern vault next to and west of Wilson's Arch, on the lower floor, there are two masonry troughs or aqueducts, which lead down through the floor by a shaft into the aqueduct we discovered at the recess in the pier of Wilson's Arch; and that underneath the southern viaduct, just before getting into the secret passage, there is another vault running east and west, in which there is a shaft running down 14 feet, and then an aqueduct leading toward a point at the southwest angle of the pier of Wilson's Arch; and at this point I expected to find some large tank where all these aqueducts would meet; but, unfortunately, they are all cut through by the modern vaults of the Hall of Justice.

ROBINSON'S ARCH.

The recovery of the pier and fallen voussoirs of this arch has in a great measure served to simplify the discussions with regard to the position of the Temple; for while Mr.

Fergusson considered it to be the entrance to the Royal cloisters of King Herod, and Mr. Williams ascribed it to the time of Justinian, there were those who denied that it had ever been a bridge at all, and said that the skewback had been placed there in anticipation of some future want.

Excavations.—Seven shafts were sunk in a line east and west across the Tyropœon Valley, opposite to Robinson's Arch, in order to ascertain the nature of the valley and search for remains of the ancient viaduct.

No. 1.—285 feet from Sanctuary wall, and close in under the eastern side of Upper City; level of surface, 2,401 feet; level of rock, 2,379 feet 6 inches. Sunk through common garden soil, and at 21 feet 6 inches came on a polished limestone slab, 6 feet square, covering the main sewer of the city; it was 6 feet high, 3 feet wide, cut in the rock, and full of very offensive sewage, through which a current of water was running to south—probably from the baths; some pieces of paper were thrown in, and in a few minutes they appeared in the main sewer, where it is uncovered, outside the Dung Gate. This seems to be the sewer through which the fellahin entered the city in the time of Ibrahim Pacha, when they appear to have penetrated up as far as the causeway of David Street, and found exit through some of the vaults there. The sewer itself runs on past the Dung Gate toward Siloam, until it opens out on the side of the hill above the Kedron, only a few feet south of the Fountain of the Virgin. It was examined by our party in 1868, and is, no doubt, the passage explored by Dr. Barclay ("City of the Great King)," as far as the Dung Gate, when he supposed it to be a water channel running into the Virgin's Fount, from the Temple or from Sion.

The sewage at present escapes from the sewer after passing the Dung Gate, and is used by the fellahin for the purpose of irrigating and manuring the beautiful cabbages and cauliflowers which are so much prized in Jerusalem; most of the lettuces and salads grown in the Kedron Valley are also periodically watered with this compound; and I have

often noticed that visitors to Jerusalem suffer for some days
after eating them. Good salads brought up on pure water
can generally be obtained from Urtas and other villages,
but they are more expensive.

No. 2.—250 feet from Sanctuary wall; line of surface,
2,406.6 feet; level of rock, 2,388.6 feet; came upon the remains of a colonnade just below the surface, consisting of
piers built on the rock, 2 feet by 3 feet, and 12 feet 6 inches
apart, with fallen arches between; piers built of well-
dressed ashlar of soft sandstone, similar to the ruins of
Kakūn, Suwaimeh, etc., in the Jordan Valley. On the
north side a plastered wall of rubble was found between the
piers, and it was not ascertained whether there were more
piers beyond; to the east they were continued (as will be
seen in the succeeding shafts), and appear to have formed
either a covered way or else to have supported the viaduct
reaching over to Robinson's Arch. The flooring was much
disturbed, and is formed of well-dressed limestone flagging
cut in squares, and laid parallel to the lay of the building,
east and west. The piers measure about 12 feet from flagging to springing of arches, and built in courses about 1 foot
each in height.

Cut in one of the piers is a little door, leading to a cylindrical cistern cut and roofed in rock, nearly filled with
camels' bones, and plastered with 2 inches of cement; diameter of cistern, 10 feet; height, 15 feet 3 inches; roof slightly
domed.

No. 3.—216 feet from Sanctuary wall; level of surface,
2,409.5 feet; level of rock, 2,377.5 feet; at 12 feet came on
arch similar to and in line with north wall at No. 2; at 18
feet came on limestone pavement similar to No. 2. Below
pavement found *débris* of cut stone, 2 feet by 1 foot by 1
foot; and the remains of a wall (melekeh) running north
and south, of well-squared dressed stones, resting on the
rock.

No. 4.—182 feet from Sanctuary wall; level of surface,
2,405.5 feet; level of rock, 2,383.5 feet; at 12 feet found

débris of stone building, and part of white marble column, 12 inches in diameter. These ruins appear to be a portion of the colonnade met with in Nos. 2 and 3. Below this at 22 feet came on a row of stones, and the mouth of a cistern cut in the rock. Cistern is square, sides 10 feet, roof flat, and 7 feet below the surface of rock, height 10 feet, plaster 2 inches thick and very hard; no entrance for water, two manholes opening down through roof, 1 foot 4 inches by 2 feet 3 inches, and 2 feet 6 inches by 2 feet. This may have been constructed for the reception of grain in early times.

No. 5.—132 feet from Sanctuary wall; level of surface, 2,399 feet; level of rock, 2,369 feet; at 13 feet 6 inches came on the walls of a plastered chamber, resting at 21 feet 3 inches on a strong wall of hammer-dressed stones, running north and south, which again, at 26 feet 10 inches, rests on a strong wall, running east and west; there are three courses of this latter remaining, and they rest on the rock; courses 1 foot 8 inches in height.

The rock here is scarped and cut into steps in a very unaccountable manner; there is a recess at the bottom of the steps covered over by a piece of flagging 3 inches thick, on which a buttress rests; the stone of walls is melekeh; the wall running east and west is about 15 feet thick, and its use is not apparent.

No. 6.—92 feet from Sanctuary wall; level of surface, 2,395 feet; level of rock, 2,354 feet 6 inches; passed some *débris* of sandstone similar to that found in Nos. 2, 3, and 4, probably forming part of the colonnade.

At 9 feet the mouth of a shaft 8 feet deep was found, and opening through the crown of a nearly semicircular arch, covering a tank 18 feet long, north to south, 11 feet 6 inches wide, and 15 feet high from bottom to springing of arch; the shaft was very narrow, and the tank full of rubbish, a great portion of which had to be brought up. A hole was then made through the plaster at western side, and rock found at $3\frac{1}{2}$ feet; it is scarped here for some feet north and south, and, as it is exactly the correct distance from the pier found subsequently, it probably is the east side of the second pier from the Sanctuary wall; no drafted stones, however, were found on it, neither were any fallen voussoirs found underneath the tank, which is quite a modern construction.

It was now desirable to drive a gallery along the face of the rock from the bottom of this tank to the Sanctuary wall, so as to make sure of coming in contact with the pier, if it existed, and to examine the wall which Captain Wilson struck on in an excavation he had made two years before. Accordingly, we broke through the east wall of the tank, and drove a staircase gallery down along the face of the rock until we were 70 feet from the Sanctuary wall, when we found the rock to be cut horizontally, and a wall of rock to our right; we continued the gallery till we were only 54 feet from the Sanctuary wall, when we found rock in front of us, and also to our left; so that we had for the last 16 feet been driving along a cutting only a few inches wider than our gallery-frames. On poking up the wall of rock in front of us to a height of 5 feet, a fine drafted stone resting *in situ* was discovered, and concluding it was the western side of the pier of Robinson's Arch, I sunk another shaft—No. 7— at 72 feet from the Sanctuary wall, with a gallery, which was directed so as to come about 8 feet above the rock at the point where we had found the drafted stone. I should have liked to drop just down upon this point from above; but unfortunately the ground here for about 68 feet from the Sanctuary wall belongs to the family of Abu Saùd, from whom Captain Wilson had experienced such trouble in 1865, and who were too greedy to listen to any moderate terms. I was obliged therefore to do this work from the grounds of the Sheikh of the Magháribins.

The shaft of the tank was left open, and the gallery from its eastern side only partially tamped up, so that we had a constant current of air coming down No. 6, and passing up through No. 7, which enabled us to get on without using the bellows and air-pipes. On reaching the drafted stone again, it was found to form part of the pier of Robinson's Arch, which I will now describe. It is 51 feet 6 inches long and 12 feet 2 inches thick; on the western side, where we touched it, there are only two courses *in situ;* on the eastern side there are three. The stones are of very hard mezzeh, precisely similar to those in the wall at the southwest angle of the Sanctuary; they have the same draft and chisel-marks, and are of the same heights. The lowest course is 3 feet 6 inches high, the second 3 feet 9 inches, the third 4 feet.

The rock on which the bottom course rests is at a level of 2,345 feet, that is, 42 feet below the springing of the arch above.

The pier stands exactly opposite the remains of the Arch of Robinson, the width of which Captain Wilson gives as 50 feet; the exact span is a trifle over 41 feet 6 inches.

The pier was examined at its northern and southern ends, and on the eastern side for 28 feet; on the western side it was seen but could not be carefully examined; it is constructed in a curious manner; apparently it was hollow, giving a space of 5 feet wide inside; the eastern side is also built in an economical manner; there are five piers of the first two courses, about 5 feet long each, and a space between each of about 6 feet, and over these spaces the third course is thrown in the form of great lintels, one of them 13 feet 9 inches long, and weighing 10 tons. By this method, only about half the bulk of the pier is occupied by stone.

Stretching from the base of the pier to the Sanctuary wall is a pavement, falling slightly to the east, and on this were found the fallen voussoirs and *débris* of Robinson's Arch. At first it was supposed that this pavement was the top of a lower level bridge, and that the spaces left in the pier were passages for getting across; but we eventually found that the pavement is laid over an immense mass of rubbish, and in all probability is the same as that which we found at the southwest angle of the Sanctuary, and which probably also extends up to the Prophet's Gateway, at some 16 feet below the sill. If the pavement does not itself extend all this distance, we at least are nearly certain from further researches that there was a road up there.

In getting across through the voussoirs of the arch we were in great difficulties, for it was quite out of the line of our fellahin, and Sergeant Birtles and I had constantly to be on the spot doing the work. We tried to get through by breaking up the melekeh voussoirs, but it was too slow work, and eventually we had to blast them; but this is a very dangerous proceeding, as the stones are all lying piled upon each other, with vacant places between, and our gallery-frames were quite unfit for supporting stones that weighed several tons each. We worked from one of the recesses in the pier, which was easily cleared out, being filled with mud; but when we touched the fallen arch, the old paving-stones came toppling over into our den, and we had to get them out with great labor; and as six of them weighed 2½ tons, it can be imagined that it was no easy matter dragging them up through the galleries, in which there was so little space for working. We had to break up several stones of 3 and 4 tons each, and get them out piecemeal; and our men would not attempt to work directly our backs were turned—in fact, it was dangerous for them to do so.

Extract of letter of 11*th January*, 1868: "East of the pier, on a level with the rock surface, is a pavement, which we have examined for about 18 feet; and on it, lying huddled together just as they fell, are the actual voussoirs of the great viaduct called Robinson's Arch; they lie in lines north and south, and between them one can squeeze with difficulty for some 10 or 15 feet each way. They are in our way going east, and, though they are of *melekeh*, they are so hard that the men cannot break them, and I have had to blast them. It will take us at least a month more thoroughly to examine this pier and all that pertains to it. To the north of pier we have tapped a tank, which has been running stones for several days; to-day it is nearly exhausted, and we have got several peeps into a big cavern."

This proved to be a tank of no great age, built against

the remains of the northern end of the pier, so as to save
masonry. On working through this cistern to east, we found
a low passage or drain leading in that direction, a few feet
above the pavement; it led direct to the Sanctuary wall,
and then branched north and south along the wall. It was
traced to the Prophet's Gate, when a breach occurred,
through which a large quantity of shingle poured without
stopping, and so we had to give up. This passage (3 feet
high and 2 feet wide) is built of rubble with flagging on the
top; it was full of mud, and could only be cleaned out by
the men crawling on their hands and knees; and at times
the air was so bad that candles would not burn, and they had
to work in the dark at the head of the gallery; the total
length was 165 feet.

The great value of this passage was that by it we saw
that the Sanctuary wall extends in one unbroken line from
Robinson's Arch up to the Prophet's Gate, for above-ground
the old wall itself cannot be seen, on account of the Abu
Saûd premises intervening. We were at this time working
night and day, and Abu Saûd complained that he could not
sleep at night, for fear his house should tumble about his
ears. He professed not to understand that we were only
clearing out a passage, and he wrote to the Pacha on the
subject; but he could not succeed in stopping our work, or
rather in levying black-mail upon us; and eventually we
became firm friends. I offered to show him the tank we
had found in his grounds, and he wanted to teach me astrol-
ogy: we did not go very deep into the matter.

We also drove a gallery along the western side of the
pier, to determine its length; then round its southern end,
and to the south of the fallen arch, in hopes of finding an
inscription on some of the stones; but we got into such a
confused heap of *débris* that we could make nothing of it.
In the pavement we found a shaft leading down into a pool
cut in the rock below. While driving this gallery along
the western side of the pier, the soil suddenly came in with
a run, and we found we had come upon the hole made by

Captain Wilson in 1865; we only got across with some trouble, and found on the surface that the earth had caved in some four feet. Abu Saûd was indignant, and said we were bringing down the Sanctuary wall, and brought the Mejelis to see the hole early the next morning; but we had been beforehand with him, and had filled it up and neatly levelled it over, so that he was unable to say where it had been. He was very much perplexed about it, as the Mejelis thought he was playing a joke on them, and did not pay much attention to him after that.

I have now to relate what we found beneath the pavement. We sunk a hole through it, and found only *débris* and old masonry to a depth of 23 feet, where we found rock, and, following it up to the east, came upon what appeared to be two fallen voussoirs of an arch, jammed in over a great rock-cut canal, running from north to south, 12 feet deep, 4 feet wide, its eastern side being about 12 feet from the Sanctuary wall; but it does not run paralled to it, and was probably in use before this portion of the wall was constructed.

The bottom of this canal (2,313 feet) is 74 feet below the springing of Robinson's Arch, and 107 feet below the level of the old road-way. It was full of mud at the point we struck it, and when we got down to the bottom we drove galleries along it; but eventually some mud fell in by accident, and we found that it was covered by an arch, and that the mud reached up to within a foot of the crown.

The examination of this canal occupied a considerable time, and we met with so many checks, that it will be more convenient to describe it all together.

The point where we opened into it was as nearly as possible opposite the centre of the pier, and about 12 feet from the Sanctuary wall. We opened it out to the south, and after 24 feet found ourselves in a square chamber cut in rock, with a segmental arch, a passage cut in rock leading due east, but cut off by the Sanctuary wall; to the west there is a passage about 3 feet square, which we could not examine, as there was a stone in front, on which the arch of the chamber rested, it having slipped. To our south we passed through a small passage, and entered a circular cistern cut in rock, diameter 16 feet, height 14 feet 4 inches, roof of rock and flat, thickness of roof 2 feet to 3 feet; in the centre is a man-hole of masonry, leading down from the pavement under Robinson's Arch; to the south is a passage lead-

VOUSSOIR OF AN ARCH FALLEN THROUGH ROOF OF ROCK-CUT CANAL.

ing off from the cistern, the bottom at the same level as the bottom of that leading in, and the bottom of the cistern is 3 feet lower, so that there would always have been a supply of water in the tank. There was a depth of 8 feet 6 inches of mud inside the cistern; and when we first entered it, and drove along the rock, our gallery being only 3 feet high, we travelled all round without finding the exit passage. This passage is 8 feet high, and passes close to the southwest angle of the Sanctuary wall; it is cut in rock, is 3 feet 9 inches wide, and has a slightly-pointed semicircular arch thrown over, of six courses. Passing the southwest angle, it leaves the rock, and is carried southeast in masonry, 3 feet wide, with an arch of five courses, falling rapidly to bed of Tyropœon; after 40 feet it turns south, and is carried along in a modern-looking drain 2 feet wide, covered over with flagging. This was examined for 59 feet, but it became too narrow and full of silt to pursue it farther.

We now examined the canal north from the point we opened into it under Robinson's Arch, and found that it runs slightly away from the Sanctuary wall, is 3 feet 9 inches wide, and roofed over by a skew-pointed arch, that is to say, an arch with five courses, the side to the east being 22 inches, to the west 33 inches. It has a very comical appearance. At 34 feet north of the north end of pier we find the canal issues from another circular pool, 12 feet 9 inches in diameter, 14 feet high, roofed in rock, with the bottom 3 feet below the bottom of canal; there is a man-hole leading down from the pavement above. Into this pool a canal comes from the north; it is 4 feet wide, flat roof in rock, and continues for 14 feet, when it turns round to the west, and has on the eastern side an entrance into another circular rock-cut pool, of which only half is to be seen, as it is *cut through* by the foundations of the Sanctuary wall. To the west of this canal, at the south end, two curious, rock-cut rectangular chambers have been

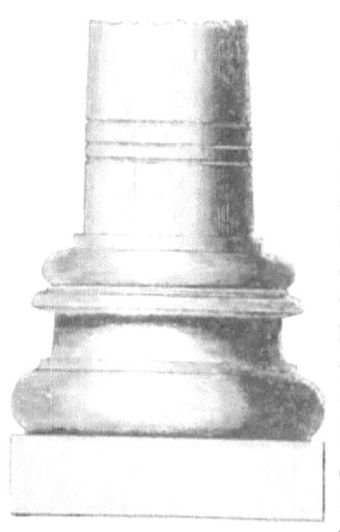

found, standing partially on top of the circular pool. They measure about 16 feet by 6 feet, and have semicircular arches; in one is a flight of steps, cut in the rock, leading up above. A base of a column, which had fallen through the roof, was lying in one of the chambers; it was too heavy to be brought home, and was used as part of the monument erected to the memory of the late Corporal Duncan (by his comrades) in the British cemetery at Jerusalem.

In following up the canal now, to the north we find that it is formed of masonry, about 3 feet wide and 8 feet high, with a semicircular arch of five courses, for 123 feet, where, in front of the Prophet's Gateway, and at 14 feet from the Sanctuary wall, the style changes, and it becomes a narrow passage 18 inches wide, with a flat roof of flagging, and runs off from the wall; it is 160 feet long, and is cut in two, a few feet south of the causeway of David Street, by the wall of a house. It would have been dangerous to break through this, and so the work was ended. Opposite to the Prophet's Gateway the bottom of the canal was found to be about 7 feet above the rock.

Several lamps, weights, jars, and an iron bar, were found in this canal, and also a stone roller for rolling *flat* roofs, precisely similar to those in use on the flat roofs of the Lebanon; so it is evident that at some period at least one house in Jerusalem was covered with a flat roof of wooden joists and mud; and I am inclined to the opinion that this was the general mode of construction of roofs until after the city was destroyed by Titus, when, wood becoming scarce, the vaulted roof came into use. 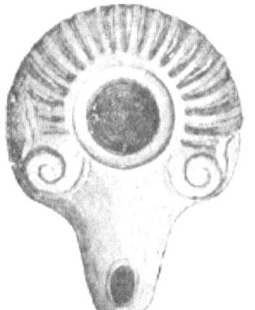 Measurements were taken of the two fallen voussoirs lying over the canal where we first struck it; one is much decayed, but the other measures 7 feet in length, and is 5 feet thick at the extrados, and 4 feet 4 inches at the intrados, and 4 feet high; there is a square joggle-hole cut on one side in the middle, 14 inches by 11 inches, and 4½ inches deep.

We could not get leave to dig alongside the wall under the arch without paying such a heavy bakshish as would have spoiled the market; but the wall was seen in several places, viz., at three points from the great canal at the foundations, at several points in the drain running along the wall above the pavement to the Prophet's Gate, and also in a gallery driven immediately under the pavement to the wall; a shaft was also sunk early one morning alongside the Sanctuary wall baring three courses from the surface. At the southwest angle, on south side, immediately outside my friend Abu Saûd's ground, a shaft was sunk down alongside the wall. The result is, that we have a correct idea of the wall under the arch; and it appears that it is built up of drafted stones, with rough faces as far as the pavement, and that above that the faces are smooth; and consequently it would appear that this portion of the Sanctuary wall was not built until the earth had filled up the valley as high as the pavement, so that it will be less ancient than the Sanctuary wall at Wilson's Arch.

The following is what the evidence before us (together with what follows in other chapters) appears to prove; and it will be noticed that, in consequence of subsequent researches, it differs somewhat from that given in letter of 13th January, 1869:

1. The winding aqueduct was cut in rock.
2. The Temple and Solomon's Palace were constructed, and a bridge leading across the Tyropœon Valley connected the Palace with the Lower City on the plateau below and east of the Upper City.
3. The arch of the bridge fell (two voussoirs still remain), breaking in part of the arch of the aqueduct.
4. The temple was reconstructed by Herod, who took in the Temple of Solomon, and built the present southwest angle of the Sanctuary; and the new wall cut-

ting across portions of the rock-cut canal, connections were made by means of masonry passages. At this time the rubbish had begun to choke up the valley at this point to 23 feet; and the wall to that height was built with rough-faced stones, the portion above being made to resemble the older parts of the wall. A pavement was laid on the rubbish, and the pier and arch of Robinson's Arch and viaduct were built. In order to obtain water readily, shafts (which still exist) were constructed at intervals from the pavement to the canal and pools.

5. The arch fell, and now rests upon the pavement.
6. *Débris* began to fill up the valley, and the pier of the arch, sticking out, was removed for building purposes—all except the three lower courses.
7. When Wilson's Arch and pier were built, a second pavement was made along the west wall of Sanctuary, level with sill of Prophet's Gateway, and a few feet above the pavement at Robinson's Arch, reaching out to the Dung Gate. Mention of this road is made in the Normal Chronicle,* and parts of the pavement still exist, and also a drain running underneath it: houses built near this pavement.
8. The houses and walls, becoming ruins and *débris*, filled the valley to its present height, which at this point is 45 feet above *lower* pavement.

The Pacha would give me no assistance of any kind, unless I entered into a written engagement not to touch the Sanctuary walls; and, as the very object of my sojourn at Jerusalem was for the purpose of examining those walls, it was impossible to come to terms on any common grounds.

We had a great number of visitors to see the ruins of the old arch; and several ladies were let down by means of a chair, but they of course could not go any lower than the pavement. On one or two occasions we had some difficulties when the chair was not used, as the close air and exer-

* Williams's "Holy City."

tion made parties get faint, and they had to be dragged up with the rope.

SUBURBAN GATES OF SECOND TEMPLE.

Gate of the Prophet.—In the west wall of the Noble Sanctuary, about 270 feet from the southwest angle, immediately under the Moor's Gate, is an enormous lintel, which, it appears, was first prominently brought to notice in this century by Dr. Barclay, of the United States, in his " City of the Great King."

In 1866 Captain Wilson excavated to a depth of about 25 feet in front of the north jamb of the gate without reaching the sill. He also explored a cistern in the Sanctuary, which proved to be the continuation of the Mosque el Burak, the two together forming the passage leading from the Prophet's Gate to the level of the Sanctuary.

A brief description of the lay of the ground at this point may be necessary. The general level of the Sanctuary is 2,420 feet above the Mediterranean, but near the Moor's Gate it is 2,416 feet. Immediately outside this gate the general surface is about 2,395 feet, and a ramp leads up to the gate from the ground below. This ramp, near the wall, is formed by two vaulted chambers, one over the other; in the lower one the lintel can be seen. The height of the lintel is 6 feet 10 inches, the total length visible is 20 feet 1 inch; the bottom is at a level of 2,398 feet 5 inches, being 5 feet 5 inches above the surface of the ground at that point. The northern jamb of the gate can be seen; it is flush with the northern side of the older portion of the passage inside, which is here 18 feet 8 inches wide, and we may reasonably suppose the gateway to be the same width. The lintel would then be 24 feet 8 inches in length.

The space below the lintel, forming the gateway, between the two jambs, is built up in rough rubble, with here and there a few cut stones. Immediately above the lintel there are no courses of bevelled stones; the masonry is modern, and the stones are small. At the Jews' Wailing Place there two courses of bevelled stones and four of square stones above the level of the top of the lintel; but these all terminate abruptly at about 12 feet from the gate.

An excavation was commenced here on 17th March, 1869. It was desirable to sink the shaft at some distance from that of Captain Wilson, as where the soil is very loose it is dangerous to work again in an old excavation. We commenced about 7 feet north of the jamb of the gate alongside the Sanctuary wall. About 5 feet below the surface we came upon a lamp and a good deal of broken pottery, of a different description to what we had hitherto met with, and bearing beautiful impressions of scrolls and other devices. At 14 feet a gallery was driven in to the south, until we reached the northern jamb of the gateway, the soil being black and very loose. We here came upon the shaft of Captain Wilson, and a rush of earth came into our gallery. On looking up into the void space a stone corbel was seen to be built into the rubble masonry under the lintel. It must, of course, have been placed there when the gate was blocked up, and was probably for the foundations of a house to rest on. I imagine that the foundations of the vaulted chambers on which the ramp leading to the Moor's Gate is laid rest upon similar corbels on the side near the Sanctuary wall.

Having made secure the gallery where the rush had taken place, a shaft was sunk down along the northern jamb, through hard earth mixed with large stones, some of them 2 feet long. At about 23 feet from the surface the sill-course was met with. This course, however, is broken, so that it cannot be said whether the top or bottom of it is the true sill of the gate. The top is 28 feet 9¼ inches below the lintel, and the bottom is 32 feet 1¼ inch below it.

We now continued our shaft, and 9 inches below the bottom of the sill-course came upon stone flagging, forming the flat roof to a drain running along the Sanctuary wall toward the southwest angle. This drain is 2 feet 4 inches wide, and 5 feet 6 inches high. It is the same drain which we found above the pavement at Robinson's Arch, and which we followed up to the Prophet's Gateway (see p. 78). Men were sent to knock at the extremity of this drain from Robinson's Arch, and they could be heard quite plainly; but we could not communicate through to our shaft at the Prophet's Gate, as rubbish had fallen in and stopped up the passage.

Sinking through this drain we came upon the top of a wall, perpendicular to, and abutting on, the Sanctuary wall, at 31 feet below the surface. We first sunk to the south of wall, and found ourselves in heavy masonry; then sinking north of it, and finding the face to be of well-dressed squared stones, in courses, we continued our shaft alongside of it, until at 66 feet 7 inches from the surface we passed its foundations. We then continued along the Sanctuary wall, and at 73 feet 7 inches struck the rock, which is cut horizontally, and the bottom stone of the Sanctuary wall is let into it.

For the last 30 feet we had passed through *débris* composed of hard earth and broken cut stones, many of them 3 inches by 2 inches by 1 foot 6 inches. On tamping up, a gallery was driven to the south, through the wall abutting on to the Sanctuary, to a distance of 8 feet, when it was found that it had been a retaining wall, about 6 feet thick, there being no southern face to it. From this it appears that the road to the Prophet's Gate from the Tyropœon Valley may have been by means of a causeway, raised 46 feet above the rock. Whether it may have been solid or supported on arches is not apparent.

The Sanctuary wall has thus been bared to a depth of 73 feet 6 inches from the bottom of the lintel of the Prophet's Gate to the rock, and the stones are of one appearance throughout, and are probably *in situ*. There are twenty-six courses of drafted stones in all, twenty-two below the lintel, two on a level with the lintel, and two above it. These two latter courses do not now exist immediately above the lintel, but can be seen a little farther to the north at the Wailing

Place. Above these, again, are four courses of squared stones, without drafts, except in portion of the fourth and lower course, at the farther end, near the Hall of Justice, where drafts are to be seen.

It is interesting to compare the stones above-ground at the Wailing Place with those we have bared beneath the ground at the Prophet's Gate, and for this purpose a tabular form is annexed (see Appendix), showing the height of each course in the wall at this point, and the width of bevel or marginal draft, and also the set-out of each stone.

The first course below the lintel is very much worn, and is shown on Plate 12 Ordnance Survey, as being 3 feet 2 inches in height. By taken it in conjunction with the courses above and below, I find it to be 3 feet 5 inches in height.

The stones we have laid bare are in a much higher state of preservation than those at the Wailing Place. It is curious that many of them are in good order at the top and damaged at the bottom.

With one exception, we have found the top draft to be a little broader than that at the bottom, and this we observed, also, to be the case in the stones uncovered on the south and east faces of the Sanctuary wall.

Gate of the Bath.—Having failed to find any entrance similar to the Prophet's Gate in the west Sanctuary wall, south of Wilson's Arch, I made a search to the north of that arch. Any examination here is difficult, as the present surface outside is generally about the same level as, or higher than, that of the Sanctuary.

Twenty feet to the south of the Gate of the Bath is a large cistern (numbered xxx. on the Ordnance Map), which was discovered and surveyed by Captain Wilson: it runs east and west, and is shown as piercing the Sanctuary wall. On plan it is singularly like the vaulted passage leading from the Prophet's Gate; it is of the same width, and runs the same distance into the Sanctuary, but it does not appear to turn round at the inner extremity, as the other passage does.

It would be very interesting to ascertain whether over this cistern (xxx.) there be a lintel similar to that at the Prophet's Gate.

When examining the Sanctuary wall on the outside, in an Effendi's house, I found a cistern which, on examination, proved to be in direct prolongation of cistern xxx., but not so wide. It was nearly empty; and I was able to go down and measure it. It is 34 feet 6 inches from surface of ground to bottom; width from north to south, nearly 12 feet; and length from east to west, 14 feet 9 inches. On the south there is a recess, so that the Sanctuary wall is exposed over a surface 28 feet in height and 12 feet in length, but it is for the most part covered with plaster. At 22 feet from the bottom can be seen the springing of a modern masonry arch, which is apparently the western extremity of the vault of cistern xxx. There are no signs of any lintel or large stones, but the surface here is over 6 feet above the general level of the Sanctuary, and the wall, free of plaster, could only be seen to a depth of 12 feet below the surface, that is to say, it could not be seen so low down as the level of the upper bevelled course at the Jews' Wailing Place. It is very necessary that the plaster covering the wall should be be removed, as by so doing the wall would be bared to a level lower than the bottom of the lintel at the Prophet's Gate.

I am under the impression that this may be one Suburban Gate, the Prophet's Gate being the other.

CHAPTER IV.

SOUTHERN WALL.

Our researches here show that the portion of the wall to the west of the Double Gate is of a different construction to, and more recent than, that to the west.

This is a matter of very great importance, and, combined with other results, appears to show the impossibility of the Temple having existed at the southwest angle, as restored by Mr. Fergusson and others.

The only solution of the question I can see, is by supposing the portion to the east of the Double Gate to have formed the south wall of Solomon's Palace, and that to the west to have been added by Herod when he enlarged the courts of the Temple.

The south wall of the Sanctuary area, 922 feet in length, is broken into nearly three equal portions by the Triple Gate to the east, and the Double or Huldah Gate to the west. At the present time the surface of the ground runs nearly level from the southwest angle to the sill of the Triple Gate (2,380 feet), and then shelves down about 22 feet to the southeast angle; but in earlier times the wall presented a very different appearance, for the rock of Mount Moriah, which is found within a foot of the sill of the Triple Gate, shelves down rapidly to the southeast angle, falling over 100 feet in 300. Toward the west from the Triple Gate the rock falls more gently; at the Double Gate, whose sill is on a level with that of the Triple Gate, the rock is probably at a depth of 30 feet; it then falls more rapidly to about 90 feet from the southwest angle, where appears to be the bed of the Tyropœon Valley—this point is 90 feet below the sill of the Triple Gate; the rock now rises again rapidly to the west, having risen about 30 feet at the southwest angle.

From the examination of this south wall, in nine separate places, there appears to be no doubt that the whole of the stones below the present surface are bevelled or marginal-drafted, though the faces are not all finely dressed, and that they are *in situ*, although, as previously observed, the portion of the wall to the west of the Double Gate appears less ancient than the remainder.

As the rock is found at the sill of the Triple Gate, it follows that we can have no course of stone running through from end to end below that level. The first through course has its bed on a level with the sole of the Triple Gate: it is nearly double the height of the courses below, being from 5 feet 10 inches to 6 feet in height.

Letter, September 2, 1868.—" The courses of stone in this wall, with marginal drafts, usually run from 3 feet 6 inches to 3 feet 9 inches in height, but between the Double or Huldah Gate and the Triple Gate, there is a course the height of which is from 5 feet 10 inches to 6 feet 1 inch; so far this is described in Captain Wilson's O. S. notes. On a recent examination of the south wall, I found this large course continued to the southeast angle, and thence running north, along the east wall, for 24 feet.

" On the elevation it may be seen that the course is unbroken between the Huldah and Triple Gates; thence to the Single Gate there is one stone *in situ*, and from a point 70 feet from the southeast angle to the angle itself, the course again is in a good state of preservation (see Ordnance Survey photograph of the southeast angle).

" I do not find that this has been made the subject of remark in any existing work, and as it bears directly upon the question of the unity of the south Sanctuary wall, I add some further particulars.

" This course is nearly double the height of the other

'drafted' courses in the Sanctuary wall. Its base is about 1 foot above the highest part of the rock of Mount Moriah (where cut by the south front), and consequently it is the first course in this front which can run uninterruptedly from east to west. It exists at present, more or less continuously, for 600 feet west of the southeast angle, but is not seen west of the Huldah Gate.

"At the Triple Gate its bed is 15 to 30 inches above what it is at the southeast angle, the line between these two points being straight or only a very gentle curve; in other words the course is not horizontal, but has a fall from centre to flank of about 30 inches. It is obvious that, on account of the peculiar nature of the ground, a considerable rise from flank to centre in the courses would be required in order to avoid offending the eye, and it is interesting to find the courses so placed, whether from accident or design.

"The sill of the Triple Gate is level with the base of this course, as are probably also those of the Huldah and Golden Gates. The sill of the Single Gate is at a lower level, but this gate has all the appearance of being quite a modern construction, the entrance found 20 feet lower, and immediately beneath it going far to support the idea that this Single Gate itself was not finished until after a considerable amount of the present *débris* in Ophel had accumulated.

"At the southeast angle, the corner-stone of this course weighs over one hundred tons, and though not the longest stone is certainly the heaviest visible in the Sanctuary wall."

Were the south wall of one construction, we ought to find this large course running through west of the Double Gate, but we have searched for it in vain. At the first and second shafts it is difficult to determine whether the stones on a level with this great course are drafted or not, and therefore they give no information; but at the third and fourth we find levelled stones apparently still *in situ*, at a higher level than the great course, and yet we find no signs of the great course itself. We have certainly a large stone at the southwest angle, the longest (38 feet 9 inches) at present known, but it is only 3 feet 3 inches to 3 feet 6 inches in height, and its bed is about 4 feet above that of the great course; it is, then, apparent that this great course did not reach so far as the southwest angle, or, in other words, that this western portion of the south wall is of a different construction to the eastern. We find this again to be the case when we examine the walls to their foundations, for at the southeast angle, and at the Single Gate, we find the wall springing from the rock, with the faces nicely worked, while at the southwest angle, and for at least 213 feet to the east of it, we find the stones up to a certain level with beautiful marginal drafts, but with rough-picked faces; and the line where these rough stones end, and the smooth-faced stones commence, is on a level nearly with the pavement on which the *débris* of Robinson's Arch rests. We have said that the rough stones are found along the west wall under Robinson's Arch, up to the level of the pavement, and it appears probable that they continue with the pavement up to the Prophet's Gate. If so, it gives the impression that the portion of the wall west of the Double Gate, and round by the southwest angle to the Prophet's Gate, was constructed after the Tyropœon had commenced to fill up, and that the lower portion, the rough stones below the pavement, were never exposed to view. In Josephus ("Wars," v. v. 1), we find: "The lowest part of this was erected to the height of 300 cubits, and in some places more, yet did not the entire depth of the foundations appear, for they brought earth and filled up the valleys, as being desirous to make them on a level with the narrow streets of the city." This passage can only apply to two sides of the Temple, the west and the north, for on the south there is no valley near, and on the east is the Kedron, the apparent bottom of which is still considerably lower than the actual bottom of the walls. Now it is just on the southwestern side (and northeastern) that we find these roughly-faced stones, reaching up to a certain level; and, finding a hard, well-squared marble (mezzeh) pavement also running along at that level, we may fairly conclude that this was the line of surface at some time after the construction of the southwest angle; and we may also infer that it was the *first* surface used after the southwest angle was completed, and that the roughly-faced bevelled stones below were never intended to be exposed to view.

At the southeast angle, and along the south walls up to Triple Gate, we find the smooth-faced stones are continued down to the rock, and it appears that when this portion of the wall was built, there was a *débris* at this point of only 12 feet in depth.

At the southwest angle, and for at least 90 feet along the south wall, we have found a second and less ancient pavement. It is about 20 feet above the first pavement, and about 23 feet below the present surface; it is nearly on a level with the sill of the Prophet's Gateway, and with what appears to have been an old surface under Wilson's Arch. This pavement appears to have been used after the destruction of Robinson's Arch, and before the building of the present Wilson's Arch.

It was under this pavement that the signet " of Haggai, the son of Shebaniah,"* was found in 1867; and in another shaft at the southwest angle we have found several fragments of pottery at a depth of about 5 feet below the pavement. Among the fragments are several Greek lamps, one of which has an inscription of Christian origin, similar to those on lamps which have been considered to be of the third or fourth centuries. These fragments may, to a certain extent, help us in ascertaining the age of this pavement. No arrangement in the laying of these pieces of pottery was noticed: they had the appearance of having been lying in the position in which they were found when this upper pavement was laid, and, if so, we must suppose it to have been made after the third or fourth century. It appears

See page 386.

possible that this may have been the level of roadway leading under Wilson's Arch, and through the present Dung Gate, spoken of in the Norman Chronicle (see Williams's " Holy City "); also there is to be seen on a line of road under Wilson's Arch along the west wall of the Haram area on the plan of Jerusalem in the twelfth century given in Fergusson's article on Jerusalem (Smith's " Dictionary "). It has been observed that the west wall of the Sanctuary at Robinson's Arch cuts through an ancient system of rock-cut water-ducts and tanks running along the western side of the Tyropœon Valley. The long aqueduct, which is described under shaft 3, and which commences abruptly at the south Sanctuary wall, was found to follow the bed of the Tyropœon for several hundred feet, and was probably also cut through at the construction of this wall.

If we are to suppose that the roughly-faced stones at the southwest angle were never exposed to view, we must presume also that the two apparent voussoirs lying on the aqueduct under Robinson's Arch belonged to a bridge which crossed the Tyropœon Valley previous to the building of the southwest angle of the Sanctuary. It is to be remarked with reference to the roughly-faced stones, that their joints and marginal drafts are quite as perfectly wrought as those to be found on the stones whose faces are finely worked.

On the west side of the Double Gate, drafted stones are only to be seen above the surface within 90 feet of the southwest angle. There are four courses visible; they suddenly cease, and are succeeded between this point and the Double Gate by several courses of large squared stones, which are jointed on to the bevelled stones in a very irregular manner. (See Captain Wilson's Plates, O. S.) The top of these squared stones ends in a line with the top of the upper bevelled stones, and above them there are courses of stone of a smaller size. These squared stones vary in height, some courses being more than 4 feet; they are not laid very skilfully, the lines of the horizontal joints having a wavy appearance, and in one case a course commencing at one end with a height of 4 feet, gradually runs out in 200 feet to a height of 3 feet 4 inches. This, however, is not a feature confined to the newer or squared work, it frequently occurs in the bevelled stones; for example, the stone at the southwest angle, 38 feet 9 inches in length, is 3 feet 3 inches high at the northern end, 3 feet 6 inches at centre, and 3 feet 6 inches at the southwest angle.

There appears to have been a considerable want of attention in the reconstruction of the wall at the southwest angle, for the joints between the squared stones are found to act as weepers. The wall is very much disfigured by the deposit left by the running water.

It is curious to find that from the Prophet's Gate to Wilson's Arch, the drafted stones have their faces finely worked, while to the south of the Prophet's Gate there are stones at a higher level which have their faces quite rough; and it only seems accounted for by supposing that the wall at the southwest angle is of later date.

The present surface of the ground between the southwest angle and the sole of the Triple Gate is now nearly on a level (2,380 feet), from thence it shelves down to a level of 2,356 at the southeast angle. As previously observed, a great course of stones runs between the southeast angle and Double Gate, partly broken away in a few places: above this great course no bevelled stones are to be seen except a few, apparently *in situ*, just at the southeast angle. As the bed of this great course is on a level with the floor of the great vaulted substructures inside the Sanctuary at the southeast angle, it can readily be seen that the original substructures are not likely to have remained after the retaining walls east and south had been destroyed, and that, therefore, the present substructures are likely to be less ancient than the great course and lower portions of the old wall, which still remain *in situ*.

A shaft was sunk, 90 feet from the southwest angle, exposing the bottom of the Tyropœon Valley.

The following is from the account which I wrote at the time:

"At 12 feet 6 inches from the surface a pavement was found, stones of mezzeh, not regularly shaped, general size 12 inches by 15 inches, well polished, probably from wear. Below the pavement a kind of concrete was sunk through, composed of stones, bricks, and mortar, for a depth of 16 feet. From 28 feet 6 inches to 33 feet 6 inches loose stones and shingle were met with, and after that large stones were found 3 feet by 2 feet 6 inches by 2 feet, one of which had a draft round it; also a wall of rubble running north and south, and abutting on the Sanctuary wall, stones about 2 feet cube.

"The courses of the Sanctuary wall exposed are as follow: the first three courses are similar to those aboveground at this point, that is, they are great squared stones without drafts, in height about 3 feet 3 inches. The courses fourth to ninth appear to be similar to those at the Jews' Wailing Place, but the first five are very much worn, though the draft can be distinguished, height 3 feet 9 inches. The face of the ninth course projects 3 inches beyond the draft. The tenth and remaining courses differ from any seen above-ground at the present day. The faces of the stones appear as when they were brought from the quarries, roughly dressed into three faces, and projecting in some cases eighteen inches beyond their drafts, which are about 4 inches to 6 inches wide, and most beautifully worked. The stones are fitted together in the most marvellous manner, the joints being hardly discernible; a section is enclosed. This work has been stopped a day or two for want of wood.

"At a depth of 22 feet was found the signet-stone of 'Haggai, the son of Shebaniah;' characters engraved in Hebrew of the transition period. Depth excavated to Thursday, 10th October, 1867, 76 feet.

"On Friday, having arrived at a depth of 79 feet, the men were breaking up a stone at the bottom of the shaft.

Suddenly the ground gave way, down went the stone and the hammer, the men barely saving themselves. They at once rushed up, and told the sergeant they had found the bottomless pit. I went down to the spot and examined it, and, in order that you may have an idea of the extent of our work, I will give you a description of our descent.

"The shaft-mouth is on the south side of the Sanctuary wall, near the southwest angle, among the prickly pears; beside it, to the east, lying against the Sanctuary wall, is a large mass of rubbish that has been brought up; while over the mouth itself is a triangular gin with iron wheel attached, with guy for running up the excavated soil. Looking down the shaft, one sees that it is lined for the first 20 feet with frames 4 feet 6 inches in the clear; farther down, the Sanctuary wall and soil cut through is seen, and a man standing at what appears to be the bottom. An order is given to this man, who repeats it, and then, faintly, is heard a sepulchral voice answering as it were from another world. Reaching down to the man who is visible is a 34 feet rope-ladder, and, on descending by it, one finds he is standing on a ledge which the ladder does not touch by 4 feet. This ledge is the top of a wall running north and south and abutting on the Sanctuary wall; its east face just cuts the centre of the shaft, which has to be canted off about two feet toward the east, just where some large loose stones jut out in the most disagreeable manner. Here five more frames have been fixed to keep these stones steady. On peering down from this ledge, one sees the Sanctuary wall with its projecting courses until they are lost in the darkness below, observing, also, at the same time, that two sides of the shaft are cut through the soil and are self-supporting. Now to descend this second drop the ladder is again required; accordingly, having told the man at bottom to get under cover, it is lowered to the ledge, from whence it is found that it does not reach to the bottom by several feet. It is therefore lowered the required distance, and one has to reach it by climbing down hand over hand for about twelve feet.

On passing along, one notes the marvellous joints of the Sanctuary wall stones, and also, probably, gets a few blows on skull and knuckles from falling pebbles. Just on reaching the bottom, one recollects there is still a pit of unknown depth to be explored, and cautiously straddles across it. Then can be seen that one course in the Sanctuary wall, near the bottom, is quite smooth all over, the stone being finely dressed, all other courses being only well dressed round the drafts; one also sees two stout boards lying against the Sanctuary wall, under which the men retire whenever an accidental shower of stones renders their position dangerous. One is now at a depth of 79 feet from the surface, and from here we commence the exploring of the 'bottomless pit.' After dropping a rope down, we found that it was only 6 feet deep, though it looked black enough for any thing. Climbing down, we found ourselves in a passage running south from the Sanctuary, 4 feet high by 2 feet wide, and we explored this passage. It is of rough rubble masonry, with flat stones at the top similar to the aqueduct from the Triple Gate, but not so carefully constructed. The floor and sides are very muddy, as if water gathers there during the rainy season.

"It struck me that it might be an overflow aqueduct from the Temple, and that there might be a water conduit underneath; we scrambled along for a long way on our feet, our skulls and spines coming in unhappy contact with the passage roof; after about 200 feet we found that the mud reached higher up, and we had to crawl by means of elbows and toes; gradually the passage got more and more filled up, and our bodies could barely squeeze through, and there did not appear sufficient air to support us for any length of time, so that, having advanced 400 feet, we commenced a difficult retrograde movement, having to get back half-way before we could turn our heads round. On arriving at the mouth of the passage underneath the shaft, we spent some time in examining the sides, but there is no appearance of its having come under the Haram wall. It seems to start suddenly, and I can only suppose it to have been the examining-passage over an aqueduct coming from the Temple, and I am having the floor taken up to settle the question. This passage is on a level with the foundations of the Haram wall, which are rough-hewn stones—perhaps rock—I cannot tell yet. The bottom is the enormous distance of 85 feet below the surface of the ground.

"Rock was found at 3 feet below the bed of the aqueduct. This is the lowest point in the Tyropœon Valley along the south front of the Sanctuary wall.

"At 350 feet along the passage, a branch gallery from the east was found, but it was impossible to clear out the deposit, as this portion was only reached by crawling. The owner of the soil began to worry about our being so long on his ground; I therefore have had the shaft filled up, much to his disgust, as he had begun to look upon it as an annuity.

"We have sunk a shaft 350 feet to the south of the Sanctuary wall, and have had the good fortune, at a depth of 60 feet, to drop directly upon our passage. The fellahin were regularly scared when they broke up a stone and found the passage with our well-known broad arrow burnt black on the roof. The passage is now being cleared out to the south.

"It appears to traverse the bed of the Tyropœon Valley; galleries were driven east and west, and the rock found to rise on each side. The passage was cleared out for a total distance of 600 feet from the Sanctuary wall, and was then abandoned.

"This aqueduct appears to have existed before the southwest angle of the Sanctuary, and to have been cut across, and rendered useless when the wall was built."

GREAT PASSAGE UNDER THE SINGLE GATE

A shaft was commenced 37 feet south of the gate, and at 22 feet a slab was found drafted on its under face; it was supposed to have covered a passage, but no walls were seen. The shingle came running into this shaft so fast that it had to be closed up, and another one commenced at 14 feet south of the Single Gate; struck the rock at 34 feet 6 inches; surface rugged.

For the first 20 feet the work was very difficult, the material sunk through being composed of rough stones and rubbish. The stones had to be broken up in the shaft, and the concussion caused the loose shingle to run like water. The workmen were continually stopping until Sergeant Birtles could come and set them going again. From 20 to 30 feet in depth the soil was very firm, of a dark-brown color. The stones are generally rough cubes from 9 inches to 18 inches, some are fragments of dressed stone, melekeh, and a few are of mezzeh; some pieces of marble have been found.

Shaft filled up for 11 feet, and gallery driven to the Sanctuary wall.

Extract from Letter, October 22, 1867.—"In a former letter I stated that I believed there was another system of vaults under the present vaults, at the southeast angle; and in a sketch at the same time I showed a point where I expected the entrance would be, under the Single Gate. I have been foiled once or twice in getting to this point; first the shaft failed, and when we had driven a second we had to wait till we could scrape together some gallery frames; finally we drove the gallery to the point I had indicated under the Single Gate, and on Wednesday, to our great delight, the hoped-for entrance was found. We were, however, both too ill to stay and explore it, and I had it covered up again. Yesterday we reopened it, and Sergeant Birtles set about getting out the *débris*. The entrance was into a passage which appeared to be blocked up—suddenly a crash, and the passage appeared clear and unencumbered, but after getting in Sergeant Birtles brought down another fall, and was blocked up in the passage without a light for two hours. It is quite clear now, the rubbish having settled at the bottom.* I send you a plan which I made yesterday immediately it was open; you will see that the stones are of great size, one of them 15 feet long, nearly all are bevelled and beautifully worked, but some of them are only hammer-dressed. The passage is 3 feet wide, and is perpendicular to the south wall of the Sanctuary, running between the piers which support the vaults above. After 60 feet the roof-stones disappear. On the east there is a passage blocked up, and also there is a second entrance above that by which we got in. The roof is composed of large stones, many of them bevelled, and laid flat on the upper course of the passage-wall. This upper course is 4 feet in height, and at the bottom of it on each side are the remains of a small aqueduct jutting out from the wall, made of dark cement. The passage is probably from 12 feet to 18 feet high, its roof is 20 feet below the floor of the Sanctuary vaults, or about 60 feet below the level of the Sanctuary. At the point B on plan, there are indications of there having been a metal gate. A check, 10-inch cube, is cut in one of the roof-stones, and there is the mark of abrasion on one of the stones, as if a metal door had swung against it; radius of swing about 13 inches.

"At present I have no clew as to the use of this passage."

There are several very interesting points connected with the Haram Area which this discovery has raised. The Single and Triple Gates are nearly (within 3 feet) on the same level as the floor within, on which the bases of the piers rest (2,379 feet), and this floor is 17 feet above the earth at the southeast angle, and 80 feet above the rock at that point. That this should be filled up solid seems improbable; and it seems more than likely that there is another system of older arches underneath those visible at present. All the masonry and arches above the level of the gates are comparatively modern.

* References to plans not published in the volume may be made at the Society's Office, 9, Pall Mall East, where all Captain Warren's plans are preserved.

The floor of these vaults is 107 feet *above* the rock on the east side of the Sanctuary wall, at about 10 feet north of the southeast angle, and 41 *below* the present level of the Sanctuary. Supposing the Great Southern Portico to have been 50 feet in height, this wall would not have been less than 200 feet in height; but probably at this time 30 or 40 feet of the basement was covered up.

CHAPTER V.

EASTERN SIDE OF THE SANCTUARY.—SOUTHEAST ANGLE.

Letter of August, 1867.—"*Galleries in western face of Kedron Valley, below the Sanctuary.*—Three separate attempts were made to find the rock at an intermediate point between the southeast angle and the Kedron. First a gallery was driven about 70 feet below the surface. At the southeast angle the substance met with was a dry loose shingle, lying at an angle of 30 degrees. The greatest difficulties were experienced in driving this gallery. The shingle, when it got a start, ran like water, and after driving the gallery 47 feet, such an immense cavity was formed above the frames, that, spite of its being filled up with brushwood and straw, the shingle eventually got the upper hand, and smashed in the frames, and I considered it dangerous to proceed with it.

"No. 2.—An oblique gallery was tried at an angle of 60 degrees, so as to be perpendicular to the layer of shingle and also to the presumed lay of the rock. After driving 14 feet, the shingle commenced running rapidly, and destroyed the frames.

"No. 3.—A perpendicular shaft was next attempted, and sunk about 14 feet 6 inches, with like results; the shingle (stone chippings, without a particle of earth) being in character almost a fluid.

"I was so much struck with what I saw in several of the wadies about Jerusalem, that I came to the conclusion that there might be water flowing in the Kedron under the accumulation of rubbish. I wished first to commence about 50 feet west of the present valley, so as to strike the natural valley in the rock; but the loose shingle prevented this, and it was considered wiser to follow the rock which crops up to the surface on the east side of the valley. Accordingly a shaft was sunk, due east of the southeast angle of the Sanctuary, and at a distance of 305 feet from it in the present bed of the Kedron. At 20 feet we found the rock falling to the west (see section)."

The work was discontinued for want of the galleryframes I was expecting from England; there was no wood fit for the purpose in Jerusalem or Jaffa.

In November, 1868, we were able to continue, and at 65 feet found the true bed of the Kedron; at 240 feet from the southeast angle, and at (2,171 feet) a depth of $38\frac{1}{2}$ feet below the present false bed. There was no stream or running water in it; but when the rains came on, the gallery at this point was much damaged; and it is apparent that at that time the water flows along the true bed.

We now found a masonry wall, 3 feet thick, in front of us; and, breaking through this, began to ascend the hill gently for the first 60 feet from the wall. Some roughly-rounded flints were found on the rock.

The rock began to rise rapidly, and the work was most difficult, as we found ourselves among loose shingle which, when it rolled, carried every thing before it to the bottom of the gallery.

At 160 feet from the entrance the air became very impure; but on going a little farther a rushing noise was heard, which proved to be a steam of pure air circulating through the ground.

We now came to several masonry walls, apparently for supporting terraces along the Kedron bank. The heavy rains again obliged us to abandon this work; and when we commenced again the rock was found to rise so rapidly at 30° that it was impossible to go up straight through the loose stones. We tried zigzags; but were finally obliged to give it up (February, 1868) when we were 175 feet from the shaft-mouth, and 130 feet from the Sanctuary wall.

In 1869 a gallery was driven down along the rock for 35 feet; and, finding it to lie at the same angle as it did below, I conclude it to be in one line (see section).

Extract from Letter of December 22, 1868.—" After having examined the Ophel wall (described p. 227), a shaft was commenced, November 14, 1868, at about 20 feet southeast of the southeast angle of the Sanctuary. The *débris* sunk through is composed principally of stone chippings, alternating with layers of fat earth, and in some places rough stones about a foot wide. On arriving at a depth of 53 feet a gallery was driven in to the Sanctuary wall passing through two rough masonry walls running respectively north and south, and east and west. The gallery reached the east wall of the Sanctuary at about 6 feet north of the southeast angle, and three letters in red paint were found on one of the stones.

"A gallery was then driven to the southeast angle, and a shaft sunk; another character in red paint was found on the wall while sinking the shaft.

"The rock (2,277 feet) is about 10 feet lower than at 16 feet west of the southeast angle. It is very soft and much decayed, but appears to be mezzeh. The corner-stone is let into the rock apparently about 2 feet; it is well dressed, and has an ordinary marginal draft of about 4 inches at the top. It shows above the rock about 2 feet. The next course is 4 feet $3\frac{1}{2}$ inches in height, with an ordinary marginal draft at bottom, but of only 1 inch in width at the top. It is very roughly dressed within the draft. The next or third course is 4 feet $2\frac{1}{2}$ inches in height, with a draft below of $4\frac{1}{2}$ inches, but none above. The character which I enclose lies on that part where the draft should be.

"The fourth course is 3 feet $7\frac{1}{2}$ inches in height, with a shallow draft of 9 inches above; it is only on this account different from any that are to be seen above-ground.

"The fifth course is similar in every respect to the best specimens of stones found at the southeast angle above the surface; it is 3 feet 8 inches in height, and on the second stone from the angle are the three letters.

"These stones are in the most excellent preservation, as perfect as if they had been cut yesterday. They are very well dressed, but except in the instances which I have mentioned differ in nowise from the perfect specimens aboveground. The marginal drafts and about 2 inches around the projecting surface have been picked over with an eight-toothed chisel, about eight teeth to the inch; within this a 'point' or single-pointed chisel, has been used.

"The letters or characters are in red paint,[*] apparently put on with a brush; the larger letters are 5 inches high. There are a few red splashes here and there, as if the paint had dropped from the brush. The general impression resulting from the examination of these marks is that they are the quarry-marks, and were made before the stones were placed *in situ*. If this be the case, then the stones must have been dressed previously to their having been brought from the quarries.

"The *débris* resting against the wall at this point is composed of stone chippings, intermixed with some black stuff looking like decomposed or charred wood. The layers of the *débris* slope in toward the Haram wall, instead of away from it.

"The color of the paint is apparently vermilion; it easily rubs off when touched with the wetted finger."

January 22, 1869.—"I have carefully tested the angle of the base course, and find it to be 92° 35′, while that at the surface I make 92° 5′. Captain Wilson, in his notes, gives the general direction of the walls 92° 50′; the eastern wall is somewhat irregular, the first 120 only being in a perfectly straight line (excluding the offsets), after which there are several slight bulges; it is, however, very probable that

---

[*] See Quarterly Statement II., Letter of Mr. Emanuel Deutsch, dated April, 1869.

the courses below the present surface are in a straight line for the first 260 feet to the north, as in that distance the inaccuracies do not amount to more than a foot; at this point there is a small postern on about the same level as the Single Gate on the south side; from this postern the wall takes a slight turn to the northeast, so that in 650 feet it is about 8 feet to the east of a line in production of the first 260 feet of the east wall (see Ordnance Survey Plan $\frac{1}{500}$).

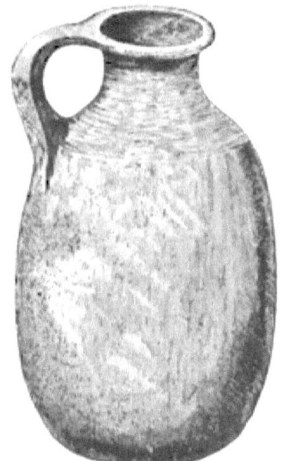

ANCIENT JAR FOUND AT SOUTHEAST ANGLE (IN THE ROCK.)

"The rock at the southeast angle into which the base course is let is very soft. At 3 feet to the east of the angle a hole was found scooped out of the rock, 1 foot across and 1 foot deep; on clearing the earth out of it, a little earthenware jar was found, standing upright, as though it had been purposely placed there.

"A gallery was driven to the east from the angle for about 8 feet, when the rock was found to slope away at an angle of about one in nine; this gallery was then tamped up, and a search was made around the corner-stone for any means of getting under it; at 4 feet north of the angle close to the wall, the rock was found to be cut away in the form of a semicircle or horseshoe, 2 feet wide and about 2 feet 8 inches deep; dark mould was found in it; on clearing it out it was found that the base course rests upon very hard rock (mezzeh), the soft rock extending only to a depth of from 2 to 3 feet: the base course is 3 feet 8 inches in height.

"Upon the soft rock there rests an accumulation of from 8 feet to 10 feet of a fat mould, abounding in potsherds; this mould does not lie close up against the Haram wall, but is at top about 12 inches from it, and gradually closes in to it; between it and the wall is a wedge of stone chippings; it is quite evident that when the wall was built, this 10 feet of mould and pottery was in existence, that it was cut through, and the soft rock also, for the purpose of laying the stones on a solid foundation, and it is probable that the horseshoe hole cut in the rock (above mentioned) was for the purpose of allowing the tackle to work when lowering the cornerstone into its bed. The pottery found in the clay is broken up into fragments, and no shapes can be recognized; a long rusty iron nail was, however, found. As this is the weather side of the Sanctuary, and there is such a deep valley below, the *débris* about here is less damp than in the Tyropœon Valley, and there is a much better chance of any articles being preserved in it. One would expect amid all the chipping to find some broken tools, or something of that sort; and it is most remarkable that so little turns up of importance.

"The layer of fat mould slopes to the east at an angle of about one in four, the layers of stone chippings, etc., above, at an angle of one in three. I find that the point where the layers slope down toward the wall is merely local, and that the general slope is toward the east. A gallery has been driven along the second course to the north; the first stone is very roughly dressed, and is 10 feet 6 inches long; the second stone is 4 feet 9 inches in length; it is well dressed and has the usual style of bevel: at about the centre is a deeply-engraved mark, like the Greek H, only that the horizontal line is about one-third of the way up the upright lines, it is cut in above ⅜ inch; on the south lower corner is another engraving; about the stone are many flourishes with red paint, but

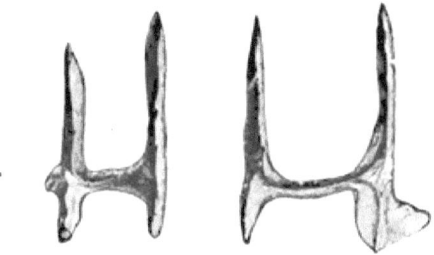

INCISED CHARACTERS.

whether they are monograms or merely "fantasia," it is difficult to say; the stone, shortly after it was uncovered, began to exude moisture, and it would not be prudent to take a squeeze of the two engraved marks until the paint is dry, as it easily rubs off.

"We are also driving a gallery along the wall to the north at a higher level, baring courses 4 and 5. Two more characters in red paint have been uncovered.

"It is curious that the third stone in the fifth course is very roughly dressed within the bevel. It does not appear that these rough stones form any pattern on the wall, and one is almost led to suppose that the builders were unable to find suitable dressed stones for breaking joint, and had to take those that were unfinished.

"There is a most beautifully dressed stone in the third course, but, as it is between the two galleries, it would be dangerous to examine it just now.

"On examining the chippings at the base of the wall, I find they are in many cases rounded and unlike what would result from stone-dressing, having more the appearance of the backing used in the walls at the present day in Palestine. Close up against the wall is a small quantity of chips, but nothing to prove that the stones were dressed after they were laid; and the fact of horizontal drafts in adjoining stones being altogether unlike is of itself sufficient to lead one to suppose that the stones were finished at the quarries.

"The third stone north on the second course was uncovered last night, and on it are found, in red paint, the marks. This stone has no draft at the top, but one of 13 inches at the bottom.

"Nazif Pacha was very anxious to know about the 'marks of King Solomon' on the wall, and I tried to persuade him to come and see them, but he would not hear of it. In his usual style of business, however, he directed one

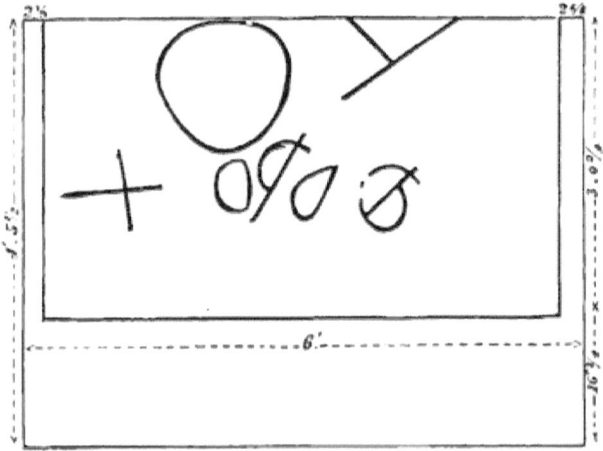

STONE C OF SECOND COURSE OF EASTERN WALL.

of the Mejelis to send a party of Effendis to report upon them, without letting me know about it. However, I got wind of the matter, and was on the ground when the inspecting officers arrived. They were rather taken aback at finding me there. They had a whole tribe of followers, as if they were expecting resistance. I asked them if they wanted to see me; but, no, they only had come to see our excavations. Had they come by order of the Pacha? After some hesitation they said they had. Then I said I would take them round to see every thing. I took them to some little shafts first, as I did not want to have the trouble of

lugging fainting men up our deep ones, and after one or
two trials there was only one who would continue to go
down, and this man was a renegade Greek from Crete, the
same man who had threatened the men when acting as a
detective. I determined to give him a dose of it, and took
him to the smaller shafts, increasing the depth each time.
When at last we got to the southeast angle shaft, the only
one at that time near the Sanctuary wall, he was fairly
beaten, but he would not give in, and went down there also,
the others waiting above and content to hear his reports.
He wanted to measure here, but this I would not allow unless he declared himself to be a competent surveyor, as I
explained to him that as he knew nothing about it he might
make out we were under the Sanctuary, when we were not.
This he quite understood, and gave up the idea of taking
any measurements. He had by this time become so friendly
that, when I showed him the basement of the Sanctuary
wall, he declared I was only making fun of him, and told
those above that we had found a wall in front of the Sanctuary, the wall of Solomon, quite distinct from the present
wall. When I showed him the paint-marks, he again
thought I was poking my fun at him, and, putting up his
finger, rubbed off the tail of a Q, and it became O; but in
my excitement I tumbled him over, and he became aware
of the enormity of his proceeding, and, fearing some other
mishap might befall him, asked to be allowed to go up again.
The party then went away to the Pacha, saying that they
were quite satisfied with what we were doing; but I did
not trust them, and I sent my dragoman to the Pacha with
a message to ask if he had really sent the Effendis to inspect, as they had brought no authority, but he was also to
find means to stop in the room until they came to make
their report, so that they might not play me false. They
were taken again aback at finding my dragoman in beforehand with the Pacha, and were obliged to make a most
favorable report. We were thus enabled to get on with this
shaft at the same time that there was still the Pacha's letter

at the Consulate that I was not to come near the Sanctuary wall.

"Our finding of these marks attracted a good deal of attention both among the inhabitants and visitors, and a great number of Europeans were taken down the shaft (see illustration heading Chapter I.); for those who were feeble, and for the ladies, we had a chair rigged up, and they were let down easy; others had to climb down the rope ladders with a rope slung round them to avoid any accident."

The illustration heading, Chapter I., gives a very clear idea of the enormous depth of the Sanctuary wall and its appearance at the bottom. For the sake of showing the stones, the division between the two galleries is not shown, and the shaft is made a few feet deeper than what it actually was, so as to open on the lower gallery instead of the upper. Visitors, however, were slung down shafts deeper than that shown in the illustration.

The lower gallery exposed the whole of the second course and the upper part of the first and lower part of the second; the latter was found to be sunk partially in the rock at the southeast angle, but as we proceeded to the north it was found to be let in entirely into the rock until at about 41 feet it ceased, the rock rising abruptly, and the second course being let into it.

There are drafts on the upper portion of the first course; on the second course there are drafts, but somewhat peculiar, for on the second stone from angle, on which are the marks H, I, the upper draft is $8\frac{1}{2}$ inches wide, while the lower draft is only $1\frac{5}{8}$ inches. In the third stone C (page 112) there is no upper draft, but the lower is $16\frac{3}{4}$ inches wide; and again on the fourth stone the upper draft is 12 inches, the lower could not be seen; the remaining stones of this course have the ordinary drafts 3 to 4 inches wide.

The third course has ordinary drafts; on the corner stone is a mark in red paint like a 4 reversed, the second stone is cut in a very superior style; the third, fourth, and

fifth stones have a few faint red paint-marks on them, and
the sixth stone has another H engraved. These four courses
are sunk in the bed of rich loam, and were evidently never
seen after they were laid. The fifth course is laid with
more regularity, but no marks were seen. On the sixth
course there are red paint-marks on nearly every stone; on
the first none, on the second the O Y Q, which is supposed

GALLERY AT SOUTHEAST CORNER OF SANCTUARY.

to be some numeral; on three to nine are single paint characters at left hand top corner; on the tenth there are a great
number of flourishes in red paint, and on the eleventh occurs something curious: the face projects about ½ inch too
much, and has been worked down over about half its surface, on the raised part is a + cut in the stone, two straight

lines perpendicular to each other; on the worked face is a painted + much larger, and with a bend down at right end of horizontal stroke.

Many of the other stones in this course have characters on them, the whole of which were carefully traced and are to be seen in the office of the Palestine Exploration Fund. Rock was found to crop up abruptly in this gallery at 76 feet from the southeast angle, and work was stopped here January 25, 1869. The gallery itself, however, was kept open for the sake of visitors until nearly a year afterward, when the gallery gave way in so many places that it was necessary to tamp it up.

In the upper gallery the remains of a semicircular pilaster were found 2 feet 2 inches in diameter. In the *débris* a good deal of black stuff was found, having the appearance of charred wood: it was sent to England.

A gallery was also driven January, 1869, round the angle of the wall to the east, when the rock was found to rise very rapidly, cutting the fourth course at 15 feet from the angle. On this course two red paint-marks were found, L's overturned and reversed; the rock now rose very rapidly, striking the top of the sixth course at 78 feet from the angle. On arriving at this point a shower of old baskets and rotten wood saluted the astonished faces of the workmen; we had arrived at the bottom of the first gallery driven to the Sanctuary wall, alongside the wall of Ophel; the stone of the 6 feet course is let into the rock at its western end, and is 20 feet long.

It is to be noticed that the batter of the Sanctuary wall on its west side is greater here than it is on its south side; that is to say, on the west each stone is set back about 3 to 4 inches behind that on which it rests, on the south side about 1 inch.

The Ophel wall appears to have been built upon the layer of rich loam overlying the rock, and not to have been based on the rock, at any rate at this point, so that we were able to go under it along the rock.

Our work at the southeast angle was not resumed until the spring of 1870, when it became a question as to whether the masonry there might not be built in the same style as it is at the northwest angle.

Details.—Commencing from our old shaft at the southeast angle, a gallery was driven on the Sanctuary wall, striking it at 32 feet north of the southeast angle, and at a level of 2,312 feet; the excavated earth was used for tamping up the galleries below. The course struck is 3 feet 8 inches in height, drafted and faced as is the wall on the surface; after running along for 32 feet 3 inches, the height of course increased to 4 feet 2½ inches; by being let down into the course below, this continues up to 108 feet from southeast angle, where there appears to be a break in the wall; that is to say, the course in continuation is only 3 feet 3⅝ inches in height, and its bed is 1 foot 10 inches above the course we had been running along; there appears to be a straight joint here through three courses, but of this we could not be certain, as the soil we were working through was of too friable a nature to allow of a close examination above and below; it is to be observed that there is a break in the wall above-ground at 105 feet 6 inches from the southeast angle, where the smooth-faced stones terminate, and the projecting-faced stones begin, and as this is the case also at the point in the gallery above mentioned, it appears probable that the break runs all the way up.

We continued along the projecting-faced stones in the wall, until at 133 feet from the angle, there is a rise in the bed of the course of 4 inches; and at 161 feet 9 inches from the southeast angle, or 129 feet 9 inches from the point we struck the wall, rock was encountered, rising to the north and cut out for the reception of the stones. At the break in the wall a strong gush of wind issued during the east wind, but not during the west.

The face of the tower at the northeast angle is 84 feet in length; and the north end of Robinson's Arch is 89 feet from the southwest angle, so that there does not appear to be any particular similarity in the dimensions at the three angles.

The northern end of the skewback (?) on the east side of the wall is just where the break occurs. A gallery was now driven to the east, so as just to catch the end of the pier if it ever existed; but nothing was to be found as far as fifty feet from the Sanctuary wall, and the span of the arch as calculated ought to be about 27 feet.

Another gallery was now driven from this last to the south, at a distance of 30 feet from, and parallel to the Sanctuary wall, for 14 feet, and then small branches from the end run east and west for 10 feet, but no signs of any pier, and the galleries were tamped up.

We were not very far from the rock when searching for this pier, but not quite on it; it cannot therefore be said for certain that there was no pier for a bridge at this point, but the probabilities are against it.

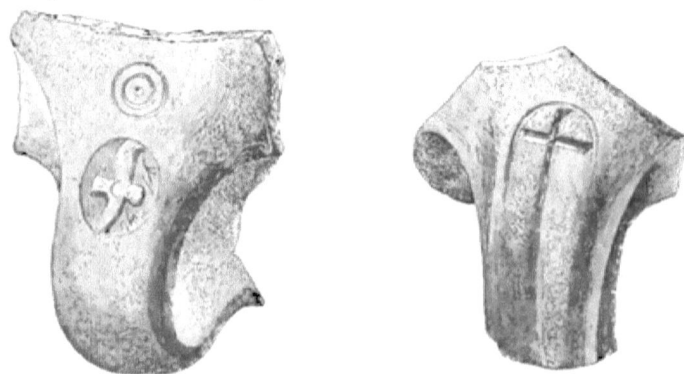

ANCIENT MARKS ON HANDLES OF VASES.

Illustrations are given of two handles of jars found in the lower gallery at the shaft, among the pottery lying on the top of the rich loam overlying the rock. The pottery lies about 2 inches thick, but it is all in fragments; however, some of the handles were found to have stamps on them, and I employed a man for some days poking into the layer for several feet on either side, and eventually got together eight of these handles; drawings were made of them and sent home at once. I supposed the jars to have been broken only a very short time after the building of the wall. In getting these handles out for the illustrations a few days ago, I was dusting the mud off one of them and found Phœnician characters to be also imprinted on the stamp: one inscription was read by an authority as "The King," and some remarks on the whole are to be found in the chapter on Pottery. It is obvious that these characters are likely in a great measure to throw light upon the age of the Sanctuary wall at this point.

The last excavation along the east side of the Sanctuary wall was commenced 300 feet south of the Golden Gate, and on the east of the cemetery, for the purpose of examining the wall somewhere in the 600 feet south of the Golden Gate, where I suppose the ancient temple wall of King Solomon still to exist. When we got to within 60 feet of the Sanctuary wall the shingle became too loose for working in, and we were obliged to desist. I consider the examination of this portion of the wall to be one of the most important investigations still required at Jerusalem.

11*th May*, 1869. *Golden Gate.*—" The Golden Gate occupies a position in the east Sanctuary wall, where an examination below the surface would probably afford much valuable information. Unhappily, the greater portion of this east wall is lined with Mahometan tombs, and we were precluded from digging near them. It is true that a shaft could be sunk through the cemetery without in any way interfering with the graves, but it is very doubtful whether permission for this could be obtained.

" It does not appear that there is any real feeling on the subject, as we find on all sides tombs, Jewish, Christian, and Mahometan, used as dwelling-places and stables by the people of the country, and sarcophagi used as watering-troughs; but there is a certain amount of sentiment involved, and the same people who see no harm in the destruction of tombs while quarrying, in using them as stables, and in building the tombstones into their houses, think it desecration for a Frank in any way to examine these interesting relics.

"It being desirable, then, to examine the wall at the Golden Gate, the only method was to sink a shaft at some distance off and drive a gallery up, so as to be altogether out of the way of the cemetery. (See plan 39.)

"The nearest convenient point was found to be 143 feet from the south end of the gate, and in a line perpendicular to its front, in a piece of ground through which a shaft was sunk in 1867.

"This point was found to be 55 feet 6 inches below the level of the ground outside the gate. The shaft was commenced 25th January, 1869, and sunk down 25 feet 6 inches, giving a total difference of level between the ground outside the gate and the bottom of the shaft of 81 feet.

"*Soil.*—First 8 feet, loam mixed with small shingle; from 8 feet to 13 feet in depth the shaft passed through stone packing 9 inches to 12 inches cube; from 13 feet to 18 feet good solid dark brown loam; from 18 feet to 22 feet 6 inches, stone packing again; 22 feet 6 inches to 26 feet 9 inches, loam mixed with stones.

"A gallery was then driven in to the west, and at 10 feet 3 inches the rock was struck, rising about one in four to the west; the gallery then rose gently with the rock until at 18 feet 6 inches a tank or rock-cut tomb was crossed. The examination of this was reserved, and the gallery continued, until at 27 feet the rock was found to present a cut scarp of 3 feet 9 inches height, on the south side, running in a northwesterly direction, the natural surface of the rock inclining to the north. The scarped rock was followed for over 10 feet, when it suddenly took a turn to the north, and it was necessary to cross over it. On the top of the scarp a rough masonry wall was found, which was broken through. At this point, 37 feet from the shaft, the total rise in the gallery was 8 feet.

"The rock is mezzeh, and on the scarp, about 2 feet 10 inches from the bottom, was found a hole cut for passing a rope through, similar to those found in the cavern south of the Triple Gate (page 233). This ring or hole was apparently for tying up animals to.

GALLERY AT GOLDEN GATE.

"The gallery was now continued on a gradual rise through a loose and dangerous accumulation of stones. At 47 feet the rock was found to rise suddenly to a height of 4 feet, and at 53 feet another rough masonry wall was encountered and broken through. At 68 feet a portion of the shaft of a column (3 feet in diameter) was met with, placed erect in the *débris*, and about 3 feet above the rock. (See woodcut.) On the bottom of this shaft of column are what appear to be masons' marks.

"From this point forward the work became very dangerous, the gallery being driven through a mass of loose bowlders alternating with layers of shingle, which on being set in motion runs like water.

"At 85 feet from the shaft, the gallery had ascended 25 feet 6 inches. The *débris* now began to run into the gallery, forming a cavity above; and to prevent further falls fifty old baskets were stuffed in, and a quantity of old timber. After a considerable amount of labor the gallery was continued, and at 97 feet (i. e., 46 feet from the Sanctuary wall) a massive masonry wall was reached, running north and south.

"An attempt was made to break through this wall, but after getting in 5 feet it was abandoned; the stones being of large size it was also found not practicable to get over the wall, as it appears to continue up to a considerable height. A gallery was then driven south along the wall for 14 feet, but there was no appearance of any break. The *débris* pierced through was of the loosest description, and the gallery had become in a highly-dangerous state. I therefore had it tamped up, leaving in all the frames for about 30 feet.

"The tamping up was continued as far as the hanging column, and at the same time a branch-gallery was driven to the north from a point immediately east of the column. At 14 feet it was turned in to the west (see plan $\frac{1}{500}$). It was found that there was here about 3 feet of solid earth between the *débris* and the rock, and by very careful management the gallery was driven on for 34 feet from the turn. At this point the massive wall was again met with, running in a northwesterly direction; the gallery followed along it, but the layer of solid earth gradually diminished in thickness, until on the 28th of April, when 55 feet from the turn, the shingle suddenly came in with a rush, quickly filling up 6 feet of the gallery, and burying some of the tools. An attempt to remove this shingle was of no avail; when touched it only ran farther into the gallery, and I have, very reluctantly, been obliged to abandon the work.

"Although we have not succeeded in our object at this point, we have at least obtained some interesting results:

"1. It is now nearly certain that at the Golden Gate the Sanctuary wall extends below the present surface outside, to a depth of from 30 feet to 40 feet (see section $\frac{1}{500}$).

"2. It appears that the rock has an inclination to the north near the Golden Gate.

"3. The massive wall where first encountered is about 50 feet in front of the Golden Gate. It appears from thence to run to the north and gradually turns in to the west, apparently following the contour of the ground.

"This wall is composed of large quarry-dressed blocks of mezzeh, so far similar to the lower course seen in the Sanctuary wall near the Golden Gate, that the roughly-dressed faces of the stones project about 6 inches beyond the marginal drafts, which are very rough. The stones appear to be in courses 2 feet 6 inches in height, and over 5 feet in length. On trying to break through the wall a hole was made 5 feet 6 inches, without any signs of the stones terminating. The horizontal joints are not close, but appear to be about 12 inches apart, and filled in with stones 6 inches cube, packed in a very curious cement, which now looks like an argillaceous stone and has a conchoidal fracture. The fellahin pronounce it to be formed of lime, oil, and the virgin red earth, and state that such is used at the present day in the formation of cisterns. Specimens of this cement have been sent home.

"It is disagreeable to have failed in reaching the Golden Gate, but to pierce through the *débris* of the nature encountered, some special machinery would have to be used; and it is dangerous to put any thing but the simplest instruments into the hands of the fellahin.

"We also cannot work more than a certain number of

days at a time at a difficult place, as the constant danger causes the nerves to become unstrung after a time, and then a few days at safer work is required; only those who have experienced the peculiar effect of the rattling of the *débris* upon the frames, with the prospect at any moment of the boards being crushed in by a large stone, can appreciate the deterring influence it has upon the workmen. The non-commissioned officers have to keep continually to the front, or the men will not venture up.

"It appears probable that the massive wall met with may continue up to the surface, as immediately above it, in the road, are some large, roughly-bevelled stones lying in the same line."

NORTHEAST ANGLE OF SANCTUARY.

Extract from Letter of May 31*st*, 1869.—"Though it would not be right at present to form a permanent theory on any of the disputed points, yet it is impossible not, and in fact most necessary, to look ahead and conjecture what we are likely to come across, for without so doing the excavating must degenerate into a wild probing of the ground, instead of a systematic investigation. And though in the following brief account I find it necessary to couple conjecture with fact, in order to give an idea what our results are, and to what they tend, yet I do so with the knowledge that each day my views must be modified by the accumulation of fresh results, and they must go on changing until by patient search we can speak with certainty of the ruins of ancient Jerusalem. I may quote, in illustration of this, my letters of the 1st and 2d February, 1869, in which I came to the conclusion that there is rock only on the western side of the Birket Israil (so-called Pool of Bethesda). I was fully impressed with the idea that on the eastern side, the valley running south from the Harat Bab Hytta ran out into the Kedron, after having been joined by the valley, which I conjecture to run east from the Gate of the Inspector, north of the platform of the Dome of the Rock. Also, in my letter of December 28th, I put the question, 'Are we to suppose this gate (of our Lady Mary) elevated 100 feet above the bottom of the wall, or does the rock break down suddenly from the gate toward the south, so as to form a deep gorge in which the pool is built?'

"In order to settle this question, I sunk shafts on either side of the Gate of St. Stephen (of our Lady Mary), and also near the road leading down to the Church of the Tomb of the Virgin, and find that the road-way at the gate is about 20 feet above the rock, and that going down the hill the accumulation of *débris* decreases from 25 feet in height to 2 feet or 3 feet. This threw considerable light upon the subject, showing that there has been no great destruction of extensive building so far north as this gate, and that the spur of the hill running from the Burj Laklah to the Birket Sitti Miriam still continues to the south. Shafts were then sunk to the east of the Birket Israil, and rock was found at a depth of 50 feet from the surface, being higher than the bottom of the Birket Israil by 40 feet. As we find the natural rock in the Birket to the west at a little below this level, we are forced to the conclusion that the valley running south does not sharply round to the east in this pool, but runs on through the Sanctuary, and issues into the Kedron somewhat north of the Golden Gate.

"I have placed on the accompanying plan the conjectural lie of this valley. That it is an important matter there can be no doubt, for on the proving of it may hang the destinies of most of the theories concerning the site of the ancient Temple.

"It is very desirable just now that we should proceed with the work with unabated vigor, and bring the question of the Haram enclosure to a proper conclusion. A few more months' work here, and we may go forward confidently, and find the old walls of the city, having fixed the site of the Temple. We expend a great deal of wood in the shafts and galleries on the east side of the Sanctuary. The shingle we pass through is often of such a nature that the frames cannot be taken out again. If it is possible to get up to the northeast angle, I propose examining it very minutely. We find the wall joining it to St. Stephen's Gate to rest several feet above the rock, the intervening space being partially filled up with concrete, and in one place at least the wall rests on the red earth. It is apparent that this wall is of no very ancient date.

"Of the city wall to the east, this northeast angle of the Sanctuary is the first sign from the northern end of any thing ancient in appearance, and it will now be very necessary to ascertain whether the whole wall of the Sanctuary to the east is built from the rock with drafted stones; if it is, we can hardly doubt that the theory of De Vogüé is correct, and that the Sanctuary is one vast platform of ancient date: if, on the other hand, we find the drafted stones in the northeast angle only extend under-ground as far south as they do on the surface, then we have the interesting problem whether this has been a tower, whether of Hananeel, as Dr. Barclay supposes, or of Meah or of the House of the Mighty (Nehem. iii. 1, 16; xii. 39). For if it should be decided that the Sanctuary wall at the southeast angle is of the time of the Jewish kings, we can scarcely give a more recent date to this wall at the northeast angle, provided we find it to be built up of drafted stones drafted from the rock."

(Subsequent research proved the stones to be drafted, but with bulging faces totally unlike those found at the southeast angle.)

"We struck the Sanctuary wall about 18 feet south of the northeast angle and at a depth of about 42 feet below the surface. We then turned north, and ran along the Sanctuary wall for 26 feet without finding any angle similar to that above. At this point a slit about 18 inches wide and 4 inches high was observed in the Sanctuary wall, formed by cutting out parts of the upper and lower beds of two courses. A stone, dropped down this slit, rolled rattling away for several feet.

"It was some time before I could believe that we had really passed to the north of the northeast angle; but there can now be no doubt of it, and that the ancient wall below the surface runs several feet to the north of the northeast angle without break of any kind.

"If the portions above-ground are *in situ*, it would appear that this angle is a portion of an ancient tower reaching above the old city wall, probably somewhat similar to the view De Vogüé gives of it (Plate XVI., "Le Temple de Jérusalem").

"We have this morning examined the slit mentioned above. At first it was impossible to squeeze through, but after a few hours it became easier, though it is now only 7 inches in height.

"The passage in from this slit is difficult to describe; the roof falls by steps, but the floor is a very steep smooth incline, falling 12 feet in 11½ feet, like the slit and shoot for letters at a post-office. The shoot ends abruptly, passing through the roof of a passage. This passage runs east and west; it is 3 feet 9 inches high, and about 2 wide; it runs nearly horizontally, and at its eastern end opens out through the Sanctuary wall. At the western end it goes (by measurement) to the east end of the Birket Israil, but is closed up by a perforated stone. This passage is 46 feet in length. On the south side of it a little to the west of the shaft, is a staircase cut in the masonry, and running apparently to the surface, but it is jammed up with stones. The roof of the passage is about 48 feet below the surface. The stones forming it are of great size, but do not show large in comparison with those of the sides, which are from 14 feet to 18 feet in length, and vary from 3 feet 10 inches to 4 feet 6 inches in height. To the west of the staircase the bottom of the passage slopes down rapidly, so that in one place it is 12 feet in height. The roof also is stepped down 4 feet, about eleven feet from the western end.

"Altogether this passage bears a great resemblance to that which we found under the Single Gate, October, 1867.

"At the eastern end, where the passage opens out through the Sanctuary wall, a rough masonry shaft has been built round, so that we can see a few feet up the wall, and about 7 feet down it below the sole of the gallery. It is evident that here there has been some tinkering at a comparatively modern date.

"In the course forming the sole of the passage there is a water-duct leading through the Sanctuary wall, about 5 inches square, very nicely cut; but in the next course, lower, a great irregular hole has been knocked out of the wall, so as to allow the water to pass through at a slightly lower level, and so run into an aqueduct 9 inches wide and 2 feet high, which commences at this point, and runs nearly due east from the Sanctuary wall. All this botching and tinkering looks as though it had been done quite recently, and the workmen have left their mark on the wall in the shape of a Christian cross, of the type used by the early Christians, or during the Byzantine period.

"At the farther end of the passage, to the west, the same large massive stones are seen until the eye rests upon a large perforated stone closing it up. This is the first approach we have yet found to any architectural remains about these old walls; and though it merely shows us the kind of labor bestowed upon a concealed overflow aqueduct, still it has a bold and pleasing effect, and, until something else is found, will hold its own as some indication of the style of building at an early period.

It consists simply of a stone closing up the end of the passage, with a recess or alcove cut in it 4 inches deep. Within this recess are three cylindrical holes $5\frac{1}{4}$ inches in diameter, the lines joining their centres forming the sides of an equilateral triangle. (See Illustration.) Below this appears once to have been a basin to collect the water; but whatever has been there, it has been violently removed. It appears to me probable that the troops defending this portion of the wall came down the staircase into this passage to obtain water.

"At first sight this passage appears to be cut in the rock, as stalactites have formed all over it, and hang gracefully from every joint, giving the place a very picturesque appearance. It seems probable that we are here some 20 feet above the rock.

"There can be little doubt that this is an ancient overflow from the Birket Israil, which could not at that time

NEWLY-DISCOVERED PASSAGE IN THE OLD WALL OF HARAM AREA.

have risen above this height, about 2,350 feet, or 25 feet above the present bottom of the pool, and 60 feet below the present top of the pool.

"It is also apparent that the Birket Israil has been half full and overflowing during the Christian period, and that for some purpose or other the water was carried away by an aqueduct to the Kedron Valley. At the present day, when there is such a dearth of running water in Jerusalem, it is rather mystifying to find that within our era the Birket Israil has probably been constantly full up to a certain point, and flowing over."

Letter of August 18, 1869.—" We have now made further progress at this angle, and have settled several points of considerable interest :

" 1. We find that the tower (so-called Tower of Antonia) at the northeast angle of the Sanctuary forms part of the main east wall, and, at near its base, the wall and tower are flush or in one line.

" 2. The wall is built up of drafted stones from the rock, but up to a certain height (nearly the same as at Robinson's Arch) the stones have rough faces.

" 3. The rock, which is only 20 feet below the surface at the St. Stephen's Gate, falls rapidly past the tower, so that at the southern angle the wall is covered up with *débris* to a depth of no less than 110 feet, and the total height of the wall is over 150 feet.

" 4. There is now no doubt that the valley at the Bab-az-Zahiré passes down through the Birket Israil into the Sanctuary, and thence out to the east between the northeast tower and the Golden Gate; and that the platform of the Dome of the Rock is at least 165 *feet* above one part of the valley in the northern part of the Sanctuary; and also that the contour trace showing the conjectural lay of the ground in the northern part of the Sanctuary, forwarded in June, appears to be nearly generally correct.

" 5. Some characters, in red paint, have been found on the bottom stones of the Haram wall under the southern end of this tower: a trace is enclosed.

" 6. It appears probable that the four courses of drafted stones of this tower, which appear above-ground, are *in situ*, and also in the wall south of the tower.

" 7. The faces of the stones below a certain line are described as rough (in paragraph 2), but they are quite unlike the roughly-faced stones at the southwest angle. The faces project from 2 to 20 inches or more, presenting a very curious appearance.

"8. The stone used does not seem to be so compact and hard as that used at the southeast angle, and the chisel-working is not so carefully done.

"The manner in which the tower becomes flush with the wall is very interesting: for the first 48 feet above the rock it is one wall, the stones being carefully drafted, the faces projecting irregularly, on an average 10 inches. The upper and lower parts of the faces are horizontal, and the sides are vertical, so that they in some instances present the appearance of one cube stuck on to a larger one.

"The wall throughout this distance has a batter formed by each course receding 4¼ inches from that below it; the tower is formed by the portion forming the wall continuing to recede from 4 to 7 inches, while that forming the tower only recedes about 1¼ inch, so that at 70 feet from the bottom (level of the gallery), and 22 feet from whence the tower begins, the projection is nearly 2 feet. If this were continued at the same rate up to the surface another 40 feet, it would give to the tower a projection very similar to what it has, viz., about 7 feet; from this it would appear as though the upper were *in situ;* but it is to be remarked that the stones in the *wall* at the surface, and also in the gallery, have projecting faces; and, as the southernmost shaft was sunk at the junction of the tower and wall, it yet remains to be seen whether the *wall* throughout is composed of stones with projecting faces, while the stones in the tower are like those at the Wailing Place.

"It is also to be remarked that the level of the point where the tower commences is only a short distance below the surface at the southeast angle, where there is a check in the wall as if just such another tower were commencing.

"There is no straight joint between the tower and wall

at the northeast angle; it is one wall for **the 22** feet we have examined, and probably continues the same up to the surface. Where the projection increases to 2 feet, the stones are cut **out to** that depth, **but** a few feet higher some other method **must have** been adopted.

"**I propose after the summer to drive the** gallery 100 feet farther to the south along **the wall, and then to sink again in search of the bottom of** the valley, which is likely to be some 30 or 40 **feet lower down: as it is, this** shaft at **the angle of the tower is the deepest yet** sunk, the bottom **being 110 feet below the surface.**

"**I have left this shaft open, so that M. de** Sauley may **have an opportunity of examining the wall if** he arrives in **time.**"

Report of 13*th December,* 1869.—*Excavations at the northeast angle of the Sanctuary.*—"**The general results of these shafts have already been noticed, and now the details of the working are given.**

"**In commencing work here we were completely in the dark as to the nature of the rock below the surface; we certainly** were **aware of the valley running down from the Babaz-Zahiré, but it was generally supposed to run out** through **the Birket Israil, turning sharp to the east, as shown** in the **Ordnance Survey Plan 1.10,000, instead of** continuing in a **southeasterly direction through the northeast corner of the Haram Area, as our excavations have shown it to do; we therefore found it necessary to sink several shafts so as to completely mark out the present lay of the rock; and it is to be remembered that the present lay of the rock** gives **very nearly the features of the ground as they appeared in early times, for it can hardly be doubted but that in those times** the rock about **here was nearly bare; covered at the most** with 2 feet **or 3 feet of red earth.**

"Wherever **we have excavated we have found the** rock at the bottom of **our shafts to be cut away in steps, or levelled, or otherwise showing that the hand of man had been ap-**

plied to it; and on this rock we generally find 2 feet or 3 feet of red earth (the natural color of the soil of this part), and all above it is stone-chippings and shingle mixed up with pieces of red pottery, or black earth formed of rubbish from the city.

"One important point these excavations have established, viz.: that outside the city wall on east to north of St. Stephen's Gate there are only a few feet of *débris*, and often none at all, while immediately south of it, and indeed all along to the southeast angle, the *débris* varies in depth from 50 to over 100 feet; this rather implies that to the north of this gate there has been very little destruction of old walls.

"Another important point with regard to the city wall at this gate is, that the present wall only goes down for 10 feet below the surface, and there rests upon 10 feet of concrete, which again is on the rock, and that there is no appearance of an older wall.

"From this it would appear that the St. Stephen's Gate may not stand upon the site of the old wall; and the line of bevelled stones found in the drain at shaft No. 10 may mark the place where the old wall turned in to the west. This idea is rather confirmed by our finding the Sanctuary wall running north from the northeast angle for at least 64 feet, so that, if it continued far enough in the same straight line, it would lie under the St. Stephen's Gate nearly.

"We come now to a question of very great interest in the East Sanctuary wall north of the northeast angle. We found an overflow aqueduct at a level of 2,341 feet, while the present level of the Sanctuary at the same angle is 2,410 feet. This aqueduct forms part of the old Sanctuary wall as seen at this angle, and every detail about it points to its having been used as a fountain or overflow aqueduct, and not as a flood-gate; and, if we admit this, we must suppose the water in the Birket Israil to have stood at the highest at 2,343 feet at the time the present northeast angle and northeast portion of the Sanctuary wall was built. If this be so, and if we might suppose the present northern end of the Sanctuary to have been built up to the same height as it is at present, when this northeastern wall was built, then we ought to find the southern side of the Birket Israil built up of the same kind of blocks as this wall.

"Now we find the inside of the Birket Israil faced with stone and plaster, so as to act as a tank up nearly to the level of the Sanctuary Area, and what may be the true face of the north Sanctuary wall may thus be covered up. The removal of a few stones here might settle this question. This question may thus be described:

"Some authorities make the limits of Herod's Temple to have extended up to Birket Israil on the north; now we have found the northern part of the east wall to be apparently *in situ*, whether it be the wall of Solomon, Herod, or Herod Agrippa. If of Herod, then the south side of Birket Israil should also be of like stones.

"In shaft No. 11 we have found a massive wall of bevelled stones, apparently not *in situ*. This may have been at a later period the line of the city wall; certainly it appears to be later than the aqueduct which it cuts in two, and which appears to run up to St. Stephen's Gate, shaft No. 10, for this aqueduct is on a level, and does not appear to have been made until the Birket Israil was made into the tank it appears at present.

"Shaft 1. Commenced 2d of April, 1869, at a point at the foot of the mound of rubbish outside St. Stephen's Gate, where some Christians say tradition places the site of an ancient church.

"Surface, 2,343 feet above sea-level. Rock was found at depth of 6 feet; it sounded hollow, and on striking with a jumper, caved in, and a grotto was exposed to view, nearly circular on plan, about 9 feet in diameter and 4 feet high; it had been used as a tomb, and is divided into five loculi by plaster partitions about 3 inches thick and 12 inches high; two of these lay about northeast to southwest, and three northwest to southeast.

"At the southern side a shaft leads down into a chamber (No. 2) 26 feet long, 6 feet broad, and divided latitudinally into ten loculi, separated as in the chamber above; one of the middle loculi serves as a passage, opening at either end into two chambers (Nos. 3. and 4) parallel and similar to No. 2; these are also divided into loculi.

"Other chambers open out from these; the largest being at the southeast angle of No. 3, where there is a shaft (about 6 feet deep) leading down into a lower range of chambers, in direct length about 40 feet. All these chambers, nine in number, are divided off into loculi, except one which appears to have been an anteroom, and in which some pieces of cut stone were found.

"The partitions separating the loculi in some cases are cut out of the rock. The chambers were found half full of earth, fallen in from above, and it is evident that they had been opened, and perhaps used, at a period subsequent to the time when they had been used as tombs. The earth was moved from one chamber into another, but we found no indications of passages into a larger grotto; the only places not explored were some shafts leading up, apparently, to the surface.

"The work was continued for twenty-four days. Six pottery lamps, apparently early Christian, and some glass vases were found; these were sent home in a box under charge of Corporal Ellis.

"The chambers are cut in the 'melekeh' of a very rotten description, nearly approaching to the 'cakooli,' and no chisel-marks were found on the rock. The system of chambers with shafts leading up to the surface is somewhat on the plan of the Greek or Phœnician tombs at Saida.

"A plan of some of the chambers, and a section, are enclosed; the whole system is not given, as they lie over each other, and are cut so irregularly as almost to suggest the idea that they may have been natural caverns enlarged by man.

"Shafts 2 and 3 were sunk at the bottom of the road, due east of St. Stephen's Gate; rock was found in each at 5 feet 6 inches and 2 feet respectively; at the first the last 3 feet 6 inches was of the red virgin soil. Shafts were now commenced higher up the road leading to St. Stephen's Gate.

"Shaft 4. Commenced 9th of April, 1869, was sunk near the road 256 feet east of the gate; at 14 feet a small aqueduct or cistern was broken into, about 4 feet 6 inches square of masonry. Rock was found at 20 feet 9 inches, the walls of the cistern resting on it, the rock levelled. Soil for first 13 feet nearly black, in layers sloping from north to south for the first 11 feet, and then from west to east to a depth of 14 feet, slope two in three; below this the color was red, and continued so for 6 feet to the rock; level of surface 2,390 feet. A shaft was next sunk higher up near the road, at a distance of 162 feet from the gate; level of surface 2,409 feet.

"Shaft 5. Rock was found at a depth of 30 feet. The top of a scarp facing to the east; this was followed down 20 feet, the rock receding under to the west, apparently the side of a tank, as it was plastered and ended abruptly to the north; large stones were found, as though they had been part of the vaulting of a tank; after getting to a depth of 50 feet below the surface this shaft was filled up. For the first 20 feet the soil was black and rotten, apparently rubbish from the city; from thence to the rock, loam mixed with stones.

"Shaft 6. Commenced 12th May, 1869, near road at 109 feet, east of St. Stephen's Gate; level of surface 2,411 feet. Rock found at 22 feet 9 inches below the surface, falling one foot in one to the southeast. At 16 feet color of soil changed from black to a reddish brown. At 8 feet some pottery found. In consequence of the finding of the wall at No. 11, it was considered desirable to drive a gallery to the west from No. 6 in search of continuation of the same.

"Rock very soft and rises to the west slightly; first 10 feet level, then 3 feet with rise of 3 inches, and then 2 feet level again; in all, 15 feet. The rock is then scarped to the west to depth of 8 feet 4 inches, is level for 10 feet, and then rises again in a small scarp of 2½ feet, and then goes on level again. Space of ditch filled in with small stones and earth. Total length of gallery to the west 25 feet 8 inches. No signs of any wall as found at No. 11; but probably we were not near enough to the west.

"Shaft 7. Commenced 24th of April, 1869; at the first angle in city wall, 43 feet north of St. Stephen's Gate; surface level 2,419 feet; wall below surface same as that seen above; at 18½ feet came on rock and concrete on which the wall rests; no signs whatever of any thing more ancient than the present city wall, as seen above-ground; soil passed through, loose rubbish.

"Shaft 8. Commenced 8th of April, 1869, at a point 200 feet due east of the south corner of tower of the northeast angle of Haram Area. Rock, cut down level, found at 29½ feet. Level of surface 2,347 feet. Some broken pieces of fresco were found near the rock. Soil passed through was black for first 8 feet, and then of a brown color, with the appearance of water having passed constantly through it with lime in suspension. A gallery was now driven to the southwest to determine the lay of the rock. Rock found to slope to the southeast; after progressing 11 feet, the gallery had to be tamped up on account of our striking a layer of loose stones with no earth among them, and which ran down in streams on being touched.

"Shaft 9. Commenced 30th of April, 1869, higher up the hill, and at a distance of 40 feet to the west of No. 8. Level of surface 2,364 feet. Sunk 23 feet through black earth, and then came upon shingle from 1 to 2 inches cube, without any earth; shaft continued 20 feet deeper, when at a depth of 43 feet the shingle changed to a layer of stones from 3 to 4 inches cube, and in getting through these the shingle commenced to run and filled in the shaft for about 1½ feet; the shaft was then filled up till the bottom was 22 feet below the surface, and a gallery was driven in to the west for

25 feet; a shaft was then sunk through stones 12 inches cube, and mud. Rock found at 25 feet, being 47 feet below the surface; rock falls one in four to the south.

"Shaft 10. Commenced 5th of May, 1869, along city wall at first angle to the south of St. Stephen's Gate, at a distance of 34 feet from the Gate. Level of surface 2,410 feet. Bottom course of ashlar of the city wall at depth of 11 feet, resting on concrete formed of stones about 6 inches cube, and hard lime; at depth of 20 feet found rock, the concrete foundation of wall resting on it: rock sloping to the south about one in four. Shaft was then filled up to the top of the concrete and a sloping gallery driven to the south along the city wall.

"In gallery, at 19 feet, came upon a strong rough masonry wall, lying east and west, about 3 feet thick, which did not reach up to the city wall by 6 feet; within this wall to the south was a pavement of rough tesseræ at a level of about 2,391 feet. Sergeant Birtles suggests that this was perhaps the remains of a house, the space between the rough wall and the city wall having been the door-way. Just before reaching the rough wall, a masonry drain 7 inches by 6 inches in the clear was crossed below the level of the pavement.

"At 38 feet the top of a barrel drain was crossed, and at 40 feet another rough wall; also large cut stones were found on the east side and bottom of the gallery.

"At 44 feet 6 inches a shaft was sunk and rock found at 4½ feet below the sole of the gallery, being 33½ feet below the surface of the ground at the mouth of the shaft; the surface of the rock therefore at this point is 2,377 feet.

"The top of the barrel-drain was now examined; after going in 2 feet 6 inches it ended, and another roof formed of flat stones at a rather higher level was seen, and after 8 feet the sides of an aqueduct running west were visible, formed of large stones; for the first 10 feet this passage is only 10 inches wide, and it then becomes larger (2 feet wide), the southern side being formed of large stones 3 feet 6 inches high and 4 feet 6 inches long, well squared, and exhibiting slight traces of a bevel; the aqueduct was traced for 39 feet in all, and was blocked up by a stone having fallen down from the roof. In the top, about 15 feet from the entrance, a cylindrical earthenware pipe, 9 inches diameter, was built in, apparently to conduct water from a higher level; also two other pipes, about 4 inches in diameter, were found laid horizontally *above* the stones forming the roof. The aqueduct was in a very decayed condition and not safe for the men to work in; it apparently leads from the Birket Israil at a level of 2,390 feet, the bottom of the pool being 2,325 feet. It is probable that it was constructed before the present city wall, but it has not the appearance of very great age, and the fact of the south side being composed of large bevelled stones rather goes to show that it was formed after the destruction of one of the old walls.

"Shaft 11. Commenced 16th of March, 1869, at a point about 100 feet to the east of the Sanctuary wall, a little north of the northeast angle. Level of surface 2,405 feet. At a depth of 42 feet an aqueduct was broken through, very rough, no plaster, roof formed by rough stones in form of an arch, runs in a northwesterly direction directly for the aqueduct found in Shaft No. 10. To the northwest 27 feet were open, and to the southeast 20 feet.

"Shaft was now continued, and at 60 feet the earth changed color, and rock found at 64 feet from the surface; cut in steps apparently for resting a foundation on. Falls to the west about one in four.

"The shaft was now filled up to the level of the aqueduct, and the clearing out of the portion toward the city wall was commenced. Passage 3 feet 6 inches high, and 1 foot 9 inches wide; stones forming sides and roof, 3 inches thick and 6 inches long, very rough.

"At 32 feet, found the passage broken in at sides; after securing this, it was found to continue and to be filled with hard silt. At 57 feet, a very massive wall of bevelled stones running north and south, and 65 feet from the city wall, was

reached—stones well squared and somewhat similar to those
found at the Jews' Wailing Place: course 3 feet 7 inches in
height. Commenced a gallery along the wall to the north;
the second stone found was not bevelled, though well
squared and dressed. At 18 feet from aqueduct, the gallery
being driven horizontally, the rock was struck, and the lowest course of the wall took a turn about 30° to the northeast,
while the second course continued straight on to the north;
the wall now was composed of small stones, and after continuing it for 8 feet farther, the gallery was tamped up by
earth taken from a new gallery driven along the wall to the
south.

"Gallery continued to the south along bevelled stones of
wall; at 19 feet reached the corner-stone, the wall now running to the west. The stones here are very well dressed, but
have a curious cracked appearance, as if they had been subjected to great heat, and they broke off in large chips when
struck accidentally. Followed up the wall to the west, and
at 13 feet 6 inches came upon what appeared to be part of
a rough wall running to the south, stones about 1 foot 6
inches high and 2 feet long. The main wall still went on to
the west, but was now composed of very rough irregular
stones of large size; the gallery was now continued for 46
feet from the angle, when the wall suddenly ended, and after
being continued for 7 feet farther, the gallery was stopped,
and another gallery driven to the southwest from the point
(47 feet from the angle) where the main hall had ended.

"Continued gallery to the southwest; progress impeded
by meeting with a concrete floor composed of black cement
and small stones; point where this floor was met with 29
feet from where the gallery branched. At 38 feet came
close on point below the northeast angle of Haram wall, and
broke into a gallery from No. 12. This was done for the
purpose of tamping up No. 9 with the soil from No. 12, and
so avoid taking it along the rough aqueduct, which had
been an awkward business.

"It does not appear that the stones of the massive wall

in No. 11 are *in situ;* they differ in height, and sometimes a squared stone is interpolated; it is probable that this wall was built after the aqueduct had ceased to be of use, as we find it cut in two by the wall; that is to say, if we are to suppose it to be one and the same with that found in Shaft No. 10.

"Shaft 12. Commenced April 24, 1869, at a point 97 feet due east of northeast angle of Sanctuary; level of surface 2,396 feet. The soil at first was very good for working (black soil) to a depth of 42 feet, where a rough wall was encountered, running east and west. Below this, rough stones were met with, and the shaft proceeded with some difficulty to a depth of 59 feet, when rock was met with: falls one in three to the east. The shaft was then filled up to 33 feet from the surface, and a gallery driven in toward the northeast angle through very good soil for 35 feet. At this point the earth gave way suddenly in front of the frames for about 9 inches, and down came a torrent of shingle, filling up the gallery for 6 feet.

"It appears that the surface of the good earth falls *toward* the Sanctuary, the shingle lying on top of it, there being, again after a few feet of good earth, another bed of shingle.

"We now had to try back, and at 29 feet from the shaft turned the gallery sharp round to the south, stepping it down each frame one in one, so as to get a few feet of good earth over our heads. After 10 feet the gallery was turned round again toward the city wall, and gradually stepped up: we were now once more in most excellent soil, the best we had come across in Jerusalem; but there was still the chance of our meeting a break of shingle and being prevented reaching the Sanctuary. Every effort was made to obviate any such accident; and Sergeant Birtles and Corporal McKenzie, putting in thirty frames in two days, arrived safely at the Sanctuary wall without encountering the dreaded shingle. What prevents progress in these galleries is not so much the work at the head of the shaft, as the difficulty in making the men carry off the soil quick enough. A gallery was now driven along the Sanctuary wall to the north; and at 26 feet the curious shaft leading to the aqueduct was met with, described at page 127.

"The gallery along the Sanctuary wall was continued to the north beyond the *light-shaft* of this aqueduct; and the stones were found to continue bevelled and well cut for 65 feet, when they changed in character from being similar to those at the Jews' Wailing Place to those found near the bottom of the tower at the northeast angle; the centres of the stones projecting from 6 to 10 inches. These were examined for 10 feet, and then the gallery was tamped up. It is to be observed that this wall was traced considerably beyond the point where the massive wall of No. 11 should have come in, and therefore they appear not to be connected.

"In the gallery to the north a concrete floor was encountered, apparently ascending to the north, at a distance of 64 feet. It was just here that the Sanctuary wall stones changed their character; and probably it may have been that the projecting-faced stones were hidden beneath the concrete floor.

"A shaft was sunk alongside the Sanctuary wall at the point where the gallery from No. 12 struck it, 18 feet south of the northeast angle of the Sanctuary (as seen on the surface). Level of the bottom of the gallery 2,363 feet 3 inches. Passed through black earth and stone about 12 inches cube; at 17 feet came on stone-chippings. Hitherto, in this shaft, the Sanctuary wall stones had the ordinary marginal draft; but at 21½ feet the first course of projecting-faced stones was met with, the projection being 25 inches.

"At 36 feet the rock was struck, having a very steep fall to the south, and being cut in steps for the reception of the stones of the Sanctuary wall. Shaft tamped.

"The gallery of the south was continued until it reached the southern corner of the tower, which at this point only projects 2 feet (page 133); and here another shaft was sunk; level of bottom of the gallery 2,363 feet. Commenced 7th of July, 1869. At first the soil was good, then some very large stones had to be broken through: at a depth of 46 feet the soil became better to work in. The face of stone 14th course X was very faulty, and its irregularities were filled up with small stones and mortar, rendered on outside so as to look like stone (specimen of mortar kept). Along the top of the Z course, which sets out $7\frac{1}{4}$ inches, a small drain was built about 6 inches by 5 inches in the clear: it runs into a little cistern about 3 feet square and 6 feet high, the sides plastered, and the top covered with a rough flat stone: depth of drain from bottom of the gallery 52 feet 6 inches. The cistern lay to the north of the shaft, its western side about 1 foot 6 inches from the Haram wall; the drain, 1 foot 4 inches wide, enters at the northeast angle of the tank, and the outlet, which is only about 6 inches square, is at the southwest angle; there was about a foot of deposit at the bottom.

"At 58 feet we got among dry shingle, and at 62 feet 6 inches came to the course, on one stone of which red painted characters were found: the face of the stone was not dressed, but in the working of it a large piece had split off, leaving a smooth face, and on this the characters were painted. In one case the letter appeared to have been put on before the stone was laid, as the trickling from the paint was on the upper side.

"Rock was found 70 feet 9 inches below bottom of the gallery: it had a steep slope of two in one to the south.

"This shaft was now tamped up and the gallery driven on to the south along the side of the Haram wall for 75 feet past the corner of the tower, the soil being very good; all at once our old enemy, the shingle, again appeared and filled up the end of our gallery, so that it had to be tamped up for 12 feet, as it is impossible to drive through this shingle with our means. Shaft now sunk (commenced 2d December, 1869) at 63 feet south of the corner of the tower, passed this loose earth and large stones, some of them 4 feet long and very nicely dressed. 13th December, got down to a depth of 28 feet.

"Wherever the wall of the Sanctuary, south of the corner of the tower, has been seen as yet, the stones have been found with projecting faces, and it seems most probable that this description of wall extends in an unbroken line as far as the Golden Gate.

"The Count de Vogüé visited the excavations at No. 12, and was shown the aqueduct; while he was down there a piece of magnesium wire was lighted at the top of the *light-shaft* so as to imitate daylight pouring in; the light, after passing down the shaft, strikes the aqueduct just where the staircase opens in, so that any person coming down it would have been able to have seen where he was going to.

"The passage has since been cleared out for 28 feet; it was filled with earth and large stones, which rolled down with great force into the aqueduct: the passage is found to be a staircase leading up toward the surface to the north, at an angle of one in one; it appears to have been cut out of the solid rock after the wall was built. The roof is hollowed a little in the centre, and ascends by great steps of about 4 feet each."

Letter of 25th February, 1870.—Conclusion of the Excavations at the northeast angle of the Sanctuary.—"Account of this work has been sent up to the 13th December, 1869; we had then failed in driving a gallery to the south along the Sanctuary wall more than 75 feet beyond the tower, and had commenced a shaft from the gallery along the Sanctuary wall at 63 feet south of the southeast angle of the tower and had sunk to a depth of 28 feet.

"The level of the gallery at the shaft-mouth was 2,363 feet 3 inches (see plan). For the first 17 feet 6 inches passed through good black earth to 2,345 feet 6 inches, then passed through a heap of broken cut stone, the faces well cut with marginal drafts. It was difficult work getting through these, as they had to be broken up with the hammer, and the concussion brought stones down upon the workmen.

"At 31 feet (2,332 feet) these large stones terminated, and to 36 feet (2,327) alternate layers of earth and gravel or small stones were met with, each layer of earth about 6 inches thick, and gravel about 9 inches.

"We now came on loose shingle and stone-clippings to a depth of 49 feet (2,313 feet). The shingle kept giving way, and running into the shaft, till it was feared the large broken stones would be dislodged; the frames were battened together and earth thrown behind them. On stone U, at level 2,326 feet, a mark was found; it is difficult to say whether it is natural or not; a squeeze of it did not show at all. A sketch has been made.

"Passed through a hard black soil, sloping to the east, till 56 feet (2,307 feet), when a layer of red clay, mixed with small stones, 3 inches thick, was reached. At 53 feet (2,310 feet) a small drain was found running along the Sanctuary wall on top of the stone Z, evidently the same drain as was met with in the shaft at the southeast angle of the tower; it was made of small stones and mortar; very hard, apparently had been mixed with oil. Just below this drain several pieces of tesserae were found; they are similar to those found about Jerusalem, supposed to be Roman. Several specimens have been kept; they have a high polish.

"We now continued below the layer of red clay (which dips to the east), and finding the soil black and hard to 60 feet 6 inches (2,302 feet 9 inches), commenced gallery B to the south at that level on 22d December, 1869.

"At 9 feet 6 inches to the south, that is, at 72 feet 6 inches to the south of the southeast angle of the tower, commenced a shaft through black earth and small stones and broken pieces of pottery. At 65 feet came on small shingle to 67 feet (2,296 feet), and then stones and wet earth to 80 feet (2,283 feet), when rock was found sloping to the north, which showed us that we had gone too far to the south. The rock is cut away in steps for the stones of the wall.

"A gallery was now commenced to the north along the rock, to find the bottom of the valley; but, after six feet, a large stone crushed through the frames, and the gallery had to be tamped up. The rock was found to continue falling to the north.

"Gallery B was now driven to the north for 18 feet when at 45 feet from the southeast angle of the tower a shaft was sunk through hard black soil, for 11 feet 6 inches (2,292 feet), when shingle was met with. The rock was found at 2,289 feet sloping rapidly to the south, and stepped down for the reception of the stones of the wall.

"Commenced a gallery to the south along rock, and at 16 feet, 24th of January; found the lowest point 85 feet below the gallery, or at a level of 2,278 feet 3 inches, or a little over 125 feet below the present surface. This is the greatest depth of *débris* we have yet found.

"The ground here was very wet, and it was to all appearances the bottom of the valley; but, to make sure, the gallery B was again driven to the south, until at 104 feet 6 inches from the southeast angle of the tower, shingle, sloping to the south one in five, was met with, and the gallery had to be stopped. At this point a shaft was sunk: the first 18 inches through black soil, then a layer of blue clay without stone or grit in it, from 9 inches to 12 inches thick, and falling to the east at one in twelve; under this was gravel, hard and difficult to get through, till at 16 feet rock was found (7th of February, 1870) at a level of 2,289, sloping to the north.

"There was thus a rise from the apparent bottom of the valley of 11 feet in 46 feet horizontal.

"There is still, however, the possibility of the bottom of the valley being farther to the south, as the rock here appears to lie in benches, with every here and there a drop. As it is, the bottom of the valley, as found by us, is over 165 feet below the Sakhra.

"In this valley at 12 we have excavated more than 600 feet run of shaft and gallery."

CHAPTER VI.

NORTHERN SIDE OF THE NOBLE SANCTUARY.

Birket Israil.—Letter of 12*th of November*, 1867.—" I have examined the passages west of the Birket Israil. The southern terminates abruptly, at 134 feet, in a masonry wall; the northern opens, at 118 feet, into a small arched

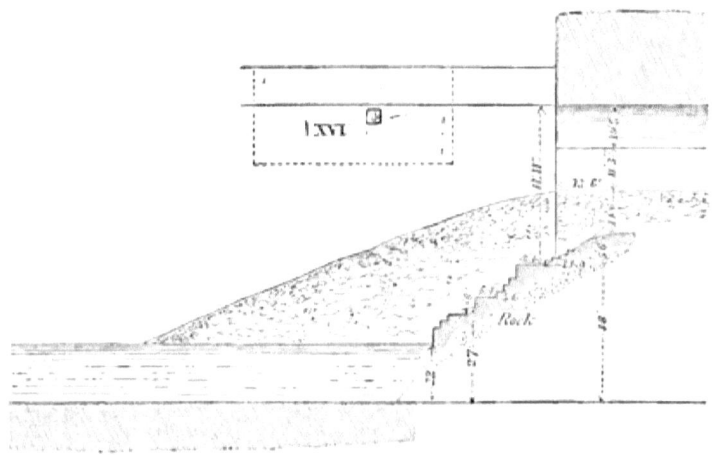

SECTION EAST AND WEST THROUGH BIRKET ISRAIL.

passage, running north and south, of modern construction, which appears to have been built to enable the rubbish to be thrown down. I am exposing the wall to the west, but at present there appear no signs of a continuation of the passage. This exploration was a very nasty piece of work, as the passage is now used as a sewer, and is choked up to the crown of the arch. In one place we both stuck for about ten minutes, not being able to get backward or forward."

January 1, 1868.—" A shaft was sunk in the pool of Israil at 20 feet from the southern side and 158 feet from the eastern end; at a level of 2,349½ feet, after getting down 16 feet through loose stones and bowlders, the rains swamped out the workmen. In November, 1868, the work was recommenced; at 21 feet water was reached, strongly impregnated with sewage."

Jerusalem, December 28, 1868.—*Birket Israil.*—" On 12th November I related to you that in sinking a shaft in this pool we had come upon filthy water, and had been obliged to discontinue the work on account of the foul smell arising. After a few days had elapsed I had this water baled out, and found that the fresh water which streamed in again on all sides was comparatively clean and pure. By feeling with a jumper, the water was found to stand at a height of 3 feet 6 inches above the bottom of the pool, and as the *débris* we had to go through was a mass of loose stones, through which the water flowed freely, it was a matter of some difficulty to get a look at the bottom, because it was not possible to get the water out fast enough to enable us to fix in frames one by one; after some trouble, the space between the last shaft-frame and the bottom of the pool (about 4 feet) was cleared out, so far as the stones are concerned, and then a small coffer-dam was let down; it consisted of four shaft-frames screwed together and rested on the bottom of the pool; clay had been got up for the purpose and was puddled in behind the frames on all sides; the water was then baled out, and the bottom of the pool was exposed.

" It has a hard, smooth surface, evidently for the bottom of a reservoir; on breaking through, we found first a thickness of plaster, 2½ inches, very hard and compact, composed of cement and broken pottery; then a kind of concrete, consisting of alternate layers of small stones and mortar, to a depth of 1 foot 4½ inches. The plaster and concrete were exceedingly hard, so much so that only small pieces could be broken off with the jumper; we were obliged therefore to have recourse to blasting, and as the water trickled slowly into the jumper-holes, the charges were put in glass bottles and rendered water-tight. We soon had a hole, about 2 feet square, made through the concrete, and there was exposed a surface of hard stone (mezzeh), either the rock or a large paving-stone, apparently the former; a jumper-hole 10 inches deep was driven into this stone, but it would have been very difficult to have gone deeper without disturbing a greater surface than our dam covered. I had the shaft partially filled in, and drove a gallery from it at a depth of 9 feet to the south wall of the pool. There we found the plaster and lining stones precisely similar to those which are seen above, and which are fully described by Salzmann."

"Specimens of the plaster and concrete from the bottom of the pool are now ready to be sent home.

"The top of the shaft was 60 feet below the Sanctuary level. At the northern end, the depth of the shaft to the bottom of the pool was 24 feet 6 inches, so that the bottom of the pool is at a level of 2,325 feet above the Mediterranean. As a result of the examination, we find that the bottom of the pool, at least in one point, is (or rather was) in perfect preservation, that the pool is upward of 80 feet deep, and that there is in it an accumulation of stones, refuse, and sewage averaging a depth of 35 feet. Should the city be again rendered wholesome and inhabitable in summer by the enforcement of proper sanitary regulations, it would be necessary to remove the rubbish from this pool, and then the Birket Israil, at the expense of rendering the sides sound, might again serve as a reservoir for water.

"The results of the examination with regard to settling the question of the position of the rock about the pool are not satisfactory: at the bottom it appears to be rock; but

at the side, where the gallery was driven, it appears that
the rock is wanting, otherwise it would not have been necessary to build it up with large stones.

"If the side of the pool to the south is not cut out of the
rock, then we have the Haram Area at this point elevated
to a height of 100 feet: and the question arises whether this
100 feet is *débris* (and most interesting *débris* it would be),
or whether it is composed of substructions similar to those
at the southeast angle, and in continuation of those we have
lately found at the north end of the Mosque Platform.

"Again, on the east side of this pool, we have the Bab
Sitti Miriam, generally called St. Stephen's Gate. Are we
to suppose this gate elevated 100 feet above the bottom of
the wall, or does the rock break down suddenly from the
gate toward the south, so as to form a deep gorge in which
the pool is built? In this latter case, how far does the
ravine extend from the southwest? Does it come down
from the Damascus Gate and pass south of the Serai, and so
join the valley from the north at the site of the pool?
These are points to which considerable interest must be
attached (see page 132).

"I find that the rock, to the north of the Birket Israil,
crops up at the side of the Church of St. Anne, at a level of
2,410 feet, and that at the gate leading to this church from
the Via Dolorosa, no rock was found at 36 feet from the
surface (2,405 feet).

"There is a question also with regard to the two arched
passages leading from the west of the Birket Israil; the
crowns of these arches are on a level with the top of the
pool, and it seems hardly probable that the piers will extend
to the bottom of the pool without a second series of arches
midway; if, on the other hand, the passages do not reach to
the bottom of the pool, it would be interesting to know
whether they are built on *débris* or on rock: a shaft is now
being sunk under one of the arches, but the owner of the
ground is a little diffident about our working there, and may
place obstacles in the way."

"*February* 1, 1869.—" Under the northern vault, 9 feet from the entrance, a shaft has been sunk, and at a depth of 14 feet 6 inches a floor of concrete has been found, which at this point is 36 feet 6 inches below the crown of the arch, and 43 feet 6 inches above the bottom of the pool.

"The floor has a slope toward the entrance, where there are four stone steps 16 inches broad and 7 inches in height; the bottom step is nearly flush with the west wall of the pool, and from this step to the crown of the arch is 49 feet; beyond this there is a landing 8 feet broad, and then a drop of 4 feet. Attempts were made to get through the concrete at this point, but the instruments could make no impression on it; the gallery was then driven down along the face of the concrete to the east, which is found to consist of irregular steps (see woodcut). The concrete was followed down until, at a point 22 feet above the bottom of the pool, the rubbish was found to be in too loose a state to work through, and the gallery has been discontinued; it is probable that in any case we could not have continued more than a foot or two deeper on account of the water in the pool.

"The concrete floor was then broken through and rock was found at 40 feet below the crown of the arch of the northern Souterrain, and also under the concrete in other places sloping to the east.

"It shows that the Birket Israil never extended farther to the west than its present limit, at its present depth; and we may draw the inference that no other enormous pools exist similar to and to the west of Birket Israil; that any ditches or pools to the west of it will be found to be cut out of the rock, and of comparatively small size, similar to that found near the Sisters of Sion Convent; and that if ever the Birket Israil was of larger extent than it is at present, it would only have been by a portion of the pool running north toward the west end of the Church of St. Anne, or south into the Sanctuary.

"The subsequent excavations at the northeast angle of the Sanctuary proved that there was also rock at the eastern side of the pool, but none on the north and south.

"On January 1, 1869, the garden, northwest of Birket Israil, on the other side of the road, was examined; and an entrance to a cistern found at 61 feet north of the Via Dolorosa, and 33 feet west of the road leading north from Bab Hytta (see Ordnance Survey Plan $\frac{1}{2500}$, the contour line 2,419 passes through the garden). The height of this entrance is 2,421 feet, for about the first 20 feet down there is a shaft 2 feet wide; below this it opens out to the west to about 8 feet, and at 36 feet is the rock, forming in part the roof of a small chamber or cistern: this chamber is cut in the rock, and is filled up within 6 feet of the top with mud: close to the shaft already described, is a parallel shaft, giving the impression that water was obtained from this chamber by means of a *n'aura* (water-wheel)."

February 1, 1869.—"We have been excavating in the cistern in the garden northwest of the Birket, where I thought there had been a n'aura, but we can find no signs of any aqueduct by which water could have been brought in; the cistern is 20 feet deep.

"At a point where the Bab el-Aten enters upon the Tarik Bab Sitti Miriam, close to the traditional tower of Antonia, I have opened another cistern, and found rock as shown on plan; running north and south on the rock is an aqueduct, which apparently filled the cistern in passing, and may have been used for the supply of the Sanctuary or of the Birket Israil; it is blocked up after a few feet at each end, and the owner of the property would not have it opened.

"Each step we take about the northeastern end of the Sanctuary tends to point out that there is a great depth from the surface to the rock."

BETHESDA ACCORDING TO EARLY TRADITION.

Wherever the original Pool of Bethesda may have been, the accounts of Eusebius and the Bordeaux Pilgrim point to the twin pools (whose existence recent researches have established at the northwest angle of the Noble Sanctuary) being the traditionary Bethesda of their day. Here are pools cut in the rock, side by side, with a pier of masonry 5 feet thick running up the centre, and arches thrown over converting them into Souterrains; the total length is 165 feet, the breadth through both pools and the pier is about 48 feet; water enters in at the northwest angle, and supplies the convent of the Sisters of Sion for all purposes except drinking, and is probably an abundant spring.

At the southwest angle a great passage leads off due south along the west wall of the Sanctuary.

Eusebius,* in his Onomasticon, gives no idea as to site, but tells us that Bethesda is "a pool at Jerusalem, which is the Piscina Probatica, and had formerly five porches, and now is pointed out as the twin pools there, of which one is filled by the rains of the year, but the other exhibits its waters tinged in an extraordinary manner with red, retaining a trace, they say, of the victims that were formerly cleansed in it."

The Bordeaux Pilgrim tells us "there are at Jerusalem two great pools at the side of the temple; that is, one on the right hand and the other on the left, which Solomon made.

"But more within the city are two twin pools, having five porches, which are called Bethsaida. Here the sick of many years were wont to be healed, but these pools have water, which, when agitated, is of a kind of red color."

If the pilgrim entered by the present St. Stephen's Gate, he would have walked along between the Birket Israil and the church of St. Anne and have turned down along the west side of the Sanctuary, and in doing so he would have to cross over the twin pools near the Ecce Homo Arch.

The red color of the water in one of the pools would be the result of the rapid influx of water after the heavy rains through the underground channels.

* Lewin, pp. 487, 488.

Several authorities (Thrupp, Williams, etc.) are in favor of water having entered the city near here; and besides this well-known spring at the Sisters of Sion Convent, there is the report of the existence of a spring in the church of the Flagellation hard by; and it is to be remarked that the Arabs have a tradition of there being a channel of running water in one of the streets close to this twin pool; the street is called Hosh Bezbezi (bubbling of water).—Wilson's O. S. O., note, p. 79.

The northern of the two great pools spoken of by the Bordeaux Pilgrim appears to have stood near the present church of St. Anne, and the traditional site of Bethesda became transferred to it, and on its destruction to the Birket Israil.

Of the existence of a pool near the church of St. Anne in the Middle Ages, north of the Birket Israil, and of its then being considered as the pool of Bethesda, we have the testimony of Sæwulf, Brocardus, and Anselm.

Mr. Williams, who goes very thoroughly into the matter ("The Holy City," p. 484), considers not only that the large pool (now destroyed) near the church of St. Anne, was the Bethesda and Piscina Probatica of the Middle Ages, but also of the earlier Christians and of the Bordeaux Pilgrim.

I cannot, however, see how he arrives at this conclusion; and as the two large pools spoken of by the Bordeaux Pilgrim are generally admitted to be the Birket Israil, and that which was near the church of St. Anne, it appears to me highly probable that the twin pool "more within the city" should be the twin pool under the Sisters of Sion Convent.

SOUTERRAIN NO. 1, CONVENT OF SISTERS OF SION.

Letter of October 28, 1867.—"I have been unable to explore the passage in the west wall of the Souterrain at 'Sisters of Sion;' it is blocked up with masonry. I have, however, examined the hitherto unexplored passage cut in

the rock at its southern end, and consider the results will be
thought very interesting. Last week I looked into this passage, and found it to open out to a width of 4 feet, and to
be full of sewage 5 feet deep. I got some planks, and made
a perilous voyage on the sewage for about 12 feet, and found
myself in a magnificent passage cut in the rock 30 feet high,
and covered by large stones laid across horizontally. Seeing
how desirable it would be to trace out this passage, I obtained three old doors, and went down there to-day with
Sergeant Birtles; we laid them down on the surface of the
sewage, and advanced along by lifting up the hindermost
and throwing it in front of us. The general direction of the
passage is due south; after 16 feet it runs to the west for 6
feet, and then pursues its original course. In some places
the sewage was exceedingly moist and very offensive, and it
was difficult to keep our balance while getting up the doors
after they had sunk in the muck. After advancing 6 feet
we came to a dam built across the passage—ashlar—about
10 feet high; the passage in continuation also containing
sewage at the lower level of 6 feet. Every thing had become so slippery that we had to exercise great caution in
lowering ourselves down, lest an unlucky false step might
cause a header into the murky liquid. After leaving this
dam behind us some 50 feet we found the sewage to be firm-
er at top, and after a few more feet we were enabled to
walk on its surface with the aid of poles. The roof now began sloping down so that the height was considerably lessened, and on arriving at a little more than 200 feet from the
commencement we found our passage diminished to only 8
feet in height and blocked up at the end by masonry.* It is

---

* The following account of recent discoveries at Jerusalem is extracted from
the *Athenæum*, October 1, 18—, and Quarterly, No. VII.:

"In this rock-cut passage, the rubbish has just been cleared out; the bottom is found to be plastered, and the dam built across has a hole in it for stopping and letting out the water.

"The extreme southern end of the passage, which was blocked up, has now
been cleared out, and is found to turn sharply to the east for a few feet, when it
meets with a massive wall of bevelled or marginal drafted stones. This wall is

cut throughout in solid rock from top to bottom, and thus we have a fair section of the contour from the Serai to the Via Dolorosa.

"It is evident that no ditch ever traversed the city across the line of this passage; and therefore the theory of a cutting from Birket Israil to Street of the Valley is untenable, unless it be supposed to have been more northerly in the direction of the arched Souterrain, whose direction, S. S. E., appears inconsistent with such an arrangement. I cannot for a moment think that this passage was originally intended as a drain; it may have been a natural cleft, utilized by cutting, and this would account for its great height, which in some places is full 36 feet above the surface of the sewage.

"Dr. Chaplin suggested that it is the passage, 'Strato's Tower,' mentioned by Josephus as leading to Antonia.

"I have examined the wall at the southern end of the Souterrain, and am convinced it is a spring of considerable capacity."

December 2, 1868.—" I visited, with M. Ganneau, the Souterrain No. 1, and found that the passage explored 28th October was comparatively dry, and we could get to the end on planks, but there was nothing new to be seen. The staircase close to this passage was in some way connected with the latrines of the Serai; it has been blocked up, and consequently the amount of sewage now oozing into the place is very inconsiderable.

"A great portion of the side of the Souterrain No. 1 to the west is rock, and I hope to be able to ascertain what it is throughout the entire length. At present it appears that the place is a deep fosse cut in the rock about 50 feet wide and 165 feet long.

8 feet thick, and lies along the western boundary of the Haram Enclosure; three courses are rubble, the middle one is 4 feet 7½ inches in height, the drafts are 7 inches wide at top and bottom, and from 3 inches to 4 inches at the sides, and sunk about ½ inch.

"The portion of the wall exposed is only a few feet south of the northwest angle of the Haram Area.

"CHARLES WARREN, Capt. R. E."

SOUTERRAIN NO 2, CONVENT OF SISTERS OF SION.

Letter of December 2, 1868.—" An important discovery has been made lately at the Convent of the Sisters of Sion (see general plan).

"In extending the buildings to the east a second souterrain was found. Through the kindness of M. Ganneau, the Frence Vice-consul, and with the permission and aid of M. l'Abbé, I have made a plan of it. It is to the northeast, and parallel to that which has already been described in Captain Wilson's notes.

"We entered from an opening in the crown of the arch, and descending 12 feet found ourselves on the top of a mound of rubbish which had fallen in from above.

"At the end to the northwest, the vault is 20 feet wide, and is filled up with rubbish nearly to the springing; the end is blocked up with a masonry wall of a later date than the arch itself. The arch appears to be semicircular, and has about thirty-one courses; at 11 feet down on the western side is a communication with Souterrain No. 1, 7 feet wide, and the pier or wall between the two is 5 feet 9 inches thick. On the eastern side of Souterrain No. 2, at this end, the arch appears to spring from the rock.

"This arch in Souterrain No. 2 continues 45 feet to the southeast; the vault then widens; the succeeding arch is 24 feet span, and the line of springing has a slope to the southeast of about one in six; the crown of the arch apparently remaining horizontal as the arch increases in span throughout its length of 36½ feet. The vault is now continued by another arch whose crown is about 4 feet 6 inches lower, and whose length is 46 feet. These two latter arches appear to be very slightly pointed; they are very nearly semicircular. The Souterrain No. 2 is thus 127 feet long, and from 20 feet to 26 feet across. The southeastern end is cut off by the same line of scarped rock which closes No. 1. Also, I believe that the springing of the arch to the east throughout its length is on the rock. For about 75 feet the Souterrain is a pool of water about 6 feet deep, with a bottom of soft mud, the water coming up to about 2 feet below the springing. We had to construct a raft, floated with inflated goat-skins, to enable us to examine this portion of the vault; and I do not feel confidence in some cross-measurements taken at the farther end, which I have not given on plan. I purpose going down again and examining the place more minutely. M. l'Abbé has offered every facility for our thoroughly exploring it.

"It is desirable to examine the arch to the northwest to see if it is continued.

"When the building of the convent was continued, over the northwest end of No. 2, scarped rock was found in continuation of No. 1, so that the inference is that this was originally a pool cut in the rock."

CHAPTER VII.

THE TANKS AND SOUTERRAINS OF THE SANCTUARY.

Captain Wilson measured and described the majority of these in 1865; and I have subsequently examined them all, with a view to determining the level of the rock in the Sanctuary, and have also surveyed those that required it.

In doing so, particular attention was paid to the accounts and plans given by Signor Pierotti in "Jerusalem Explored;" and I have come to the conclusion that his plans of tanks (Plate XI.) are rough sketches of those he entered or looked into, as they are totally unlike any thing at present existing. Also with regard to the passages he shows cut in the rock (in Plates IV. and XXVII.), as connecting the tanks in the Sanctuary with Siloam, etc., I should suppose he does not intend the reader to imagine that he explored them throughout; but, for example, finding a drain at one place and a walled-up opening, 200 yards off, he concluded the drain "must have corresponded with the opening" ("Jerusalem Explored," p. 99); and showed it accordingly on the plan. There are several instances in his text where conclusions of this kind are leaped at, and the doubtful portions in plan or section are in no way distinguished from what he actually discovered; and hence from this oversight his very valuable researches are, for the most part, rendered worthless. One of the most tantalizing instances of this is at tank No. 1, when, what would otherwise have been a most important discovery, is thus rendered liable to rejection.

He tells us how he found two tanks, opening one into the other (see No. 1 on plan) by a passage 4½ feet high and 3 feet wide, and on plan 15 feet long; how he found two openings to the southern end, down one of which he penetrated, until he found himself in a chamber below the Sakhra, and looking up *saw* the marble slab above him which covers " the Well of Spirits."

He does not tell us how he could recognize the under surface of a marble slab of which he had previously only seen the upper surface; neither does he say that he had anybody placed over the Well of Spirits to make signals to him, nor that he used tape or compass; and it is remarkable that tank No. 1, which he describes as two tanks with a passage between, is now a long rock-cut tunnel, with no vestiges of the passages or partition. I am of opinion that a passage from tank No. 1 to a chamber under the Sakhra does exist, and think it highly probable that the marble slab seen by Signor Pierotti was the stone covering the Well of Spirits; but I do not feel satisfied until some further data are given: and as to the blood having been led from tank to tank to stagnate and putrefy and poison the courts of the Temple, there seems no reason for such a system. Apparently all that would be necessary would be a receiving chamber opening into a culvert, running as straight as possible from the inner court of the Temple, with here and there openings where conduits of water might flush it out.

I will now briefly relate any information with regard to the tanks of the Sanctuary which has not already been published in Captain Wilson's O. S. notes.

No. 1. Rock 2,427 feet above Mediterranean, and 12 feet below surface of Dome of the Rock platform. This tank is a tunnel about 130 feet long and 24 feet wide, cut in rock for 18 feet from bottom to springing of arch, which is segmental. Signor Pierotti describes a passage connecting this tank with a chamber under the Sakhra; and I have to suggest that this Sakhra cave is the gate Nitsots, from whence there was a passage through the tunnel to the gate *Tadi*.

TANKS.

No. 3. Rock 2,426 feet; 9 feet from surface. A channel cut in the rock, leading into this tank, was examined November, 1867; it runs north and south, and conducts into the tank surface-water from small ducts which run east and west. There are three chambers in this tank, which are separated by piers, through which there are low-arched door-ways. I have to suggest that this may have been the House of Baptism, communicating with the room of Beth Mokad and the gate Tadi.

It is to be noticed that the tanks Nos. 1 and 3 would, if produced north, meet together at the northern edge of the platform, where there is a hollow-sounding piece of ground. Under this may still be the gate Tadi, opening out through the scarped rock, one portion of which was found somewhat to the east at Souterrain 29.*

No. 2. Rock 2,429; 6 feet from the surface. This is a large tank cut in the rock, but there was too much water in it for us to measure it. Length about 60 feet; breadth about 50 feet. The sheikh of the Mosque said it communicated with No. 34 hard by; but it does not appear to do so.

No. 4. A small retort-shaped cistern; rock 2,417 feet; 18 feet below the surface. At 11 feet below the surface is a more ancient entrance-mouth to this tank, somewhat above the general level of the Sanctuary.

No. 5. At the northwest entrance rock is 2,425 feet; 10 feet below the platform; at the southeast entrance rock at 2,408 feet, 8 feet below the surface of the Sanctuary; and at 20 feet below the surface a conduit for water opens into the cistern.

It is over the northwestern end of this tank that I have to suggest was the position of the Altar of Burnt-offerings.

It is extremely interesting to find the following in Mejir ed Din, as it possibly refers to an older legend, which some readers may have heard of ("Mines d'Orient," p. 94):

"The Dome of the Roll. This is on the platform of the

* See Appendix II.

Sakhra on the southwest. I have been told that it is so called because one of the ancient kings, on a visit to Jerusalem, having ascended the Mount of Olives, threw a roll which fell here; which gave occasion to the building of the Dome and to its name. Men have invented divers accounts of the matter; God only knows the truth."

This Dome of the Roll would have stood over cistern M, very near where it is suggested the altar stood; and the legend appears likely to be older than the Moslem era. It is evident that Mejir ed Din relates only one account of many that he knew. The Jews at the present day affirm that the volume of the Sacred Law is buried somewhere in the Sanctuary, for which reason it is forbidden to them to enter; and there is a legend given in one of the works of Jerusalem stating how this volume was found.

No. 6. Rock 2,410 feet 6 inches; at 5 feet 6 inches from the surface.

No. 7. Rock 2,411 feet; at 5 feet from the surface.

No. 8. Rock generally 2,411; at 5 feet below the surface. This is called the Great Sea. The rock was viewed at the entrances and at the steps.

No. 9. Rock appeared to be about 2,400 feet, but not for certain. This is called the Well of the Leaf.

No. 10. Rock 2,387 feet; at 31 feet below the surface. This tank communicates with Solomon's Stables and the canal under the Triple Gate.

No. 11. Examined 11th November, 1867. Situate on the east of the Mosque of Aksa. Rock 2,397; at 19 feet below the surface; bottom 61 feet 6 inches below the surface of the ground. It consists of three tanks, each about 26 feet by 40 feet, lying east and west, connected by a passage 14 feet wide, running north and south; it is capable of holding about 700,000 gallons of water. The roof is cut in the rock, in the form of arches. Steps cut in the rock run up along the west side, and issue close to the mouth of the cistern. There is the foundation of a massive wall on the rock to the west of the steps.

The vaulted passage from the Triple Gate runs over this cistern.

No. 12. Rock, partially on the surface, 2,406 feet.

No. 13. Rock on the surface 2,409 feet; of an irregular shape, about 30 feet square; sides perpendicular, roof partially domed in the rock, ribs of rock springing from angles. A conduit for surface-water comes in from the east; it comes from a receiving-tank 250 feet farther to the north, between Nos 15 and 18. It is built close in under the surface of the Sanctuary.

No. 14. Rock 2,409 feet; on the surface.

Signor Pierotti, Plate XI., shows the cisterns Nos. 12, 13, and 14, as communicating one with another. They have no connection with each other at present, neither is there any sign of the conduit running in from Nos. 1 to 13, which he shows on his plate.

No. 15. Cistern near the Golden Gate, nearly circular; about 18 feet in diameter, and cut and roofed in rock.

Rock about 2,393 feet; about 15 feet below the surface.

Nos. 16 and 17; near Birket Israil; no rock found. See letter of February 1, 1869.

Substructure in the Sanctuary, near Bab Hytta (extract).—" At the northern end of the Sanctuary east of Bab Hytta are two tank-mouths, 16 and 17, which were not examined by Captain Wilson. They are closed by heavy stones. To the west of these is a private garden which projects out into and forms part of the Sanctuary; in this garden are two other tank-mouths. I examined one of these some months ago, but was unable to get down the other on account of the small size of the opening. On Monday last I went again to this garden to have another trial at these cisterns, and first examined that to the west, which is simply a tank about 8 feet by 15 feet, with a semicircular arch over it, and no appearance of rock about it. I then went to the other, situate at the southeast angle of the little garden, which at this point is elevated about 10 feet above the Sanctuary at the mouth of 17 (the mouth 17 appears to be at an elevation of 2,413 feet). On sounding, I found it 42 feet down to the water. I tried to descend, but to no purpose, until I had nearly stripped to the skin, and even then in my contortions I managed to slip the rope over one arm. The narrow passage was only for 3 feet, and 10 feet from the surface I came on the floor of a little chamber about 6 feet square, apparently on a level with the Sanctuary. The shaft down to the cistern continues through the floor of this chamber, and is a moderate-sized opening. On getting down to the water I found it only 3 feet deep, and concluding from the size of the cistern that help would be required in measuring, I signalled for Sergeant Birtles to come down.

"On lighting up the magnesium wire and looking about me, I was astonished, my first impression being that I had got into a church similar to that of the cathedral (formerly a mosque) at Cordova. I could see arch upon arch to the north and east, apparently rows of them.

"After floundering about some little distance, however, I could see that there was a limit to these substructures at no great distance to the north and east. In the mean time, Sergeant Birtles was making great efforts above with very little result; do what he would, he could not get past the narrow opening to the cistern, and at last had to give up the trial and go and get leave from the owner to pull down the upper mouth of the shaft, and then he very soon appeared at the bottom, his shoulders considerably injured in his exertions. In the mean time the excitement of our 'find' had begun to wear off, and the water felt cold. I was just giving the sergeant some sage advice as to how he could direct his steps to the best advantage, when I stumbled over a large stone and fell into the water flat on my face. As just at present the weather is frosty, and the rain is generally accompanied by sleet or hail, a bath in one's clothes is any thing but pleasant. I found the stones on which I stumbled to be about six in number: they average about 7 feet in length, and 3 feet in depth and width.

I could see no inscriptions on them; they appear to have fallen in by accident.

"The substructure, now used as a tank, is 63 feet from north to south, and 57 feet from east to west, thus being nearly square; its northern wall is 23 feet 6 inches from the south side of the Birket Israil. It consists of nine rectangular bays, formed by four piers, cruciform on plan, equidistant from each other and from the walls from which spring arches. The arches between the piers and between the two northern piers and walls are stilted and pointed; those from the two southern piers to the walls appear to be flying buttresses, unless the remainder of these arches are concealed behind the east, west, and south walls of the substructure. The dimensions of arches and piers all vary somewhat, which may arise from the thick coat of plaster which exists up to the tops of these arches, that is, to about 14 feet above the floor of the tank. These arches support nothing, they merely strengthen the piers and resist any lateral thrust against the side-walls.

"The whole of the substructure is covered in by vaults intersecting in groins over the bays. Surface-ribs (of cut-stone) are thrown over from the piers to the sides, the remainder of the arches being composed of rag-work; the vaults are pointed. The springing of the vault surface-ribs is 14 feet above the floor of the substructure, and the cement does not reach higher than that point. The vaults from springing to crown are also about 14 feet in height, giving a total of 28 feet from floor to crown.

"In the south wall is a staircase leading up to the surface of the Sanctuary, which I understand has been open within the memory of man. Near the bottom of the steps is a shaft leading up to entrance No. 17, and in the centre bay is an opening leading up to entrance No. 16. There is no appearance of an open continuation of these vaults in any direction. There is an opening on the northern side about 2 feet in height and 1 foot wide, on a level with the top of the cement, which lets in light; and on examining the pool Birket Israil I find a grating in the south wall (2 feet square) exactly opposite the opening in the substructure, and which undoubtedly communicates with it, but whether directly through the thickness of the wall, or whether through another chamber in the wall, has yet to be determined; through this opening any superfluous water in the substructure would flow into the Birket Israil.

"These vaults are unlike any known tanks in Jerusalem, and so very different from the substructions at the southeast angle of the Haram Area. I do not think that such a structure as this was built merely for a tank; and if it was simply to support the present surface of the Haram, then there is probably more of it to be found to the south and east.

"We were altogether three hours in the water measuring, and I took every thing I could get at, and have put the most important measurements on the 10 feet to an inch plan.

"The vaults look small when compared to the Birket Israil in section, but then the Birket is really an enormous reservoir, nearly 100 feet deep.

"The large stones I found huddled together at the bottom in the water, are, I think, evidence of the roof having once fallen in and been replaced."

See woodcut, showing section through the Birket Israil (page 149).

No. 18. Near the Serai. Rock 2,414 feet; 4 feet from surface: a small tank 7 feet by 10 feet and 38 feet deep.

Nos. 19 and 20. These are described in the Appendix to Captain Wilson's O. S. notes. In No. 19 there is no appearance of rock at 2,374 feet.

No. 21. South of Birket Israil, 21 feet deep, 24 feet by 12 feet of masonry; no appearance of rock.

No. 22. Near the gate of the Inspector. A large cistern of the type found down by Beit Jebrin and Deir Duban. It is cut and roofed in rock, domed. A flight of rock-cut steps runs round the curved wall; there are two openings into it from above, now closed up. Rock 2,416 feet ; 4 feet below the surface.

No. 23. Rock 2,429 feet, on surface; tank retort-shaped, about 8 feet in diameter and 35 feet deep: situated at the northwest angle of the platform.

No. 24. Rock 2,425 feet ; 9 feet below the surface of the platform. The rock is here exposed under the vault of a building; it falls at an angle of about 30° to the west ; this is probably referred to by Mejir ed Din ("Mines d'Orient," p. 91): "On the west side of the *Mesjid* are rocks said to be of the time of David. It is evident they are natural rocks rooted in the ground and never removed."

No. 25. Rock 2,416 feet ; 20 feet from surface : a small tank about 12 feet in diameter, and 37 feet deep ; situated a few feet south of No. 24.

No. 26. In the garden east of Nos. 16 and 17 ; a small tank ; no rock seen.

No. 27. In the garden at the northwest angle of the Sanctuary ; it is cut in the scarped rock.

No. 28. Rock 2,412 feet ; 3 feet from the surface ; situated at the northeast angle of the platform ; it is cut in the rock, and is about 10 feet in diameter. Its position is of importance, as it shows that the scarped rock found in No. 29, along the northern edge of the platform, did not extend so far east as this point.

No. 30 is the cistern which pierces the Sanctuary wall, south of the gate of the Bath ; it is described in Captain Wilson's notes ; rock was not found there.

No. 32 is a small tank in the Aksa (place of women): it apparently leads from the Well of the Leaf.

No. 33 is a small tank north of the Aksa, under the stairs going down to the double-passage rock.

Double Passage below the Aksa.—Search was made on all sides of this passage. The "Well of the Leaf" was examined, and at the bottom was found a curious arch of tiles (like Malaga bricks) : it has the appearance of having acted as an outlet to some subterranean flow of water. In examining the aqueduct which leads through the double passage to the well, a blocked-up passage was found, and, on removing the rubbish, it was found to lead into several ducts, which the plan * will best describe: they are about 5 feet below the present Haram surface, and are similar to those beneath the Sakhra platform: one of them is rendered with a very curious plaster of broken pebbles, and somewhere in its length it is possible there may be the shaft to a tank beneath, as the inclination of the ducts appears to be toward this passage.

An the north end of the double passage, to the east, there is a vestibule or vaulted chamber 17 feet square; its arch is similar in construction to that of the northern part of the double passage. It may perhaps have been built to serve as a guard-room or porter's lodge to the gate.

Entrance to the " Tomb of Aaron's Sons," at south end of double passage below the Aksa.—" Within the gate I have removed the stones and examined the passage through the wall; it is about 10 feet 6 inches thick, and very rough on the inside. It is backed up with earth. I do not see any signs of the continuation of vaults or buildings to the west of this passage: this is an important negative discovery."

"*Standing-place of Elias*" in the *Aksa.*—" The end of the passage or door-way here was broken through; it is about 1 foot 6 inches thick. Behind it is a mass of loose rubbish, and after removing about a ton of it I was able to get through, but could see nothing to lead me to suppose that there is anything beyond but made earth.

" The conclusion I have come to after making these excavations is that the " Double Passage " is a tunnel built through the made earth of the Haram Area, and quite unconnected with any vaults on either side. I can only account for the ducts I have found to the west of it by supposing that at one time the passage only extended for 190 feet from the south wall of the enclosure (at which time the Aksa Mosque could not have been in existence), and that

* Lithograph No. 9.

the ducts were used for collecting the surface water. When the Aksa was built, it appears that the passage was extended to its present length (260 feet), but on the east side only, as a heavy mass of masonry supporting a considerable portion of the Mosque rests just where the western passage should come; also, it appears that in order to prevent the arch of this extended passage cropping up above the Haram surface, it was necessary to cut down the old ramp to a gentle slope, and by that means to cut through the duct leading to the Well of the Leaf. I find there is a break in the arch of the eastern passage just where the western terminates, and the ramp at that point also changes its inclination.

"No. 34 is close to No. 2, at the northeast angle of platform; it was examined, but not measured; it is of an irregular shape, cut in the rock, and perhaps 60 feet in diameter: at the northeast angle is a passage cut in the rock which appears to terminate after about 10 feet. Rock 2,431."

13

CHAPTER VIII.

IMPORTANT DISCOVERY NORTH OF THE PLATFORM OF THE DOME OF THE ROCK ("MOSQUE OF OMAR").

No. 29. *Letter of December* 8, 1868.—" Going over the noble Sanctuary to see if I could trace any resemblance between the plan in Dr. Lightfoot's " Prospect of the Temple" and the present form of the ground, and passing by the northern edge of the " Mosque of Omar " Platform, I saw that the earth had been lately disturbed at the foot of the eastern steps, and, on asking the Sheikh of the Mosque about it, he said that after the heavy rains, three days before, the ground had given way, and that they had found an entrance to substructions as large as those at the southeast angle. I suggested to him that the hole had been badly filled in, and that it would probably give way again. This morning we went early to the Haram Area, and happened to come upon this place just a few minutes after the hole had opened a second time. We went down into it and made an examination.

" It is a souterrain running east and west in the line of the northern edge of the Mosque Platform. It consists of an arched passage of 18 feet span, with bays to the south of 12 feet by 17 feet, arched over, the piers between being 3 feet 6 inches thick. The southern side of these bays is scarped rock, and on it the wall supporting the northern edge of the Mosque Platform is built. Portions of the piers are also scarped from the rock, which appears to shelve down rapidly to the north; so that, if the earth and these vaults were removed, the northern end of the Mosque Platform would present the appearance of a perpendicularly scarped rock, with excrescences on its face 3 feet 6 inches thick, 12 feet apart, and projecting about 6 feet.

"The vault was examined for about 70 feet east and west, and four bays were surveyed. The crown of the arch of the vault and also of the bays is about 2 feet below the surface of the ground, which is there about 8 feet below the level of the Mosque Platform; the distance from crown to springing of the arches is 9 feet 6 inches, those (arches) of the bays being perpendicular to and forming groins with that of the vault. The arch over the vault has a span of 18 feet, but it is not semicircular. It appears to have a parabolic curve, while the arches over the bays are decidedly pointed (spans from 12 feet to 13 feet).

"The voussoirs of the arches are small, presenting about 15 inches by 4 inches on the soffit.

"On the northern side of the vault I could see no appearance of rock, except in one place for about 5 feet, where there is either rock or a large stone, the top of which is about 10 feet below the springing; the northern portions of the piers are also of masonry, but from their centres to their southern ends they are cleanly scarped from the rock, just as is the southern end of the bays.

"The masonry in the walls is of very miscellaneous character; in some cases large and small squared stones, and in some places coarse rubble. On the northern side of the vault are two passages, about 2 feet wide and 6 feet high, which are blocked up after about 8 feet; they have the appearance of being in connection with other vaults to the north; they are roofed over with stone slabs.

"To the east and west the Souterrain is blocked up with rubbish, fallen in from above; but it appears to extend in both directions, though toward the west there is an indication of a portion of the arch having given way. To the south the rock rises to about the springing of the arches; that is to say, to about 12 feet from the surface of the ground, or to about 18 feet below the Mosque Platform. Above the rock, the ends of the bays are filled in with coarse rubble, and it is doubtful whether they extend beneath the Mosque Platform. In the eastern bay there is an arched door-way, or communication, which is filled up with coarse rubble.

"The Souterrain has no appearance of having been constructed for a tank; there is not a sign of plaster about, and the rock appears to have been scarped for view; it differs in most respects from the tanks in the Sanctuary, and was apparently built for the purpose of raising up the Sanctuary to a general level. The arches appear to be Saracenic. For several months I have been seeking an opportunity to examine the ground on the northern side of the Mosque Platform, near the western steps, as I am convinced there are vaults there (from the hollow sound of the ground), and my impression now is that the Souterrain just discovered extends all along the northern edge of the platform.

"I do not see that the Souterrain supports the position of the Temple, obtained by the application of Dr. Lightfoot's plan to the existing plan, as sent home by the mail. It may with reason be claimed by one party as the ditch on the northern wall of the Temple, and by the other as the northern ditch of Antonia. It, however, limits the space on which the Temple could have stood, and as other knowledge is gained it may become a strong point in settling the matter.

"N. B.—The scarped rock was only visible to a depth of 12 feet, but there was no indication of any termination."

IMPORTANT DISCOVERY ON THE SAKHRA.

"On Thursday, April 8, 1869, I visited the Dome of the Rock with a view to examine two pieces of flagging which appeared to be lying upon it. They are horizontal, and extend in a northerly direction for 5 feet in prolongation of a gutter shown on the Ordnance Survey detail plan; this gutter is cut out of the solid rock, and leads from the western upper side to the northern lower plateau. The flagging was very heavy, and was found to conceal an opening in the rock 5 feet long and 2 feet wide; it continues due north for 11 feet more, and is roofed in rock; the rock is cut down perpendicularly at both sides and also at the southern end, where the gutter leads immediately into it; the pavement round to the Sakhra cuts off this passage to the north.

"When visited it was about 3 feet deep, but it was filled up at the bottom with soft earth or rubbish, and the real depth could not be ascertained. It is not easy to determine the object of this passage or cell; it is unlike the tombs and loculi seen about Jerusalem, and it can hardly have been for draining the rain-water off the surface into a tank, as the gutter commences from the higher portion of the rock.

"Sir John Maundeville relates (apparently of this Dome of the Rock), A. D. 1322:

"'And in the middle of the Temple are many high stages, 14 steps high, with good pillars all about, and this place the Jews call the Holy of Holies. No man, except the prelate of the Saracens, who makes their sacrifice, is allowed to come in there; and the people stand all about in divers stages, according to their dignity or rank, so that they may all see the sacrifice.'

"From this it would appear that the present exposed rock was then concealed by a raised dais, with steps leading down all round, in which case the gutter may have been used for carrying away the water when the dais was washed after the Moslem sacrifice.

"The chief Effendis, however, of Jerusalem have told me that sheep are never sacrificed in the precincts of the Sanctuary, and deny that they ever have been.

"It appeared to me that there was another piece of flagging lying on the rock some feet to the east of the two pieces I have described, but I had no opportunity of examining it, as this rock is very holy, and the dust gathered from it once a year is swept off by the Pacha, and given or sold for the cure of ophthalmia; it is therefore very seldom that any thing can be done there. There is a story about a hole somewhat corresponding to the place where I thought I saw the piece of flagging, through which an Effendi told me his father had let down a plummet for a great number of feet, until he had no more string left.

"I was in great hopes that there would have been an opportunity for examining the Well of Spirits, under the Sakhra, this spring. When the great dearth commenced, an Effendi came and asked my advice with regard to getting water for Jerusalem, his only idea being that of *pumping* it up from the Jordan, 18 miles off, and 4,000 feet below us. After showing him that there was sufficient water at the sealed fountain above the pools of Solomon, near Urtas, provided there were proper pipes, I asked him if he had thought of any place nearer than that. No; that was the reason he had come to me. He wanted me to sink an Artesian well. I asked him where was the source of all the rivers of the earth. 'Under the Sakhra!' 'Then why don't you go there and get it? Would Allah be angry?' He would not care if Allah were angry, for he had been mocking the people for two months by sending clouds without rain, and was not good; why should he mock the people?' 'Then why do you not try and get water from under the Sakhra?' 'Because—did I think there really was water there?'

"I read to him the account of Jerusalem given by Tacitus and also that given in the Mishna. He began to be convinced, and said that at that time the people would think it sacrilege, but that in another month they would, like him, think Allah was mocking them, and would be glad to get at the hidden waters. Rain, however, came in small quantities, and when I left Jerusalem, on April 8th, the country was covered with snow, consequently this Well of Spirits could not be examined.

"Under the Dome of St. George, at the northwest angle of the platform, is a chamber of which I never could get the key; it deserves examination.

"At the southwest angle of the platform a tank is spoken of by Mejir ed Din, and is shown on Pierotti's map. I could hear nothing of it. It is to be noted that we now know seven cisterns on the platform, which is the number given by Mejir ed Din. Search, however, should be made for this tank; it should be somewhere under where I suppose the Holy of Holies to have been.

"There yet remains a considerable amount of work to be done in the Sanctuary alone; all the surface drains should be examined, and new tanks might be found. Being so fully employed excavating, I had very little time for examining this place.

"It is perhaps worth noting that the Souterrain under the Convents of the Sisters of Sion is directed straight upon the Sakhra.

"The scarped rock on the northern end of the Sanctuary is found to extend from the northwest angle to the east for 352 feet, when it turns sharp to the north.

"On 12th November, 1867, I noted, 'There is a point somewhere north of the Dome of the Rock platform, where there may probably be a deep ditch filled up with earth; if not, it must be a natural valley, as the rock is entirely wanting on the surface.' I have since come to the conclusion that this is a natural valley, for if it were cut it would probably have been made parallel to some of the walls. There can be no doubt about its being a hollow of some kind. The rock, cut horizontally at the northwest angle of the Sanctuary, suddenly terminates in a line running northeast from the Gate of the Inspector, and there is a space 150 feet wide, where no rock is visible on the surface; then again it suddenly appears near the northwest angle of the platform, also running northeast.

"In reference to the contoured plan, it will be seen that the rock slopes rapidly down from the northern end of the platform, and I am under the impression it is scarped all along from the steps at the northwest angle to nearly the northeast angle. We know from the Souterrain No. 29 that at least 80 feet of this length is scarped. It is suggested that the northern edge of the platform is the northern front of King Herod's Temple, and that here was the house of King Hezekiah, spoken of by the early writers. I imagine that here was the exhedra of the temple spoken of by Josephus in the attack by Titus, and that it was joined to the Antonia, by cloisters across the natural valley already spoken of."

SOLOMON'S STABLES.

M. de Saulcy ("Voyage en Terre Sainte," p. 9) describes some remarkable rock-cut passages under the Temple Gate, and Captain Wilson gives a plan of them (O. S., Plate XV.). Our first work in Jerusalem, 1867, was the examination of these canals; we found them blocked up to the north by walls of hard old masonry, and we were fortunate enough to be able to get through these before our Vizieral letter arrived excluding the Sanctuary from our excavations.

They were evidently the overflow canals connecting the several tanks in the Sanctuary, and were arranged so that the water might be let off at different levels. It appears quite out of the question to suppose they were used as channels for carrying off the refuse from the sacrifices; and it is possible they may have been used as ducts for supplying water to the portion of the city to the south of the Sanctuary, and also for flushing the blood-channel, which appears likely to have been that discovered under the Single Gate.

The canal appears to run from tank No. 11 along the western passage of the Triple Gate, and enters tank No. 10 by two ducts, one very small, along which I crept sideways until I found it to open into No. 10, just below the roof, and the other is about 3 feet wide and 5 feet high, and, besides entering into No. 10, also branches off into two rock-cut passages, the western one being for water, and joins another leading from No. 10 at a lower level, and thence runs south; the eastern one turns sharply to the east just outside the Sanctuary wall, and, when clear of the east arch of the Triple Gate, zigzags along just under the surface of the ground, which here is close to the rock: this last passage does not appear to have been a water-channel.

We were able to clear out these passages for 60 feet north of the Triple Gate before we were finally stopped.

In the centre of the floor of the western canal there is a duct cut down to a depth of 18 inches, with about the same width; this was also the case with the passage under the Single Gate, with the old aqueduct discovered south of the Cœnaculum, and also with one of the passages in the so-called "Cave of Adullam," at Khureitun (noticed by Mr. Eaten). It can be understood that with a moderate stream the water would flow in the duct, while a person could walk from step to step on either side without rendering it impure.

At this time the entrance to the "stables" was by a hole through the crown of one of the arches opening down from the Sanctuary above, and visitors used generally to come down and see the place. The young Sheikh of the Mosque, who acted as guide, used often to be asked where our excavations had been, and he invariably showed visitors a dangerous hole made under the pier of one of the arches by somebody, I suppose, in search of treasure. I was frequently taxed with having made this hole, and had to refer people to the Ordnance Survey Plan, No. 15, of 1865, where it is shown as having then existed; or else give them the answer the Sheikh of Siloam gave the Chief Rabbi when the Tomb of Jehoshaphat had been opened by somebody in search of old copies of the law (for here they are said to be interred). The Rabbi sent down word to the Sheikh that it must be closed up at once, and suggested that I was the guilty person. The Sheikh replied, "You may be sure that *el Captán* did not open the tomb, for if he had he would have closed it up again, and nothing would have been known of it."

"Solomon's stables" are now very difficult of access. The entrance from the Sanctuary through the hole in the arch was closed up in 1868, in consequence of reports of some of the troops having secreted themselves in the vaults when sent to prayers, and of having eventually deserted. There is an entrance from "the Mosque of the Cradle of our Lord Jesus," but it has been plastered up for some years.

At present there are only two means of entry, the one through a loop-hole (9 inches wide and 19 inches high) on the staircase leading to the "Mosque of the Cradle" by a drop of 40 feet, past an overhanging mass of crumbling masonry—an entrance which, having once accomplished in safety, I would not wish to try again.

The other entry is by getting down tank No. 10 from the floor of the Sanctuary, and then up again by the Triple Gate canal (already mentioned) into the "stables."

Letter 38; *February* 11, 1869.—"A few days ago, finding that I still required some measurements for the completion of an elevation of the western wall of the vaults, I went in through tank No. 10. You enter from the surface of the Haram Area. There is first a shaft about 16 inches square, and about 31 feet to the top of the tank (rock), then a drop of 24 feet to the bottom of the tank, and 18 feet up again to the aqueduct leading to the vaults. The small ladder we could get down was only 12 feet long, and another, which we eventually got to lash on, was of slender proportions, having been made to assist young pigeons in getting up to their cote; the two together did not reach up to the hole, and we had considerable difficulty in getting up.

"In tank No. 10, in the roof of rock, is a space of 4 feet, covered by a flat white stone, and Sergeant Birtles observed some carving upon it. It can only be seen in a certain light, but I have made an approximate sketch of its appearance. It must be nearly 30 feet below the surface of the Haram Area, and is probably very ancient, as it would appear to have been put over the cistern before the *debris* accumulated.

"On this occasion we examined and made elevations of

the inside of the Triple Gate and west wall of the passage; no traces could be found of any 'colossal monoliths' about the gate-way ('Murray's Hand-book,' latest edition, p. 110); but there are the remains of engaged columns in the gate-way and the west wall of passage, which appear to show that there was originally a vestibule here somewhat similar to that at the Double Gate.

"As the west wall of this Triple Gate passage is supposed by Mr. Fergusson to have been the east wall of Herod's Temple, and, as it has never been described, it will be necessary to go into the matter.

"The Triple Gate has three semicircular arches on the exterior; in the interior they are elliptical, and have a greater span, so that the doors might fold back flush with the points.

"The west wall of the passage is formed of piers 4 feet wide and about 10 feet apart, with semicircular arches thrown over, on which rests the vault covering the passage; between the piers rough walls of ashlar are built up, forming recesses about 18 inches deep. There is nothing ancient in the construction of these piers or of the wall, except the remains of an engaged column, which is apparently *in situ*, at 60 feet from the south wall of the Sanctuary; there is only the lower course of this left, it rests on the rock and has no base mouldings. After 192 feet from the Sanctuary Wall the piers and arches terminate, and the wall is built up of ashlar very irregular in size; here and there a stone of considerable size being worked in, and on one of these false joints are cut. The passage on the west side has been cut down through the rock to a depth of about 3 feet, and it is found here and there in the wall to that height. The point in the wall where a lintel of a door-way has been supposed to have existed is simply where the rock crops up with a horizontal crevice running along it at the line of the road-way.

"The west side of the passage lies almost entirely on the rock, and rises at about an angle of one in twelve; at the sill of the gate it is 38 feet below the level of the Sanctuary; at 192 feet from the Triple Gate to the north the original passage terminates, and it is continued by a more modern arch and wall. It is to be remarked that at very nearly the same distance from the Double Gate the original double tunnel terminates.

"On either side in the piers of the western arch of the Triple Gate are engaged columns similar to that in the wall, only the lower course of each is left, and they have no base mouldings.

"Underneath the passage in the rock is tank No. 11, whose roof is only about 4 feet thick, and runs under the western wall of the passage. An excavation was made a short distance through the wall, under an arch in the western side of the passage; it appears to be built up merely to retain the earth and rubbish which exist to the west.

"There is nothing whatever in this wall that can give it the slightest pretensions to be considered as the exterior wall of the Temple, and the remains of ancient engaged columns, *in situ*, tend to show that it was a gateway of about the same style as the Double Gate, and is very likely at that time to have exactly corresponded to it in only having two passages.

"Mr. Fergusson shows very clearly that the Royal Cloisters of King Herod could not have stood on the southeastern portion of the Sanctuary as it now exists, on account of the irregularity in the spans of the vaults, but it seems hardly necessary to prove that Herodian work did not stand upon work which is evidently of a much later period. It is quite evident, with the exception of the large course running along the level of the floor of the stables, and the bit of masonry exactly at the southeast angle, that the whole of Solomon's Stables is a reconstruction from the floor upward, and it is probable, from the remains of an arch (described p. 37, O. S. Notes by Captain Wilson) at the southeast angle, that the original vaulting was of a much more solid and massive character. It is to be recollected that the floor of the stables is found to be 107 feet above the base of the wall, so that the 40 feet of reconstruction is in comparison slight; but at the southeast angle itself the stones appear to have never been displaced since the building of the wall, and I have to suggest that this may have been the so-called pinnacle of the Temple alluded to by so many of the early writers, as most authorities of the present day concur in supposing that some object at the southeast angle of the Sanctuary is alluded to.

"Signor Pierotti ('Jerusalem Explored,' p. 77) tells us that the chamber containing 'the Cradle of our Lord Jesus' is partly excavated in the rock, but our excavations show that its floor is nearly 120 feet above the rock."

CHAPTER IX.

THE WATERS OF JERUSALEM.

These have been classed by Captain Wilson in O. S. Notes, under the heads of Springs, Tanks, and Aqueducts.

The aqueducts are supposed to have been three in number, leading at different levels from near Solomon's Pools; of these the low-level aqueduct is still in use—that is to say, it was repaired a few years ago, but in so ineffectual a manner that it is very seldom that it carries water into Jerusalem, and, when it does do so, it runs to the Pacha's Palace, the Judgment Hall, and the Great Sea under the Mosque, from whence it is drawn up and sold to the people about the place, but it is of no advantage to the Jewish and Christian inhabitants. This low-level aqueduct is for the most part carried along near the surface of the ground about Jerusalem, but there is no doubt it originally was dug in the rock with shafts at intervals for supplying the houses it passed under.

Extract of Letter, September 2, 1867.—" I have made what I consider to be a very important discovery, viz., an ancient aqueduct, southeast corner of the Cœnaculum, and about 50 feet north of the present aqueduct—I have no doubt the original aqueduct from Solomon's Pools to the Sanctuary. We dug out the earth from a cut-stone shaft 2 feet square, and at 16 feet was a channel running from the west to the northeast, precisely similar in construction to the passages under the Triple Gate. It varies very much in size; sometimes we could crawl on hands and knees, then we had to creep sideways, again we lay on our backs and wriggled along, but still it was always large enough for a man of ordinary dimensions. In parts built of masonry, in parts cut out of solid rock, it is generally of a semicylindrical shape; but in many parts it has the peculiar shoulders which I have only seen under the Triple Gateway, but which I told you in my last letter had been noticed by Mr. Eaten, in the channel leading toward Tekoah. To the northeast we traced the channel for 250 feet, until we were stopped by a shaft which was filled with earth; to the west we traced it for 200 feet, till it was stopped in the same manner. In part of this passage we could stand upright, it being 10 or 12 feet high, with the remains of two sets of stones for covering, as shown in M. Piazzi Smyth's work on the Great Pyramid; the stones at the sides being of great size—12 feet by 6. This channel is evidently of ancient construction. It is built in lengths, as though the work had been commenced at several points, and had not been directed correctly. The plaster is in good preservation.

"The aqueduct was traced for 700 feet, and at either end it was found to be crossed and used by the present low-level aqueduct, it being at the same time level, but the entrances are much farther up the hill on account of the cutting being so deep, in one place 29 feet below the present surface.

"It is apparent that the builder of the present low-level aqueduct made use of the original one wherever it was convenient.

"This rock-cut aqueduct (discovered in 1867) has no appearance of being a Roman work, though we are informed by Josephus (Ant., xviii., 3, 2) that Pilate, the Procurator of Judea, brought water into Jerusalem from a distance of 200 furlongs.

"The high-level aqueduct was traced by Captain Wilson to a short distance beyond Rachel's Tomb, and we have since traced it along the right-hand side of the road for several hundred yards, until about half-way between Mar Elias and Jerusalem, where it has been ploughed up. It is supposed to have crossed from hence the plain of Rephaim (so called), and to have flowed into a pool lately discovered on the high ground to the west of the citadel; from thence it would naturally flow into the Birket Mamilla, or Upper Pool of Gihon, and so be carried along the line of the existing aqueduct from that pool to the citadel."

Extract of Letter.—" Nothing could be seen anywhere of the third aqueduct, and I could find no trace of any outlet in its supposed direction in the passage leading from the Sealed Fountain to Solomon's Pools, which we explored for nearly 500 feet, until we were close to the head of the upper pool. Here we were unable to proceed, the mud and water being up to our hips, and the accumulation of bats all driven into a small space being more than we could contend against, our candles being blown out by the nasty little animals, which got entangled in our hair and beards, and were most unpleasant in their antics. We left a mark on the walls, and I intend reëxamining the passage from the end close to the pool, where there is an opening and vault very like that covering the Souterrain under the convent of the Sœurs de Sion. I have made a plan of the chambers and entrances for water at the Sealed Fountain. There is a very small flow at present, but near the Upper Pool of Solomon it is joined by a rush of water from a higher level, apparently from the aqueduct of Wady Byar, which, however, is dry a few hundred yards higher up. Probably there may be another sealed fountain to the southeast of that known at present. There is plenty of water at this point to keep the high-level aqueduct going all the summer, should it ever be repaired, and that without interfering with the supply to Bethlehem and Jerusalem by the low-level conduit.

" During the late dearth of water in Jerusalem (1870), it was reported that the flow from this sealed fountain was greater than usual, and yet the Mejelis took upon themselves to refuse the munificent offer of Miss Burdett Coutts to supply Jerusalem with water. The passive resistance of these local Moslem authorities is easily explained: the water supplied to the city would come in at the higher level, and would supply the Christian and Jewish part of the population who inhabit the higher portions of the city. The richer Moslems, who live for the most part around the Sanctuary, are able to obtain water from its tanks when their own run dry, and can command a further supply from the Great Sea at any time, by repairing the low-level aqueduct; they therefore would to a certain extent lose money (the monopoly of the low-level stream) by the scheme, and they think they might run also the chance of losing the supply altogether from the low-level aqueduct.

"The water from the Birket Mamilla appears, after passing the citadel, to have flowed as at present into the pool of the Bath, or, as it is called, of Hezekiah. This pool, I am under the impression, was Gihon-in-the-valley, where Solomon was anointed king. It is to be noticed that the Gihon-in-the-valley is often shown as the Birket-es-Sultan, but this is not in accordance with 2 Chron. xxxiii. 14: 'Now after this he built a wall without the city of David, on the west side of Gihon, in the valley,' which shows that the lower Gihon is to be looked for within the city.

"It has been suggested by some that the pool of Siloam is the lower Gihon, but this can hardly be called the west side of Sion, neither is it apparent how a wall would then have been built to its west. By supposing Sion to be identical with Acra of the Maccabees, the lower pool of Gihon at once falls into its place on the site of the pool of the Bath, and the wall of Manasseh would be the supposed wall to its west, shown as the *second wall* by many authorities on Jerusalem.

"After passing into the lower Gihon, or Gihon-in-the-valley (the valley which runs down from the Jaffa Gate to the Sanctuary), the overflow water probably was conducted along this valley until when near Wilson's Arch it turned to the south along the rock-cut canals we have found under

Robinson's Arch; from thence down the Tyropœon Valley to the pool of Siloam, where it would be met with the waters from the Virgin's Fount.

"There are two pools of Siloam, a small one into which the waters from the Virgin's Fount fall after issuing from the tunnel, the other a larger pool now nearly filled up. This latter I suppose to have been the pool dug by King Hezekiah, and to be that going under the name of Siloam in Josephus (*Wars*, v., 10, 4) and the 'king's pool' in the first chapter of the prophet Nehemiah.

"The question of the origin of the Virgin's Fount aqueduct is a very interesting one; it appears to me to have been constructed in the following manner:

"First, an intermittent fountain on the east side of the Kedron issuing into the valley. When the Assyrians were expected by King Hezekiah, the fountains outside the city were stopped and the water brought inside. This applies completely to this fountain, for we find a canal cut in the rock leading due west till it is well under the hill of Ophel, then a shaft down to this canal with a place scooped at the bottom for water to lie in, and an iron ring at the top to tie the rope of the bucket to; leading from this shaft is a great corridor cut in the rock, and then also a staircase leading up until it is under a vaulted roof, the exit being on the hill of Ophel, a few feet from the ridge, and almost certainly within the ancient walls. Below the vaulted roof is another rock-cut shaft shown on the illustration, but this was only examined to a depth of about 35 feet.

"Apparently after this had been in use for some time, it was considered insufficient for the supply of the city, as the receiving-hole at the bottom of the shaft is so small and the corridor so confined for a large number of people; and so a rock-cut channel was cut through the hill, 1,700 feet long, to carry the water into the pool of Hezekiah, which already received the overflow water from the Gihon Pools. This pool was probably without the wall, but being at the mouth of the valley it would be surrounded on three sides by the outer wall, and would thus be as secure for the people as though it were inside; at the same time it would act as a wet ditch to protect a very vulnerable part of the fortress. This passage from the Virgin's Fountain to Siloam has been examined by several gentlemen, but to most of them some accident happened, so that only measurements were taken. Le Frère Liéven (author of the very useful French Guide to the Holy Land), apparently took angles with an ordinary compass, and I found his plan of the canal, which he lent me to compare with mine, to be very correct."

Extract from Letter of December 12, 1867.—" I have examined and surveyed the rock-cut passage leading from the Virgin's Fount to Siloam. We entered from the Siloam end, so as to have as much clean work as possible. For the first 350 feet it was very plain sailing; the height of passage sloping down from 16 feet at the entrance to 4 feet 4 inches; the width 2 feet; the direction a wavy line to the east. At 450 feet the height of the passage was reduced to 3 feet 9 inches, and here we found a shaft leading upward apparently to the open air. This might be made use of to great advantage by the owners of the soil overhead. From this shaft the passage takes a northeasterly direction, and at 690 feet is only 2 feet 6 inches high. Our difficulties now commenced. Sergeant Birtles, with a fellah, went ahead, measuring with tape, while I followed with compass and field-book. The bottom is a soft silt, with a calcareous crust at the top, strong enough to bear the human weight, except in a few places, where it lets one in with a flop. Our measurements of height were taken from the top of this crust, as it now forms the bottom of the aqueduct; the mud-silt is from 15 inches to 18 inches deep. We were now crawling on all-fours, and thought we were getting on very pleasantly, the water being only 4 inches deep, and we were not wet higher than our hips. Presently bits of cabbage-stalks came floating by, and we suddenly awoke to the fact that the waters were rising. The Virgin's Fount is used as a sort of scullery to the Silwân village, the refuge thrown there being carried off down the passage each time the water rises. The rising of the waters had not been anticipated, as they had risen only two hours previous to our entrance. At 850 feet the height of the channel was reduced to 1 foot 10 inches, and here our troubles began. The water was running with great violence, 1 foot in height, and we, crawling full length, were up to our necks in it.

"I was particularly embarrassed: one hand necessarily wet and dirty, the other holding a pencil, compass, and field-book; the candle for the most part in my mouth. Another 50 feet brought us to a place where we had regularly to run the gantlet of the waters. The passage being only 1 foot 4 inches high, we had just 4 inches breathing-space, and had some difficulty in twisting our necks round properly. When observing, my mouth was under water. At 900 feet we came upon two false cuttings, one on each side of the aqueduct. They go in for about 2 feet each. I could not discover any appearance of their being passages: if they are, and are stopped up for any distance, it will be next to impossible to clear them out in such a place. Just here I involuntarily swallowed a portion of my lead-pencil, nearly choking for a minute or two. We were now going in a zigzag direction toward the northwest, and the height increased to 4 feet 6 inches, which gave us a little breathing-space; but at 1,050 feet we were reduced to 2 feet 6 inches, and at 1,100 feet we were again crawling with a height of only 1 foot 10 inches. We should probably have suffered more from the cold than we did, had not our risible faculties been excited by the sight of our fellah in front plunging and puffing through the water like a young grampus. At 1,150 feet the passage again averaged in height 2 feet to 2 feet 6 inches; at 1,400 we heard the same sound of water dripping as described by Captain Wilson, the Rev. Dr. Barclay, and others. I carefully looked backward and forward, and at last found a fault in the rock, where the water was gurgling, but whether rushing in or out I could not ascertain. At

1,450 feet we commenced turning to the east, and the passage attained a height of 6 feet; at 1,658 feet we came upon our old friend, the passage leading to the Ophel shaft (see next page), and, after a further 50 feet, to the Virgin's Fount. Our candles were just becoming exhausted, and the last three angles I could not take very exactly. There were fifty-seven stations of the compass. When we came out it was dark, and we had to stand shivering for some minutes before our clothes were brought us; we were nearly four hours in the water. I find a difference of 42 feet between my measurements and those of Dr. Robinson, but if he took the length of the Virgin's Fount into account, we shall very nearly agree."

The discovery of a shaft down to the water of the Virgin's Fount threw considerable light upon the object of the rock-cut canals about Jerusalem, as proving them as, had been conjectured by some, to have been for conducting away the refuse and blood from the temple.

Extract from Letter of October 11, 1867.—*Virgin's Fount or Ain Um-ed-Deraj.*—" This was an excavation under the lowest step leading to the pool, in order to examine the communication by which the water enters. As the pool is usually occupied by water-carriers during the daylight, we went down about an hour after sunset on Friday, the 4th instant, and with three fellahin of Silwân, commenced removing the pebbly deposit from under the steps. The Silwân people, however, got wind of our proceedings, and came trooping down in a very excited state and requested us to begone. By dint of chaffing they eventually changed their tone and sent us coffee. After three hours' work I found that there would be more difficulty in opening the space under the steps than I had anticipated, and hearing that during this month there are few persons taking water from the pool, I ordered the work to be resumed in the morning.

"It appears that the village was divided on our account,

one cantankerous Sheikh taking it into his head that we had
no business out of our own country, and in the morning our
men found that he had effectually stopped our resuming the
work by sending a bevy of damsels there to wash. His
scant wardrobe, however, did not take long to beat up, and
sending down the men again in the afternoon, the pool was
found untenanted, and we resumed the work and continued
it on Saturday, the village taking our working anywhere as
a matter of course, the Sheikh vowing vengeance on the men
and threatening to get them placed on "the Road," which
is just being commenced from here to Jaffa by forced labor. After removing the deposit under the steps for 4 feet, a
hard substance was reached, either masonry or rock, and
without the assistance of divers, or letting the water off, it
would be very difficult to continue the search in this direction any farther. The other point of entrance of the water
is a deep hole of 4 feet in the middle of the pool, at which
nothing can be done. Finding our attempts thus abortive,
I had part of the rock cut passage to the pool of Siloam examined, and Sergeant Birtles found two passages leading
into it from the northwest, the farther one being the largest,
and being about 50 feet from the entrance to the pool. At
this we commenced to open. It was difficult work, full of
hard mud, which had to be carried for 50 feet through the
water of the passage, and then taking up the steps leading
to the pool. The men seldom have much more than their
heads above the water when removing the soil, and sometimes the water suddenly rises, and there is danger of their
being choked. The passage was cleared out 17 feet to-day,
and a small cave was arrived at, being the bottom of a deep
shaft cut in the solid rock. It is difficult at present to
form an opinion on the subject. We must erect a scaffolding to get to the top of the shaft, which appears at least 40
feet in height, and is cut in the rock. The magnesium wire
has come at a very opportune time."

Extract from Letter of October 28, 1867.—"To-day,

October 24th, having managed to obtain a small quantity of wood after infinite trouble, we went down to the Fountain shortly after sunrise; we had some 12-feet battens 2 feet square, but were obliged to cut them in half, as 6-feet lengths could only be got into the passage; the water was unusually low, and we managed to crawl through on our bare knees without wetting our upper clothing very much, which was fortunate, as we had the whole day before us. After passing through the pool we had to crawl 50 feet, and then came upon the new passage, which is 17 feet long, opening into the shaft. The bottom of this shaft is (now that the deposit is removed) lower by about 3 feet than the bottom of the aqueduct, and was evidently filled from the Virgin's Fountain. The length of the shaft averages 6 feet, and width 4 feet. We had a carpenter with us, but he was very slow, and quite unused to rough-and-ready style of work, and the labor of getting up the scaffolding devolved on Sergeant Birtles and myself, the fellahin bringing in the wood and handing it to us. Once, while they were bringing in some frames, the spring suddenly rose, and they were awkwardly placed for a few minutes, being nearly suffocated.

"By jamming the boards against the sides of the shaft, we succeeded in getting up 20 feet, when we commenced the first landing, cutting a check in the rock for the frames to rest on, and made a good firm job of it. Then, with four uprights resting on this, we commenced a second landing. On lighting a piece of magnesium wire at this point, we could see, 20 feet above us, a piece of loose masonry impending directly over our heads; and as several loose pieces had been found at the bottom, it occurred to both of us that our position was critical. Without speaking of it, we eyed each other ominously, and wished we were a little higher up. The second landing found us 27 feet above the bottom of the shaft. The formation of the third was very difficult; and, on getting nearly to the loose piece of masonry, we found it more dangerously placed than we had im-

agined, and weighing about 8 cwt. So we arranged it that
the third landing should be a few inches under this loose
mass, so as to break its fall and give us a chance. This third
landing was 38 feet above the bottom of the shaft. We
floored it with triple boards. It was ticklish work, as an in-
cautious blow would have detached the mass; and I doubt
if our work would have stood the strain. About 6 feet
above landing No. 3 the shaft opened out to the west into
a great cavern, there being a sloping ascent up at an angle
of 45°, covered with loose stones about a foot cube. Having hastily made a little ladder, I went up; and very cautious I had to be. The stones seemed all longing to be off;
and one starting would have sent the mass rolling, and me
with it, on top of the Sergeant, all to form a mash at the
bottom of the shaft. After ascending about 30 feet, I got
on to a landing, and the Sergeant followed. We found the
cave at this point to be about 20 feet wide, and to go southwest and northwest. The former appeared inaccessible;
the latter we followed; and at 15 feet higher came on a level plateau. From this is a passage 8 feet wide and 3 feet to
4 feet high, roof cut in the form of a depressed arch, out of
the rock. We followed it for 40 feet, and came to a rough
masonry wall across the passage, with a hole just large
enough to creep through. On the other side the passage
rose at an angle of 45°, the roof being at the same angle and
still cut in the same manner as before. The space between
the roof and the bank is about 2 feet. There are toe-holes
cut in the hard soil, so that, by pressing the back against
the roof, it is easy to ascend. Fifty feet up this found us at
the top, where was another rough masonry wall to block up
the passage; and on getting through we found ourselves in
a vaulted chamber 9 feet wide, running about south for 20
feet; arch of well-cut squared stone, semicircular; crown
about 20 feet above us; below us was a deep pit. We had
now to go back for ropes; but, on getting near the shaft,
found it impossible to get down with safety. Luckily the
Sergeant had a faja on, which, torn up in four pieces,

just reached down to the ladder; and we hauled up the rope and took it to the vaulted chamber and descended into the pit about 20 feet deep, and then into a smaller one about 8 feet deeper, where we found the appearance of a passage blocked up. Coming back, we explored another little passage, with no results.

"The sides of the horizontal portion of the passage are lined with piles of loose stones, apparently ready to be thrown down the shaft; on these we found three glass lamps of curious construction, at intervals, as if to light up the passage to the wall or shaft; also in the vaulted chamber we found a little pile of charcoal as if for cooking, one of these lamps, a cooking-dish glazed inside, for heating food, and a jar for water. Evidently this had been used as a refuge. Two other jars (perfect), of red pottery, we found in the passage; and also overhanging the shaft an iron ring, by which a rope might have been attached for hauling up water. Having now explored this passage, there only remained that going southwest. To get to it, it was necessary to go down half-way to the shaft and then up again for about 15 feet. I had a rope slung round me and started off; the use of the rope was questionable, as it nearly pulled me back in climbing up. On getting into the passage we found the roof (of rock) had given way, and nothing definite could be seen but pieces of dry walls built up here and there. In coming down, part of a dry wall toppled over into my lap as I was sitting on the edge of the drop. Sergeant Birtles was 6 feet lower down, and narrowly escaped them; they were each about a foot cube; three of them came on me, but I managed to hitch them back into the passage. We now heard, to our surprise, that the sun had set, so getting together our delf, we made all haste down. On coming out, great was the commotion among the people of Siloam, who wanted to have a share in the treasure, and would not believe we had only got *empty jars*. We got into town some time after dark."

October 28*th*.—" On going up the scaffold next day a

stone over 2 feet long was found lying on the top landing; it had fallen during the night. The men are now working at the blocked-up passage in the vaulted chamber. Two more jars have been found."

Rock-cut passage above *Virgin's Fount.*—(*Extract from Letter, October* 2, 1868.).—"This has already been described in letter of November 1, 1867; perhaps another brief description may help to establish it in the minds of those who are interested in the subject. (Plans 18 and 19.)

"The hill, which is generally called Ophel, extends in a southerly direction from Mount Moriah, gradually sloping down through a horizontal distance of 2,000 feet until it becomes lost at the pool of Siloam. Its highest point, near the Triple Gate, is 300 feet above its foot at the Siloam Pool; it is bounded on the east by the Kedron, and on the west and south by the Tyropœon Valley, these two valleys meeting at the pool. The descent into the valley of the Kedron is very steep (about 30°), and the natural surface of the rock is covered up by *débris* from 10 to 50 feet in height.

"About the centre of the Ophel hill, to the east, in the Kedron, is the Fountain of the Virgin, an intermittent spring whose waters communicate with the Siloam Pool by means of a rock-cut canal running in a serpentine course through the hill. About three-quarters of the way up the hill, due west from the Virgin's Fount, is a vault running north and south, the crown of which is 22 feet below the present surface of the slope. This vault spans a chasm or cutting in the rock, and the springing is from the rock; the chasm, when discovered, was over 40 feet deep, and beyond that depth was filled up with *débris;* it, and the vault also, is 8 feet wide; the arch was originally semicircular, but is now very much distorted. The length of the arch is about 11 feet, but 4 feet farther to the south the vault is open, the roof being self-supporting, earth and stones, and is in a very dangerous condition. It appears that the southern wall, on which the voussoirs overlapped,

ROCK-CUT PASSAGE ABOVE VIRGIN'S FOUNT.

has given way and fallen into the chasm, taking with it a quantity of rubbish from several feet above the crown of the arch at the south end; the voussoirs here project irregularly, and a slight fall of rubbish from above them would probably displace one of them, and thus cause a further fall, and so the arch would collapse. Some time in June, or July, or August, a fall of stones took place, when the work was not going on.

"It is not apparent at present in what manner the vault was reached from the outside, but it is likely that there was an entrance through the southern wall which has been described as having fallen.

"About 17 feet 9 inches below the crown of the arch at the north side is the commencement of a sloping rock-cut passage leading northeast by east. The earth has been cleared out, and we find the passage to be 8 feet wide and from 10 to 12 feet high. There are several rock-cut steps for the first part of the descent, then a landing and a drop of 10 feet (see p. 195). The horizontal length of this passage is 39 feet, the fall is 37 feet. At the bottom is a passage whose roof slopes about 5 feet in its length of 68 feet. This passage is on a plan nearly semicircular, bending round from northeast by east to south-southwest. Then there is a sloping passage for about 18 feet, the fall being at an angle of 45°, and we arrive at the top of the shaft, 44 feet deep. All these passages, canals, shafts, etc., are cut in the solid rock, the nature of which is a hard silicious chalk called *mezzeh*, except near the top of the shaft, where the rock is soft and decayed.

"As yet the rubbish has only been cleared out of the staircase passage, so that we know nothing about the bottom of the passage leading to the shaft, but probably it is 10 feet high.

"It was very desirable to know how far the chasm under the vault extends, and for what purpose it was cut out, and also what there is to the south of the vault. The vault, however, was in too dangerous a condition to work under, so I arranged to fill up the chasm with the *débris* from the staircase passage. This we have already partially done. On the soil reaching to the top of the staircase landing, gallery-frames were fixed up through the length of the vault, and battened together, and soil filled in at the side and top, so that the men can now work to the south, or sink a shaft without danger from the arch giving way. I hope the arch will be filled up to the top and quite secure in a week.

"We have now commenced the prolongation of the before-mentioned gallery to the south; if we find nothing in particular, I shall make steps up to the surface, so that any visitors this year to Jerusalem may go and see these passages without descending a vertical shaft.

"I should have mentioned that the voussoirs of the arch are of *melekeh*, very much decayed, and capable of crumbling on the slightest extra pressure.

"It is a curious circumstance that the landing at the top of the staircase is unconnected with any door-way or other means of exit, so that it suggests itself whether there has been a wooden bridge across the vault from the southern to the northern side, as it appears as if this chasm is of great depth, and any very temporary means of getting across would have been disagreeable with such a drop down below.

"Should we find that our rock-cut canal below Bir Eyûb is unconnected with that well, we may hope that it extends from and forms part of this system of passages at the Virgin's Fount. It will be observed on the plan (No. 19) that the vault comes quite to the southeast of the canal from Virgin's Fount to Siloam, and may, therefore, very well be connected with other passages.

"The work of excavation here has been going on at intervals. In May, under Dr. Chaplin's superintendence, the rock was bared for 30 feet on the surface down toward the Kedron, and the rubbish in the passages was moved from side to side in search of other branches. The gallery along the surface of the rock had eventually to be abandoned on account of the treacherous nature of the soil. The work was resumed about a fortnight ago.

"A shaft was sunk at 40 feet to the south of the vault, and at the same time the space under the vault was filled up by the earth from the rock-cut passages. On getting up to the level of the entrance down by the staircase, a gallery was laid on the top of the soil and then laid over with earth until it was filled in right under the arch. This was very dangerous work, as the arch appears ready to fall at each concussion of the falling earth. The gallery was then driven to the south, when it was found we were in a rock-cut passage without a roof, the original entrance to the vault; after ascending rough steps we cut in upon the shaft we had sunk south of the vault, joined them, and then filled up the shaft, which was over the vault. Having now the arch made secure, we commenced a shaft directly underneath it to examine the rock-cut shaft, but the made earth was allowed to fall in, and a slip took place throughout the whole of the gallery, so much so, that the work had eventually to be abandoned.

"A very great number of visitors went down to see these rock-cut passages.

"I cannot take leave of the Virgin's Fount without calling attention to a mistake in the standard work on Jerusalem, which has led to theories upon the position of the Temple, etc.

"There are three parallel paragraphs in the 'City of the Great King,' bearing on the Virgin's Fountain, at pages 309, 518, and 523.

"Page 309, Dr. Barclay states: 'In exploring the subterranean channel conveying the water from the Virgin's Fount to Siloam, I discovered a similar channel entering from the north a few yards from its commencement, and on tracing it up near the Mugrabin Gate, where it became so choked,' etc. Again he states, with reference to the same channel, page 518: 'On closely examining a passage turning north, at a distance of 49 feet from the upper extremity, it was found to be the termination of the channel leading across Ophel from Mount Sion, and explored as far as a point near the present Mugrabin Gate.'

"In both these instances he states that the passage was traced from the Virgin's Fount to Mugrabin Gate.

"Now turn to page 523, and read how he came to this conclusion: 'I then observed a large opening entering the rock-hewn channel, just below the pool, which, though once supplying a tributary quite copious—if we may judge from its size—is now dry. Being found too much choked with tesserae and rubbish to be penetrated far, I carefully noted its position and bearing, and on searching for it above, soon *identified it on the exterior*, where it assumed an upward direction toward the Temple, and entering through a breach, traversed it for nearly a thousand feet.'

"From this it appears that finding a subterranean passage branching off from the main aqueduct about 40 feet below the surface of the *rock*, and not being able to get into it, he went on the hill of Ophel outside and *identified* as one and the same passage the main drain of the town, which is built of masonry, and generally only a few feet below the surface of the made earth.

"This aqueduct, then, the mouth of which Dr. Barclay discovered was filled with the deposit of years, was opened up by our working-party, and found not to be a tributary to the fountain, but a conduit for water from the Virgin's Fount to the shaft, which apparently was the ancient draw-well of Ophel."

December 18, 1869.—*The Great Rock-cut Aqueduct in the Kedron Valley.*—"A description of this was given at the public meeting held at Willis's Rooms, June 11, 1868. An extract from it is given below:

"'*Rock-cut Aqueduct.*—Down the valley of the Kedron, and south of Siloam, there is the Well of Job, or Joab, about which there are several curious traditions which connect it in many ways with the ancient Temple. It has been examined, but to my mind there is yet a mystery concealed there.

It is a well 100 feet deep, without appearance of connection with any surface-drains, and yet after heavy rains it fills up and overflows in a voluminous stream.

"'South of this well, about 500 yards, there is a place called by the Arabs, "The Well of the Steps," about which they had a tradition that there were steps leading up to the Well of Joab. I had the ground opened, and at 12 feet below the surface came upon a large stone which suddenly rolled away, revealing a staircase cut in the solid rock leading to a rock-cut chamber and aqueduct, running north and south. It was filled up with silt or fine clay. We cleared it out to the north for about 100 feet, and found it to be a great aqueduct 6 feet high, and from 3 feet 6 inches to 4 feet broad. When the winter rains came on, a stream burst through the silt, and, completely filling the passage, found its way up the steps and rolled down the valley in an abundant stream, joining that from the Well of Joab. In April the stream abated, and in May we were able to commence again; and, working day and night, we may expect to reach the city in six months. We are working with English barrows in this aqueduct, much to the delight of the Arab workmen, who take a childish pleasure in using these new toys. We clean out at present about 15 cubic yards in twenty-four hours. Looking at this aqueduct from a sanitary point of view, we might suppose it built for carrying off the sewage of the city, and, from a military point of view, for carrying secretly off any superabundant water to the nearest crevice in the rocks; possibly it may have been used for both purposes. Looking into the Bible history, we find in the Second Book of Chronicles that Hezekiah stopped the brook that ran through the midst of the land, saying, "Why should the King of Assyria come and find much water?" Again, we find from the other account that the refuse from the burnt-offerings was carried down to the Kedron by a subterranean channel; and, as water would be wanted to run it down, it may be supposed that the aqueduct in question might have been used for some such purpose. At

JERUSALEM.
REMARKABLE ROCK-CUT TOMB ON WEST SIDE
OF THE KEDRON ABOUT ½ MILE BELOW
BIR EYUB

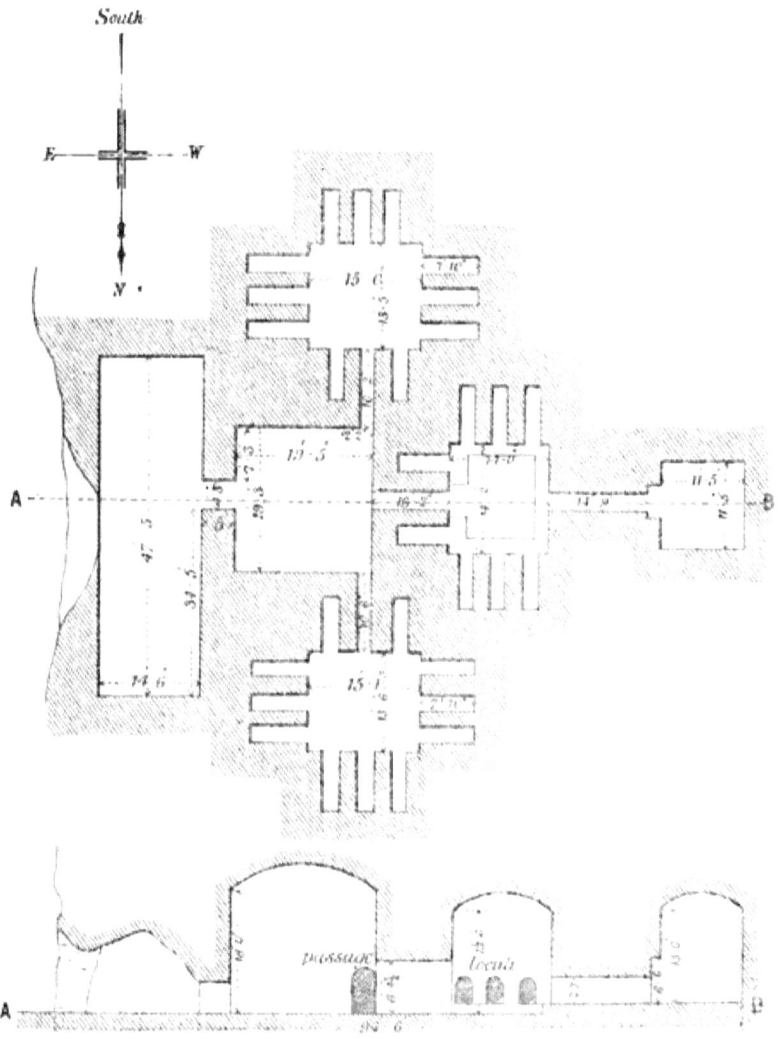

SECTION ON A B

Scale $\frac{1}{320}$ = 26.66 F^t to an Inch

any rate, it is highly important that we should discover for what purpose; and we have the chance of its being a clew to the Altar of the Temple, and—which is of more practical value to the inhabitants of Jerusalem—to the hidden springs of Hezekiah, which, if found, might again supply the city with living water.'"

A further account is given in Letter XXV., January 1, 1869.

Rock-cut Passage at 'Ain el Luz'h.—" The passage was followed up until 170 feet from Bir Eyûb, where another staircase was found, the steps of which are in very good preservation : the passage was then continued to the north, for upward of 100 feet, until 12th of December, 1868, when a heavy down-pour of rain stopped the work, Bir Eyûb overflowed, and the rock-cut passage was filled up with a stream of water, which found vent by the two lower staircases.

" The rainfall in December of 1868 was much greater than usual ; up to the 15th of the month 8.703 inches had fallen, and it is interesting to find that the overflowing of Bir Eyûb is due, not so much to a steady, long-continuous rain, as to a sudden heavy fall.

" It is now nearly certain that the rock-cut passage does not communicate with Bir Eyûb, as we are only 70 feet to the south of it, and at least 70 feet to the west. Since that time the work has not been resumed until within the last few days, when I recommenced in order to obtain a correct idea of the probable expenditure that would be incurred in continuing the work.

" It took a few days to get quit of the mud which lay in the passage; for, all through the summer there has been a little water trickling into the tunnel : on going on to the north we had not cleared away 3 feet before a large grotto was discovered, out of which the aqueduct opened.

" Apparently this grotto was originally natural, but afterward cut out so as to form a receiving-tank. It is 35 feet from east to west, and 20 feet from north to south, nearly oval on plan; it is about 45 feet in height, the roof being formed by the sides gradually approaching each other. At the highest point there appears to be a shaft upward, about 2 feet square, covered by a white stone. The bottom of the passage by which we entered is about 9 (or more) feet above the bottom of the cistern, so that there would always be a depth of 9 feet of water retained in it. At the northern end are two aqueducts running into the cistern: the upper and eastern one has its bottom 12 feet above the bottom of the outlet aqueduct; below it (the upper) by 9 feet and 6 feet to the west, is the lower aqueduct, which, after a few feet, runs in under the upper one; they both come from the same point (about 80 feet north-northeast of the cistern), where they are in one, forming a passage 15 feet high, and nearly 6 feet wide. This point is 90 feet due west of Eyûb.

"The way in which these two aqueducts run together is very curious: at the point where it is one passage, there is a little staircase cut in the rock going up about 9 feet on to a landing where the upper aqueduct begins; this is 3 feet 10 inches wide, and 5 feet 9 inches high; it is very well cut, the roof is curved a little, and it runs nearly straight to the cistern, falling about 2 (?) feet in its length: about midway it is blocked up by a masonry wall 3 feet thick, and composed of cut stones set in a hard black mortar, apparently mixed with oil. The lower aqueduct starts from the same level as the bottom of the high passage. It is only about 3½ feet high (apparently), and the top is about 6 feet below the bottom of the upper aqueduct; for some distance it runs immediately under the upper one, and then, with some winding, comes out to its west by 6 feet: just before it enters the cistern, it opens into a natural cleft in the rock, which appears to be part of the original cavern. This cleft is nearly perpendicular, and is about 4 feet wide, and over 15 feet high. Corporal MacKenzie went up it 48 feet to the northwest; it then gets too narrow to be followed up.

"The rock throughout is a hard mezzeh, and the passages appear to have been cut out with the chisel. The surface of the rock appears to be not less than 70 feet above the aqueduct.

"This tunnel, as we have now examined it, extends from near Bir Eyûb to a point 1,800 feet down the Kedron Valley: it has been judiciously cut under one side (the west side) of the valley, so that, though it is from 70 to 90 feet under the surface of the rock, yet the staircases being commenced to the east (nearer the bottom of the valley), have not to descend by more than 40 to 50 feet. In the 1,800 feet we have cleared out, seven staircases have been exposed; they are about 3 feet wide, and descend at about an angle of 35°. The steps are about 1 foot in height, and the tread is about 15 inches; in some cases the steps are much worn and broken. At the bottom of some of the staircases the aqueduct is deepened a little, so as to form a shallow pool.

"In one place, between the third and fourth staircase, there is a branch tunnel leading across toward the east side of the valley in a southeast direction; this was only followed for 30 feet.

"It is apparent that this aqueduct was of considerable importance, for the labor in cutting it so far below the surface must have been enormous. That it was for water I think there can be no doubt, and probably for pure water.

"The cistern we have just found is similar in its construction to those found under Robinson's Arch, and the aqueduct altogether has the same appearance as the rock-cut aqueduct found there. The staircases, too, may have originally been used for bringing up the chippings, but they appeared to be very much worn, as if they had been in constant use.

"We have not as yet found there is any connection with Bir Eyûb, and if we do find any, it will probably be a communication by which the water from the aqueduct flows into it, and cut at a later period; neither is there any appearance of its being connected with the Virgin's Fount Aqueduct, for they differ in height and width, the tunnel we have found being nearly twice as wide and very much higher; also the Virgin's Fount Aqueduct winds very much more than this one, and there are shafts instead of staircases.

"It would be a most important point to establish the direction from whence this great aqueduct comes; at present we do not know whether it comes down the Kedron Valley, the Tyropœon, or by the valley from the Jaffa Gate.

"It is currently reported in the city that a Jewish blacksmith descend Bir Eyûb a few years ago, when it was dry, and found a passage at the bottom from whence a strong wind was blowing. However this may be, it is evident that the man has some curious tradition about the place, as he has been trying to buy the land over where we have lately found the grotto, and the fellahin of Siloam say they refused twelve napoleons for it. This man sent a messenger a short time ago to ask if we were going on with the clearing out of the great aqueduct, and to say that if so he intended to raise the money to continue our work. He probably had been reading the accounts of Jelal and Mejir ed Din."

December 21, 1869.—"In continuing our work a staircase at an angle of about 45°, and 90 feet on slope, has been found. The top is walled up with masonry: near the top another staircase leads off toward Bir Eyûb, branching into two. The rains have suddenly set in, and if Bir Eyûb overflows, this work will have to be stopped for the present.

"N. B.—It has been stated that the bottom of the cistern or grotto is 9 feet below the bottom of outflow aqueduct, but 9 feet is the depth to which we have sunk. The water in the cistern prevents our sinking deeper, and the jumper cannot be driven on account of the large stones met with."

The great Rock-cut Aqueduct south of Bir Eyûb.—"Account of this was given up to December 21, 1869, when some rock-cut staircases were found 86 feet north of the cistern or grotto.

"A shaft was now sunk at 75 feet north of the pool at Bir Eyûb, and at a depth of 22 feet came on head of staircase. The soil sunk through was black earth and stones, mixed with a great quantity of red potsherds. The staircase was found to be closed at top by a masonry wall, and, on breaking through this, the steps, after going 6 feet to the west, branch off north and south. That to the north has again a branch staircase to the east.

"The northern staircase has sixty-seven steps. It descends 39 feet vertical, in 56 feet horizontal, and ends abruptly, having never been finished. At 16 feet 6 inches down this staircase the branch to the east commences, and falls (with twenty-two steps) 19 feet vertical in 27 feet horizontal; it then turns to the north, and falls 5 feet 10 inches in 10 feet 6 inches, and ends abruptly.

"The staircase to the south (with fifty-four steps) falls 41 feet 5 inches in 72 feet, and ends in the aqueduct, where the upper and lower join together, at about 86 feet north of the grotto. These staircases were only partially filled up with mud and broken jars and pottery.

"There only now remained the continuation of lower aqueduct to the north to examine. This was continued for 148 feet, where it was also found to end abruptly, rock on all sides. It is generally about 3 feet 7 inches wide and 6 feet high. It appears, then, that this great work has never been completed. It is to be presumed that the great volume of water which now issues from the aqueduct in the spring, enters through the rifts in the rocky sides of the grotto. The reasons for the wall stopping up the upper aqueduct having been built are not apparent. This aqueduct, leading into the grotto, is 86 feet long; that is, 44 feet from grotto to first wall, 4 feet thickness of wall, 32 feet to the second wall, 3 feet thickness of wall, and 3 feet to small steps.

"In the first wall at the bottom a hole or duct was left

6¾ inches by 4 inches, and on the northern side a stone plug to fit and 12 inches long was found in it."

Letter of August, 1867.—*Chasm in Rock*.—"This was the continuation of an excavation commenced by Captain Wilson, R. E., and followed up by Mr. Schick. It is a natural perpendicular cleft in the rock, and was filled with red earth, stones, and pottery. After arriving at a depth of 135 feet a storm partially filled the cleft with water, the clay swelling smashed in the shoring, and the work was rendered too dangerous to continue during the wet weather.

"There are several traditions with regard to this shaft. It is supposed by some to be the site of a sealed fountain. I consider the results that are likely to accrue are too problematical to allow of my continuing this work at present, while money can be spent more profitably elsewhere."

Letter of December, 1867.—"About a mile south of the village of Lifta, on the crest of a hill, is a chasm in the rocks, about which there are many traditions, and which we failed to explore in the spring. We went there last Monday, provided with three ladders, reaching together 120 feet, and a dock-yard rope 165 feet long. We had three men to assist in lowering us on the rope. The entrance from the top just allows of a man squeezing through, but as you descend the chasm opens out until at 125 feet it is about 15 feet by 30 inches. At this point is a ledge, and we rested there while we lowered the ladders another 30 feet, to enable us to descend to the bottom, which is at the great depth of 155 feet from the surface. The chasm is exactly perpendicular, and the bottom is horizontal. Water was dripping quickly from the rocks, but ran out of sight at once. On the floor was a rough stone pillar, and near it the skeleton of an infant; close to the pillar is a cleft in the rock, very narrow, into which the water was running. I got down into this, but it is a crevice which gets narrower and narrower, and there being no hold, I slipped down until my head was about 4 feet below the surface. Here I stuck, every movement jamming me tighter down the cleft. Ten minutes of desperate struggling, and the help of a friendly grip, brought me to the surface again, minus a considerable portion of my skin and clothing. On ascending, we had some little excitement—at one time the grass rope-ladder caught fire; at another, the men suddenly let me down about 3 feet, the jerk nearly wrenching the rope out of their hands.

DORIC CAPITAL, SILOAM.

"I cannot help thinking that this cleft is partially artificial. I have not yet ascertained its level with reference to Jerusalem, but there is the possibility of its being in connection with the cleft where we were excavating near the Russian buildings, which some suppose to be the shaft of an aqueduct by which the town used to be supplied with water.

"Some other clefts in the rock to the north of Jerusalem have been found, and it appears probable that they are natural."

The capital above appears to have formed part of the buildings about the pool of Siloam. It was pointed out to me by Prof. Donaldson, and was secured for the Palestine Exploration Fund.

———

Note.—The conclusions at which I have arrived as to the topography of the Holy City, especially with reference to the site and identity of Zion and Acra, are given in detail in a paper entitled "The Parallel Holiness of Mounts Zion and Moriah," which was first published in the *Athenæum*, and afterward reprinted in the "Quarterly Statement" No. III. Statement of Palestine Exploration Fund.

CHAPTER X.

THE HOLY CITY.

Our excavations in the city have established the certainty of a valley running down from the citadel to the Sanctuary. It appears to commence a few yards to the north of the citadel; it runs through the pool of the Bath and the Muristan, and eventually into the Tyropœon, near Wilson's Arch.

On the southern side of this valley rock was seen in the lower chamber of a house in Harat ash Sharaf, 2,450 feet, where there are some rock-cut chambers, and a tradition of a passage passing under the Tyropœon to the Sanctuary: it overlooks the Wailing Place. Rock was found at the so-called Gennath Gate 2,449 feet; it was also seen under the house of the Incumbent of the English church, 2,510 feet, where it was traced by Captain Wilson for about 300 feet east and west.

On the northern side of the valley it was found along the northern end of the Muristan 2,430 feet at the east to 2,450 feet at the west. It is seen in the Church of the Holy Sepulchre 2,477 feet, and was found by Captain Wilson in the Russian property marked 75 on Ordnance map, 2,460 feet. It is also to be seen on the surface at the top of the street at Takeyeh 2,474 feet, and also in several places at Takeyeh, the present palace of the Pacha. It was found in the street al Wad, in front of the Austrian Hospice.

In the valley itself rock was not found. On the north side of David Street, immediately in front of David's Tower, there was no rock at 2,510 feet; in the pool of the Bath there is only the appearance of rock at the northwest angle, and its depth is about 2,450 feet. In the Greek convent of St. John the Baptist the floor of the old church is 25 feet below the line of Christian Street; there is a tank in this church, and, roughly speaking, there is no rock here at 2,455 feet. In the southern part of the Muristan no rock was found at 2,460 feet; there is therefore no doubt of the existence of a considerable valley separating the Upper City of Josephus from the Acra.

Details of the principal excavations in these parts are here given.

MURISTAN.

This piece of ground, now given up for the most part to the plough, was once the site of the hospital of St. John and the convent of St. Mary the Greater. Local tradition says that it was cursed by the Moslems after their capture of the city, and this may account for its not having been built over.

The ruins of the chapel, etc., at the northeast angle have lately been given over by the Turkish authorities to the Grand Master of the modern representatives of the order of St. John, under whose happy auspices, and by the aid of the Kaiserswerth deaconesses, so many beneficial institutions have been established in Turkey—hospitals, schools, etc. The arable land is in the possession of the Greek Patriarch. On the west side it is on a level with Christian Street, about 2,500 feet: it slopes greatly to the east, when it is raised about 20 feet above the Street of the Bazaar.

The first excavation was made to the west of the old arch discovered by Mr. Williams ("Holy City," p. 56, vol. ii.), alongside the more modern arch, but we soon came to rough masonry, and a second excavation was commenced still farther to the west, and quite clear, as we thought, of the vaults of the Bazaar below; but there happened to be an inner chamber just under us, and alongside of this we sank one shaft, and it was only discovered when, on breaking through the wall, Sergeant Birtles found himself in a blacksmith's smithy, and recognized the workman as a man from whom he had been buying some tools shortly before. The man was transfixed with terror at the apparition of the Sergeant bursting through the wall of his subterranean workshop, and thought he was a gin come to torment him for having driven too hard a bargain, and fell on his knees before him. The affair had such an effect upon the blacksmith that he was only too glad that the story should not get about; otherwise, I suppose, we should have been sued for heavy damages. This was one of our first experiences in Jerusalem, and I took care afterward always to make a careful search, lest after going down several feet through *débris* we might come in through the roof of an inhabited dwelling. For example, in a garden to the west of the French Consulate, when I was asked to dig, I found that the stables at a lower level run in from the street for several yards under the soil.

We could do nothing at the Muristan until the crop was off the ground, and then we had some little difficulty in getting permission to dig in the arable land. The Patriarch had no objection if the Pacha had none, the Pacha had none if the Patriarch did not object; but neither would give leave. Eventually deputies were sent from each side, who met together, and would come to no decision, but after some days they pronounced there could be no danger for our work, but still I could get no formal permission until September 24, 1867; not until the Government inspector had paid me a visit, and had been convinced of the advantage of our work at what I considered a very expensive rate.

Our object was now to cut from north to south across the vacant space in search of any signs of the second wall, and accordingly shafts were sunk in line and afterward joined by trenches. The trench from north to south was 350 feet long, 25 feet deep on an average, and at about 200 feet distance from the Bazaar. At two points to the southern end shafts 40 feet deep were sunk without finding rock;

a branch trench running east up toward the arch of Mr. Williams was also cut.

The general result was unsatisfactory. There appears to have been a great number of vaults corresponding to those seen now forming the Bazaar; the floor line about 28 feet to 30 feet below the surface of the ground, the piers of well-dressed ashlar about 12 to 14 feet apart; the arches very rough, of rag-work grouted in. At the northeast angle a shaft was sunk to a depth of a little over 70 feet, where rock was found at 2,430 feet; at the northwest angle a shaft was sunk, and at 28 feet below the surface a man-hole was found leading into large tanks, the bottom at the level of 2,440 feet. The sides are partially cut in the rock, the highest point of which is 2,450, falling to the south and east. The first tank entered lies north and south, and is 40 feet by 17 feet, semicircular arch, and in the northwest angle a flight of twenty-five steps. To the northeast lies another tank east and west, 68 feet by 17, and north again another tank not cleared out: to the south of the first tank is a smaller one 16 feet 6 inches by 6 feet 6 inches. I sent to tell the Greek Patriarch of our finding what I considered to be so valuable a treasure; but he replied that he had quite enough tanks, and only wanted me to get out of his ground as soon as I could, as the rains were expected. At the end of November the rains came down so heavily that they commenced ploughing in the Muristan in spite of our trenches, and we were obliged to fill up in hot haste.

We cannot be certain, on account of our trench not reaching the rock, that the second wall does not cross some part of the Muristan. It does not, however, appear to me to be probable, as the rock is proved to fall to the south. The most probable site, as far as I can judge, for the position of the Second Wall, is along the northern wall of the Muristan, and in this case the architect building for the Knight of the Order of St. John may find that the old chapel partially rests upon it.

Extract of Letter, October 2, 1867.—" I now send you a progress report of the works, which are getting on well. I only want gallery-frames to make great way ; opposition has ceased for a season, and we are prosecuting the work with all dispatch. I have now about twenty men turning up the ground at the Muristan, which has assumed the appearance of Chatham Lines after the commencement of the second parallel.

" I have found a great change in the Effendis lately : they seem to be fast losing the apprehensions with which they were at first possessed, when they thought we were here for political reasons. They begin to appreciate our efforts now they see we do nothing to harm their religion ; and the strict discipline to which the workmen are subject, and the prompt payments that are made, have invested our employment with a mysterious novelty.

" We are getting really good work out of the men ; they are gradually adopting our European notions, and a spirit of emulation has sprung up among them ; instead of all wishing to be paid at the same rate, they now work hard to get on to the first class of pay. On Monday the measured work for the day showed 6 cubic yards per man dug up, and thrown out from an average depth of 3 feet 6 inches. During the whole summer we have worked English hours. Sergeant Birtles is indefatigable in his exertions ; he has an amount of tact and discernment of character seldom to be met with, and I have always the satisfaction of knowing that what I leave to him will be done well. The work throughout has been of a dangerous nature, and we have hardly had an accident."

Letter of February 11, 1869.—*The Gate Gennath (so called).*—" H. R. H. the Archduke of Modena, through the Austrian Consul, Count Caboga, expressed a wish that we should reëxamine the Gate Gennath (so called), and he gave a donation in furtherance of that object.

" On Thursday week a shaft was sunk down alongside

the northern end of the gate-way, and the arch, which is very
much battered and weather-worn, where exposed, was found
to be in very fair condition immediately below the surface
of the road, and to spring from an impost or capital 2 feet 1
inch in height; below this the door-post is composed of
three stones, giving together a height of 7 feet 4 inches. The
lower stone of the door-post rests on a stone forming a sill,
which projects into the road-way and under the arch about
12 inches. No pavement has been found.

"The arch of the gate is composed of eleven stones, 2
feet 3 inches long, and also 2 feet 3 inches wide at the extrados. The keystone is 2 feet 6 inches in length, the extra 3
inches appearing to project beyond the archivolt (as shown
in elevation); but of this I cannot be quite certain, as a settlement in the arch might have produced this effect. The
arch is semicircular, the span being 10 feet 8 inches. The
springing of the arch is flush with the door-post, the abacus
and mouldings projecting 3 inches. The impost is in good
preservation; a sketch of it is enclosed.

"The height of the gate-way from sill to top of impost
is 9 feet 5 inches; and, adding to it the rise of the arch, we
have a total height from sill to crown of 14 feet 9 inches.

"On getting down to the sill of the gate-way a gallery
was driven to the south, when it was found that there was a
second door-post of more modern construction within the
first. On getting under the centre of the arch some earth
fell in, and, on its being cleared away, it was found that we
were under a pointed arch. On examination, I found that
the Gate Gennath (so called) is cased inside with door-posts
and a pointed arch of comparatively modern construction,
as shown on plan. This inner door-way is recessed 4 inches;
a simple moulding (astragal) runs down the jamb, projecting
4 inches, so as to be flush with the front of the outer gate-way. I cannot see if the moulding runs round the arch, as
there is some masonry in the way. This inner pointed arch
forms part of the roof of a dyer's shop; and I understand
that it was under the arch inside that the first excavation

two years ago was made. Except at the point where our shaft is sunk, there is masonry encasing the old gate-way, and one might dig about it for a long time without getting upon the old gate-way, as we have had the luck to do.

"The sill of the gate-way (Gennath) is about on a level with the Sûk al Biyar, and also of the floors of the two towers to the west of the gate, described in Lewin's 'Siege of Jerusalem by Titus,' p. 216.

"This is not the only instance where I have found old works smothered in on all sides by more modern masonry; and it has sometimes occurred to me that the pointed arches at the Makhama conceal more ancient arches above—certainly in two places this can be observed.

"From the battered condition of the exposed portion of the Gate Gennath, it is evident that a vast number of years must have elapsed since the two gate-ways were closed up; and as the inner gate was probably built to be used when the outer gate became decayed or distasteful in its architecture, we may safely assume that the gate-way is of early construction, especially as its style is Roman.

"The jambs of the gate do not rest on the rock, but on made earth mixed with pottery, similar to what we found at the lowest point southeast angle of Haram Area. The rock we found at a level of 2,449 feet, the old road-way going under the gate being 2,474½ feet, and the surface of ground at the mouth of the shaft 2,486 feet.

"No walls of any kind were found near the rock, and no signs of any wall older than the Gennath Gate within 13 feet to the east, and 20 feet to the south. If the first wall of the city was built up from the rock and was not totally destroyed, it was not within the above-mentioned distance of this gate."

DAMASCUS GATE.

Letter of August, 1867, 1, 2, *and* 3.—*Excavation at Damascus Gate.*—"1 and 2. Eastern side of the road; 3. On western side. They will be spoken of as one excavation.

"It appears that in the twelfth century the present Damascus Gate went by the name of St. Stephen's, and the only large buildings near it that are spoken of were the Church of St. Etienne and the Asnerie, or Donkey House, which was used by the knights in the execution of one of their threefold duties, viz., that of conducting pilgrims between Jerusalem and the sea-coast. It is also supposed that there was at one time near this gate a tower called 'Maiden's Tower' (Josephus), which may have been made use of as the Asnerie. As it is probable that the church was at some distance from the Gate, any massive walls found near to the latter would appear to belong either to the ancient tower or to the Asnerie, always supposing that the present Damascus Gate stands on its former site. This Gate is at present built of two very different styles of masonry, the older portion of which is probably of the same age as portions of the Sanctuary Wall.

"An excavation was commenced near the mouth of the cistern close to the wall at point A, east of the road, where a solid wall was discovered with a relieving arch, blocked up with masonry. A passage was jumped 5 feet into this wall, nearly as far as the foundations of the present wall, with no results. To the north of this was found a flight of steps, leading down to the tank. When these steps were used, the tank was probably an open pool or sea. North of these steps was found a very ancient wall running east and west. The stones are drafted and similar to those at the wailing-place, but appear not to be *in situ*, there being other stones in the wall of more recent date. Nearly opposite the Gate the wall suddenly stopped, and on digging round was found to be 10 feet 6 inches in thickness, the north side being of a different style of masonry to the south, but of similar age. The foundations of this wall are 3 feet below the road-way at the Damascus Gate, and it is improbable that the ground line there was ever lower than it is at present. Although a great part of this wall is above the road-way leading through the Gate, an immense quantity

of rubbish had to be cleared away, because it has been the
custom to throw refuse from the city outside the Gate on
either side, and consequently it has accumulated until it has
formed two little hills, the great North Road to Damascus
running between them. I should place the date of the
building of this wall at an intermediate interval between
those of the two styles of masonry at the Damascus Gate.
Taking every thing into consideration, I consider this wall
was built by the Crusaders, and was destroyed when they
were compelled to leave the Holy City. A stone with a
Templar's Cross on it was found at the foot of the wall
among the rubbish; it had formed part of the wall. On
the west side of the road the core of the wall was traced,
but the hill of rubbish rose so suddenly, and the authorities
got so nervous about the city wall, that I considered it prudent to close the excavation.

"The only accident which occurred on our works happened here. I had just come up from Gaza and was measuring this wall, there being to our east a portion of the
bank cut through over 20 feet in height. We had but just
come out, and the fellahin were getting down to their work,
when the bank gave way and fell in upon the wall, but prov-
identially no one had got down to the bottom, and only
about six men were at all covered in. One man, the lowest
down, we saw swallowed up, his ghastly face remaining for
a second or two in view before another slip covered him up;
the others we got out easily, but this man was only rescued
after some digging, and when out had to be carried by his
brother and friends to Bethlehem. For two weeks we paid
his wages to his brothers, and then I sent Sergeant Birtles
to see how the poor man fared, having told them the day
before to be on the lookout for him; but on arrival at
Bethlehem, Sergeant Birtles found no trace either of the
man or his brother, and we heard of them no more: either
the man had died immediately, and his brother, having drawn
two weeks' pay, had fled for fear of the consequences, or
else the man had been less hurt than we supposed; in either

case we were deceived in the matter, and I made some new
rules about accidents, as we found that the men, finding
we had paid for a sick man, were getting reckless. The
next affair, however, cured them. At one of the shafts, our
first deep one, we had not sufficient rope ladders, and the
order was that the men were to be hauled up by a strong
rope, but this they found too much trouble, and, whenever
they thought nobody was on the lookout, they came up the
shaft by pressing fingers and toes against the side. They
were told that, if any accident occurred, they only would
be responsible, and they would be turned off the works if
found out; but it was of no use, and at last one man fell the
whole depth of the shaft from top to bottom and broke his
back. It was necessary to appear cruel in this case to save
the others, and so the man's friends had to find a donkey
and carry him off at their own expense, and their working
pay was stopped. This effectually cured them, and we had
no more trouble on that score; had we taken any care of
the sick man, we should probably have had many accidents
of the same kind."

Excavation at British Cemetery.—" This was the continuation of the laying bare of some steps cut in the solid rock, discovered when the cemetery was levelled. The rock here appears to have formed part of the ancient wall of Zion. These steps are considered by some to be those of the prophet Nehemiah, but the Rev. J. Barclay has shown me steps at Siloam which answer more nearly to the Biblical description.

" The excavation reached a depth of 18 feet, and on arriving at the thirty-sixth step a landing was found, and a gallery was driven along it for 17 feet without any results. This landing was probably the foot of the rock scarp, which must have presented to the enemy a perpendicular face of 29 feet in height."

Letter of December 20, 1869.—" Commenced a shaft May 19, 1869, at the side of the street 'The Valley,' close to the 'Bath of the Sultan' (see Ordnance Survey Plan $\frac{1}{2500}$, 27): level at the surface 2,418 feet.

"Passed through black soil mixed with large rough stones: came on rock at $17\frac{1}{2}$ feet: it shelves down rapidly to the west-southwest at about 45° by steps 2 feet 6 inches high. Drove a gallery in to the west for the purpose of discovering the lowest parts of the valley: found the soil very hard and mixed with large stones. At 5 feet 6 inches broke into a passage or old sewer running north and south, apparently down the Valley Street, which runs from the Damascus Gate to the Hall of Justice. This passage is of rough stones: it is 4 feet 9 inches high and 2 feet wide, and has a slope to the south of about one in six; the bottom is the natural rock: the roof is formed of stones, about 14 inches in breadth, laid across from wall to wall.

"Continued the gallery to the west; rock still falling. At 17 feet broke into a masonry shaft (plastered), about 4 feet square, leading down toward the rock. On climbing up this shaft 7 feet a drain was found opening into it from north to south; cleared the shaft out and descended: found the rock scarped to the south and east of the shaft, and found rock bottom at 15 feet below our gallery: the rock bottom is cut level: level of rock 2,378 feet.

"It is probable that this place was an old cistern, the scarps facing to the north and the west being the sides. The soil passed through here was wet mud mixed with stones. Shaft now tamped up; and the first passage found was examined to the south.

"This passage runs down under the Valley Street. At first the soil was like silt or clay; but after 50 or 60 feet, it became like sand left by a running stream; it was quite filled up. After continuing the passage for 130 feet to the south under the Valley Street, it was tamped up.

"Three shafts leading down into this passage were passed: the first at 16 feet south of one shaft; it is circular, 2 feet in diameter, and is closed by a flat stone at 8 feet 3 inches from the top of the passage: the second, at 62 feet from the entrance, is 1 foot 8 inches square, and covered by flat stone at 5 feet 3 inches from the roof of the passage: the third at 76 feet, and connecting a drain from the east with the main drain. It does not seem certain whether this passage had originally been for water or for a sewer. It does not appear to have been used for many years.

"Although we did not find the natural course of this valley, yet I am inclined to think that the passage we first found runs nearly along it, and the Valley Street defines it. The scarped rock we found may have been for other purposes, but I think it probably is the inside of a cistern cut in the rock. It was a peculiar arrangement to have had a sewer running in from both north and south if this had not been a tank. The gallery to the west was not continued on account of our having reached nearly to the west side of the street.

"We had a difficulty at this shaft which might have resulted fatally. There was a squabble just then between the Turkish soldiers and the military police of the city, and our government zapti was standing near the mouth of the shaft, when a great stout soldier of a north Syrian tribe came rushing by in a very excited state, and seeing our zapti rushed upon him like a wild beast, and in doing so knocked Corporal Ellis, who was just descending, down the shaft. Corporal Ellis had the presence of mind to hook out his arm in falling, which luckily stuck in the rope ladder before he had fallen more than a foot or two, and thus saved himself a severe tumble.

"The zapti and soldier then grappled together and were left to fight it out, but at last the former became completely exhausted, and the soldier proceeded to take out his bayonet with the intention apparently of pinning the zapti through the middle; but then Sergeant Birtles rushed forward and secured the weapon, and with the assistance of Corporal Ellis fastened on the soldier hand and foot; in a few seconds a great crowd had gathered round, and a patrol of soldiers came by, who were appealed to, to take their comrade

in charge, but they did not like the look of him and went
off. Then the interpreter was sent up to the military Pacha to ask him to send a file of the guard down to take the
soldier away, and he was marched off to the Serai, and there
formally accused our corporals of having set upon and beaten
him. Knowing, however, from experience what would occur, we sent round and obtained the evidence, of all the re-
spectable persons who were about, to the transaction, and I
then preferred a complaint against the soldier for assaulting
our zapti. The case was heard at the Serai, when the officer commanding the troops insisted that the soldier was
only just out of the hospital and incapable of committing an
assault.

"By good fortune there had been some Franks belonging to the Austrian Hospice looking on at the time, and I
sent word to the Serai that their evidence would be brought
forward if some measures were not taken to settle the matter, for our zapti had been removed and imprisoned under
the pretence of his having been the cause of the disturbance.
By dint of the exertions of the Dragoman of the Consulate,
M. Jirius Salāmé (who always did exert himself when matters were put in his hands), this affair was put straight, but
it was some time before I could get back our zapti on the
works, and not until I expressed my intention of leaving
Jerusalem if he were punished any further."

It may be necessary to mention that, when the questions
of the excavation were transferred from the Pacha's secretary's department to that of the Mejelis, I applied for a
government zapti to be employed on the works, in order to
prevent any of the offenders belonging to that court interfering, and thus upset again their arrangements for obtaining bakshish from us.

It was significant that, although the Pacha had insisted
at one time upon my having zaptis on all the works, yet
when I applied for *one* I could not get him sent to us for
several weeks.

CHAPTER XI.

OPHEL.

The term Ophel is used by Dr. Robinson as the name for the southern end of the hill Moriah between the Temple and Siloam, bounded on the east by the Kedron, and on the west by the Tyropœon Valley; and in this sense it has been used when referred to in our excavations—the wall of Ophel, the shafts on Ophel, etc. The term, however, appears to have originally been used in a more restricted sense, and I have to suggest that it was the name by which the Palace of Solomon was known, a building which, if I am right in my location of it, would, in the age of the later kings of Judah, have commanded the Kedron Valley by a wall of at least 150 feet in height, increased subsequently by King Herod to 200 feet by the building of the Royal Cloisters.

King Solomon's Palace was evidently at a lower level than the Temple (Lewin, p. 263), and therefore (2 Chron. xxvii. 3) King Jotham may have still built much upon the wall. (2 Chron. xxxiii. 14) King Manasseh "compassed about Ophel, and raised it up a very great height;" that is, I suppose, he built the wall which we have exposed in our excavations, at the present day over 70 feet in height, and, in conjunction with which, there is a great tower of drafted stones, perhaps that "which lieth out."

In confirmation of this idea in 2 Chron. xxvii. 3, the Targum has for Ophel "the wall of the Interior Palace."

Mr. Williams, in summing up on the subject (page 365),

considers the southeast angle to have been a fragment of
"the great outlying tower," which, says he, "must have occupied a space not far from the original Ophel;" and, page
368, suggests that there may have been "ruins of the original
Ophel or interior palace." And from his other remarks on
the subject, I gather that he is not averse to the idea that
this may have been Solomon's Palace, which also appears to have been the opinion of Dr. Robinson. I cannot
help feeling that had Mr. Williams, at the time he wrote his
book, known of the existence of the wall which we have
lately discovered, it would in a great measure have brought
him to view this southern wall as the southern wall of
Herod's Temple, for his more serious objection to this is the
absence in his time of this very wall (page 364). It is
very gratifying to find how the reasonings of Messrs. Robinson and Williams, and also in many cases of Mr. Fergusson, dovetail in together by the new light thrown upon the
Temple Area, and appear to bring out a plan of the holy
mount and of the city, differing in part from the plan of
each, but yet embracing and combining so many of their
ideas.

EXCAVATIONS.

After we were driven away from the Sanctuary wall
in March, 1867, I sunk a shaft 37 feet to the south of the
southeast angle, and to this no objection could be made, as
it was just without the line given to me. My object was to
sink down and then drive into the Sanctuary wall and run
along it. At that time our powers of mining were quite
unknown, and the workmen, having been told by the local
authorities they would have three months' imprisonment if
they touched the Sanctuary wall, were not much looked
after. This very threat just suited my arrangements, as it
secured the silence of the men; and, as it was only considered that we could touch the wall by working along it from
the surface, we proceeded merrily. My object was to get
up to the wall, have published the results, get copies sent to

the Porte, then to come nearer to the wall and sink a shaft, and when ordered away to resist passively, asserting that we had already been working alongside the wall from underneath, that the matter was published, known to the world and to the Porte, and that it was now an established custom; for custom is almost a law in this part of Turkey. And on one or two occasions, when waiting to get leave to do a difficult job, I did an easier one first without leave, and when given the usual answer that it was contrary to custom, I showed that it had been done already, and so laid that objection aside.

This method succeeded admirably; our next shaft was 20 feet from the wall, then 10 feet, then 3 feet, and finally at the wall itself.

On sinking the first shaft at 37 feet south of the southeast angle, we by good luck at once struck upon the remains of an ancient wall (the Ophel Wall), and went down along its eastern side for 53 feet until we struck the rock; we then ran horizontally alongside the wall to the north, until, when 15 feet from the Sanctuary wall, we came across a wall running east and west, 4 feet thick, of hard mezzeh. The stones in this were of large size and thorough-bond, and, as the fellahin were only commencing their mining lessons, Sergeant Birtles had infinite difficulty in preventing an accident. The large stones had to be dragged along the gallery and broken up at the bottom of the shaft, where there was room for the hammer to be used; when we did arrive at the Sanctuary wall it was found similar to what is found on the surface at the southeast angle, and at the Wailing Place.

Our men, on finding themselves actually at the wall, were profoundly impressed, several of them refused to work with us any longer, some from fear of present punishment, others from superstitious motives, and there were left with us a lot of reckless men, who stuck to us throughout our labors, and were ready to do any thing they were bid *aboveground*, provided they were paid, for they reasoned among themselves that, if I could act in defiance of the Pacha's orders, and that openly, I must have some secret "firmaun" from the Sultan, which was not generally known; and this was the key to our success with these people. I was not at all sorry that this idea should gain ground until our influence with them might be fully established, and on that account I was most careful never to run any risk of being stopped by "the Pacha." And when extreme measures were adopted, and our men were threatened individually by one of the *detective police*, I found a man who had been threatened, and asked his permission to dig in his ground, where there could be no objection. He refused, telling me the reason why. I then went to the Pacha, and represented to him that the firmaun recommended him to persuade the men to let me work in their grounds; and he, finding there was no possible objection, said he would send a man. I asked if the *detective* might go; the Pacha acquiesced at once, and I had the satisfaction of making this man, before several witnesses among our men, say that the Pacha ordered the fellah to allow us to work in his grounds. After this our influence was reëstablished, and the *detective*, when he again threatened the men, was only laughed at by them. It must be recollected that it is only the outside villages that the Pacha would venture to give an order of that sort to; the townspeople are a sturdy lot, who have their own ideas about Turkish rule.

The Ophel Wall was found to be 14 feet 6 inches thick at the bottom; it is perpendicular. At the southeast angle it is found at 4 feet from the surface (level of top 2,352 feet): the top course is drafted, and is 3 feet 9 inches in height, and serves as a coping, as the stones below only average 1 foot 9 inches in height. It was examined down to a depth of 30 feet on the western side close to the southeast angle; below this point the stones are not squared, and, as this is the case all along, it is apparent that this wall was not built until long after the building of the Sanctuary Wall at the southeast angle. This wall is in some parts of melekeh, and in others of mezzeh, at the bottom it appears to be of the latter; the 4-feet wall met with is of the same age apparently; it was supposed that there might have been a road-way between it and the Sanctuary, but no signs of any gate were found in the Ophel Wall. The wall abuts on to the Sanctuary Wall exactly at the southeast angle; at the top it is 1 foot 6 inches in advance of it, but as it is perpendicular, and the other has a batter, it gradually becomes flush with it and then behind it, until at 70 feet it is a couple of feet in rear. It is to be noted that it is not built on the rock as in the Sanctuary Wall, but on the hard layer of clay resting on the rock; this is proof that this wall is more modern than that of the Sanctuary. When we were digging at the southeast angle, our gallery round the corner to the west was driven just under the Ophel Wall for its whole breadth, until we came upon the remains of the gallery we had driven months before along the western side.

Extracts from Letter, October 2, 1868.—" Upward of fifty shafts were sunk about Ophel in search of the wall, etc. To describe the result of each shaft would only be to confuse the account; it will suffice to say that eight of these shafts were in connection with the line of wall which is now found to extend as far as 700 feet from the first tower in a southeasterly direction along the eastern ridge of Ophel.

"The wall commencing at the southeast angle extends in prolongation of east wall of Sanctuary for 76 feet, where there is a tower with a front of 23 feet 9 inches, and projections of 8 feet and 6 feet. The wall then turns with the ridge in a straight line and southwest direction for 700 feet, where it ends abruptly. About 200 feet southwest, and in the same line, some massive walls have been uncovered; they have been built over subsequently, and it would be very difficult to determine their original objects. At this point there is a rocky knoll, and the earth is only about 12 feet in depth. Looking at the remains from a professional point of view, I am inclined to think that what we call the

Ophel Wall was here terminated by a tower, placed on the rocky knoll, and that from thence the wall ran up toward the Dung Gate. (Plan 30.)

"We have found, however, no trace of the wall with 200 feet of the rocky knoll, but it is exceedingly unlikely that the wall would terminate in a hollow with rising ground a few feet in front of it; as the earth about here only covers the rock to a depth of from 12 to 15 feet, it is possible that the wanting portion of the wall may have been taken up and sold for building-stone by the fellahin, who at the present day frequently go down to that depth in search of cut stone. Cut stone in Jerusalem is much in demand, and on the grounds of the fellahin all traces of walls at or near the surface are fast disappearing. The rock-cut steps and caves which existed along the slopes of Ophel are also fast becoming obliterated: the farmers find that these are the places where they have least trouble in blasting and quarrying the rock, and within the last few years many old features on the southern side of the old city have vanished; thus, year by year, the old Jerusalem will become more difficult to be understood.

"It appears likely that the Ophel Wall was built in two or more steps, with a road at the bottom of each wall, as we find that in the first wall the stone is roughly dressed to a certain height above the rock, and that to this height there is an outer wall of cut stone about 20 feet to the front of it.

"Projecting beyond the line of the wall in the 700 feet three small towers are found; they project about 6 feet beyond the wall, and have fronts of about 22 to 28 feet: the first is 310 feet from the bend, the second 425, and the third at 575.

"A peculiarity about this wall is that, for 20 feet on an average above the rock, it is of rough rubble of moderate dimensions, then there is a plinth of well-cut stones. The plinth sets in about 6 inches, and on it is the first well-dressed course of the wall. (Plan No. 21.)

"As the plinth is in many places only a few feet below

the surface of the ground, the wall above it is naturally only a few courses in height. In some cases there is only one course, in some four or five. These vary from 1 foot 9 inches to 2 feet 6 inches in height, the length of the stones averaging 2 feet to 4 feet. Many of the stones are polished, and that generally at the angles of the towers, reminding one of the ' polished corners of the Temple.' It is, however, to be remarked that in the south wall of Jerusalem polished stones are to be met with in a few places, and indeed the Ophel Wall in many respects bears a striking resemblance to the present south wall of Jerusalem.

"The stones in the south wall are probably not *in situ*; nor, I think, are those of the Ophel Wall; that is to say, they appear to be stones used in the building of a previous wall.

"There is a point to which I would draw attention. The plinth is about 20 feet above the rock, and the inference to be drawn is, that up to the plinth the wall was covered from view. Now, the wall stands on the edge of the east ridge of Ophel, the rock sloping down steeply to the Kedron, so that, in order that these 20 feet of foundations may have been covered, it is necessary that there should have been an outer wall which would retain the earth up to the height of the plinth.

"The method of exposing these walls is very slow and tedious. We can only get at them by mining; and to examine a wall 50 feet high by mining it is necessary to have several shafts and galleries. We can at best get but an outline of what there is, leaving the parts of more exceeding interest to be examined minutely subsequently. We are still at work at these Ophel walls and towers." (1868.)

EXTRA TOWER.

Letter of October 2, 1868.—" At 312 feet from the bend we have found at the plinth-level the top of a tower projecting 16 feet beyond the tower. The stones are of a large description, having a marginal draft or bevel; the face within the draft being rough-hewn, similar to some in the Haram Wall. The stones of this *extra* tower are from 2 to 3 feet in height, and 4 to 8 feet long; the face of the tower is 26 feet. It has been examined to a depth of 25 feet, that is, 5 feet below the rock-foundation of the Ophel Wall, and it is of one description throughout.

"At the southeast angle of this *extra* tower we have found another wall going down toward the Kedron; it is 19 feet long, and then takes a turn to the southwest. We have not yet followed it farther. It has been examined to a depth of nearly 40 feet. The stones are well-dressed ashlar; in size about 1 foot 6 inches to 2 feet high, and 2 feet to 3 feet long. An isometric projection of the extra tower and the projecting wall is enclosed. It can be seen that, if the *débris* were to be shovelled into the valley, there would still be a scarped wall for Ophel of from 40 to 60 feet in height, which is only dwarfed by the stupendous height of the Haram Wall alongside."

Letter of January 16, 1869.—" This tower was found to rest upon rock, which is so scarped as to overhang 18 inches at the top. There is a perpendicular scarp of 14½ feet, and then a small gutter for water; below this the rock is cut away so as to form a water-channel, 10 feet high, and about 18 inches wide, open at the top. This channel was found to be too narrow to follow up. The rock scarp was traced to the north-northeast for about 25 feet, when the rock was found to be wanting, a rough wall taking its place.

"With regard to the *extra* wall beyond the tower, it is found to be at present 66 feet in height and 80 feet in length. At its southern end it turns to the west toward the Ophel Wall, and becomes so much decayed that further excavations about it were considered undesirable. It is partially plastered on the outside, and so likewise are the large bevelled stones of the extra tower.

"I have to suggest that this may be the remains of 'the tower which lieth out.'"

IN FRONT OF THE TRIPLE GATE.

Letter of February, 1869.—" Two shafts were sunk in search of any traces of a wall running south from the west side of the Triple Gate. The upper shaft, No. 34, was commenced 132 feet south of the Triple Gate, and to the west of a cistern; rock was found at 22 feet, and a drain at the same level was broken into, in which were found a great number of glass bottles and earthen-ware lamps, which are supposed to date from about the third century of our era. A gallery was then driven along the surface of the rock for 25 feet to the west, but no wall was found. Objections were made to our continuation of the work to the west under the adjoining property.

" To the east of No. 34 shaft is a cistern in which there is a large cross (of St. John) moulded on the plaster, and also some hieroglyphs, a sketch of which was forwarded home in the spring. The cross is placed in a little alcove in the cistern, so that it would only be seen by persons looking for such marks. This cistern would appear, then, to have been plastered in the times of the Crusaders or of the early Christians; if of the time of the Crusaders, the cross would probably be that of the Templars, who were quartered just above. It may perhaps be attributed to the early Christians, as we find the drain with the early Christian pottery so near to it.

" The second shaft, No. 42, was sunk at a distance of 260 feet from the Triple Gate, and in the production of a line perpendicular to the eastern jamb of the centre arch. As soon as the rock was reached a gallery was then driven to the west, and at ten feet a drain was broken through, the same as that met with in shaft No. 34; also a branch drain coming from the northwest; this was followed up until at 30 feet from the shaft a massive stone wall was met with, running apparently in the direction of the eastern jamb of the centre arch, Triple Gate; the wall was then followed 34 feet to the south, where it becomes lost, and 35 feet to the north, where it is succeeded by a wall of rubble masonry, and there lies on it (not *in situ*) a small well-cut bevelled stone about 2 feet by 3 feet 6 inches. The wall was then followed 10 feet farther to the north, but apparently it still continues of rubble masonry; just at the point where is the bevelled stone the mouth of a shaft was found leading down to a rock-cut cavern, which will be described.

"The wall is not yet examined thoroughly; one stone appears to be 15 feet long and 3 feet high (without a bevel); but there is a good deal of cement on the stones, and the joints may be concealed; the wall appears to consist of one course of larger stones resting on a wall of rubble, and the impression it gave me at first was that it might be the wall of a ramp leading from the wall of Ophel up to the Triple Gate. I shall perhaps be able to judge better in a few days.

"At the point marked on the trace No. 40, a shaft was sunk for the purpose of examining the rock under the hollowed piece of ground south of the Double Gate; rock was found at 27 feet 6 inches, and to the east some rock-cut cisterns and a passage with steps leading down into them. A gallery was then driven to the north, and another cistern, about 17 feet square, met with; the gallery was continued along the rock for 60 feet in search of the steps leading up to the Double Gate, but without result; the rock was found to have a scarp or steep down to the east along the line of the gallery; I have since found the rock cropping up to the present surface about 100 feet higher up the hill, so that there is no chance of the steps from the Double Gate having extended so far down.

"Is there any chance of the theatre of Hadrian having been located near this spot? It is the only place that I have observed near the walls of Jerusalem where the ground takes the form of a theatre.

"At No. 38 a shaft was sunk and rock found at 12 feet, but we just lighted upon a place where it is scarped down toward the west for 12 feet to 14 feet; this scarp was traced for about 15 feet to the northwest and southeast.

"I have elsewhere suggested that the Ophel Wall may have terminated on a rocky knoll about 200 feet south of the point to which we have traced it, and that then it may have taken a turn up toward the southwest angle of the Haram Area; it would in such a case run very close to this scarp at 38 (see Contour Plan), which might have been cut to give additional height to the wall; the plan gives the contours as obtained from the several points of the rock we have at present met with.

"At shaft No. 31 rock was found at 33 feet and a drain cut in the rock, in which some lamps were lying. (For the direction of the drain, see General Plan.) The rock is stepped out in a puzzling manner, and to the west the jambs of a gate-way were found; width from post to post 12 feet.

"At the point where the rocky knoll is we have found cisterns and strong walls, but they are built over with more modern masonry, and the whole is so blended together that I can make nothing of it; the more modern building has a floor paved with tesseræ.

"At each shaft sunk south of the Haram Area we have found the remains of buildings, drains, scarped and cut rock, and we may draw the inference that this portion was once covered with houses. We have, however, found no architectural remains *in situ*, and nothing that would repay the expense of keeping the ground open. As the work is generally 20 feet to 40 feet below the surface, it can only be got at by driving galleries at such depths, and, as in this country the wooden frames quickly decay, it becomes a matter of necessity to tamp up the galleries soon after we have opened them. I am now tamping up all the galleries south of the Sanctuary, except two, where the wall of Ophel can be seen by any travellers who come here during the ensuing spring months."

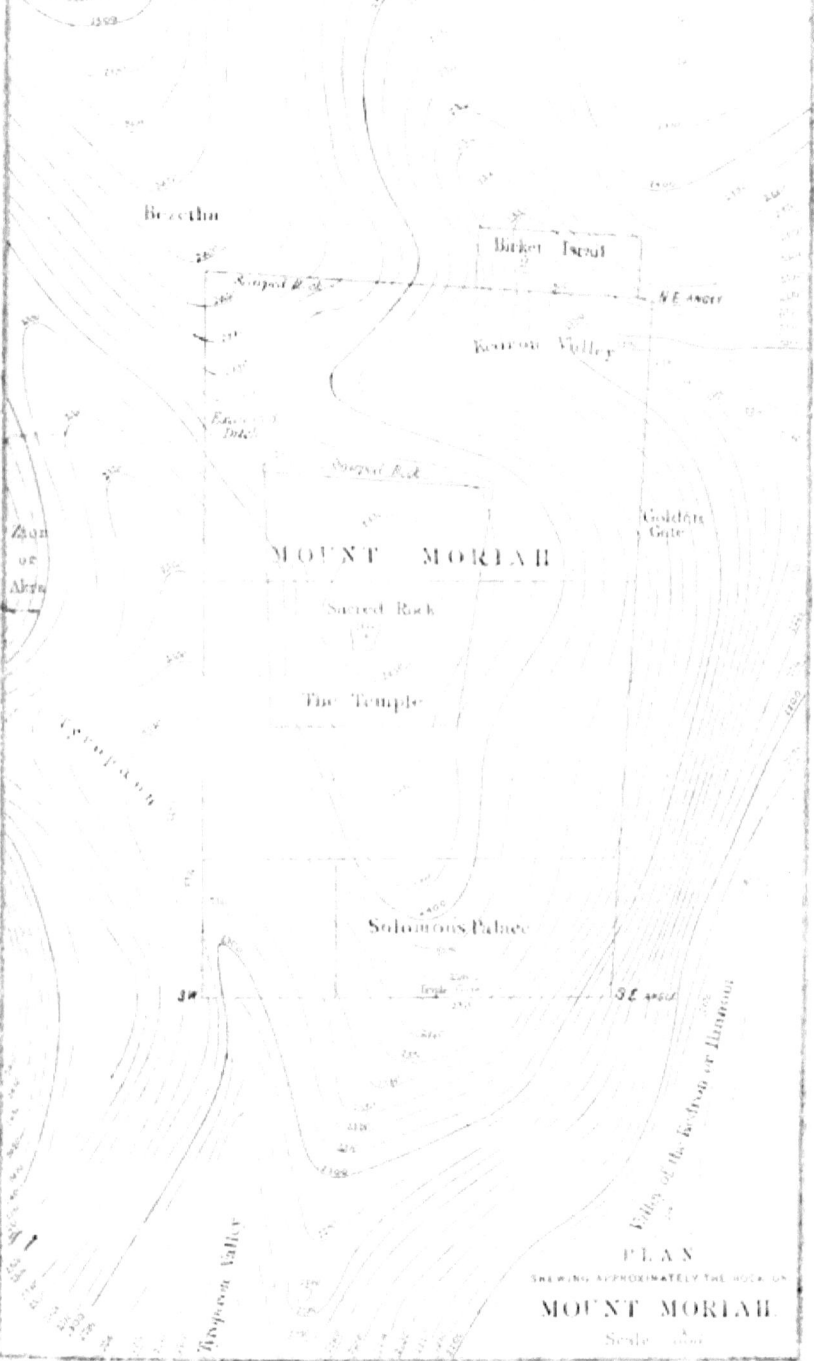

CAVERN SOUTH OF THE TRIPLE GATE.

Letter of February, 1869.—"The cavern previously mentioned as having been met with in the gallery from the shaft No. 42, is cut out of the rock. The roof is flat; it consists of two chambers: the northern appears to have been about 12 feet square, but a portion is taken up to the east by a masonry wall; on the sides of the rock are small holes punched as though for some instrument to rest.

"The southern chamber is irregular in shape, and a portion of it is divided off by stone columns cut from the rock. Mangers or shallow vats exist round the chamber; in some cases the rock is cut in under, and in other cases the troughs are cut out of the steps projecting from the face of the rock. They are from 18 inches to 20 inches wide, and where unbroken are 6 inches deep; in one I found a plug-hole, which shows that the vat was intended for the reception of some liquid. In the roof, on the walls, and at intervals under the troughs are eyes cut in the stone through which a 1½ inch rope may be drawn. These eyes are formed by cutting two groves in the rock about 2 inches apart, and then connecting them by a small hole, half an inch in diameter, about 1 inch below the rock-surface.

"As we find the cave at present, it has the appearance of having been last used as a stable, and the floor is about 2 feet below the level of the mangers, but it cannot originally have been cut for such a purpose, as we find that the true floor of the cavern is 11 feet below the troughs; so that it is apparent that the original object was not connected with housing and feeding of cattle.

"On entering a dyer's shop in Jerusalem you will find vats ranged round the room, and staples let into the wall, from which lines are stretched for hanging up the cloth to dry. The difference is, that at the present day the vats are circular, and those of the cavern are long and narrow. I have to suggest that this cavern may have been a fuller's shop, where clothes were cleaned or made white. Tradition relates that St. James was cast over the outer wall of the Temple enclosure, and that 'a fuller took the club with which he pressed the clothes, and brought it down on the head of the Just One.'

"The eyes made in the walls are similar to those cut in the piers of the substructions at the southeast angle of the Haram, which are sometimes called Solomon's Stables, described in Captain Wilson's notes.

"At the southeastern side of the cavern there is a masonry wall, perhaps to support the rock roof, which here appears to have cracked. Attempts were made to go through this wall, but it was not considered safe to continue the work.

"About half the earth in this cavern has been turned over and a considerable amount of pottery has been found, but all in fragments. Also the lower part of a copper candlestick,* which was found in two pieces that had originally been soldered together. The upper part has been turned in a lathe, the lower part has been probably pressed on a block.

"The rock above this cave is 4½ feet thick, and in the earth above is a drain containing glass and pottery, supposed to be early Christian; it must then have been some time back when this cave was used as a stable, and farther back still when it was used for its original purpose.

"In the roof is a peculiar cutting, as though for a piece of metal; and I cannot at present ascertain whether such a hole is made in oil-pressing rooms, etc.; but I have observed a similar cutting in the lintel of a door-way in Hârat ad Dâwâyeh, and perhaps some person may be able to explain it; but the dyers, fellahin, and others about Jerusalem, say that they do not know its object."

Sculptured Slab.—In 1868, a fellah, when digging on the southeast side of Cœnaculum, found in a hewn cave a slab of sculptured marble, in size and appearance very similar to those found built into the walls of the mosques in the

---

* See below, Mr. Greville Chester's paper.

Noble Sanctuary (see Plates 13 and 14, Ordnance Survey Plans).

It has a cross upon it; and also the ornament inside the wreath appears to be a cross coupled with a fleur-de-lis, similar to one of the ornamented sides of the great red marble font which is now to be seen at Tekoa. (See Illustration.)

December 22, 1869.—" 1. Commenced 3d of July, 1869. A trench was dug in front of the core of an old wall appearing above the surface of the ground just outside the city wall,

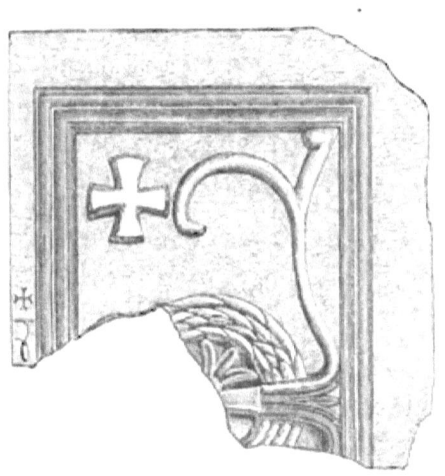

MONUMENTAL SLAB.

north of Kalât al Jalud. Rock was found at 4 feet, and between it and the core of the wall is a space of about 2 feet, probably where the cut stone rested. The rock was examined for a distance of 20 feet, but no appearance of any old foundations.

"2. Commenced the same day in the Greek garden outside the city wall to the northwest, a little north of the Latin Patriarch's Palace, where a core of a wall crops up on the surface; rock was found at 4 feet, the core resting on it with a space in front where the cut stone had been; rock scarped in front; followed it down and found it bevelled at the bottom at 12 feet below the surface: **no signs** of any old foundations."

THE HOLY CITY.

I have great diffidence in presenting this sketch of Jerusalem in the time of King Herod, because I have not had time to go thoroughly into the subject since I came to a conclusion as to the position of the Temple.

There are a few remarks necessary for explanation of the sketch. One, two, and three, together form the temple courts of Herod, but there is also four, which joined to the Temple but a secular portion of it; this, I suppose, was the armory of King David, the Baris of later days, perhaps the palace appertaining to the Temple of Nehemiah, the *tower* of Antonia, which was joined to the *castle* of Antonia by cloisters. It is the northern portion of the platform of the Sanctuary, and as it is for the most part rock, with a scarp to the north, I imagine it to have formed the line of defence; it is, perhaps, the palace of King Hezekiah mentioned by the Bordeaux Pilgrim. I only put this forward, however, as an idea, for I am very unwilling to attempt to elaborate any plan of this position of the Temple until I see how the general idea is received by the learned public, for perhaps now that all the details of our work are accessible in one volume, some other views and arguments may be started which will capsize the theory I have at last formed; and I must acknowledge that I only put forward a theory which appears to me to be less open to objection than any other, and I should be very willing to see a more perfect solution of the question. The principal difficulty I find—but this is common to all theories—is, that in the Book of Nehemiah the city of David, the house of David, and the sepulchre of David, all appear to be on the southeastern side of the hill of Ophel, near the Virgin's Fount or En Rogel, and yet such a position for Zion appears at first sight to be out of the question.

The contour lines are not put in very accurately, but I

JERUSALEM AT THE TIME OF KING HEROD

SKETCH SHEWING APPROXIMATELY THE LIE OF ROCK.

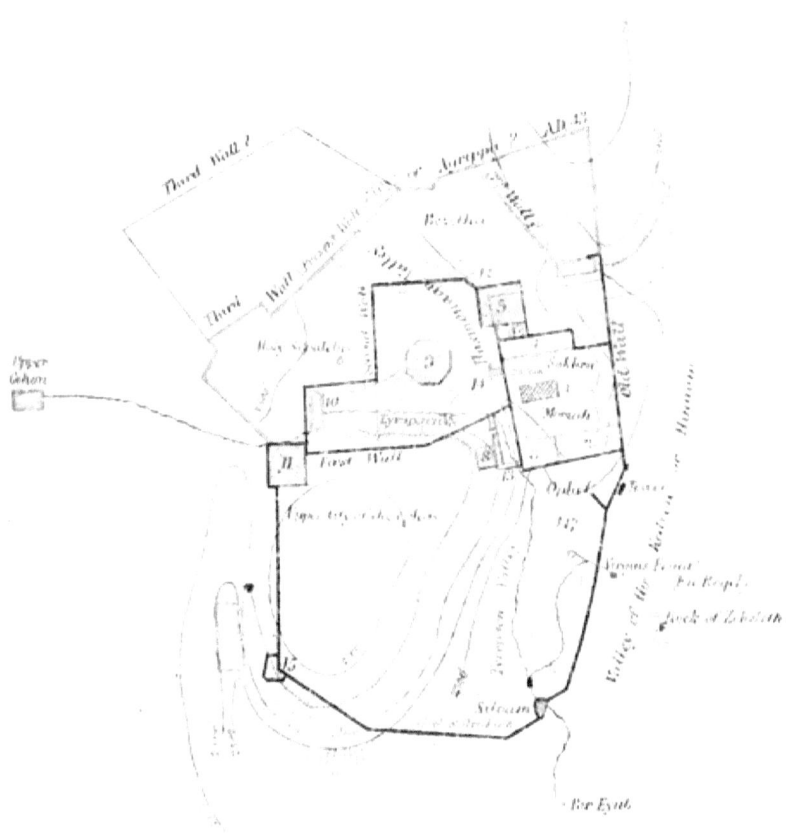

Scale 1/20000

REFERENCE

1. Temple of Solomon
2. Palace of do } Herods Temple
3. Added on by Herod
4. Eschedra (The Tower Baris or Antonia)
5. Antonia (The Castle)
6. Cloisters joining Antonia to Temple
7. Xystus
8. Agrippa's Palace
9. Zion, Akra
10. Lower Pool of Siloam or Amygdalon
11. Herods Palace
12. Bethesda or Struthion
13. Bridge built by Herod
14. The Lower City called sometimes Akra
15. British Cemetery A.D. 1876

think they give a truthful idea of the position of the rock in the city.

It will be seen that Zion and Acra stand upon a slope 2,400 to 2,450 feet, thus a little below the level of the Sacred Rock on Moriah. It appears, however, probable that this portion may have been a rocky knoll overlooking the Temple by 50 feet before it was cut down by the Maccabees.

I cannot yet make up my mind as to whether the Acra of Josephus was in his time used to represent the crescent-shaped hill, including Zion, Moriah, and Ophel, but there seems much in favor of the idea.

Josephus tells us that the third wall, after turning at the northeast angle, was joined on to the *old* wall which I suppose to be the prolongation to the north of the porch of Solomon. This old wall may have existed in early times, and certainly must have existed in the time of Pompey, B. C. 65, for he was *within* the walls of the city when he attacked the Temple on its northern side, which Josephus tells us was protected by towers.

The third wall I think to have been on the site of the present northern wall of the city, but we have no very decisive evidence on the subject.

With regard to the other walls, I follow very closely the outlines given by Mr. Lewin ("The Siege of Jerusalem"). In his disposition of the gates and pools, however, I cannot quite agree with him, but at the same time I am not yet sufficiently convinced on the subject to illustrate my present ideas.

January 20, 1870.—" A sarcophagus* was presented to the Palestine Exploration Fund on January 19, 1870, by Mr. Hay, acting consul for the United States, and Captain Walker; they found it near the Convent of the Cross, in a rock-cut tomb.

"This tomb is situated on the east side of the valley

---

* See below, Mr. Greville Chester's paper.

running up from the convent to the third tower on the Jaffa road; it is cut out of a soft rock like the melekeh.

"The entrance is 1 foot 9 inches wide, and opens into a chamber 8 feet 4 inches square, and 3 feet 10 inches high; on the south side are three loculi 7 feet 6 inches long, 1 foot 4 inches wide, and 2 feet 10 inches high; on the east side are two loculi (see plan) of about the same dimensions. The roof is flat; the sarcophagus is only 2 feet 6.9 inches long, 1 foot 0.4 inches broad, and 1 foot 3.5 inches high, and appears to be less ancient than the tomb.

"Nothing else was found inside but a lamp of earthenware.

"The ground belongs to the Lifta men, and the tomb appears to have been opened for some years; but the sarcophagus was not removed, as they thought it to be Moslem. It was amusing to find that the fellah Sergeant Birtles took with him to remove it was the owner of it and the soil, and had often wished to make a little money out of his property. The sarcophagus is of soft stone, similar in general appearance to those found in great numbers about Jerusalem, but more skilfully cut than any I have seen. A squeeze has been taken of it.

"It is noticeable that these sarcophagi are seldom found close to Jerusalem, but generally at a distance of about a mile. We have found them on the east side of Olivet, north of the Russian Building, near Mar Elias, and now at the Convent of the Cross. They have generally been ascribed to the third or fourth century of our era. M. de Saulcy found one very similar to the east of the Dead Sea; at Kerak, I think."

Mr. Greville Chester (paper on Pottery, etc.) assigns these sarcophagi found near Jerusalem simply to the Christian period. A sketch of the sarcophagus whose history is given above will be found in his Notes.

Some holes were opened in the marly rock on the east side of Olivet. They are simply egg-shaped holes, about 8 feet high and 5 feet in diameter: in them we found a variety of pottery of several shapes (see chapter on pottery). Two of the pots are similar to some I have seen in use at Mogador, northwest coast of Africa.

A few words are perhaps necessary on my impression concerning the boundary-line of Judah and Benjamin, running through Jerusalem.

In June, 1869, I came to the conclusion that the valleys of Kedron and Hinnom were identical, and made the suggestion in an unpublished letter. In February, 1870, M. Ganneau also came to the same conclusion, from finding a rock (Zehwélé) close to the Virgin's Fount, thus identifying them respectively with the rock Zoheleth and the fountain En Rogel. M. Ganneau's letter of February 22, 1870, is given at length in the "Quarterly," No. V., P. E. Fund.

The question is of too great a length to go into here, but I may give the direction I suppose the line of boundary to have taken, viz., across from the rock Zoheleth in Siloam to (En Rogel) the Virgin's Fount, thence up the (Valley of Hinnom) Kedron, until nearly opposite the southeast angle of the Noble Sanctuary, where it crossed over the hill of Moriah at the southern side of the Temple, thence up the Tyropœon Valley to the Jaffa Gate, and so on to (Niphtoah) Lifta.

The Arabic accounts speak of the Kedron as the Wady Gehinnom, and the prophet Jeremiah (xxi 11) says: "Go forth into the valley of the Son of Hinnom, which is by the entry of the East Gate;" which does not apply to the modern valley of Hinnom.

The head of this valley of Hinnom, or Kedron, commences up the Jaffa road, a mile and a half northwest of Jerusalem, and runs along the northern side by the Tombs of the Kings.

Mr. Lightfoot, quoting from the Talmud, tells us: "*For most part of the courts was in the portion of Judah, but the altar, porch, temple, and most holy place, were in the portion of Benjamin;*" and further, that the part which lay in the portion of *Judah* was made hollow "*with arches upon arches underneath.*"

This appears exactly to apply to the position I have assigned to Herod's and **Solomon's Temple Enclosures**, and to the boundary-line between the **two tribes.**

CHAPTER XII.

CONCLUSION.

BEFORE stating the impressions which the details of the excavations have made upon me, I think it right briefly to relate what my views have been with regard to the topography of the Holy City.

On landing in Palestine in 1867, I was impressed with the work of Mr. Fergusson, "The Holy Sepulchre;" but after further study, the historical account of Mr. Williams, in "The Holy City," and the architectural reasoning of the Count de Vogüé, in "Le Temple de Jérusalem," appeared to me entirely to refute the idea of the present Dome of the Rock having been placed by Constantine over the supposed site of the Holy Sepulchre.

I still, however, considered the Temple of Herod to have been in a square of 600 feet at the southwest angle of the present Sanctuary, and considered the plan of Mr. Lewin, in "The Siege of Jerusalem," to give the nearest approach to an idea of how the temples and walls once were placed. But each result of our researches tended to prove that the Temple area of Herod was more than 600 feet square.

In every thing, except the Temple of Herod itself and parts adjoining, I still think that Mr. Lewin's plan of the old walls is nearer correctness than any other; but, with regard to the Temple of Herod, I agree more with Robinson, Kraft, Barclay, and Porter, except that I do not think the Sacred Rock of the Moslems to have been the site either of the Altar or of the Sanctum Sanctorum, but rather of the gate Nitsots of the inner court opening into the northern gate Tadi.

The change in my views, from supposing Herod's Temple to have been on a square of 600 feet to that of 900, and thus occupying the whole southern portion of the present Sanctuary, arose entirely from the result of our excavations, for it appears to me that, if it were only 600 feet square, it would have had to be in three or four places at once. For example, its western wall must have been coincident with the present west wall, because of Robinson's Arch leading over to the upper city, which appears undoubtedly to be the bridge over which Titus parleyed with the Jews after he had taken the Temple; its northern wall must have been near the present northern edge of the Dome of the Rock platform, for here only is there a great valley, as described in the attack on the older Temple by Pompey. Its eastern wall must have coincided with the present east wall of the Sanctuary, so as to have overlooked the Kedron ravine, and because on that wall we find marks ascribed to times earlier than Herod, and, if this enormous wall had only been the outer wall of the city, the Temple cloisters could not have overlooked the Kedron: again, the southern side of the Temple must have coincided with the present south wall of the Sanctuary, because we find the wall of Ophel coming in at the southeast angle, and we find the south wall to have been of one construction from the southeast angle to the Double Gate.

With regard to the Antonia, I still feel in considerable doubt whether it stood on the northwest angle of the present Sanctuary or on the northwest angle of the Dome of the Rock platform, and the only solution I can see to the difficulties is by supposing that it did both: that the castle of the Antonia stood at the northwest angle of the Sanctuary, and that at the northwest angle of the platform was a tower called Antonia, and joined to the castle by passages or cloisters.

As a proof of this, we have the account of Josephus (*Bel.* vi. 3. 7), where Titus, after he had possession of the Antonia, erected banks against the outer court of the Temple; one of which was "at that northern edifice (ἐξέδραν) which was between the two gates." This evidently refers to some tower of the kind suggested.

The account (*Bel.* v. 5, 8) would be incomprehensible without some explanation of this kind. We are there told that Antonia is connected with the Temple at the junction of the northern and western cloisters by passages down to them both, and that the *southeast* tower of the Antonia was built 70 cubits high, so as to overlook the Temple, and was evidently not joined to the Temple; therefore the castle of Antonia must have been only connected by cloisters, as shown in the plan of Mr. Lewin. As a further proof of this, we have (*Bel.* ii. 16, 6) an account of the cloisters joining the Temple to Antonia being cut off, by which Florus was unable to get into the Antonia from them. Now if the Antonia had projected into the court of the Temple, as shown on the plans of De Vogüé and Fergusson, it does not appear that cutting off the cloister would have done much harm; but if Antonia was separate from the Temple by a ditch over which cloisters were built, the cutting of them down would fulfil the requirements of the case.

THE TEMPLE OF SOLOMON.

The Noble Sanctuary of Jerusalem is a raised plateau, measuring about 1,500 feet from north to south, and about 900 feet from east to west, sustained by a massive wall, rising on the exterior from 50 to 80 feet above the present level of the ground; the general level of this plateau is about 2,420 feet, but toward the east, at the Golden Gate, it is not filled up to this level by some twenty feet or so.

Almost in the centre of this plateau is an irregular four-sided paved platform, rising some 16 feet above the general level of the plateau; and above the centre of this platform the Sacred Rock crops out, over which is built the celebrated Dome of the Rock, generally ascribed to the Moslem chief Abd al Melek, but claimed by Mr. Fergusson as the church of Constantine.

There is no question but that within the present Noble Sanctuary the Temple of Herod once stood, and that some part of the remaining wall is on the site of, or actually is, a portion of the old wall of the outer court; but, with regard to its position, there are the most conflicting opinions.

Some authorities, as M. de Saulcy, Sir Henry James, the Count de Vogüé, Messrs. Menke, Sepp, and Kraft, suppose the whole Sanctuary to have been occupied by the Temple courts, and that Antonia was joined on at the northwest angle, or projected a little into the outer court.

Then Mr. Williams supposes the northern portion of the Sanctuary, about 950 feet square, to have been occupied by the Temple courts, while the remainder was the work of Justinian, based upon the ruins of Ophel.

And Messrs. Robinson, Kraft, Barclay, Kiepert, and Porter, suppose the Temple courts to have occupied the southern portion of the Sanctuary on a square of about 925 feet, or thereabout.

Again, Messrs. Tobler, Rozen, etc., suppose a Temple of about 600 feet a side, nearly coincident with the present platform (where I suppose King Solomon's Temple to have been).

And Messrs. Fergusson, Thrupp, Lewin, etc., suppose Herod's Temple courts to have been about 600 feet a side, and situated at the southwest angle of the Sanctuary; but as to the position of Antonia all differ.

Amid all these views, that of Dr. Robinson appears to be most nearly correct, so far as Herod's courts are concerned, with the application to them of Mr. Lewin's plan of the Antonia, changed in position, and somewhat modified in form.

It is necessary to state, before proceeding further, that the Holy City is built upon a series of rocky spurs close to

the water-shed or backbone of Palestine; and it appears to
be quite certain, from the nature of the surrounding country, that in early times the site of Jerusalem was a series of
rocky slopes, the ledges covered here and there with a few
feet of red earth. When, therefore, we get down to the surface of the rock at the present day (provided it has not been
cut), we get down to that surface which presented itself to
view in olden times, before the first inhabitants built their
city.

Now this being the case, it is only necessary to throw
away all the *débris* forming the vast plateau of the Sanctuary, and we get a view of the rock of Moriah, as it would
have appeared to the eyes of King David: although this is
of course impracticable on the ground itself, we have been
able to do so on paper, and on a model: for, having obtained the height of the surface of the rock in all the tanks
of the Sanctuary, where rock was to be found, and having
obtained the height of the rock along the wall, we have been
able to produce a very approximate contoured plan of the
rock over all this area; and on some part of this area the
Temple of Solomon once stood.

We find, then, that the ridge of the hill of Moriah runs
along from the northwest angle, nearly in a straight line
southeast by south, until it reaches the Triple Gate in the
south wall, and that it falls away from this ridge very
steeply, northeast and southwest, so that a point of rock
near the northeast angle is no less than 162 feet below the
Sacred Rock; a point of rock at the southwest angle is no
less than 150 feet below the Sacred Rock; and again, at
the southeast angle, it is no less than 163 feet below this
rock. I have to submit, then, that where the sides are as
much as one in two or three, where the ground slopes very
nearly in the same degree as does the rock of Gibraltar to
the west, it seems incredible that the temple, a building
which was so conspicuous, and which was to perform such
an important part in the fortifications of the city, should
have been placed down in a hole, or even along the sides of

the hill, or anywhere except on the ridge, where there is just enough room for it to have stood, for it is somewhat flattened on the top.

It certainly may be said that the site was not selected for a fortress, and that its position depended on that of the threshing-floor of Araunah; but it seems reasonable to suppose that Divine Providence would have caused the threshing-floor to have been placed in such a position as would have been afterward favorable to the dominance of the Temple: and again, it is well known that threshing-floors in Palestine are so placed on the ridges of hills or on the highest points that, by exposure to every puff of wind which may be straying about, the corn and chaff may be separated; for, there being no machines, the winnowing at the present day, as of old, is effected by tossing up in the air the well-trodden corn and chaff, when the latter is carried away. Dan. ii. 35: "And became like the chaff of the summer threshing-floors; and the wind carried them away."

Supposing the Temple, then, to have been built on the ridge, we must give up all idea of its having stood at the southwest or northeast angles, for there are the beds of the Tyropœon and another valley. It could not have stood at the northwest angle, because Josephus tells us that at the north of the Temple was a valley which Pompey, in his attack, B.C. 65, was obliged to fill partially in (*Bel.* i. 7, 3); and the only valley which exists about there is that which the northern end of the platform of the Dome of the Rock overlooks. The position, therefore, where the altar could have stood lies somewhere in a line of about 300 feet, between the Sacred Rock of the Moslems and a point 100 feet east of "The Cup."

There are reasons for supposing that it stood somewhere on the northern portion of this line, for we know that the Temple of Herod stood on the site of that of Solomon, and the Mishna also tells us that the Temple of Herod lay in the northwest angle of its enclosure, and therefore, if the latter be a square of about 920 feet, forming the southern portion of the Noble Sanctuary, then the Temple of Solomon would fall somewhere very near the Sacred Rock.

The position which appears to me to fulfil most nearly the several requirements is that by which the Altar of Burnt-offering would have stood over tank No. 5 at its western end—the Dome of the Roll (see page 161).

Then the Sacred Rock of the Moslems would have formed part of the Chel, through which the gate Nitsots led under-ground to the gate Tadi, over which, on the northern portion of the platform, were the towers attacked by Pompey when he took the Temple, and which afterward became the citadel, until the fortifications at this point were still further enlarged, and the castle of Antonia built.

The position, therefore, I suppose to have been occupied by the courts of the Temple of Solomon is a rectangle 900 feet-odd from east to west, and 600 feet from north to south, its southern end 300 feet north of the south wall of the Noble Sanctuary.

This would suppose the wall at Wilson's Arch and the Wailing Place to be the work of Solomon, or of the kings of Judah, and also the portion of the Sanctuary on the eastern side and opposite.

It would perhaps have appeared more in keeping with the account to suppose a square for Solomon's Temple; but there is this difficulty: The present east wall of the Sanctuary has Phœnician characters on it, and has all the appearance of being a portion of the oldest work, so that if it were not Solomonic it would have formed part of the *old wall* spoken of by Josephus, which I suppose to have been the work of the kings of Judah. But Josephus tells us (*Ant.* xv. 11, 5) that the Porch of Solomon in the time of Herod overlooked the Kedron, and therefore would have to overlook this east wall of the Sanctuary, if it were not identical with it.

But a person standing to-day at the southeast angle of the platform would have to be raised up 200 *feet* before he could see over the present east wall into the Kedron; therefore it is apparent that, if the east wall is as old as the time of King Herod, then it must have formed the east wall of his temple enclosure; and, if so, then it was the wall on which the cloister called Solomon's Porch rested, and is the actual wall built by King Solomon himself. For this we have a chain of evidence running throughout the account of Josephus; and we have most clearly the information that this porch, in the time of King Herod Agrippa (A.D. 63), rested on the wall of Solomon, which was 600 feet long. (*Ant.* xx. 10, 7.)

My impression is, that this wall commences at 300 feet north of the southeast angle, and extends up to the break in the east wall for 600 feet, and that there the *old wall* of the kings of Judah commences and runs up to the northeast angle, and, turning to the west above the Birket Israil, formed the second wall up to the time of Herod, when the castle of Antonia was built; and that it was within this wall that the camp of Pompey was pitched when he attacked the northern side of the Temple.

It is to be observed that, at both the northeast and southeast angle, characters in paint have been found at the foot of the walls, which are pronounced by *savants* to be Phœnician.

The evidence with regard to the temple enclosure of Solomon having been 600 feet a side, and the enclosure of Herod being enlarged, was originally given here more fully, as I had never seen the subject broached previously; but, just before sending this to press, the supplement to No. 8, vol. ii., of the "Museum of Classical Antiquities," 1853, was put into my hands, and I find it there brought out very clearly, so that there is no occasion for me to do more than allude to it.

The next question which arises is as to the disposition of the portion of the Noble Sanctuary, 900 feet by 300 feet, lying between Solomon's Temple Enclosure and the south wall.

A square of 300 feet at the southwest angle I suppose

to have been built by King Herod, together with the arch of Robinson and the passage to the Xystus and the Upper City.

The remaining portion, 600 feet by 300 feet, extending from the Double or Huldah Gate to the southeast angle, I suppose to have been the site of

SOLOMON'S PALACE.

It is very remarkable that there is a disposition among many authorities, however much they may differ in other respects, to place the palace somewhere near this point.

Mr. Lewin, in his exhaustive argument, shows that the palace evidently must have stood to the south of and lower than the Temple; but, placing the Temple on his plan at the southwest angle, the palace has to follow, and is outside the limit of the Noble Sanctuary. Remove his temple to the position I suppose it to have held, and the palace occupies the southeast angle.

Mr. Williams also considers the palace to have been very near this point; see *supra*, page 222 (Ophel).

Dr. Robinson also appears to favor the same idea, and alludes to the general name of "Palatium sive Templum Salomonis," given to the Aksa by early writers.

It certainly does appear that all tradition agrees in placing the Palace of Solomon here; and we are indebted to Mr. Fergusson for showing how carefully we must distinguish between *Templum Domini* and *Templum Salomonis*; but it is interesting to note that the inference he draws is, that the one is the *Church of Our Lord*, the other the *Temple of Solomon*, while it appears to me that the real rendering should be the Temple of the Lord (built by Solomon) and the Palace of Solomon.

This difference is not a small matter; for, if his rendering should be right, then it would be evident that the opinions of all travellers from A. D. 333 till the Middle Ages were in favor of the Holy Sepulchre being on the Sacred

Rock of the Moslems, and the Temple of Solomon at the southwest angle, according to his disposition.

It appears to me, however, that all the early writers support each other in placing the Holy Sepulchre where it is at present, making the site of the Temple of Solomon identical with that of the Dome of the Rock, and the Palace of Solomon with the portion of the Noble Sanctuary reaching from the Aksa Mosque to the southeast angle.

Care must be taken to distinguish between *Porticus Salomonis* and *Palatium Salomonis*; the first, evidently referring to the Porch of Solomon on the east wall of Herod's Temple Enclosure; the other, to the portion of the enclosure where Solomon's Palace once stood.

From the anonymous description of the Holy Places, published by Dr. Titus Tobler, we extract the following:

"Ab hoc loco (the Holy Sepulchre), quantum potest arcus bis mittere sagittam, in orientali parte est Templum Domini a Salomone factum, in quo a justo Simeone præsentatus est Christus. In dextra parte hujus templi Salomon templum suum ædificavit et inter utrumque templum porticum speciosam struxit columnis marmoreis. In sinistra parte est probatica piscina."

This portion Mr. Fergusson appears to think may have been written in the fourth century. The account, however, closely resembles those of the time of the Crusades, and it draws a distinction between the Temple of the Lord built by Solomon, and Solomon's Temple or Palace. This distinction will be marked throughout the following quotations, and shows that the Templum Domini had no reference whatever to the Church of Our Lord, the Church of the Resurrection, or Holy Sepulchre.

The Bordeaux Pilgrim, about A. D. 333, speaks of the site of the temple built by Solomon, but before this he describes the southeast angle (Lewin, p. 490), and says: "Ibi est angulus turris excelsissimæ ubi Dominus ascendit;" and then further tells us: "Item ad caput anguli et sub pinnâ turris ipsius sunt cubicula plurima ubi Salomon palatium habebat." Here we have the palace again placed at the southeast angle, and distinct from the temple built by Solomon.

A. D. 700. Bishop Arculf evidently describes the present Church of the Holy Sepulchre, but his reference to the Temple is obscure.

A. D. 1102. Sæwulf describes the present Dome of the Rock as the Temple of the Lord, and places the Temple of Solomon to the south, near the southeast angle.

M. de Vogüé, in " Les Églises de la Terre Sainte," gives us two accounts: the first A. D. 1157, where, after speaking of the *Templum Domini*, it relates, page 413, from an account of date 1157: "A parte quoque meridianâ est palatium Salomonis;" the second, "La Citez de Jherusalem" (A. D. 1187), tells us the same: " Entre le mur de la cité et le mur des Portes Oires si estoit les Temples, et si y avoit une grant place qui plus estoit d'une traictie de lonc et le giet d'une pierre de lé, ainz que on veigne au Temple. Cele place si estoit pavée, dont on apeloit cele place le Pavement. A mein destre, si come on issoit de ces portes, estoit li Temples Salemon, là où li Frere du Temple manoient. A la droiture des Portes Specieuses et des Portes Oires estoit li moustiers du Temple Domini, et si estoit en haut, si que on i montoit a degrez."

William of Tyre also carefully distinguishes between the Temple of the Lord and the Palace of Solomon; and Brocardus (A. D. 1283) tells us: " Mons Moriah in quo Templum Domini et Palatium Regis ædificata erant."

A. D. 1163. Benjamin of Tudela (a Jew) tells us that the Templum Domini (Dome of the Rock) is the site of the Holy Temple, and that the hospital of Solomon (the Aksa), occupied by the Knights Templars, is the palace originally built by King Solomon.

A. D. 1521. Mejir ed Din (xxiv.) describes the substructions at the southeast angle under the name of Solomon's Stable, and says: " It is probably Solomon's building." He also tells us that " remains of the works of Solomon may still be seen on the inside of the enclosure (the Golden Gate), the only remains that are found within the Mesjid." He also supposes that the stonework in the Double Passage may be the remains of Solomon's buildings.

We have also at the present day the name of "Solomon's Stables" attached to the vaults at the southeast angle, and the Double Passage is still shown by the Moslem guides as part of Solomon's work.

It is also to be noted that the southern cloisters of Herod's Temple Enclosure were called the Royal Cloisters. This name, I presume, was obtained from their being built over the remains of the Royal Palace.

Herod's Temple Enclosure appears then to have consisted of the old enclosure of King Solomon's Temple, the old palace, and a piece built in at the southwest angle to make the whole a square of about 900 feet a side. And, besides this, there was the portion on which the towers protecting the side of the Temple rested, called by Josephus the Exhedra, and connected with the main castle of Antonia by a double set of cloisters.

It has already been shown (p. 242) that this position exactly meets the requirements of the account of Josephus; it now only remains to compare the several walls of the Noble Sanctuary.

The wall from Wilson's Arch to the Prophet's Gate is of one construction, and is built up from the rock of smooth-faced drafted stones. The wall is continued in the same straight line to the southwest angle, and along that portion, and round to the Double Gate, it is built up, as far as the pavement under Robinson's Arch, with rough-faced drafted stones, and above that they closely resemble those at the Wailing Place.

From the Double Gate to the southeast angle, and about 105 feet round the corner to the north, the stones are built up smooth-faced from the rock; and beyond the point as far as we examined, they are built up from the rock to the present surface with slightly projecting faces (of 2 to 3 inches).

At the northeast angle the stones of the tower have projecting faces up to a certain level (see p. 132), and after that they resemble those at the Wailing Place; but in the wall south of the tower the stones have projecting faces (of 12 to 24 inches), from the rock up to the present surface, a height of more than 125 feet.

The inference I draw from these walls is, that the portion from Wilson's Arch to the Prophet's Gate is of the time of Solomon, being the west wall of his temple enclosure, and that the portion from the Double Gate round by the southeast angle is also Solomonic, having formed the wall of his palace. The wall at the northeast angle I suppose to have been the work of the kings of Judah, the *old wall* to which Josephus (*Bel.* v. 4, 2) tells us the wall of Agrippa was joined.

It is to be remarked that, though there are projecting faces to the stones both near the southeast and northwest angles, yet they differ very much in appearance, for the former only project 2 to 3 inches, the latter from 12 to 24 inches: the fact of the northeast angle tower being built up from the rock with stones whose faces project also implies that it is a later construction than that of the southeast angle, where the stones are as well dressed at the bottom as at any other point.

With regard to the rough-faced stones at the southwest angle, they differ entirely from any in the east wall, and I suppose them, for reasons already given, to be Herodian.

Levels were taken all round the wall of the Sanctuary, and the relative heights of the several courses are given in the abstract which will be found in the Appendix.

In conclusion, I may observe that my endeavor has been to give the details of the excavations only, together with any new combination of old facts which may have happened to strike me. I have avoided, as much as possible, repeating any thing that has appeared previously in the standard works on Jerusalem, because the account here given cannot pretend to do more than act as an *Addendum* to those works;

my references have therefore generally been made to them when I considered it necessary to correct some error into which the writers have fallen from their want of knowledge of facts, which the excavations have opened up; and, in consequence, a casual reader may be led to think that I do not thoroughly appreciate them. To put the matter, however, beyond a doubt, I beg to express my gratitude to those whose former labors in the same field in history, architecture, topography, archaeology, criticism, and controversy, have so ripened the several questions as to render the excavations of some service; and, not least, to the lady by whose munificent gift the Ordnance Survey under Captain Wilson was enabled to be carried out, for without that survey nothing satisfactory in excavating could have been undertaken.

It may appear to some, who have already formed their ideas on the topography of the Holy City, that it was unnecessary for me to give more than the details of our work. I have, however, given the few opinions I possess for the information of those who have not been yet convinced either way; and I may conscientiously say that I have carried on the work entirely without any strong bias toward any particular theory, for my opinions have changed whenever our researches, throwing new light upon the several questions, have shown that I was in error, and I have not hesitated to say so in my letters.

Appendix I.

Allusion has been made, p. 38, to the vizierial letter which professed to give us the necessary authority to carry out our exploration of Jerusalem. An examination of its terms will serve to bring into yet stronger light the difficulties interposed by the Government, which cramped our operations at every turn.

Copy of Vizierial Letter received in February, 1867.

[Translation.]

"Excellency,

"The British Embassy has informed us that Lieutenant Charles Warren, an English Officer of Engineers (with a few employés and workmen), has been appointed to make certain scientific researches in Jerusalem and its neighborhood, and requests that the needful assistance may be given them; and that as they will require, in order to complete their investigation, only to excavate and examine certain localities from which no objectionable consequences would result, the Embassy likewise requests that the necessary permission may be given for that purpose. As the object of the mission of these persons is to make useful scientific inquiries, it is needful that facilities and support should be afforded them. You will accordingly extend to these persons consideration and regard, and the necessary facilities in regard of the object of the mission, and, as above stated, permission and every possible facility to dig and inspect places, after satisfying the owners, with the exception of the Noble Sanctuary and the various Moslem and Christian shrines.

"(Signed)　　Mahomed Russad.

"27 *Ramazan,* 1283."

A letter accompanied the vizierial letter, stating that an order could not be given for us to excavate in the Noble Sanctuary of Jerusalem, because the Prince of Wales was the only Frank who had visited it; thus confusing the Sanctuary of Jerusalem with the more jealously-guarded one at Hebron. A letter was written to the Porte explaining the mistake, but no satisfactory answer was obtained. As long as this lasted I thought I was justified in endeavoring to examine the hidden portion of the Sanctuary. In 1869, however, a firmaun arrived forbidding excavations there, signed with the Sultan's own hand. I at once wrote home to state that after this I could not undertake any more work there beyond a survey. The following is the substance of this document. It is dated the 19th Muharrem, 1283, or May 1, 1869:

"Lieutenant Warren proceeds to Syria for the purpose of carrying out archæological researches, and excavating for antiquities. The authorities in Syria are enjoined to give an officer to accompany him on his mission. He should be allowed to make excavations, under certain conditions, at localities where antiquities are likely to be found; but he should on no account be permitted to make excavations at the Haram-esh-Shereef, at the Musjed-el-Aksa, the Kubbet-es-Sakhra, or any other places in the immediate vicinity of the said Haram-esh-Shereef. Lieutenant Warren is empowered to carry on such archæological researches as are mentioned above during the period of one year from the date of this firmaun."

C. W.

Appendix II.

Letter of December 4, 1868.—Extract from Athenæum.—"We are told that the meaning of the word *Tadi* is 'obscurity.' The Jerusalem translation of the Mishna says: 'Tadi served for no (ordinary) purpose,' and further, 'that it was used by the priests to retire by, should they have become defiled during their service in the Temple.' We read further on: 'All the gates there had lintels, except Tadi; there two stones inclined one upon another.' There we read again that the gate Nitsots 'had a door into the Chel, and that to the house Mokad were two doors, open to the Chel.' Again, with regard to the house Mokad: 'In the northeast (chamber) they descended to the House of Baptism;' and again, the priest 'rose and went out in the gallery that ran under the arch, and candles flamed on either side until he came to the House of Baptism.' Rabbi Eleazer, the son of Jacob, says: 'In the gallery that went under the Chel he passed out through Tadi.' Dr. Lightfoot, in his Commentaries, says that the priests after suffering defilement 'were to bathe as was said before, and the way to the bathing-place is expressed in these words: "He goeth down a turning staircase that went under the Temple." Therefore it is hard to say which way this passage to the bathing-place lay, since the word will enlarge it to any part of the Temple. It appeareth it was some vault underground through which they passed; into which vault they went down by a turning pair of stairs, out of the northwest room of Beth Mokad. And from thence whither they went, whether under the Chel, as Rabbi Eleazer conceiveth, or under some part of the court or mountain of the house, it is but in vain to search; it seemeth the bath was under-ground, and a room by it with a fire in it to warm themselves at when they had done bathing.' We have, then, the certainty that the passage from Mokad to the House of Baptism was under-ground, and the inference that Tadi was on the same level and under-ground also. Now, looking at Dr. Lightfoot's plan, placed over the Sanctuary, we see that Nitsots is over the passage down into the Sakhra, and that there is a passage running in the direction of Mokad, and which appears to unite with Tadi above the northern edge of the Mosque Platform, at a point where there is a hollow sound as of vaults underneath."

Return showing the height of courses in the Sanctuary

No. of letters given to each course.	1st Epoch. Wilson's Arch.	1st Epoch. Prophet's Gate-way.	2d Epoch. Southwest Angle.	2d Epoch. 64 ft. 6 in. east of S. W. Angle.	2d Epoch. 90 ft. east of S. W. Angle.	2d Epoch. 213 ft. east of S. W. Angle.	1st. W. of Triple Gate.	1st. Triple Gate.
	1	2	3	4	5	6	7	8
	Ft. in.	Ft. in.	Ft. in.	Ft. in.	Ft. in.	Ft. in.	Ft. in.	Ft. in.
8	...	3 5	...	...	...	...	...	...
7	...	3 5	...	...	...	...	...	...
6	...	3 10	...	...	...	...	...	...
5		3 6	...	...	...	...	...	...
4	3 4½	3 4	...	...	...	...	...	...
3	. .	3 6	...	...	...	...	...	...
2	3 6	6 10*	...	...	...	...	...	...
1	3 3		3 2¼	3 2½	3 2	3 2	...	...
A	2 6	3 5	3 4	3 3	3 3	3 3	...	...
B	3 6	3 8	3 4½	3 6½	3 6½	3 5½	...	...
C	3 6	3 7	3 7	3 6	4 0	3 4	...	...
D	3 4	3 3	3 6	3 4	3 9½	3 10½		
E	3 9½	3 8	3 8	3 6¾	3 2½	3 2	5 10	5 9½
F	3 8½	3 8½	3 7½	3 7¾	3 0	2 10½		
G	3 8	3 8	3 6¾	3 5½	3 9	3 9	3 6	
H	3 9	3 9½	3 8½	3 6½	3 9	3 9	3 9	
I	3 3	3 4½	3 6½	3 4	3 9	3 8	3 9	
J	4 1	. .	4 0	3 11	3 8	3 8	. .	
K	3 11	. .	3 10½	3 11	3 9	3 3½	. .	...
L	3 11½	3 10½	3 10	3 10	3 9	3 6		
M	3 10	3 9½	3 9	3 9½	3 6	3 8¾		
N	3 9	3 11¼	3 8¼	. .	3 11	3 10		
O	3 9	3 6¾	3 4	. .	3 8	3 4½		
P	3 6	3 6½	3 9	. .	3 9	3 7½		
Q	2 10½	3 5	. .	. .	3 9	3 6¾		
R		3 6½	. .	. .	. .	3 9		
S		3 6	. .	. .	. .	3 8½		
T		3 5½	. .	. .	. .	4 0		
U		3 7½	. .	. .	. .	3 8½		
V		2 5½		. .	. .			
W				. .	. .			
X				. .	. .			
Y				. .	. .			
Z				. .	. .			
a				. .	. .			
b					. .			
c					. .			
d					. .			
e								
f								
g								

* Lintel.

III.

wall as exposed on surface and in the several shafts.

EPOCH.		3D EPOCH.		
Single Gate.	Southeast Angle.	South end of Tower, N. E. Angle.	N. E. Angle, 19 ft. to south.	
9 Ft. in.	10 Ft. in.	11 Ft. in.	12 Ft. in.	
...	...	3 7½	3 7½	
...	...	3 10	3 10	
...	...	3 10	3 10	
...	...	3 1½	3 1½	
...	, ,	3 9	3 9	
...	, ,	, ,	, ,	
...	, ,	, ,	, ,	
...	, ,	, ,	, ,	
...	, ,	, ,	, ,	
...	...	, ,	, ,	
5 11	6 1	, ,	, ,	
...	...	, ,	, ,	
3 5½	3 5½	, ,	, ,	
	3 9½	, ,	, ,	
	3 9	, ,	, ,	
, ,	3 8½	, ,	3 4	
, ,	3 8½	3 5	3 5½	
Opening	3 9	3 4½	3 6	
3 8	3 8	3 5	3 5	
Opening to channel	3 9	3 5	3 9	
	3 9	3 5	3 9½	
3 9	3 9	4 0	4 0	
3 9	3 9	4 0	3 11½	
3 9	3 9	4 0	3 4½	
	3 9	3 2½	2 10	
	3 8	3 0½	3 5½	
	3 9	3 4½	In rock.	
	3 9	3 4½		
	, ,	4 0		
	, ,	3 6½		
	4 6	3 11		
	4 0	3 1½		
	4 0	2 11		
	3 6	2 10½		
	4 2½	3 1½		
	3 7½	2 10½		
	4 2½	2 7½		
	4 3½			
	3 8			

The wall would appear to have been built at three epochs, and therefore the courses are not of the same height all round; the bottom of course D is nearly on a level throughout.

Some of the more important levels are given:

Bottom of B, springing of Wilson's Arch . . 2391.6 ft.
" of 1 and 2, Hutel Prophet's Gate . . 2338.5 ft.
" of C, springing of Robinson's Arch, and at S. W. Angle . 2388 ft.
" of E and F, great course, Triple Gate 2380 ft.
" of course J in columns 11 and 12 . . 2363.2 ft.

... New work.
— · — Top of drafted work.
▬▬▬ Present surface of ground.
∿∿∿ Top of rough-faced work.
· · · Stones not measured.
▨ Rock.
▩ Presumed line of Rock

LINES OF ROCK.

1.—2396.75	*7.—2331. ft.
2.—2320. ft.	8.—2350 ft.
*3.—2321 ft.	9.—2361 ft.
*4.—2300 ft.	10.—2272. ft. 3 in.
5.—2289.8 ft.	11.—2292 ft.
6.—2322.4 ft.	12.—2327. ft.

* Presumed.

APPENDIX IV.

Return showing the height, etc., of Courses of Stone at Barclay's Gateway, exposed by an excavation commenced March 17, 1868, and completed. The stones 1 to 8 are above-ground, and were observed about 40 feet from Barclay's Gate to the north; the remainder, from B to V, are beneath the surface of the ground.

FORD OVER THE JORDAN.

PART II.

THE HOLY LAND.

THE SEA OF GALILEE.

BY CAPTAIN WILSON, R.E.

WITH the exception of Jerusalem, there is no place in Palestine which excites deeper interest than that lake district in which our Lord passed so large a portion of the last three years of His life, and in which He performed so many of His mighty works. "What is the Sea of Galilee like?" is one of the first questions a traveller is asked on his return from the Holy Land; and a question which he finds it extremely difficult to answer satisfactorily. Some authors describe its beauties in glowing terms, while others assert that the scenery is tame and uninteresting; neither perhaps quite correct, though representing the impressions produced at the time on the writer's mind.

There are, it is true, no pine-clad hills rising from the very edge of the lake; no bold headlands break the outline of its shores, and no lofty precipices throw their shadow over its waters; but it has, nevertheless, a beauty of its own which would always make it remarkable. The hills, except at Khan Minyeh, where there is a small cliff, are recessed from the shore of the lake, or rise gradually from it; they are of no great elevation, and their outline, especially on the eastern side, is not broken by any prominent peak; but everywhere from the southern end the snow-capped peak of Hermon is visible, standing out so sharp and clear in the bright sky that it appears almost within reach, and, toward the north, the western ridge is cut through by a wild gorge, "the Valley of Doves," over which rise the twin peaks or horns of Hattin. The shore-line, for the most part regular, is broken on the north into a series of little bays of exquisite beauty; nowhere more beautiful than at Gennesareth, where the beaches, pearly white with myriads of minute shells, are on one side washed by the limpid waters of the lake, and on the other shut in by a fringe of oleanders, rich in May with their "blossoms red and bright."

The surrounding hills are of a uniform brown color, and would be monotonous if it were not for the ever-changing lights and the brilliant tints at sunrise and sunset. It is, however, under the pale light of a full moon that the lake is seen to the greatest advantage, for there is then a softness in the outlines, a calm on the water in which the stars are so brightly mirrored, and a perfect quiet in all around, which harmonize well with the feelings that cannot fail to arise on its shores. It is perhaps difficult to realize that the borders of this lake, now so silent and desolate, were once enlivened by the busy hum of towns and villages; and that on its waters hostile navies contended for supremacy. But there is one feature which must strike every visitor: and that is the harmony of the Gospel narrative with the places which it describes, giving us, as M. Renan happily expresses it, "un cinquième évangile, lacéré, mais lisible encore."

The lake is pear-shaped, the broad end being toward the north; the greatest width is six and three-quarter miles, from Mejdel, "Magdala," to Khersa, "Gergesa," about one-third of the way down, and the extreme length is twelve and a quarter miles. The Jordan enters at the north, a swift, muddy stream, coloring the lake a good mile from its mouth, and passes out pure and bright at the south. On the northwestern shore of the lake is a plain, two and a half miles long and one mile broad, called by the Bedawin El Ghuweir, but better known by its familiar Bible name of Gennesareth; and on the northeast, near Jordan's mouth, is a swampy plain, El Batihah, now much frequented by wild-boar, formerly the scene of a skirmish between the Jews and

Romans, in which Josephus met with an accident that necessitated his removal to Capernaum. On the west there is a recess in the hills, containing the town of Tiberias; and on the east, at the mouths of Wadys Semakh and Fik, are small tracts of level ground. On the south the fine open valley of the Jordan stretches away toward the Dead Sea, and is covered in the neighborhood of the lake with luxuriant grass.

The water of the lake is bright, clear, and sweet to the taste, except in the neighborhood of the salt-springs, and where it is defiled by the drainage of Tiberias. Its level, which varies considerably at different times of the year, is between 600 and 700 feet below that of the Mediterranean —a peculiarity to which the district owes its genial winter climate. In summer the heat is great, but never excessive, as there is usually a morning and evening breeze. Sudden storms, such as those mentioned in the New Testament, are by no means uncommon; and I had a good opportunity of watching one of them from the ruins of Gamala on the eastern hills. The morning was delightful; a gentle easterly breeze, and not a cloud in the sky to give warning of what was coming. Suddenly, about mid-day, there was a sound of distant thunder, and a small cloud, "no bigger than a man's hand," was seen rising over the heights of Lubieh to the west. In a few moments the cloud appeared to spread, and heavy black masses came rolling down the hills toward the lake, completely obscuring Tabor and Hattin. At this moment the breeze died away, there were a few minutes of perfect calm, during which the sun shone out with intense power, and the surface of the lake was smooth and even as a mirror; Tiberias, Mejdel, and other buildings, stood out in sharp relief from the gloom behind; but they were soon lost sight of as the thunder-gust swept past them, and rapidly advancing across the lake lifted the placid water into a bright sheet of foam: in another moment it reached the ruins, driving myself and companion to take refuge in a cistern, where, for nearly an hour, we were confined, listening to the rattling peals of thunder and torrents of rain. The effect of half the lake in perfect rest, while the other half was in wild confusion, was extremely grand; it would have fared badly with any light craft caught in mid-lake by the storm; and we could not help thinking of that memorable occasion on which the storm is so graphically described as "coming down" upon the lake.

The Sea of Galilee now, as in the days of our Saviour, is well stocked with various species of fish, some of excellent flavor. One species often appears in dense masses which blacken the surface of the water, the individual fish being packed so closely together that on one occasion a single shot from a revolver killed three. These shoals were most frequently seen near the shore of Gennesareth; perhaps not far from that place where the disciples let down their net into the sea, and "enclosed a great multitude of fishes; and their net brake."

There does not appear to be any thing volcanic in the origin of the lake, which is simply part of the great Jordan depression. The hills on either side are lime-stone, capped in places with basalt, which has three distinct sources: one at Kurn Hattin, or in its neighborhood; another near Khan Jubb Yusuf, north of the lake; and a third in the Jaulan district. Earthquakes are frequent, and sometimes extremely violent; as, for example, that of 1837, which laid Tiberias in ruins, and caused the death of seven hundred persons; and the scarcely less terrible one which occurred in 1759. There are in the basin of the lake a number of warm springs, which are said to have increased both in volume and temperature after the earthquake of 1837.

The above description will, it is hoped, give the reader some idea of the general character of the lake district, and enable him, with the assistance of the map, to realize the position of the places in the following narrative. I have at the end added a few notes on the sites of the three cities, and the probability of the identification of Capernaum with Tel Hum and Chorazin with Kerazeh.

TELL HUM.

WEST SIDE OF LAKE FROM JORDAN'S ENTRANCE TO ITS EXIT.

At the mouth of the Jordan, on its western bank, are a few small mounds and heaps of stones called Abu Zany, the site, according to Dr. Thompson, of the Galilean Bethsaida; and not far from the eastern bank, shaded by palm-trees, are traces of an ancient village, and foundations of old walls, among which are scattered a few Arab tombs, and fragments of basaltic columns. This place the same author identifies, and with great probability, with Bethsaida-Julias, the burial-place of Philip the Tetrarch, who had rebuilt the town and called it Julias, after the emperor's daughter. From the Jordan to Tel Hum, a distance of two miles, there is little of interest, no ruins, and but scant vegetation, except where two small springs, Ain Zany and Ain Aysheh, run down through the basaltic rocks to the lake. Tel Hum was the first of our many pleasant camps on the shores of the Sea of Galilee. We had left Safed, on the heights above, in a keen easterly wind, chilled by the snow which still lay on the Jaulan plateau, and were delighted with the genial climate which we found at the lake when we had descended to its level. We were soon among those ruins which, if they are, as we believe them to be, those of Capernaum, must always have such a lasting interest. The season was favorable for an examination, the tall thistles which hide the ruins in early summer not having yet reared their heads; and we readily made our way to the "White Synagogue" and the more conspicuous building at the water's edge. It needed but a glance to show that the latter had been almost entirely built with limestone-blocks taken from the Synagogue, and to this therefore we principally turned our attention. A party of Arabs, brought down from Safed, were set to work, and cleared out a large portion of the interior, sufficient to enable a plan to be made. Excavation with no means but those the country could provide was no easy matter; no picks or shovels, not even a crow-bar, or a piece of wood large enough to be of any use, could be pro-

cured; the earth was laboriously scraped into baskets and
carried away, while the heavy stones were turned over by
our living crow-bar, a man of great strength, with a short
neck, who appeared to have been born for the purpose. He
would dig a hole at the foot of the great limestone-blocks
to receive his head and shoulders, and then, raising his feet
against the face of the stones, exert all his power to move
them, rarely failing to do what he attempted.

The Synagogue, built entirely of white limestone, must
once have been a conspicuous object, standing out from the
dark basaltic background; it is now nearly level with the
surface, and its capitals and columns have been for the most
part carried away or turned into lime. The original building is 74 feet 9 inches long, by 56 feet 9 inches wide; it is
built north and south, and at the southern end has three entrances. In the interior we found many of the pedestals of
the columns in their original positions, and several capitals of
the Corinthian order buried in the rubbish; there were also
blocks of stone which had evidently rested on the columns
and supported wooden rafters. Outside the Synagogue
proper, but connected with it, we uncovered the remains of
a later building, which may be those of the church which
Epiphanius says was built at Capernaum, and was described
by Antonius, A. D. 600, as a Basilica enclosing the house of
Peter. It may be asked what reason there is for believing
the original building to have been a Jewish synagogue, and
not a temple or church. Seen alone there might have been
some doubt as to its character, but, compared with the number of ruins of the same character which have lately been
brought to notice in Galilee, there can be none. Two of
these buildings have inscriptions in Hebrew over their main
entrances; one in connection with a seven-branched candlestick, the other with figures of the paschal lamb, and all
without exception are constructed after a fixed plan, which
is totally different from that of any church, temple, or
mosque, in Palestine. For a description of the very marked
peculiarities which distinguish the synagogues from other

buildings I would refer the reader to an article on the subject in the Second Quarterly Statement of the Palestine Exploration Fund. If Tel Hum be Capernaum, this is without a doubt the synagogue built by the Roman centurion (Luke vii. 4, 5), and one of the most sacred places on earth. It was in this building that our Lord gave the well-known discourse in John vi., and it was not without a certain strange feeling that on turning over a large block we found the pot of manna engraved on its face, and remembered the words, "I am that bread of life. Your fathers did eat manna in the wilderness, and are dead."

Round the Synagogue, and stretching up the gentle slope behind, are the ruins of the ancient town, covering a larger extent of ground than we had been led to expect. The whole area, half a mile in length by a quarter in breadth, was thickly covered with the ruined walls of private houses, among which we thought we could trace a main street, leading in the direction of Chorazin. At the northern extremity of the town two remarkable tombs were found, one constructed with limestone-blocks below the surface of the ground, which must have been a work of great labor, as the hard basalt on the surface had first to be cut away; the other, a rectangular building capable of holding a large number of bodies, which is above-ground, and appears to have been whitewashed within and without. It is possibly this description of tomb to which our Lord refers in Matt. xxiii. 27, where He compares the Scribes and Pharisees to "whited sepulchres," beautiful in outward appearance, but within "full of dead men's bones:" a similar building may also have been the home of the demoniac at Gergesa.

The shore was eagerly searched, but without success, for traces of an artificial harbor. The boats which formerly belonged to the town must always have taken shelter at Et Tabigah, or, as is just as probable, have been drawn up on the bank when not in use. There are, however, along the shore several fish-traps made by the Bedawin, which some travellers have taken for the remains of piers; they consist of enclosures, made with large stones, in the shallow water, an opening being left for the fish to enter by; in this manner a few fish are caught each night.

Before leaving Capernaum we cannot help drawing attention to the additional force and beauty which our Lord's words in Matt. xi. 23 derive by adopting the reading of the two oldest known MSS. of the New Testament (the Sinaitic and Vatican): "And thou, Capharnaum! shalt thou be exalted unto heaven? thou shalt be brought down to hell." There is a reproach conveyed in this question to "His own city" which is lost in the rendering of the authorized version; and it is impossible to draw from it the fanciful conclusion that Capernaum was on a hill, as a late writer has done, from the words, "And thou, Capernaum, which art exalted unto heaven."

An hour's journey (2½ miles) north of Tel Hum, and on the left bank of the valley which falls into the lake near it, are the ruins of Kerazeh, Chorazin. As early as 1740 Pococke heard the name of Gerasi, and identified it with Chorazin; and since his time the place has been mentioned and visited by more than one traveller; but perhaps, owing to the peculiar character of the masonry, barely to be distinguished at one hundred yards' distance from the rocks which surround it, and the shortness of their visits, they have failed to appreciate the extent and significance of the ruins. They cover an area as large, if not larger, than the ruins of Capernaum, and are situated partly in a shallow valley, partly on a rocky spur formed by a sharp bend in Wady Kerazeh, or, as it is called lower down, Wady Tel Hum, here a wild gorge eighty feet deep. From this last place there is a beautiful view of the lake to its southern end; and here too are gathered the most interesting ruins — a synagogue, with Corinthian capitals, niche heads and other ornaments cut, not as at Tel Hum, in limestone, but in the hard black basalt. Many of the dwelling-houses are in a tolerably perfect state, the walls being in some cases six feet high; and, as they are probably the same class of houses as that in which our Saviour dwelt, a description of them may be interesting. They are generally square, of different sizes—the largest measured was nearly 30 feet— and have one or two columns down the centre to support the roof, which appears to have been flat, as in the modern Arab houses. The walls are about two feet thick, built of masonry or of loose blocks of basalt; there is a low doorway in the centre of one of the walls, and each house has windows 12 inches high and $6\frac{1}{2}$ inches wide. In one or two cases the houses were divided into four chambers.

Almost in the centre of the ancient town is a fine tree with spreading branches, beneath which a spring rises up and flows down the valley; by its side are the tombs of two Bedawi sheikhs, over which passing travellers have hung shreds from their many-colored garments, and a few yards to the south a large building with remnants of Ionic capitals. On the north we found traces of the paved road which connected Chorazin with the great caravan-road to Damascus.

Westward along the shore of the lake, a mile and a half from Tel Hum, is the charming little bay of Et Tabigah, and the great spring which is without a doubt the fountain of Capharnaum, mentioned by Josephus as watering the plain of Gennesareth. The bay is about half a mile across, and on its western side is shut in by the cliff of Khan Minyeh, the only place at which the shore of the lake cannot be followed. There is a small tract of fertile land, but we could find no ruins except those connected with the mills or water-works. There are five fountains, all more or less brackish, and varying in temperature from $73\frac{1}{2}°$ to $86\frac{1}{2}°$; four are small, but the one mentioned above is by far the largest spring in Galilee, and was estimated to be more than half the size of the celebrated source of the Jordan at Banias. It rises to the surface with great force, at a temperature of $86\frac{1}{2}°$, which can hardly be considered warm in such a climate as that of the lake district. Most of the

water now runs to waste, producing a quantity of rank
luxuriant vegetation; but some of it is collected in a small
reservoir, and is thence carried off by an aqueduct to a mill
owned by a man of Safed, the only one in working order of
five that were built by the great chieftain Dhaher el 'Amr.
The mills are small towers with two circular shafts, to the
top of which the water is brought by aqueducts, and then,
falling down, turns the machinery at the bottom. Connected with this fountain are the remains of some remarkable works which at one time raised its waters to a higher
level, and conveyed them bodily into the plain of Gennesareth for the purposes of irrigation. The source is enclosed
in an octagonal reservoir of great strength, by means of
which the water was raised about twenty feet to the level
of an aqueduct that ran along the side of the hill. Strong
as the reservoir was, the water has at last broken through
it, and there is now little more than two feet left at the bottom, in which a number of small fish may be seen playing
about. After leaving the reservoir the aqueduct can be
traced at intervals following the contour of the ground to
the point where it crossed the beds of two water-courses on
arches, of which the piers may still be seen; it then turns
down toward the lake, and runs along the hill-side on the
top of a massive retaining wall, of which fifty or sixty
yards remain, and lastly passes round the Khan Minyeh cliff
by a remarkable excavation in the solid rock, which has
been noticed by all travellers. The elevation of the aqueduct at this point is sufficient to have enabled the water
brought by it to irrigate the whole plain of Gennesareth;
and, though we could only trace it for a few hundred yards
inland, it was not improbably carried right round the head
of the plain: the same causes which have almost obliterated
it in the small plain of Tabigah would fully account for its
disappearance in Gennesareth.

On passing round the cliff mentioned above, the first object which strikes the eye is the rich green of the turf
which borders the fountain of the Fig-tree, "Ain et Tin," a

fitting commencement to the rich plain of Gennesareth which stretches out beyond it. The spring is small, and, although there are two heads, it is not more than one-fourth the size of the fountain of Et Tabigah. It is very little above the level of the lake, which at times, judging from the old water-marks, rises into it, and it is slightly brackish, and considered unhealthy by the Bedawin, who invariably use the water of the lake in preference. A short distance north of the spring is Khan Minyeh, almost a ruin, though inhabited by a few Arabs. The Khan was doubtless built for the convenience of travellers to Damascus, and is at least as old as the twelfth century, being mentioned by Bohaeddin in his "Life of Saladin." West of the spring are the ruins which Dr. Robinson, the learned American traveller, identifies with Capernaum. They form a series of mounds, covering an extent of ground small in comparison with either those of Tel Hum or Kerazeh. We made some small excavations in these, but did not succeed in finding the remains of any building of great size. The walls were rudely built, and the fragments of pottery dug up appeared to be modern. There were traces of a thick well surrounding the site. No fragments of columns, capitals, or carved stones, were found in the ruins, nor could any be seen in the walls of the Khan, or round the tombs close by—a fact which seems to indicate that the ruins are of modern date, or at any rate never contained any building such as the synagogues or churches found elsewhere, as in all other places old material is invariably found built into the walls of later buildings where they are near old sites.

On the hill above Khan Minyeh are a few unimportant ruins, with a small platform, to which there is an ascent by rude steps, called Tel Lareyné. About a mile north of this, on the hills above Et Tabigah, are other ruins, Khurbet Khureibeh, remnants of walls, with a few door-posts and lintels, and fragments of columns of basalt. Not far from this are several tombs cut, like modern graves, in the rock, and covered with stone lids after the manner of sarcophagi.

Southward from Khan Minyeh stretches the plain of Gennesareth, with its charming bays and its fertile soil, rich with the scourings of the basaltic hills; the plain is now thickly covered with brushwood, and a few isolated patches of corn are cultivated by the Bedawin, who depend on the winter rains for success in raising it; but formerly it was watered by irrigation, and must have been extremely productive, equalling, if not exceeding, in this respect the larger plain of Damascus. Josephus describes the district in glowing terms, and in this case at any rate he does not appear to have exaggerated. The hills, which rise rather abruptly from the plain, are broken by three valleys or wadys, down which in winter small streams of water flow to the lake. The first of these from Khan Minyeh is the "Valley of the Column," Wady Amûd, which rises in the recesses of Jurmuk, the highest mountain of Galilee, and forces its way down through a deep cleft in the limestone. Next in order comes Wady Rubudiyeh, which drains a large district to the west, and runs through an open valley with thickets of wild olive near its head, strikingly in contrast with the wild gorge, through which the waters of the third, Wady Hamâm, pass. From the mouths of each of these valleys aqueducts are carried to the right and left, for the irrigation of the plain. Some appear to be very old, and may formerly have been connected with the aqueduct from the Tabigah spring, which would supply water when the streams were dry. Between Wady Rubudiyeh and Wady Hamâm is the "Round Fountain," Ain Mudawarah, which is held by some travellers to be the fountain of Capernaum. There are, however, no ruins of consequence in the vicinity, and the wall which surrounds the spring is not sufficiently strong to raise the water to a higher level; there are no traces of aqueducts, and it seems never to have been used much for irrigation, as the water from the two streams on either side was brought almost up to it. The fountain is about one-third the size of that of Et Tabigah; the water is sweet, and rises at a temperature of 73°: a number of small fish were seen, and Mr. Tristram tells us, in his "Land of Israel," that he found several specimens of the Coracinus—a fish common also to the waters of the Nile.

At the southern extremity of the plain is a heap of ruins, now called Mejdel, the site of Magdala, once the home of that Mary whose history is so touchingly recorded in the New Testament. There are several mounds of rubbish along the shore of the lake toward Khan Minyeh, perhaps marking the sites of those towns and villages in which our Lord taught; and on the hills close to Wady Rubudiyeh is a village, Shusheh, inhabited by a band of Algerines who followed the fortunes of their Emir when he took up his home in the East, but evidently built on the *débris* of an ancient village or town. On the level ground below are five deserted mills, built like those at Tabigah by Dhaher el 'Amr.

From Mejdel, we made an expedition to the caves in Wady Hamám, once inhabited by robbers, but afterward the resort of hermits and monks. The cliffs on either side of the little stream rise almost perpendicularly to a height of about 1,200 feet, and in their faces are the curious system of caverns sometimes called Kalat ibn Ma'an. Our visit was paid to those on the right or southern bank, a short distance below the ruins of Arbela (Irbid). After climbing up the steep side of the valley we reached a flight of steps which led to the first tier of caverns; from this there was a circular staircase to a second row, and higher still were two other sets of chambers inaccessible from below: we were for some time at a loss to find out how the inhabitants reached their homes, but after a good search found the remains of some rock-hewn steps, which came down through a narrow cleft from the ground above. The caverns are of considerable extent, and those on the same level are connected by narrow passages cut in the face of the rock, the sides next the valley being protected by walls. The mouths of the caverns are closed with masonry, in which a number of basaltic stones brought from the plain below are used; the interiors appear to have been plastered, and there are recesses in their sides which may have been sleeping-places. The appearance of the masonry and other details gave us the impression that the caverns had been used by Christian communities after the robbers had disappeared, and reminded us strongly of the similar establishment in the Mount of Temptation near Jericho. As a robbers' den the place is perfect; a sheer precipice, with only a few steps to give access to the caves, inaccessible and perfectly safe from all attacks, except that one which Herod the Great so successfully employed. The robbers were strong enough to meet Herod in open battle, but after a sharp encounter they were defeated, and retired to the caves, in which they were besieged. Herod, finding all approach from the valley impracticable, had a number of large boxes prepared, and in these he let down his soldiers, by means of a strong chain, from the top of the cliff. Then ensued one of the most extraordinary fights which perhaps ever took place: the soldiers swinging in mid-air attacked the robbers with fire and sword, or with long hooks tried to pull them out over the precipices; the latter tried in turn to break the chains which connected the boxes with mother earth, but all to no purpose—they were completely subdued. Toward the end of the fight one of those strange scenes occurred which are almost without parallel in the history of other countries: a father stands at the mouth of his rock-cut home, and orders his seven children to come out one by one; as each appears a sword is thrust into his side, and he falls headlong over the precipice; then follows the wife, and last the stern parent, after upbraiding Herod with his low origin, springs forward, and is dashed to pieces, sooner than surrender to the victor.

The series of caverns on the north or left bank of the valley we did not visit, but we made an examination of the ruins on the height above which were first described by Irby and Mangles. They consist of a thick wall with flanking towers, designed apparently to prevent an enemy from ap-

proaching the caverns from above, and enclose a triangular
piece of ground bounded on two sides by inaccessible precipices. These may perhaps be the fortifications which Josephus says he built to protect the caves.

Opposite on the southern heights lie the ruins of Irbid,
the ancient Arbela, a place once of some importance; part
of the surrounding wall is standing, and there are two small
pools, several cisterns, and the remains of numerous houses
belonging to the old town, among which, easily discernible,
are those of a later Arab village. Close to the edge of the
steep descent to Wady Hamám is an old synagogue, similar
to those found in other places, except that the door is on the
eastern side instead of the southern, an arrangement necessitated by the rapid rise of the ground to the south. The
building was at one time used as a mosque, and many changes
appear to have been made in it at that time, as we found
both Corinthian and Ionic capitals in the rubbish; there
were too the same semi-barbarous mouldings, and peculiar
arrangement of columns, which are distinctive marks of the
Galilean synagogues.

From Irbid a fine rich plain stretches westward to the
village of Hattin and the foot of the steep ascent which is
crowned by the "Horns of Hattin." This curious peak
with its twin horns is, according to tradition, the mount on
which our Lord delivered the beautiful discourse in Matt. v.
7, and is also remembered as the scene of the last expiring
struggle of the Christians at the fatal battle of Hattin. Apparently an ancient crater, and one of the centres from which
the lava flowed down toward Tiberias, "the Horns" with
the hollow between them form a sort of natural fortress;
and there is no doubt it was formerly used as one, for in the
interior is a cistern, and round the edge of the depression
are the remains of walls. On the south the peak rises not
more than 40 or 50 feet above the great plain on which the
battle was fought, but on the north there is a sharp descent
to the plain of Hattin and "Valley of Doves;" from the
summit there is a commanding view, on one side over the

rich plains toward Tabor, and on the other over the ruins of Arbela, the plain of Gennesareth, and the northern coast of the lake.

The tradition which makes Kurn Hattin the Mount of Beatitudes is of Latin origin, and not older than the twelfth or thirteenth century; but the place is so well adapted for the delivery of a discourse to a large multitude, that in this case we may well believe it was correctly chosen by those who first selected it.

The battle of Hattin, which was fought under the fierce heat of a July sun (5th July, 1187), and resulted in the loss of the cross, the capture of the King of Jerusalem, and the almost total destruction of the Christian host, is one of those curious encounters in which the fate of one side seemed ordained from the commencement. Never perhaps could the old saying "Quos Deus vult perdere, prius dementat" be applied with more justice than to the leaders of the Christian army: encamped round the springs of Sefuriyeh, the ancient Sepphoris, they learned that Saladin had taken Tiberias; a council of war was at once called, and Count Raymond's advice to remain near water and fortify their camp adopted: it was now midnight, the knights and barons had retired to rest, when suddenly a trumpet sounded through the camp, and the heralds gave the word to arm. The King, influenced by the Grand Master of the Templars, had changed his fickle mind and determined to march at once to Tiberias, and would not even give an audience to the knights who wished to warn him against the danger of such an advance. It must have been daybreak before the army was in readiness to march, and at that time of the year the sun soon makes its power felt. The road from Sefuriyeh to Tiberias passes up a long open valley till it reaches Lubieh, whence it commences its descent to the lake, at first gradually over the plain in front of Kurn Hattin, then rapidly to the town of Tiberias. Up this road, where there is no water, no shade, and where the glare of the limestone-rocks adds to the intense heat of the sun, the Christians advanced, harassed on all sides by the light-horse of the Saracens. In the afternoon they reached Lubieh, exhausted by the heat and want of water, and found the army of Saladin drawn up on the heights above Tiberias: then again evil counsel prevailed; instead of at once attacking, wearied though they were, and forcing their way to the lake, the soldiers lay down for the night on the bare, waterless heights; those who, tormented with thirst, tried to search for water, were cut off by their active enemies, and, to add to the horrors of the night, the dry grass and shrubs to windward were fired by the Saracens. The result of the next day could not be doubtful; the Christians fought with their usual valor, but two days' exertion under a Syrian sun was, without water, too much for the bravest; the footmen and archers failed first and threw aside their arms, then the knights retired to the height of Kurn Hattin, where prodigies of valor were performed; thrice the attacks of the Saracens were driven back; then, the cross lost, the Bishop of Ptolemais who bore it dead, and Count Raymond with his followers fled, the King, with the few knights who remained, surrendered to Saladin. The black basaltic rocks which surround the summit seem in keeping with the last scene of the sad drama—the death of two hundred Templars and Hospitallers who were executed after the battle. Dean Stanley, in his notice of the battle, has drawn attention to the touching circumstance that the last struggle of the Crusaders occurred " in the presence of the holiest scenes of Christianity."

We must now return to Mejdel and continue our journey southward along the lake. About half-way between Mejdel and Tiberias, a distance of three miles, a small ravine comes down from the hills, and opens out on to a small triangular plain covered with the richest verdure; it is now studded with nebek-trees, but wanting these would be a "level grassy spot," such as it was when pointed out to Arculf as the scene of the miraculous feeding of the five thousand. Within a few yards of the lake, and surrounded by thick brushwood, are three springs; the centre one, called

Ain Barideh, the "Cold Spring," has a temperature of 80°.

Two of the springs are surrounded by walls, apparently to raise the water for mill-purposes, as there are circular shafts similar to those seen at Tabigah. The water is sweet and pleasant to the taste. Tradition at present points out a spot on the brow of the hill between Kurn Hattin and Tiberias as that where the multitude "sat down in ranks, by hundreds and by fifties," apparently following the reading of John vi. 3, where it is said, "Jesus went up unto a mountain." The earlier tradition of the end of the seventh century, as given by Arculf, was that the scene of the miracle was at Ain Barideh, where the five thousand "drank after they had eaten their fill." All late writers on Palestine have agreed that the site should rather be looked for on the eastern side of the lake, but the Sinaitic version of Luke ix. 10, and John vi. 22, 23, places the old tradition in a different light, for in the former there is no mention of Bethsaida, and in the latter it is said that the place was close to Tiberias. This question will come more fully before us when discussing the site of Capernaum, on which it has an important bearing.

Following the road from Ain Barideh to Tiberias, three small springs on the side of the hill are passed, and to each is attached a fragment of an old duct for irrigation purposes.

The modern town of Tiberias, or Tabariyeh as the Arabs call it, occupies only a small portion of the ground covered by the ancient city, the remains of which may be seen stretching southward toward the hot springs. The houses are surrounded on the land side by a wall with flanking towers, toward the water they are open; the strong wall is now of little use, as it has never been repaired since the great earthquake of 1837 shook it to its foundations, and the usual road by which visitors enter passes through one of the rents. At the time of the earthquake the bed of the lake appears to have sunk in front of the town; we noticed that one of the towers at the southeast corner had been thrown violently forward; and Mr. Macgregor, at a lower stage of the water, was able to distinguish from his canoe the remains of a mole or sea-wall which had quite disappeared. Tiberias, founded by Herod Antipas, played a conspicuous part in the war with the Romans, and was fortified at that time by Josephus; on the approach of Vespasian, however, it surrendered without a blow. It afterward became, and remained for several centuries, the chief seat of Jewish learning in Palestine; and has remained to this day one of the favorite places of residence of those Jews who return to the land of their fathers. The town is now chiefly remarkable for the filth of its streets and the activity of its vermin, who are in such numbers and so rapacious that even the Arabs noticed them, and have a saying that "the king of fleas holds his court at Tiberias." A small church, said to stand on the site of St. Peter's house, and a mosque half in ruins, with its court-yard and fountain, are the only buildings which attract attention; but lying about may still be seen some traces of the grandeur of the ancient city —here a magnificent block of polished granite from Upper Egypt, cut into a basin 6 feet 4 inches in diameter, there a hunting-scene carved on the surface of a hard black lintel of basalt. To the south the ruins cover some extent of ground; there are the remains of a sea-wall, and of some portions of a city wall, 12 feet thick; many traces of old buildings, broken shafts and columns, half buried in rubbish; and at one place, foundations which appear to belong to a church, perhaps to that which was built during the reign of Constantine on the site of Adrian's unfinished temple. The present water supply of Tiberias is derived from the lake, but during the Roman occupation the inhabitants were far more particular in the quality of what they drank; and we find extensive remains of a fine aqueduct which brought the sparkling waters of some fountains at the foot of the Ard el Hamma, below the southern end of the lake, into the ancient city. The length of this aqueduct is about nine miles, and in places it is cut with great labor in the rock, running along the side of the hills which border the lake.

A mile and a quarter south of modern Tiberias are the well-known hot springs; we counted and took the temperature of seven distinct springs, ranging from 132.2° to 142.2° Fahr. A strong smell of sulphur rises with the water, and as it flows down to the lake a green deposit is formed; the springs rise from the limestone formation. Three of the fountains have been enclosed, but only one of the buildings, that erected by Ibrahim Pacha, is in a decent state of repair; in this the water is received into a circular basin about three feet deep, round which there are marble columns and a paved marble floor; the temperature is 136.7°, and the steam given off is so dense that it was difficult to read our thermometer with the aid of a candle. This bath is much frequented by the poor Jews of Tiberias, and is said to give great relief in cases of rheumatism.

A short distance south of the springs are the remains of a wall, 11 feet 6 inches thick, running from the lake to the mountain, and to the north of it above the springs are extensive ruins, which may have been suburbs of old Tiberias. The wall has been considered part of the camp which Vespasian established in this neighborhood; but it seems to have a more permanent character than a camp-wall would have had.

Between the baths and Kerak, at the point where Jordan leaves the lake, there are two places with some inconsiderable ruins. Kerak, or Tarichææ, commanding as it did the southern end of the road which ran along the western shore of the lake, and also the three bridges over Jordan in its immediate vicinity, was formerly of great importance, and we find it repeatedly mentioned in the account which Josephus gives of his campaign in Galilee. The position of the place is naturally strong; a mound about 30 feet high, surrounded on three sides by water, and on the fourth by a broad ditch, through which a branch of Jordan appears to have passed: this feature is produced by the eccentric course of the Jordan, which soon after leaving the lake takes a sharp turn and flows nearly northeast. The land approach was by a causeway, well provided with culverts, across the ditch, and this was defended by a small fort or tower on the land side. There are also the remains of a bridge connecting the town with the eastern side of Jordan. Of the town absolutely nothing remains but a heap of rubbish covered with broken pottery and fragments of sculpture, offering probably a rich field for excavation.

Tarichéae was taken by Titus after a sharp fight with the Jews on the plain outside (B. J. iii. 10, 1–6), and a day or two afterward there was a sea-fight near the same place, which is graphically described by Josephus (B. J. iii. 10, 9); 6,500 men are said to have been killed in the two engagements; the lake was colored with blood for some distance round, and the air tainted with the number of bodies on the shore.

EAST SIDE OF LAKE FROM JORDAN'S ENTRANCE TO ITS EXIT.

While staying at Tiberias we had endeavored to obtain from the Modir of the town an escort sufficient to enable us to examine the eastern shore of the lake at our leisure, but that worthy gentleman, who seemed to have a horror of the dwellers in black tents, threatened us with a guard of 100 sabres, an honor which we politely declined. Whether it was that our present was not large enough, or that it had diminished in passing through the hands of our dragoman, we could not find out; but our relations came to a close by the Governor's refusing to have any thing to do with two Englishmen who were insane enough to venture among Bedawin at open war with the Turkish Government. We were, however, determined to proceed, and after some trouble succeeded in hiring a boat to take us to the mouth of the Jordan, and meet us each night at certain fixed points with blankets and a tent; we were thus enabled to examine

on foot and in comfort a large portion of the eastern shore,
and our excursion turned out to be a remarkably pleasant
one, though brought to a rather abrupt conclusion. Our
friend the Modir we afterward came across when visiting a
Bedawin camp in the Jordan valley: much against his will
he had been ordered out to fight the Adwan; an order he
successfully obeyed by making his horsemen empty their
muskets every morning across the Jordan.

Leaving our heavy baggage at Tiberias in charge of
Corporal Phillips, whose name is well known from the beautiful series of photographs which he has taken for the Fund,
we (Lieutenant Anderson and self) embarked in one of the
three boats which represent the fleets which at one time
passed to and fro over the waters of the lake. Our crew
consisted of two Jews and an Arab boy, who was shortly
afterward accidentally shot by an English traveller; our
outfit, the clothes on our back, a tent, a couple of blankets,
and three days' provisions. A pleasant breeze was blowing
as we started, and, all sail set, we soon made our way to the
mouth of the Jordan, and landed on its eastern bank. Here
we made an examination of the ruins which have been described above (page 267), but soon found that our farther
progress was stopped by marshy ground and creeks with
deep water which ran in from the lake. We had, therefore,
to reëmbark and ascend the Jordan in the boat to a point
near Et Tel. At the mouth of the Jordan we found a large
number of Bedawin trying to escape from a body of Turkish
horsemen who were beating up the neighborhood for con-
scripts, and were able to help them across by lending our
boat after we had landed, the water being too deep to ford,
in consequence of a sudden freshet. This lucky accident
placed us at once on the most friendly terms with the Bedawin, and enabled us to make our friend the Modir some
return for his want of civility.

Et Tel lies on the slope of the hills at the point where
they break down to the plain of Butiha; there are here a
modern Bedawi village and a number of rude remains; no

shafts of columns, or fragments of sculpture, and with the
exception of a few door-lintels no dressed stone; all is of
basalt, and there is no appearance of its ever having been a
place of any importance. At the foot of the hill are two
springs, and round these a large number of the Tel Hum
Bedawin who had already escaped across the river were
encamped. We were received with much kindness, and allowed to go anywhere without being troubled with even a
cry for "bakshish." Et Tel has been identified with Bethsaida Julias, but it appears to be too far from the mouth of
the Jordan, and there is no trace of that magnificence with
which, according to Josephus, Julias was built.

The plain of Butiha, which lies on the east side of Jordan, is about two and a half miles long by one and a half
wide. Near the lake it is extremely swampy, but at the
upper end it is, like all basaltic soils, rich and productive.
Several streams cross it on their way to the lake; one, that
which comes down Wady Hajaj, larger than either of those
of Gennesareth. The coast-line is not nearly so beautiful as
that of the western plain, the bays being larger and not so
deep; and there is an absence of that pearly white beach
and fringe of oleanders which give such a charm to the
latter.

Our route from Et Tel lay along the base of the hills to
the stream of Wady Hajaj, which we forded, and shortly
afterward we crossed a smaller stream issuing from Wady
Daly. On the left bank of this are the ruins of an old
town; part of the wall which surrounded it remains, and
there are also fragments of columns, capitals, and some
blocks of stone with a variety of mouldings and ornament—
one with a well-cut scroll of vine-leaves with bunches of
grapes; the material is basalt, and mortar has been used in
building the walls. From this point we pushed on over
the beds of several small wadys to a fine terebinth-tree,
which is a conspicuous object from the western shore of the
lake, and had been one of our landmarks for the last three
weeks. Under its shade are several Arab tombs. We re-

mained some time making observations, and before reaching
our tent on the margin of the lake darkness had set in; the
ground was excessively swampy, and we had constantly to
wade up to our knees in water. Next morning we visited
a small grove of palm-trees, and some ruins near it called
Kefr Argib, consisting of a few rude foundations, fragments of columns, and a broken olive-press. From this
point there is a fine view northward of the Jordan valley
and the snow-capped peak of Hermon. A couple of hundred yards to the south is a curious oval mound, partly artificial, and built in two terraces supported by loose stone
walls; in the centre is a large tree, and the tomb of some
Bedawi sheikh. Here we turned up the side of the eastern
hills, and, after passing a broad level terrace well covered
with grass, reached the summit near a deserted Arab village called Sebba. A short distance beyond the gorge of
Wady Semakh was reached, and we had to descend its
almost precipitous side by a rough goat-track. A very good
geological section is exposed at this place, showing the
basalt overlying the white limestone, through which run
bands of flint conglomerate; it appears to contain no fossils.
At the point at which we struck it the valley is almost half
a mile wide, with a stream running down the centre; there
was good pasturage on each bank, which was covered with
the flocks of a Bedawi camp close by. The astonishment of
these people at seeing two Franks appear in the middle of
their tents without any warning was most amusing; but
here, as elsewhere among the dwellers in tents, we experienced nothing but kindness.

On the left bank of Wady Semakh, and at the point
where the hills end and the plain stretches out toward the
lake, are the ruins of Khersa (Gergesa). The site is enclosed by a wall three feet thick. The remains are not of
much importance, with the exception of those of a large
rectangular building lying east and west. On the shore of
the lake are a few ruined buildings, to which the same name
was given by the Bedawin. About a mile south of this, the

hills, which everywhere else on the eastern side are recessed from a half to three-quarters of a mile from the water's edge, approach within forty feet of it; they do not terminate abruptly, but there is a steep even slope, which we would identify with the " steep place " down which the herd of swine ran violently into the sea, and so were choked. A few yards off is a small intermittent hot spring.

That the meeting of our Lord with the two demoniacs took place on the eastern shore of the lake is plain from Matt. ix. 1, and it is equally evident, on an examination of the ground, that there is only one place on that side where the herd of swine could have run down a steep place into the lake, the place mentioned above. The eastern coast has since been carefully examined by Mr. Macgregor in his canoe, and he has come to exactly the same conclusion. A difficulty has arisen with regard to this locality in consequence of the different readings in the three Gospels. In Matthew our Saviour is said to have come into the country of the Gergesenes; in Luke and John into that of the Gadarenes. The old MSS. do not give any assistance here; but the similarity of the name Khersa to that of Gergesa is, as Dr. Thomson points out in the " Land and the Book," a strong reason for believing that the reading of Matthew is correct; and we have also the testimony of Eusebius and Origen that a village called Gergesa once existed on the borders of the lake. Perhaps the discrepancy may be explained by supposing that Gergesa was under the jurisdiction of Gadara. There do not appear to be any rock-hewn tombs near Khersa; but the demoniacs may possibly have lived in one of those tombs built above-ground which have been noticed under the head of Tel Hum, a form of tomb much more common in Galilee than has been supposed. I have entered into this question rather fully, as travellers have alternately asserted and denied the existence of a suitable locality on the eastern shore; and even such a carefully-compiled work as the " Dictionary of the Bible " has made the extraordinary blunder of placing the scene of the miracle at Gadara, now Umm Keis, a place from which the swine would have had a hard gallop of two hours before reaching the lake.

After passing the night at the water's edge nearly opposite Tiberias, we crossed the low ground at the mouth of Wady Fik, and commenced the ascent to Kalat el Husn, Gamala. Our way lay up a small valley on its southern side, and we soon came upon fragments of the old walls which had rolled down from above. The position is one of great strength, the only approach being over a narrow neck of land, which connects the town with the plateau on the east; on all other sides there is a rough, almost precipitous descent to the valleys below, and the rock has in places been scarped or cut away to give additional security. Josephus (B. J. iv. 1, 1) compares the shape to that of a camel's back, the hump representing the hill on which the town stood; and he gives a vivid description of its capture by the Romans, who, repulsed on one occasion with great loss, eventually took the place by assault, and put all the inhabitants to the sword. The space on the summit was larger than we had expected to find it, and was enclosed by a strong wall, of which there are many portions left. The town itself is a confused mass of ruins; at one point there are a few prostrate columns and capitals which appear to mark the site of a synagogue, at another a large building which may have been a church, for there are remains which leave no doubt that the place was occupied after its destruction by the Romans. The direction of a main street running from the neck down the centre of "the hump" can be easily traced. On the neck are several broken sarcophagi, and in the cliff on the left bank of the valley to the south are a number of rock-hewn tombs.

It had been our intention from this point to continue our journey round the lake to Tarichea, but the sudden storm which I have previously described (page 265), completely drenched and chilled us, and we were glad, as evening drew in, to return to our camp at Tiberias. Lieutenant Anderson, before the commencement of the storm, had gone off toward a village, Kefr Harib, on the heights to the south, and when it broke had been obliged to seek shelter among the fellahin. While in the village he was well treated, but on leaving he was followed by several of the men, who attempted to throw him down and rob him; fortunately, however, he was able to draw his revolver, and, taking advantage of the momentary pause which the sight of it caused, he succeeded in getting over the edge of the hill and making his way to the boat. From Wady Fik the distance between the base of the hills and the lake continually increases till it widens out into the broad plain of the Jordan Valley.

We were anxious before leaving Tiberias to pay a visit to the ruins of Umm Keis (Gadara), and, finding it impossible to obtain assistance from the Modir, we determined to go without escort, and started off one morning at daylight, followed at a respectful distance by our dragoman and muleteer, who had been pressed into the service, and looked any thing but happy. We crossed the Jordan at Kerak, having to swim our horses in consequence of the depth of water in the river, and then followed the shore of the lake to Semakh, a large village of mud huts. Here we met with fresh difficulties; our two attendants refused to proceed, and the sheikh of the village wished to inflict a large escort on us, which we politely declined. Our only chance was to push on by ourselves, and trust to finding Gadara from our knowledge of its general direction. We had hardly, however, gone one hundred yards when our trusty Nijim rode up to say that a boy would act as guide if he could get a horse; this was all we wanted, and, dismounting Nijim, we started across the plain with our new companion at a hand-gallop, which soon brought us to the mouth of the Jarmuk gorge. Immediately on entering the valley we were struck by the appearance of the stream, which had all the character of a mountain-torrent, rushing in places through deep chasms in the chalk, and flowing lazily along in others through small plains, where the contrast between the bright green of the spring verdure, the brilliant white of the chalk, and the sombre hue of the basalt above it, was very pleasing. After travelling some distance we reached the hot springs of Gadara, prettily situated on a small open space on the left bank of the river. The main spring, which gives off a body of water larger than that of Tiberias, rises in a basin, partly natural, partly artificial, whence it flows down to the river. The temperature is 110°, and the water being strongly impregnated with sulphur is extremely unpleasant to the taste and smell. The medicinal properties of the spring are highly valued by the Bedawin, who have made the place a sort of neutral ground, to which any one can resort, when ill, without fear of molestation; we found several men taking a course of hot baths. Close to the spring are the remains of baths, and all around are the ruins of houses, covering so large an extent of ground that we were led to believe this must have been a favorite watering-place, to which the inhabitants of Gadara resorted when the driving wind and rain of winter made the plateau above uncomfortable.

We now forded the Jarmuk, the water running strong over a rough slippery bottom and rising up to the horses' bellies, and ascended the steep face of the hill by a Bedawi track which led directly to Umm Keis. On reaching the summit we found ourselves in front of the eastern theatre, the form of which is perfect, though the upper part has fallen down and covered the seats with stones. A few yards to the east of this is the large cemetery, which forms one of the most peculiar features of the place; there are both rock-hewn tombs and sarcophagi; the former are cut in the limestone, without any attempt at concealment. A flight of steps leads down to a small court, from which two or three doors give access to the tomb chambers; the doors are of stone, and many of them are still almost perfect. These tombs are now occupied by fellahin, who bear rather a bad character, but we seemed to attract little attention. There are a large number of sarcophagi, ranged in two rows, one on either side of the great military road, which, after passing through the city, went eastward. The sarcophagi are all of basalt, and the universal use of this material, which though more enduring does not take such a fine polish as the limestone on which they rest, can only be accounted for by a caprice of fashion. The best general view of the ruins is from the eastern theatre, from which the western and larger theatre is about three hundred yards distant. This building is in an almost perfect state of preservation, and were it not for a little rubbish on the floor we might imagine that the earthquake, which appears to have ruined the city, was an affair of yesterday. The seats, which are very comfortable, appear to have left the mason's hands but a few hours, so fresh and sharp are the mouldings. In the vaults of the passages and vomitories hardly a stone is out of place, and they are so wide and lofty that we rode through them with ease. The approach to the theatre must have been extremely grand, passing from the main street over a grand platform, on each side of which were columns with Corinthian capitals. The main street running east and west through the city can be easily followed. The basalt pavement is in places quite perfect, and retains traces of the marks of chariot-wheels; along each side of the road lie a row of columns just as they fell. There are many other buildings toward the west, and a modern cemetery, said to be the favorite burying-place of the Beni Sakr Bedawin. A short ride westward from the city brought us to the brow of the hill over the Jordan Valley, from whence there is a magnificent view of the lake district, and also over the eastern plateau, seamed with the deep gorges of the Jarmuk and its tributaries. We were particularly struck with the appearance of the Jordan Valley, over which far and wide was spread a bright-green carpet of turf, a sight we had not seen before in Palestine. On our way down we came several times upon the old Roman road to Beisan (Scythopolis), and after crossing the Jarmuk by a deep ford reached Semakh as the sun was going down. We found our two men anxiously looking out for us, and were much amused at the change in their manner on the way home; there was no hanging back now, they pushed on in front, and as we approached Tiberias Nijim became greatly excited, firing off his gun, and telling every one he met how bravely he had taken his "Hawájahs" to Umm Keis, and how, after innumerable perils, he had brought them back again in safety.

CAPERNAUM, BETHSAIDA, CHORAZIN.

I now pass to an examination of the sites of the three cities, Capernaum, Bethsaida, Chorazin, and may at once state that no inscription has yet been found which enables us to say with certainty where any of them stood. Many facts have, however, been lately discovered, or more prominently brought forward, which seem to throw some gleams of light on what has hitherto been involved in such darkness. I allude especially to the identification of the spring at Et Tabigah with the fountain of Capharnaum, mentioned by Josephus; the extent and importance of the ruins at Kerazeh, and the different aspect which our Lord's journey across the lake, after feeding the five thousand, assumes in the Sinaitic version of the Gospels. For this last information, and much more, I am indebted to the Tauchnitz edition of the New Testament, a book which should be in the hands of all who study their Bible.

The sources from which it is possible to obtain any clew to the sites of the cities are—I. Josephus; II. The Bible; and III. Tradition, as represented by writers before the commencement of the Crusades. I place Josephus first, as his description of Capernaum is fuller than that contained in the Bible.

I. Josephus states (Vit. 71) that, hurt by a fall from his horse in a skirmish near Julias, on the banks of the Jordan, he was carried to a village called Capharnome; that he remained there that day, and was removed during the night

to Tarichea. There may have been many reasons why he
should not have been taken to Julias, then in his possession,
but rather carried to the next nearest town on the shore of
the lake, whence he could take ship to Tarichea; for it can
hardly be supposed that, having the command of the lake,
Josephus would make the journey by land. Travelling
westward from the Jordan, the first place one comes to is
Tel Hum. With this must be compared the account which
Josephus gives of the plan or district of Gennesareth.
After describing its wonderful fertility, he goes on to say
that it was watered thoroughout—such seems to be the force
of διάρδεται—by a fertilizing fountain called Capharnaum,
which some held to be a vein of the Nile, as it contained
the fish called Coracinus, also found in the lake near Alexandria. He gives the extent of this district along the border of the lake as thirty furlongs, a distance which agrees
almost exactly with that from Et Tabigah to Mejdel; and I
take it for granted that this district, or at any rate the plain
of Ghuweir from Khan Minyeh to Mejdel, is Gennesareth.*
It seems to me that there must have been something remarkable about this fountain of Capharnaum which called for
notice; and, on comparing the description of Josephus with
what is known of the ground, we find that there is nothing
peculiar about the Round Fountain, or Ain et Tin, while
there is at Et Tabigah a large spring, the water of which
was raised by artificial means, and carried across the low
ground and round the cliff of Kahn Minyeh, by a striking
piece of engineering, at a sufficient altitude to irrigate the
whole plan of Ghuweir from end to end. Had the Round
Fountain ever watered the plain, there must have been some
traces left of the aqueducts which conveyed the water; nothing of this kind could, however, be seen. The supply of
water from this spring is now not sufficient for irrigation,
and the land close to it is irrigated by water brought from

* I am aware of the view put forward by Dr. Tregelles and Mr. Thrupp
that the Batihah is Gennesareth, but I think their arguments are not sufficiently
forcible to disturb the claims of the plain of El Ghuweir.

the streams which run down Wadys Hamâm and Rubadiyeh. It may be said that the volume of water was formerly greater; but it is hardly probable that, if such had been the case, the labor and expense of making the aqueduct from Et Tabigah would have been incurred. As to Ain et Tin, it is a small, weak spring, and could never have irrigated any thing. The next question is that of the presence of the Coracinus, on which Dr. Tristram lays so much stress in his endeavor to fix the site of Capernaum. He obtained several specimens from the Round Fountain, and one from the lake near Tiberias. That the fish lives in the lake there can be little doubt; and there is no reason why it should not have lived at one time in the spring at Et Tabigah; the water is not too hot, for the temperature is only $86\frac{1}{2}°$; not greater than the shade temperature of the lake district in summer, or than that of the Round Fountain would be at that time of year. Dr. Tristram found none of the fish at Et Tabigah; but his search does not seem to have been exhausted, and the disappearance of the fish might easily be accounted for by the mills and the aqueducts and dams connected with them, which now all but close any direct passage from the lake to the spring. Under these circumstances, I think that, wherever the town of Capernaum may have been, the fountain of Capharnaum must be identified with the spring at Et Tabigah.

Josephus also gives some valuable indications as to the site of Bethsaida. He tells us Bethsaida was a village, raised to the dignity of a town by Philip, who changed its name to Julias, and built himself a tomb there, in which he was afterward buried with great pomp. We also gather that it was a town of Lower Gaulonitis (B. J. ii. 9, 1), that the Jordan passed by it (B. J. iii. 10, 7), and that it was situate at the Lake of Gennesareth (Antiq. xviii. 2. 1). With this also agrees the account of the battle with the Romans under Sylla (Vit. 70–72), which requires that Julias should be close to the Jordan, and not far from its mouth.

II. The Bible does not give much assistance in the identification of the sites of the three cities. In Matthew iv. 13, Capernaum is said to be "on the sea-coast, in the borders of Zabulon and Nepthalim." The word used for borders (τα ὅρια) does not mean the line of division between the two tribes, but rather the district occupied by them; and it is used in this sense in other passages, as "the coasts of Tyre and Sidon," "the coasts of Decapolis," etc. In addition it is not known where the boundary of the tribes was; so that this passage only helps us in so far as it makes Capernaum on the shore of the lake. So, also, "the way of the sea" in Isaiah's prophecy, quoted in Matthew iv. 15, can only mean generally the districts in which our Lord passed the greater portion of the three years of His ministry. From other passages we gather that Capernaum was in or near the district of Gennesareth on the west side of the lake; that it had a synagogue built by a Roman centurion, which indicates that a detachment of troops was quartered there; and that there was a customs station, where dues were gathered; but this there may have been, and probably was at all towns of any size under the Roman occupation. All this seems to show that Capernaum was of more importance than either Bethsaida, or Chorazin, which were probably not far distant, from the manner in which they are mentioned in connection with it. We have seen before (page 270) that, with the new and beautiful reading which the Sinaitic and Vatican versions give to Matthew xi. 23, it is hardly possible to suppose any allusion was made on that occasion to the height of the position in the town itself; and here I may state that the same two versions enable us to settle a point which has been doubted by some writers, that the Capernaum of the Bible and the Capharnaum of Josephus are the same. In every passage in which the word occurs these give it, without exception, in the form Capharnaum. I now come to the details contained in the accounts given in the three Gospels of the feeding of the five thousand, and our Lord's journey across the lake afterward, and propose examining them with the new light which the Sinaitic version throws on them.

The first point to decide is where the miracle took place. Matthew states that our Lord departed by ship to a desert (that is unfrequented) place; so also Mark: John adds that He went up a mountain; and Luke says that the place belonged to the city called Bethsaida. This last allusion has induced all writers, up to the present day, to place the scene of the miracle on the eastern side of the lake, not far from the supposed site of Bethsaida Julias. On turning, however, to the Sinaitic version we find that the words "belonging to a city called Bethsaida" are omitted; and in the same version we have a remarkable reading of John vi. 23. Instead of "Howbeit there came other boats from Tiberias nigh unto the place where they did eat bread," as in the Authorized Version, we read, "When therefore the boats came from Tiberias, which was nigh unto where they did also eat bread." Adopting these readings, we arrive at the conclusion that the place was near Tiberias, and had no connection with Bethsaida; a result which is in striking accordance with the tradition of Arculf that it was on the grassy plain behind Ain Barideh. It has unfortunately happened that the sites of many Biblical events have for convenience been transferred to other places where the events could not possibly have taken place, as the scene of the destruction of the swine from the eastern shore of the lake to Khan Minyeh, the Cliff of the Precipitation from Nazareth to a hill over the plain of Esdraelon, and many other cases which are familiar to all who have travelled in Palestine. Was this the case with the scene of the feeding of the five thousand? When we consider that Arculf visited the country at the end of the seventh century, little more than fifty years after the Muhammedan invasion; that shortly before that invasion, and possibly after it—for the first conquerors do not seem to have persecuted the Christians to any great extent—not only was Gadara a large and flourishing city (a bishop of Gadara is mentioned in 536), but the Hauran was inhabited by the remarkable race of Christians (Japanides) who built the stone houses, we cannot help coming to the conclusion that a place of such interest must have been well known at that time; and that there could then have been no motive, such as arose afterward, for transferring the tradition from the eastern to the western shore of the lake had the miracle been performed on the former.

With regard to the voyage home, Matthew says the disciples were directed to go before to "the other side," and that they came "into the land of Gennesareth;" Mark "to go to the other side before unto Bethsaida," and that they came "into the land of Gennesareth;" and John informs us that they "went over the sea toward Capernaum," and that after the storm "immediately the ship was at the land whither they went." It is perhaps impossible to reconcile these passages exactly; but a glance at the map will show that, taking Ain Barideh as the starting-point, Tel Hum and the mouth of the Jordan are much in the same direction. The expression, going over "to the other side" might be very well used for a passage across the water in front of Gennesareth, and the force of the storm may have obliged them to land at Et Tabigah or Khan Minyeh; it would not in this case be necessary to suppose that there were two Bethsaidas.

In John it is said the storm overtook the boat after they had rowed twenty-five or thirty furlongs; in the other Gospels it is said to have been in the midst of the sea: this certainly shows that it was some distance from land, for the expression "immediately" in John appears only to mean that, when the storm ceased, the rowers had no further difficulty, not that the boat was by a miracle brought instantaneously to the shore. Taking a mean of the distance given by John, we get about three and a half miles; and, if this is measured from Ain Barideh toward Tel Hum, it would leave the boat still some distance from the land.

There may be many objections to this view, which is

put forward for the sake of drawing attention to the great
difficulty experienced in fixing the point from which the
boat started, and, this being uncertain, it is of course impossible to draw any correct conclusion as to the site of Capernaum from the narrative.

III. The notices contained in the works of the oldest
writers appear to place Capernaum at Tel Hum, Bethsaida
at the mouth of the Jordan, and Chorazin at Kerazeh. Eusebius and Jerome merely mention that the three cities
were on the shore of the lake, which need not imply that
they were at the water's edge; Jerome adds that Chorazin
was two miles from Capernaum, which agrees with the distance of Kerazeh from Tel Hum. Epiphanius mentions
that in the reign of Constantine a Jewish Christian obtained
permission to built a church at Capernaum, then inhabited
by Jews; and Antoninus in the sixth century says that he
visited Capernaum and found there a Basilica, including the
house of Peter. It is hardly probable that this building can
have entirely disappeared; and, as only one important ruin,
that at Tel Hum, has yet been found north of the lake, we
must hold it to be the church mentioned by Antoninus and
Epiphanius till another is discovered.

The next account is that of Arculf, a French bishop, who
visited Palestine toward the close of the seventh century.
He says that "those who wish to go from Jerusalem to
Capernaum take the direct way by Tiberias, and from
thence, along the Sea of Gennesareth, to the place where the
loaves were blessed, from which Capernaum is at no great
distance." Arculf saw this place from a neighboring hill,
and observed that "it has no walls, but lies on a narrow
piece of ground between the mountain and the lake. On
the shore toward the east, it extends a long way, having the
mountain on the north and the water on the south." As
we have seen above, the place where the loaves were blessed
is Ain Barideh, and the "neighboring hill" is probably one
of the hills above it.

As we looked down from these heights on the northern

shore of the lake, the hills appeared to rise uniformly and rapidly from the water's edge; the little cliff at Khan Minyeh stood out prominently, but a town at this point could not have been described as lying east and west along a narrow piece of ground between the mountain and the lake. The description would apply better to a town at Et Tabigah or Tel Hum. Arculf says that Capernaum had no walls; while the ruins at Khan Minyeh appear to have been surrounded by one, and they are moreover confined to a limited area instead of stretching along the shore of the lake as those at Tel Hum do.

The only other traveller who visited the country before the Crusades and has left an account of his journey is Willibald (A. D. 722). He says: "And thence (from Tiberias) they went round the sea, and by the village of Magdalum to the village of Capernaum, where our Lord raised the prince's daughter. Here was a house and a great wall, which the people of the place told them was the residence of Zebedæus and his sons John and James. And thence they went to Bethsaida, the residence of Peter and Andrew, where there is now a church on the site of their house. They remained there that night, and next morning went to Chorazin, where our Lord healed the demoniac, and sent the devil into a herd of swine. Here was a church of the Christians." They afterward went on to the sources of the Jordan at Banias. Here we at once see that Willibald, whose account was written after his return home, has confused Chorazin with Gergesa; and we may suppose either that he visited Capernaum, Bethsaida, and Gergesa, or Capernaum, Bethsaida, and Chorazin. In the latter case, if the towns were respectively at Tel Hum, the mouth of the Jordan, and Kerazeh, he would naturally visit them in the order in which they are mentioned, and then strike the Roman road to the north above Kerazeh; for if he had gone from Tel Hum to Kerazeh, and then to the mouth of the Jordan, he would have had to retrace his steps, there being no regular road up the Valley of the Jordan.

In conclusion, I would briefly call attention to the three ancient sites still existing on the northern shore of the lake, which undoubtedly represent Capernaum, Chorazin, and the Galilean Bethsaida—if there were two places of that name, for Bethsaida Julias must have been close to the Jordan. At Kerazeh, a name strikingly similar to Chorazin, there are extensive ruins, including those of a Jewish synagogue. At Tel Hum there are also extensive ruins, a regular cemetery, and a remarkable Jewish synagogue, built of limestone brought from a distance, and partly enclosed by a later building of the same material. The name Tel Hum has also been considered a relic of the original Hebrew, Tel taking the place of Caphar, or Kefr.* At Khan Minyeh there are certainly the ruins of a town, but, as far as we could judge, they appeared to be comparatively modern, and not to contain the remains of any important building. In addition, they cover a much smaller extent of ground than those of Tel Hum or Kerazeh.

I have omitted touching on three points which may be considered of some importance. The Roman road from Tiberias to Damascus certainly left the lake at Khan Minyeh, and struck up over the hills to Khan Jubb Yusuf; and, if Capernaum was situated on this, it would at once decide the question in favor of Khan Minyeh; but there is no direct evidence that the road ran through the town. An objection urged against Tel Hum is that it has no harbors or places where boats could lie, and that there must have been something of the sort at Capernaum: the simple answer to this is, that there are the ruins of a town nearly as large as Tiberias on the shore of the lake, without any harbors, and if they are not those of Capernaum it is difficult to say what they are. Those who maintain that Et Tabigah or Khan

---

* A deserted site or mound marking ruins is generally called "Tel," while the Arabs apply the term "Kefr" to an inhabited village; it also often happens that the final syllable in old names is alone preserved, as, for example, Achzib becomes Zib. Kefr or Caphar-na-hum would by a change of this kind naturally become Tel Hum.

Minyeh were the sites of important towns explain the absence of dressed stone, columns, capitals, carved stone, etc., by saying that it has all been carried away to build Tiberias. They forgot, however, that the people of Tiberias have within easy reach among the ruins of the old town enough material to build their houses twice over, without crossing the lake for it. A similar report was current with regard to the synagogue at Tel Hum; but we could not find any trace of the blocks in the houses at Tiberias. We afterward heard that some of them had been burned for lime at Tel Hum, and conveyed in that state to Tiberias.

It is very desirable that extensive excavations should be made both at Khan Minyeh and Tel Hum, as, until this is done, it is impossible to say with certainty which is Capernaum. I think, however, in the present state of our knowledge, the evidence is in favor of the latter place, and I would place Chorazin at Kerazeh, Bethsaida Julias at the mouth of the Jordan, Capernaum at Tel Hum, and the Galilean Bethsaida, if there were one distinct from Julias, at Khan Minyeh.

THE ARCHITECTURAL REMAINS OF PALESTINE.

BY R. PHENE SPIERS, A. R. I. B. A.

THERE is no phase of the results obtained in the exploration of Palestine likely to prove of more value than that which tends to elucidate the history of architecture in that country. The great difficulties attending all travelling in the East have hitherto caused the notes and records on the monuments which abound there to be of too slight a nature to enable us to determine, with any degree of accuracy, either their date or their style; and although the works of Dawkins and Wood, published in 1753, and of Cassas, in 1799, on the ruins of Palmyra and Baalbec, ought, by the great beauty and richness of the monuments therein delineated, to have encouraged others to follow in the same path, till within the last few years the field has been entirely neglected. We hail therefore with pleasure the drawings and photographs published by the Palestine Exploration Fund, under the direction of Captain Warren, of the Ordnance Survey, under Captain Wilson, and, among other works, those by M. De Vogüé on Jerusalem and Central Syria. To the photographs especially, which now form a very valuable series, we are indebted for the most faithful record hitherto obtained of the masonry and sculpturesque decorations of Syrian architecture; and we cannot but feel that, in conjunction with historical records and inscriptions, they will prove to be of the greatest assistance in fixing a date and an origin to all the architectural remains in Palestine.

The chief works of interest which have been undertaken, and on which we propose now to make a few remarks, are, 1st, the careful examination down to the foundation of the enclosing walls of Haram-esh-Shereef, the site of the ancient Temple of Jerusalem; 2d, the small temples in Cœle-Syria and other Roman buildings at Baalbec, Damascus, and Jerash; and, 3d, the Jewish synagogues and tombs in Galilee.

The results of the excavations down to the foundations of the Haram wall—in some cases 80 feet below the present surface of the ground—although astounding us by the stupendous nature and extent of the masonry, do not lead to any more definite conclusions, as regards the architectural style of the Jewish nation, than can be learned by those portions hitherto exposed to view. It is scarcely necessary to point out that constructive masonry alone, without any architectural features, is not sufficient to constitute a style, and that its nature can only assist us to form conclusions as to the race of people by whom it was worked. Mr. Deutsch's* discovery of Phœnician characters, similar to those on the walls of ancient Sidon, enables us to ascribe the execution of the Haram wall to that race; but for whom they worked, or at what period, remains still an open question.

The peculiarity of the masonry of the enclosing wall of the Haram-esh-Shereef is the sunken face or groove, varying in width and depth, forming a border worked round the face of each stone. The earliest dated example of such work is found in the walls of Passargadæ, erected by Cyrus in the sixth century B. C.; a similar sunken face is found in the best Greek work, and in Rome and Pompeii; in later days it seems to have been very constantly introduced by the Arabs in the walls of their towns and citadels. It is not found in Egypt, and was rarely employed by the Goths.

A clear distinction should here be drawn between this

* Quarterly Statement. No. II., p. 35. Palestine Exploration Fund.

sunken face and the ordinary bevel, which exists more particularly in masonry of the Florentine and Italian Renaissance periods. Other instances of this sunken face of early date in Palestine are found in the mosque at Hebron, the Propylæa at Baalbec, the palace at Arak-el-Emir, and other places. The sunken face of the stone varies in width from 2 to 5 inches, and is always finely chiselled. The central face of the stone varies considerably in finish; sometimes being left in "*bossage*," or, as we call it, "rusticated," sometimes axed or roughly chiselled, and sometimes hammer-dressed. At Hebron and Arak-el-Emir it is hammer-dressed or finely chiselled all over, at Baalbec roughly chiselled, and in the Haram wall all three kinds of work are found.*

The object of this sunken face was probably either to assist the workmen in obtaining a finer joint, or else to run less risk of chipping off the arrises of the stone when finishing the work. It is customary now to work round the face of a stone with a chisel first, leaving the centre to be hammer-dressed or finished afterward; and that would seem to have been the original object in view with this Jewish masonry. The central face, however, never seems to have been worked down to the same plane as the sunken face, but left as an ornamental feature.

Captain Warren has noticed in one of the temples of Cœle-Syria a small bevelled edge at 45° in addition to the sunken face; this bevelled groove, however, we believe to be an exception to the general rule, and, although an additional precaution against the chipping of the arris, would destroy the breadth of the masonry, and look like a coarse joint. The masonry of the Haram wall is laid in courses of various heights, with a precision and fineness of joint surpassed only by the early Egyptian work of the Pyramids, or by Greek work. In his description of the methods employed to obtain this fine joint in the latter, Mr. Penrose † informs us that the stones, before being fixed, were rubbed

---

* Quarterly Statement. No. V., p. 193. Palestine Exploration Fund.
† Penrose's " Principles of Athenian Architecture."

backward and forward on the course immediately beneath, and that the ancones, or projecting bosses on the face of the stone, gave the masons a hold on them. In many cases these bosses are still left on unfinished Greek work; and we find similar features on the Haram wall, though the immense size of some of the blocks would in the latter case cause us to doubt whether such a working of them were possible.

The temples of Cœle-Syria delineated and described by Captain Warren* form a valuable addition to our store of knowledge, because, although they are mentioned and described by Burckhardt and other travellers, no series of drawings has before been published of them. These temples are found in the country which lies between Baalbec, Tyre, and Damascus; they all date from the period of the Roman domination, and although more debased in style than the remains of Baalbec and Palmyra, have several peculiarities of interest about them. The greater number are Ionic; and this is curious, because, with the exception of four semi-detached columns at Palmyra, neither this town nor Baalbec possesses any temple of this order. It is possible that the absence of sculpture and the greater simplicity of the Ionic order may have led to its adoption, for the carved work in the capitals is poor in the extreme, and the mouldings, though profuse in number, have no carved ornament on them.

All the temples of Cœle-Syria face the east. This was the universal custom in Greece, though in Rome it was frequently departed from. The chief reason for this orientation would seem to have been, that the rising sun should cast its first rays on the statue of the god inside the Sanctuary. Prof. Cockerell, in his work on the temples of Jupiter at Ægina, and of Apollo at Bassæ,† explains that " the orientation of this latter temple north and south, instead of the usual direction of the fronts to the east and west, was prob-

---

* Quarterly Statement. No. V., pp. 183–210.
† " Temples of Ægina and Bassæ." By the late Prof. Cockerell.

ably due to its position on a narrow ridge, and to insure its better appearance when seen from the plains of Messina and the Mediterranean," and notices, further, that "it is remarkable (as if in conformity with the usual practice in Greece of entering the temple from the east) that a door-way of scarcely secondary importance both in magnitude and decoration is placed in the eastern peristyle; forming an important entrance into the sacrarium, and receiving the first rays of early dawn upon the image of the deity within: thus fulfilling, as respects its entrance from the east, the usual condition of the Grecian temple." He remarks also in a note that "the Temple of the Sun at Palmyra stands north and south, with four entrances from the east, the principal 32 feet high by 15 wide."

While in Greece the temples were always placed away from the crowded thoroughfares of the city, in Rome we find them in the busiest parts; and hence their orientation was made subservient to the monumental decoration of the public places in which they were erected. The Roman being essentially practical in all he undertook, was more likely to make as great display as he could, by turning the entrance portico where it would best be seen, and where it would better add to the magnificence of his city, than sacrifice its effect to a religious tradition. No rule for orientation therefore is to be found in Rome: in Cœle-Syria the ancient tradition seems to have been kept up, and the temples always built facing the east.

Of the twelve temples measured by Captain Warren, seven are of the Ionic order, two Corinthian, and the others doubtful. Five of the Ionic order have all porticos "in antis;" that is, the north and south walls of the cella are continued beyond the east wall, and form antæ, which, with two columns between, carry the cornice and pediment, and constitute the eastern façade. Four other temples, two Ionic and two Corinthian, are prostyle; that is, have porticos of four columns in front. All these temples are raised on a stylobate or podium, varying in height from 5 feet 6 inches to 11 feet. One of the chief peculiarities in these temples, excepting that of Husn Niha, is, that the mouldings of this stylobate are continued close round in front of the portico. Now in all Roman temples elsewhere, the stylobate is carried on in front of the main façade, and forms pedestals as it were on either side, between which are flights of steps leading to the interior; but here there was apparently no means of ascent, and we are bound to suppose, either that the faithful were not admitted into the cella, or that temporary wooden stairs were provided as a means of access.

The entrance for the priest was on the south side, at the western end of the temple, through a door in the stylobate, which led into the chambers under a raised dais or platform at the west end, and from thence through doors into the cella. Similar raised platforms are still to be seen at Pompeii, in the temples of Jupiter and of Isis.

The chambers at the west end of these temples are specially interesting. Some of them are described as vaulted or arched over,* but no sections are given, to show the nature of the arch or vault. In the Temple of Thelthatha these chambers are about 7 feet in height, and are covered with stone landings similar to those in the stone houses of Central Syria. In order to diminish the bearing of these landings, a series of corbels carry a projecting cornice, on which they rest; so that, while the chamber measures 9 feet in width, the corbelling out reduces the bearing of each landing to 4 feet 7 inches. The size of these landings, 9 feet by 4 feet, and 2 feet 6 inches thick, corresponds to those in Central Syria.

In comparing the mouldings of cornices, etc., of these temples in Cœle-Syria with those of Baalbec and Palmyra, we are struck by the total absence of carved ornament in the former; while, too, the capitals and cornices show considerable ignorance of Roman work, the mouldings of the

* Quarterly Statement. No. V. Palestine Exploration Fund.

bases and of the stylobate are remarkable for their good contour, which is almost Greek in feeling.

In the Temple of Ain Hershah, for instance, the corona of the cornice is carried up the pediment only, and the first horizontal member of the cornice is what would be (if so carved) the dentil fascia. In the Temple of Thelthatha, the cornice is unusually heavy; the dentil fascia is not carved, its lower edge projecting outward; and in the place of the small fillet and cyma reversa, usual in the Ionic entablature, is a huge bead, resembling the bowtell of English mouldings; the crowning mouldings of the architrave also are clumsy and ineffective. When, however, we examine the base or stylobate mouldings of these two temples, they are not only refined in contour, but good copies of the best type of Roman examples. There is one peculiarity in three of the temples, viz., Hibbariyeh, Aiha, and Deir-el-Ashayir—and there is a similar example at Baalbec—in the stylobate cornice; instead of there being a horizontal plane above the upper projecting fillet, we find an ogee or ovolo moulding reversed, carrying back the projecting mouldings to the face of the pilaster or wall-base by a raised curve instead of a horizontal plane; this is often found in Renaissance, and invariably in Gothic work, but never, we believe, in Greek or Roman. The cushion frieze, rarely if ever used with the Ionic order, here exists in all the examples; but it is not carved, as in the Corinthian examples at Baalbec, Palmyra, and elsewhere; the carved ornament, in fact, seems to be confined to the heads of the door-ways, the niches, and capitals of the columns, and is extremely poor, showing an attempt to copy Roman work, without sufficient knowledge of it, or talent to invent any thing new. The Corinthian capitals have only the outline of the leaves (they are not simply blocked out), and the abacus has no moulding. The Ionic capitals are just sufficiently detailed to show they were intended for that order.

In the Temple of Husn Niha, about 5 or 6 feet above the base, are two projecting courses of masonry, the lower

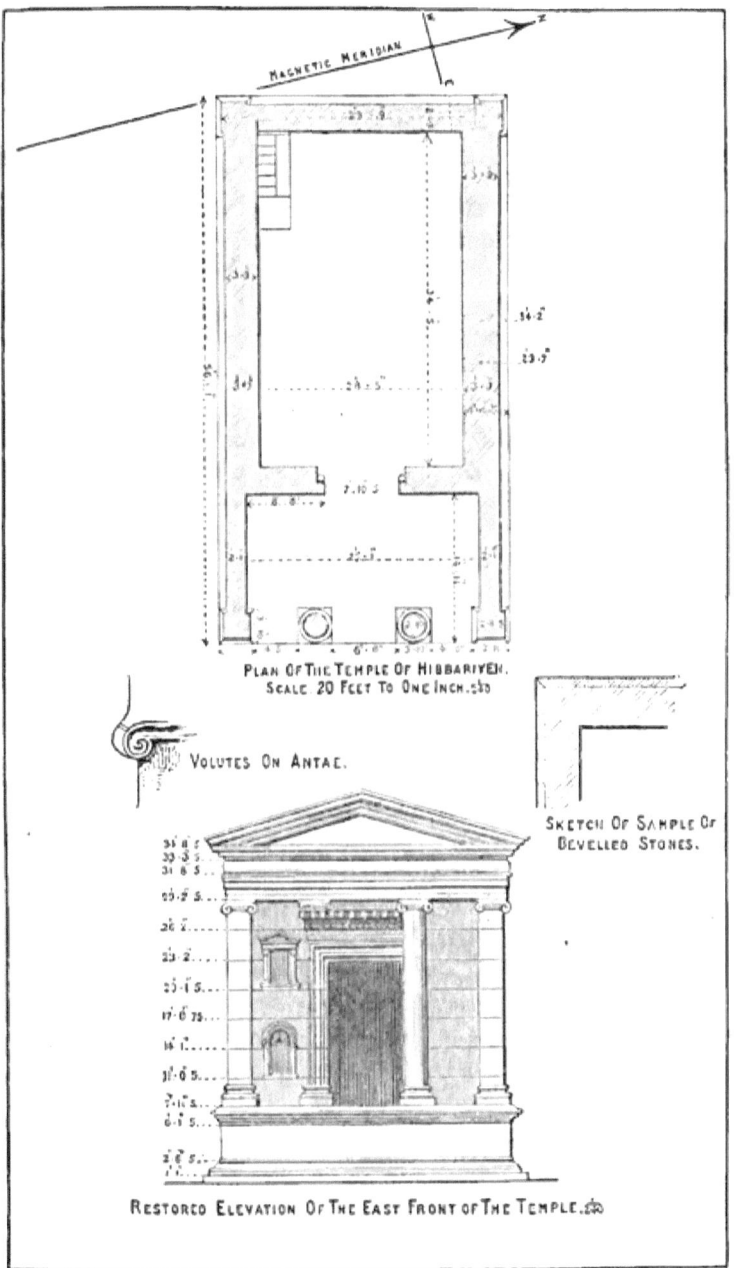

PLAN OF THE TEMPLE OF HIBBARIYEH.
SCALE 20 FEET TO ONE INCH.

VOLUTES ON ANTAE.

SKETCH OF SAMPLE OF BEVELLED STONES.

RESTORED ELEVATION OF THE EAST FRONT OF THE TEMPLE.

one moulded and bevelled, running along the north and south walls, round the antae, but not continued across the east end. A similar feature is found in the Temple of Jupiter at Baalbec; it would seem to have been a "motif" derived from the customary dado mouldings in Pompeiian interiors, and sometimes round their temples. As regards the interior of these temples of Cœle-Syria, there are no sections which would enable us to judge of their architecture. From the plans we are able to ascertain that in Deir-el-Ashayir the walls were decorated with flat pilasters similar to those in a building south of Forum, Jerash,* and in Husn Niha, and Niha with semi-detached columns. The purpose of the double engaged columns in the four corners of these temples was to give a better bearing to the two ends of the architraves than is usually the case when a single column has to receive them; this object must not be confounded with that of the clustered column in English-Gothic architecture, where two or more orders of arches have to be carried in parallel planes.

In the drawings and photographs of the synagogues of Galilee, described by Captain Wilson,† one cannot fail being struck by their resemblance in plan, accidental or otherwise, to the palaces of Persepolis, and to the House of the Forest of Lebanon, built by King Solomon—"rectangular buildings," as Captain Wilson describes them, "the interior, divided into five aisles by four rows of columns," recalls precisely similar dispositions to the two examples above named; the columns, however, are of far more sturdy proportions, averaging from 4½ to 6 diameters in height. They carried apparently stone architraves, some of which we found among the ruins, and the roof was constructed of wooden beams with rafters and planks covered with earth, probably similar to the roofs of modern Arab houses in Syria and Egypt, and ancient ones also, to judge from the carved imitations in stone in some of the tombs near the great Pyra-

---

* Photograph. No. 333. Palestine Exploration Fund.
† Quarterly Statement. No. II., pp. 37-41. Palestine Exploration Fund.

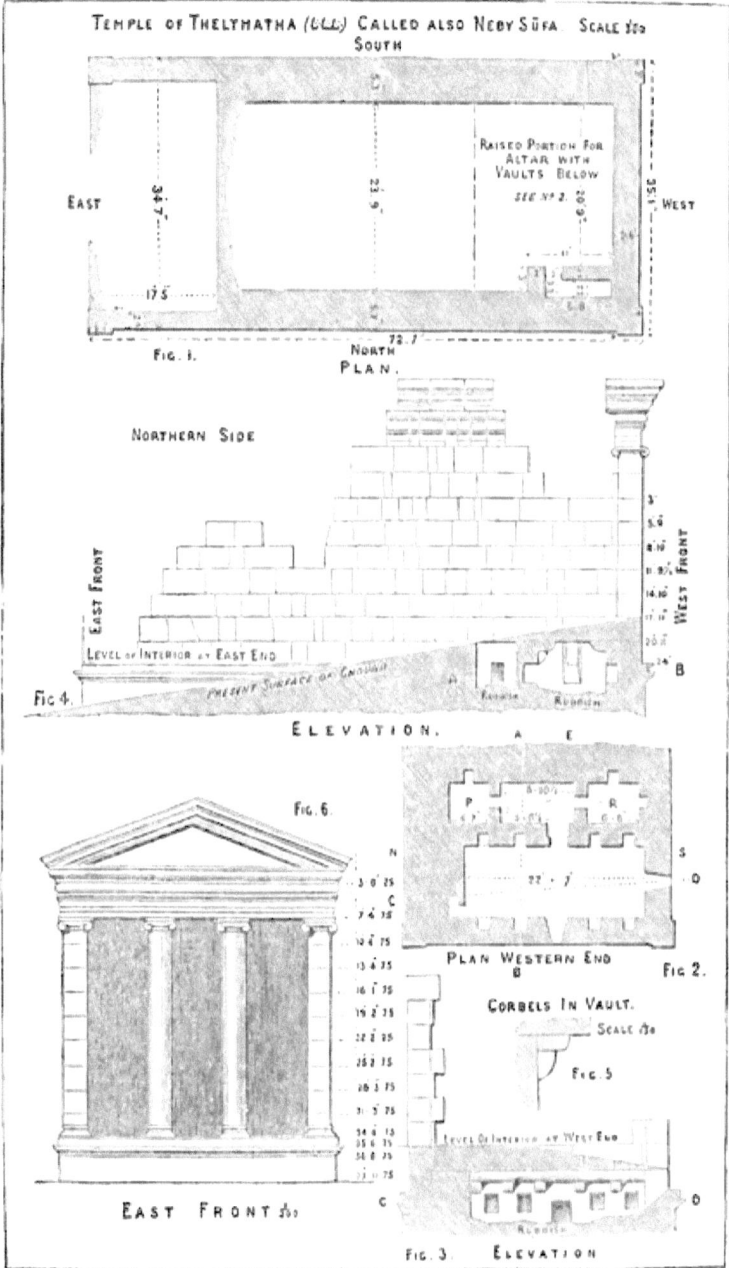

mids. The proximity of one of the columns to one another, and their proportion, are explained by their having to carry stone architraves; the intercolumniation, centre to centre of columns, varies from 3¼ to 5 diameters; in the Egyptian temples at Karnak and elsewhere, where the roofs are entirely in stone, the intercolumniation varies from 2¼ to 3 diameters; the relative proportion of height to diameter in both cases being about the same. The proportion of the height of these columns to their diameter is the same as in the examples of Tourmanin, Serdjilla, and Babouda, of the fifth and sixth centuries, A. D., shown in De Vogüé work on Central Syria; and there is a marked resemblance between all these examples in the capitals and the mouldings of the bases.

These synagogues are paved with lime-stone flags; they cover areas of from 4,800 to 2,200 square feet, rather larger than the temples of Cœle-Syria; and we may suppose that at the time they were built they constituted buildings of considerable importance. The richness and beauty of their mouldings and of their carved ornament place them among the finest examples of Syrian architecture. The two internal supports at the northern extremity of these synagogues, instead of being single columns, consist each of a square pier with semi-engaged columns on two faces; and this, Captain Wilson remarks, "is invariably the case in these synagogues." The object for this additional strength is not apparent, except that some special arrangement of the roof for light or ventilation at this end of the synagogue might have been required; in the south façades of these synagogues are small windows.

The tombs of Galilee have no special architectural value except so far as regards the decoration of their external elevations; for here alone are we able to trace those features which constitute architectural style. As these bear the strongest resemblance in detail to the decorative features of the Jewish synagogues, we propose to treat of them together.

Looking through the whole series of photographs taken

for the Palestine Exploration Fund, and confining our attention to those in which architectural ornament is detailed, we seem to recognize two distinct styles of work: the one, rich but debased Roman work, the other Greek of the bas-empire, or Byzantine. Examples of the former will be found in photographs Nos. 5, 12, 24, 44, 45, 263, 322, 326, 327, and 334; of the latter in Nos. 13, 39, 51, 53, 54, 56, 57, 60, 63, 68, 69, 71, 97, 110, 141, 143, 149, 151, 297, 298, and 320.

All those in the first class belong to the large Roman cities of Baalbec, Damascus, Jerash, and Amman, where, from the extent and importance of these places, we may suppose Roman architects and sculptors of ornament to have been employed. To this class belongs also the work of the temples of Cœle-Syria, though executed by inferior workmen.

To the second class belongs the architectural ornament of the buildings of the Jewish (?) or Byzantine style.

Except noticing that, in many cases, the " motifs de décoration," such as bunches of grapes, vine-leaves, the pot of manna, and one or two other emblems, have been borrowed from Jewish work, and treated in the Roman manner, the first class (Roman work) does not call for any special attention here. In the second, however, we find the germs of a style which, whether Jewish or Greek in its origin, ultimately led to the development of the Byzantine style, as found in the Mosque of St. Sophia, and other buildings of the same date at Constantinople, in the buildings of Central Syria published by De Vogüé and in the Golden Gate-way of the Haram-esh-Shereef at Jerusalem—the latter a little less pure in style than the first, because away from the architectural centre at Constantinople.

The earliest examples, to judge from their purity and simplicity of mouldings, would be those of Arak-el-Emir (297), the date of which we believe is known—176 B.C.; and the oldest portion of the Mosque of Damascus (13). Next to these (though from 50 to 100 years later, perhaps) would come the rock-cut tomb near Shafat (143), the Tombs of the

Kings (illustrated in De Vogüé), the Tombs of the Judges (141), Tomb of Jehoshaphat (149), and the Tomb of Ananias (151). This series would bring us down to the time of Herod, or up to and including the half of the first century of our era. The synagogues would all appear to be of a later period, and date from the third to the sixth centuries inclusive.

The reason we have for this order is shown in the gradual development of the style known as Byzantine, which can be traced step by step through all these examples. The archaic and debased periods of the style are easily distinguished in the treatment of the architectural ornaments and mouldings. Take, for instance, the two first-named examples (297 and 13); no one can fail to see the resemblance between them and the early Greek work at Pompeii (which, it must be remembered, is late and slightly-debased Greek); the mouldings are similar, and there is the same crisp character in the carving of the dentils. In the tomb near Shafat, again, the whole entablature, and notably the triglyphs and the shallow architrave, is almost a copy of one at Pompeii (Triangular Forum).

Following out the development of this Byzantine style, however, we recognize the introduction of features which are not Greek in origin; such as the constant representation of the grape and vine-leaves, of the olive, of a vase, supposed to be the pot of manna, and of other emblems which may safely be said to be Jewish. We notice also a change in the ancient Greek mouldings, which become vigorous and bold, and a modification of the constructive features of the classic entablature.

The sculptured ornament in the tympana of the Tombs of Jehoshaphat (149) and of the Judges (141), with the acroteria in the latter, is not Jewish, but debased Greek. The ornament on the architrave of the Tombs of the Kings is Jewish, but executed probably by Greek artists, if we may judge from similarity in the carving to those above mentioned.

There is no reason why Jewish artists should not have possessed similar powers; but we should not then have found copies of Greek ornament; for that the examples in the Tombs of Jehoshaphat and of the Kings are copied from the foliage in the Greek steles and elsewhere cannot be denied. M. De Saulcy we believe reverses the order, and holds that the Greeks copied from the Jews; but no one who has had any practical acquaintance with the design of architectural ornament could possibly agree with him in his conclusions; the archaic period and decadence of every style being totally distinct in character. Let us take an instance: the tombs of Beni Hassan in Egypt and the tombs of Lydia show the wooden origin of the dentil moulding, afterward employed decoratively by the Greeks; we trace it again in the examples before mentioned of Arak-el-Emir and Mosque of Damascus with almost the same purity as in Greek work. Compare these examples with those in the Tombs of the Judges (141), or in the head of a niche of the ruined synagogue at Kerazeh (50), where it is mixed with a variety of mouldings and ornament belonging to other orders. It has there become thoroughly debased, with no trace of its wooden origin; or look again at the Tomb of Ananias (151), how the triglyphs and cornice have been changed from their original type, and have lost all trace of the distinctive character which they possess when employed in the Parthenon or other Greek temples. The continual copying of a conventional feature like the triglyph is sure, in debased architecture, to lead to its being employed with quite a different feeling and object from its original type. To reverse the order, and to agree with M. De Saulcy that the Greeks obtained the triglyph and other conventional ornaments from those debased specimens of Jewish art, could only lead to a complete chaos in the history of architectural art.

The drawings and photographs of Palestine architecture are specially interesting, as enabling us to trace the changes and modifications of the original Greek mouldings—changes which took place prior to the Roman domination in Syria,

and, when cotemporaneous, apparently in spite of it. One
of the earliest examples is found in the door-way of the
Triple Gate in the Haram wall, and others are found in the
tombs before mentioned. As these changes are gradual, and
would take long to detail, we will proceed at once to the
examination of the ruins of the synagogue at Kefr Birim,
dating probably from the fifth or sixth century of our era,
and which are specially noted by Captain Wilson as worthy
of remark. They are shown in the photographs Nos. 67,
68, and 69.

We find here in the door-way (68) the three divisions of
a classic entablature, viz., architrave, frieze, and cornice.
The architrave (or lintel in this case, being a door-way) has
here acquired a totally different proportion from a classic
example; being the main support, it is three times as deep
as either frieze or cornice: the two latter, in fact, have become mere decorative features. The relieving arch above,
always masked and hidden in classic work, if possible, has
here become accepted as a necessary element of construction, and is accentuated accordingly by a bold circular arch.
The mouldings of this arch, as well as of the door-way, are
vigorous and effective, showing a remarkable contrast to the
flat planes and reliefs of any Greek example.

There is in this central door-way a noticeable feature not
found in Central Syria or Constantinople, and that is the
wide projection of the lintel on either side of the door-posts,
and the extension of the mouldings on either side. The
door-way of the Propylæa at Athens has the same projection of lintel and moulding, though not so accentuated as in
this example. The carving on the lintel of the animals
(Paschal lambs?) on each side of a central flower is also
peculiar, and probably Jewish in idea. The column still
standing in front of this synagogue, and which formed part
of a portico similar to that at Mezrah (110), shows a great
change from classic work in the sturdy proportions and simplicity of its capital; the depth of the architrave also shows
the importance given to that constructive feature. As sim-

ilar mouldings of capitals are found in Central Syria, we should be inclined to class them as Christian Greek, and not Jewish, as Captain Wilson would seem to infer in his description of them.*

Our chief reason for attributing these and other features to the Christian Greeks (Byzantine) rather than to the Jews rests on the unmistakable proofs that the former people developed in Central Syria and elsewhere a perfectly distinct and homogeneous style, in which, although we are able to point out the source of many of its decorative features, these are so altered and modified as to have changed their original character, and assumed a new one. In Jewish work such is not the case; we find in all those buildings, such as tombs and synagogues, in which it may be assumed that the Jew was the paymaster and directed the work, a heterogeneous mixture of all styles without any study in design. Thus, for instance, in the so-called Tomb of Absalom, we find an Egyptian cavetto cornice mounted on a Doric entablature, carried by Ionic semi-detached columns, with corner pilasters of the Græco-Syrian type. In the Tomb of Zacharias we have an Egyptian entablature on similar Ionic columns and Græco-Syrian pilasters. In the Tombs of the Kings we find three acanthus-leaves † performing the duty of triglyphs. These and many other instances, in which the original features have been copied in each case as far as possible, and not worked up and modified, as in Byzantine work, show clearly that the Jews had no style of their own, but borrowed on every side, and made such compositions as we see often at the present day, when in one single building the details of many different styles or periods of a style are found jumbled up together without rhyme or reason.

In any comparison which might be made between the development of the Byzantine style in Syria and of the Romanesque and Gothic styles in Western Europe, it is

* Quarterly Statement. No. II., p. 59. Palestine Exploration Fund.

† Not palm-leaves, as usually described; the original copy is found in the centre of the tympanum of the Tomb of Jehoshaphat.

curious to notice how, working on the same principles though at different periods—the first arriving at such perfection as was possible before the Arab invasion; the second, in consequence of the civil wars and troubles in Western Europe, delayed until the eleventh to the fifteenth centuries—in both styles somewhat similar results were arrived at.

The strong accentuation of all constructive features, as the architrave, lintel, and arch, and their appropriate mouldings—the selection of door-ways and windows as special objects for architectural decoration, no longer to be rendered subordinate or second in importance to purely ornamental features, such as columns or pilasters decorating a façade—and the development of a stone-vaulted roof of the same material as the walls, and forming therefore a covering in keeping with the latter—in all these elements of architectural style, based on the same principles, though differing in detail and form, we recognize similar results; both were Christian, and both progressed hand in hand with the advance of science.

Had the further development of the Byzantine style, with its magnificent crowning feature, the dome, been left in Christian instead of Moslem hands, and allowed the same time and opportunity as we have witnessed with the Gothic style, there can scarcely be any doubt that its results would have, in grandeur and magnificence, at least equalled, if not surpassed, the cathedrals of Europe.

It would scarcely be possible to overrate, therefore, the value of the publication of all Byzantine architecture in Syria and elsewhere. There is now, in this archæological age, when all tradition of style is gone, a tendency to study the best examples of ancient art, to learn the principles on which they were designed, and thus to recover if possible the lost thread of architectural style. We know of no field more likely to afford satisfactory results as regards its exploration than that which is offered to us in Palestine, where so many relics abound of what we believe to be a partially-developed style.

THE HAURAN.

BY THE COUNT MELCHIOR DE VOGÜÉ.*

AMONG the lands which are more or less directly connected with the events recorded in the Scriptures, there is not one more interesting or less known than the Hauran. Its riches, both natural and archæological, its retired position, and the manners of its inhabitants, all combine to render it, above all other places, worthy of exciting the curiosity of the traveller; who, when once he has made up his mind to get over the first difficulty, and to give up those comforts which surround the nineteenth-century pilgrim, is quite sure to be rewarded for his trouble. Not only will he find there volcanic features of the most singular interest, ruins in the best preservation, and inscriptions in great numbers, but also scenes of life and manners which will enable him to penetrate, more perfectly than in any other part of Palestine, into the details of pure Oriental life. Here there are no pachas and no consuls: neither passports nor firmans are demanded; and, above all, no theatrical displays, got up by interested dragomans, for the amusement of travellers, to create an imaginary East on the beaten roads of Jerusalem and Nazareth.

* The names of places in this paper are spelt as in Count de Vogüé's manuscript. The paper itself is unfinished, wanting the concluding paragraphs, which were to have been supplied by the author when revising the proofs. Recent events in France have, as is well known, called for Count de Vogüé's services with the army, and his Essay has therefore not received his final revision.

In these regions is found a population which depends entirely on itself; Druses or Arabs; nomadic Bedouins or stationary agriculturists; brigands or farmers—all, in point of fact, are independent; they have their own chiefs, and their relations are regulated by their reciprocal wants, their ability, or their vigor. The feudal life, with its display of individual energy; the pastoral life, with its adventures; the life of brigandage, with its dangers, all have their representatives here. In the absence of any central government, and of any regular police, each chief has, individually, to provide for every thing—the administration of the land, the security of his vassals and himself, the defence of the country, and the duties of hospitality. These last are, indeed, largely exercised, though one can hardly say that they are entirely disinterested as regards the European traveller; but I can affirm, from my own personal experience, that they are practised with sincerity; when once the symbol of friendship—the Khoué—has passed between the sheikh who gives his protection and the Frank who brings his presents, the latter may sleep at ease; he has nothing more to fear, even in the midst of tribes who live by pillage, if he will but agree to the conditions of living with his host, and as his host; of keeping out of local quarrels, and of making an accurate acquaintance with the statistics of the alliances and enmities of each family. By following this line of conduct, Mr. Waddington and myself were enabled to explore the country in every sense; to visit regions previously unvisited, and reputed inaccessible, such as the Ledja and the farther volcanoes of the Safa, and to remain there during the time necessary for scientific observations; to make sketches; to copy inscriptions; and even to make excavations at several important points.*

But before giving the principal results of our visit, it

* "Syrie Centrale." Par le Comte de Vogüé. Paris. Baudry. I. Architecture Civile et Religieuse. II. Inscriptions Sémitiques.
"Inscriptions Grecques de la Syrie." Par W. Waddington. Paris. Firmin Didot.

will be well to define with some accuracy the limits of the country over which our journey extended, and the points at which these regions touch on the history of the Bible.

The massive block of mountains designated by European travellers as the Hauran rises to the south and southeast of Damascus, out of the great plain which lies between the desert on the east, and the mountains of the Jordan on the west. This mass is composed of three distinct groups, which we may as well call by their native names.

The centre of the whole system is the Jebel Hauran. This is volcanic in its origin, though without apparent craters, and is composed of mountains of moderate elevation and easy gradients, the slopes of which are covered with wood and cultivation. It is the district of the Druses, whose chief towns are Qennawât, Soueida, Schehbah, and Schagga. To the north of these mountains, and at the foot of the farthest slopes, close to the city of Schehbah, is a group of extinct volcanoes, the still open craters of which have thrown up, at an epoch geologically recent, an enormous stream of lava, which, in process of cooling, has formed the plateau of the Ledja. This latter is a vast triangle, 22 miles broad by 25 long, entirely composed of basaltic rocks, which have hardened into the most picturesque forms; their height is hardly forty or fifty feet above the level of the plain; but the thousand clefts which furrow them, the rents of their lace-like edges, and the broken character of their elevations, render them a natural labyrinth, and an inextricable haunt for brigands. The Druses, and, above all, the Soulout Arabs, inhabit this retreat, which they call Qalat Allah—the Fortress of God.

To the east of this group is situated another, called the Safa, the product of a series of formidable craters, extending over a length of more than thirty miles. Here are found the same plateaux of lava, with its cleft elevations, as in the Ledja; but the volcanoes are more numerous, and of larger size. The Safa is occupied by tribes of Bedouins, among whom it is sufficient to name the Shtayeh and the

Rheyât. Beyond the Safa begins an immense steppe, called the Hamâd, which stretches as far as the Euphrates, and forms the Desert of Syria.

The great fertile plain which extends to the east and the south of the Jebel Hauran is called the Nongra Hauran. Its principal town is Bostra; it is inhabited by stationary Arabs, and cultivated by the Bedouin. It is bounded on the west by the chain of mountains which forms the basin of the Jordan. The chain bears different names: the Djaulân, which commences on the east slopes of the Anti-Lebanon, and borders the left bank of the Sea of Galilee, as far as the river Yarmouk (the Hieromax of the ancients); the Jebel Ajloun, from the Yarmouk to the Jabbok; and lastly the Belgâ to the south.

The plain situated to the extreme north, between the point of the Ledja and the Anti-Lebanon, bears the name of Djeddour.

The greater part of these names preserve traces of their ancient appellations; and by the aid of these indications and of historical information, we can arrive at a determination of the site of each province. The country appears in the Bible, at the two extremities of the Hebrew history—at its *début*, in connection with the conquests of Moses and Joshua, and, at its close, with the ambitions and disasters of the Idumæan dynasty.

Of the sovereignties destroyed by Moses, the kingdom of Bashan was the most important: King Og, the Amorite, ruled from the Land of Moab to Mount Hermon. By comparing Deut. iii. 10, Josh. xii. 5, xiii. 11, and 1 Chron. v. 11–23, it is found that the northern limit of Bashan, properly so called, was a line running from east to west, and passing by Edrei and Salchah. The place of these two cities is perfectly determined. Mr. Waddington has proved from the inscriptions that Edrei was the modern Derat, an important town on the Yarmouk, which commands the entrance of the mountains of the Ajloun, and of the Djaulân. Salchah is the modern Salchad, an isolated fortress at the entrance of Jebel Hauran, and on a winter affluent of the Yarmouk: it is evident that this line of rivers, formerly much more abundant, formed the frontier of Bashan, just as the Jabbok formed that of the ancient territory of Moab, and the Arnon that of the later territory of Moab. These parallel affluents of the Jordan form natural limits for the local subdivisions. Og possessed also the mountains of the Jaulân, which were beyond the limits of Bashan to the north (1 Chron. v. 23). The half-tribe of Manasseh had, in the division, a part of the land of King Og, that is to say, the portion of the Nougra which surrounds Bosra, as far as the Sheriat el Menadire, the beautiful plain conquered by Moses, and the mountains of the Djaulân, which enclose the city of refuge; it had also the half of Jebel Ajloun, the ancient Gilead, whose fair pasturage and oak-forests still justify the ancient reputation of Bashan.

I do not think that the Hebrews ever passed across this line, or occupied the Jebel Hauran. No remains exist in the country to indicate their rule; for there is no monument to be found there anterior to the Idumæan dynasty. It was under the reigns of the Herods and the Agrippas that the Hauran began an era of prosperity which was further developed under the Roman Empire, and only stopped by the Mahometan invasion. The geographical divisions of this epoch are found under the modern nomenclature.

The Auranitis, properly so called, is the plain of the Nougra. Batanæa is the Jebel Hauran, whose northeast slopes have preserved the name of Bathaniyeh. The researches of Herr Wetzstein ("Hauran und Trachonen," p. 85) justify this identification, and prove that the name formerly extended over the whole Jebel. Trachonitis is the Ledja, and the modern Soulouts are the worthy descendants of the brigands of Zenodorus. Ituræa is Djedour, augmented by a part of Anti-Lebanon. Gaulanitis is identical with Jaulân, and its name has never varied from the most remote times.

It is not my business here to give the history of these

regions during the agitated government of the little Greco-Oriental dynasties which disputed their possession. Idumæan princes, Nabathæan kings, Arab chiefs, each ruled in their turn. Monumental proofs of their reigns are preserved in the inscriptions. King Herod is mentioned on one at Siah. The two Agrippas, his successors after Philip, are found cited in at least ten inscriptions; the most interesting is the fragment of a decree discovered at Qanatha by Mr. Waddington, and running as follows:

"King Agrippa, friend of Cæsar, and friend of the Romans, says: . . . . of a life like that of the wild beasts . . . . I am ignorant how up to the present time, in many parts of the country, dwelling in caves . . . . nor altogether . . . ."

It is very much to be regretted that this document should be so mutilated; it would have given curious information on the social state of the country; even as it is, it confirms the description given by Josephus of the savage manners of the inhabitants of Trachonitis, and confirms at the same time the opinion that I have put forth, namely, that before the advent of the Idumæans no monuments at all were erected in the country. At the most they may be looked for only at the south of the Hauran, toward the frontiers of the Nabathæan States. That the Nabathæan princes, from the first century before Christ, had a certain culture, is proved by their medals, and their monuments at Petra. They reigned at Bosra, without doubt, from 100 B. C. to the Roman conquest in 109 A. D., and often pushed their arms as far as Damascus. The coins and medals which I have collected establish, during these two hundred years, the succession of six kings: Harethath (Aretas), Malikou, Obodas, Harethath-Philodemus (Aretas Œneas), Malkou (Malchus), Dabel (Zabelus). Four of these sovereigns are mentioned in the inscriptions found at and around Bostra and Salchad; Malikou, the adversary of Herod the Great, appears on an altar consecrated in the eleventh year of his reign. Harethath-Philodemus and Malkou are on the gate of an edifice constructed in the seventeenth year of the reign of the latter, Dabel on a tomb dated the twenty-fifth year of his reign. Harethath-Philodemus is a Biblical personage. He it was who held Damascus, and governed it by an ethnarch at the time of St. Paul's escape (A. D. 39); his son Malkon brought reënforcements to Vespasian during the war against the Jews; an assistance which by no means prevented Dabel from being dethroned by Cornelius Palma, legate of Trajan, and from seeing his states annexed to the Roman empire.

The Roman conquest gave these lands three centuries of tranquillity, during which a kind of architectural fever traversed the country from end to end. The triumph of Christianity added still more to this ardor for building, and it stopped only with the approach of Islamism.

The period exhibits the phases of the remarkable architectural movement which I have studied in its monuments, and which I propose here rapidly to describe.

This most ancient monument of the Hauran is a great tomb, situated at Soueidah. It is a massive cube of masonry, decorated with Doric columns, and formerly surmounted by a pyramid, of which nothing now remains but the lowest course. A bilingual inscription in Greek and Aramaic teaches us that it was built by a certain Odeynath for his wife, named Hamrath. The form of the letters and the style of the architecture announce an epoch near the Christian era. This Odeynath was, without doubt, a chief of the Arab tribe of the Beni-Samaideh, which established itself in these countries about the same time. Greek inscriptions, which announce the existence at Soueidah of a $\Phi \acute{v} \lambda \eta$ $\Sigma o \mu a \iota \delta \eta \nu \hat{\omega} \nu$ under the Antonines, authorize this inference. The monument was built on the unit of the Greek foot; it measures 33 feet at the base, the half columns are 15 feet in height, the entablature 4 feet. The pyramid was originally 14 feet high, so that the total height, with the two steps, was 39 feet. The use of unequal numbers will be remarked, and the predominance of the number 3. This remark, indeed, is general. In reducing to Greek measures the dimensions of all the monuments of Central Syria, we are led to recognize the use of mystical and conventional numbers; and in tracing the principal lines of the monuments, it is very seldom that we cannot establish the employment of certain geometrical figures, to which the whole of antiquity has attributed a special virtue; such, for instance, as the square, the right-angled triangle, whose sides satisfy the formula $3^2 + 4^2 = 5^2$, and the Egyptian isosceles triangle, whose height is equal to $\frac{5}{8}$ of the base.

The tomb of Hamarath proves that at the epoch of the Herods Greek art had taken possession of the country. But while applying Hellenic methods and forms, the Syrian artists preserved in certain details the remembrance of former traditions. This is proved by the curious temple of Siah.

The temple of Siah is situated near Qennawât, the ancient Kanatha, in a picturesque country, at the summit of a hillock. It is perhaps the most interesting monument of this region. In order, therefore, to understand it better, we caused it to be almost entirely cleared of rubbish. Our researches were actively conducted during a week by a squad of Druse laborers, and resulted in the complete exposure of the façade, and of the undisturbed approaches to an ancient temple, a spectacle hitherto new to modern eyes.

A monumental gate, preceded by steps, opened upon a large court surrounded by porticos (αὐλη, atrium), and paved with regular slabs. At the end rose the temple on a basement of two steps. On the top of the steps was a deep προναος, sustained by two columns, and included between two broad pavilions of peculiar arrangement. In the centre was the door of the Sanctuary. The interior of the temple was transformed in the middle ages into a fortified post, and was therefore past examination. The stones obtained by the demolition of the edifice had been blocked one beside the other, so as to form a compact mass, which even our mechanical means would not enable us to attack. But from the study of the surrounding *débris*, and the text of the inscriptions, we have been able to deduce with certainty the principal features of the construction.

It is certain that the Sanctuary was of two stories; if not over the whole surface, at least over the façade. A construction decorated with pilasters crowned the two pavilions and covered the πρόναος. This disposition is peculiar, and does not exist, to my knowledge, in any ancient monument. The only one which offers any resemblance to it is the Temple of Jerusalem. It is clear from Josephus's description that the pronaos of the temple built by Herod—doubtless in remembrance of the *Oulam* of Solomon—was higher than the Sanctuary. For myself, I cannot but think that there is an evident connection between these two buildings, constructed at the same time, and under the influence of the same dynasty (as the inscriptions prove). The resemblance is not confined to the simultaneous existence of the second stage, but extends to other essential points—the monumental gate, recalling "the gate of Nicanor," the cloisters of the court, and a well-sculptured vine-branch, which adorns the gate of the Sanctuary, just as the golden vine did that of the Temple of Jerusalem.

The identity of dates is established, as I have already explained, by inscriptions found during our researches. I have already published the texts, and have no occasion to reproduce them here; they are engraved in Aramaic and in Greek, on the bases of the statues which we discovered ranged under the πρόναος. They testify that the edifice was built by two Arabs, named Maleikath, of whom one was the grandson of the other, in honor of the god Baal Samin. Besides this, a statue had been raised to King Herod; the pedestal which bore it was overturned; the statue broken in pieces; there remained nothing but the right foot, still adhering to the base, on which was engraved the inscription. The image was evidently overthrown by the early Christians.

Other inscriptions cut upon accessory parts of the monument mentioned the two kings Aggripa.

At the foot of the steps, the altar was found still existing in its original place: it is a block of stone decorated on its two faces with two wild-goats—an animal sacred to the Asiatic Venus. The style of the construction is as strange as its general disposition: although built under Greek influence, it has nothing of the Greek sobriety and good taste, but displays an accumulation of ornaments, leaves, and fruit, mixed up with figures of every kind; birds, lizards, locusts, winged genii, human busts, heads with solar rays, eagles, and lions, being scattered in profusion over all the architectural lines. The capitals of the columns are a very distant imitation of the Corinthian, but the elegant Corinthian volute is replaced by a *corde tressée*, the central flower by a human bust, and the acanthus-leaf by large and coarse foliage. The bases are yet more singular, being surrounded by a cincture of foliage, which gives them the appearance of a capital upside down.

All this sculpture is executed in the hard black basalt of the country, which makes its want of delicacy still more apparent: the English reader may form an idea of the style, since one of the heads obtained in our researches is at present placed in the British Museum. At Soueideh, a short distance from Siah, there still exists the remains of a temple of the same period and the same style: the capitals exhibit the same winged busts, and the same *corde tressée;* the architrave offers the same overcharged lines, and in examining the bases we found the same foliage. Here, however, the resemblance stops; the plan of the temple is that of a Greek peripteral temple, thereby establishing the transition from the strange style of the Herodian epoch to the more regular style of the Imperial. In order to seize these differences and appreciate the progress of style, a few steps only are necessary. Qennawat is only half an hour distant from Siah, and this city contains one of the most complete collections of ruins conceivable. Here are found two temples of the Antonines, an Odeum, a Nymphæum, a large basilica of the fourth century, tombs, cisterns, churches, private houses.

nameless and numberless ruins, all grouped among the rocks on the two sides of an embanked stream. A little farther on, at Shahbeh, the present residence of the powerful Sheikh Fares Amer, and formerly Philippopolis of Arabia —the native place, as Mr. Waddington has shown, of the Emperor Philip, and embellished by him—are baths, a theatre, temples, and monumental streets. Farther on still, at Shagga, basilicas, houses, a Roman prætorium, and sanctuaries of various forms, attest the fertile activity of the architects of the Imperial epoch. Everywhere, in short, in every village, ruins and inscriptions testify to the same labor, and when, leaving the mountain, the traveller goes on to Bostra, he may there contemplate Imperial monuments, among them an immense theatre, in almost complete preservation, the imposing effect of which is doubled by the noble girdle of towers with which the Ayûbite Sultans have surrounded it.

In a rapid sketch of the present, it is of course impossible for me to describe these interesting monuments in detail; I reserve this for the volumes on which I am engaged; and to which I beg to refer the reader. All I can do here is to indicate rapidly the special characteristics which distinguish these constructions from those erected in other parts of the Roman empire. The style of the ornamentation is nearly the same: the Ionic and Corinthian orders, the latter especially, with their ordinary accessories, are nearly exclusively employed; here, therefore, there is little to detain us.

The striking feature in the architecture of the Hauran is the exclusive use of stone. The country produces no wood, and the only rock which can be obtained is a basalt, very hard and very difficult to work; reduced to this single material, the builders were obliged to resort to combinations of arches as a means of covering great spaces. The elementary combination is the following:

Parallel arches are constructed at a distance varying from 6 to 10 feet; on these arches are built walls which are levelled to the same height; and from wall to wall are laid slabs, fitting perfectly and forming the ceiling. When the bearing is great, or the building more careful than usual, each levelled arcade is surmounted by a line of moulded corbels, forming a cornice; they then support the slabs on the extremity of the corbels, taking care to load the centre so as to counteract the leverage. Sometimes the line of the corbels is double, an upper layer projecting over the lower,

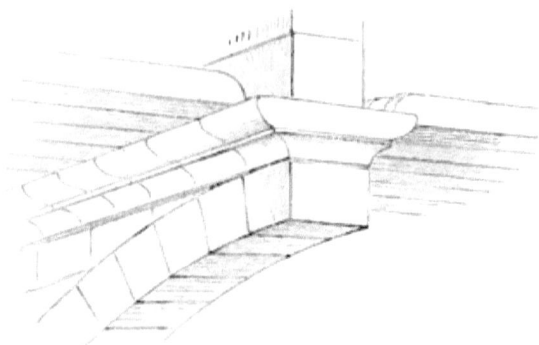

so as to give greater breadth to the cornice. The inscriptions designate this fundamental arcade by the name of ἄψις, and the joist, or slab of stone, by that of στρωτήρ. It is by the aid of these two elements, the arcade and the slab, that the architects were enabled to carry out all their designs, varying the distance of the arches, their radius, and their superposition, according to the plan and resources at hand. By way of roof they placed a layer of earth on the slabs which formed the ceiling of the top story.

The doors are also of stone, with either one or two leaves; each leaf is formed of a single slab, bearing two projections cut from the solid, and fitting into two sockets, one in the lintel and the other in the sill, so as to permit the whole to turn easily, as on a hinge: a great number of these doors exist still, *in situ;* the inscriptions call them θύρα, and often speak of their construction, which was one of the most difficult operations in their style of architecture, and one on which the builders were most disposed to pride

themselves. The closets formed in the inner walls of the
chambers were closed by similar, smaller, doors. I brought
away a specimen, finely sculptured, of this kind of cabinet-
work in stone. The windows were closed either by shut-
ters of the same kind, or more generally by fixed slabs,
pierced with holes, after some sort of design, more or less
elegant; and in these openings panes of glass were doubtless
adjusted.

Such are the methods of procedure in the buildings of
the Hauran. We find them applied to the most diverse
monuments, the basilica, with three naves and higher galleries, the private house, with reception and residence chambers, stables, out-houses, public and religious edifices. For
these last, in order to conform to the traditional Greek tem-

ple, certain modifications in the general plan were necessary. The fundamental arch, instead of being levelled horizontally, received on its extrados a pointed pediment, forming almost a gable, the space between the gables being oc-

cupied by a roof of sloping slabs. As for the façade, the
central intercolumniation being larger than the others, and
exceeding the length of the architrave, the latter was re-

placed by an arch, giving the temple that curious appearance so often seen on Syrian coins.

Lastly, in cases where the architects had to cover square or circular spaces, or halls, the purpose or interior effect of which would have been spoiled by the multiplication of parallel arcades, they had recourse to the cupola.

It is well known that the cupola or cap in masonry is of very ancient usage. Under the hemispherical or conoidal form, it is found on the Ninevitish bass-reliefs. From the East it passed over to the West, and was variously employed by Roman architects up to the day when, under the Byzantine revival, it became the principal element in modern Oriental art. The radical difference which distinguishes the ancient cupola from the Byzantine one is that the former rests upon a circular drum, while the latter is supported on a square by means of *pendentives*, or spherical triangles. We know that this feature of architecture was invented in 548 by the architects of St. Sophia, Anthemius of Tralles and Isidore of Miletus; but we do not know clearly by what series of tentative efforts the solution was discovered. The Hauran gives us several illustrations of these rudimentary essays.

The most interesting is that furnished by the "Kalybeh" of Umm-Ez-Zeitûn.

The inscriptions designate, under the name ἱερὰ καλύβη, a sort of sanctuary, composed of a cubical chamber covered by a cupola, open on one side by a great arcade, and flanked by two wings pierced with niches; the central arcade is gained by steps; brackets fitted in the wall formerly bore statues. It is difficult to pronounce on the liturgic use of these chapels; but it is probable that they served to preserve the mystic symbols of the divinity, whether images or conical stones, and also to give oracles, for they generally have a subterranean floor, in which the interpreter of the divine will could place himself.

However this may be, the Kalybeh in question, dated by two inscriptions engraved on the façade, is of the seventh year of the Emperor Probus, 282 A. D. Its cupola is in part preserved, and the system of construction is perfectly visible. First, the angles of the square were covered by means of slabs of stone, so that the space inside was brought to an octagonal form; then on this octagon a first layer was made by placing a stone across each of the angles: two layers laid in the same manner transformed the original square into a polygon of thirty-two sides, near enough, in practice, to a circle to serve as a base for a hemispherical cupola, constructed of blocks of concrete, and forming a structure which was supported at all the points of its lower perimeter, and consequently complied with the ordinary conditions of domed cupolas. The largest cupola constructed according to this system is that of the Palace of Shagga, called by the Arabs Kaisarich: it dates, like that of Umm-Ez-Zeitûn, from the third century, but is also in ruins.

It is in the Hauran that the most ancient cupolas applied to the architecture of the Christian churches are found. St. George of Ezra is of the year 515, the Cathedral of Bosra of the year 512—prior in date to those of St. Vitale of Ravenna, and St. Sergius of Constantinople, with which, however, they have some points in common.

The Christian period appears to have been the most fertile in buildings of every kind—at least, it has left the greatest number of monuments. The larger number of the private houses and tombs still standing date from this period, as the inscriptions testify. Another argument in favor of this opinion is, that the greater part of the pagan inscriptions are not *in situ*, but are generally found in later buildings. Christianity penetrated very early into these regions, and it counted numerous adepts, organized in hierarchic order, when Constantine gave it peace; and accordingly from the second half of the fourth century inscriptions are found pointing out the existence of a strong and active Christian society, building houses, porticos, cisterns, hostelries, basilicas, churches, tombs, etc., in honor of the Holy Trinity, and of the saints who were most widely worshipped

—St. George, the Martyrs Sergius and Bacchus, St. Elias, St. Theodore, and, lastly, the Virgin Theotokos. The hierarchy which conducted the building and governed the faithful is also complete. We find in a text of the year 354, the names of an archimandrite, a priest, a deacon, a steward; and at Shagga, about the same period, is a bishop named Tiberinus, who transformed a pagan kalybeh into a church, and dedicated it to St. George and his companion martyrs—ἁγίων ἀεθλοφόρων μαρτύρων γεωργίου καὶ τῶν σὺν αὐτῷ ἁγίων.

One of the causes which most favored this Christian development was the conversion of the principal tribes which had migrated from Arabia. We know that from the first century of our era a current of migration set in steadily toward the north from the most retired parts of the Arabian peninsula. It was the precursor of the great Mahomedan invasion; but, far from having the disastrous effects of the latter, it was, on the contrary, very salutary; and it shows what might have been the destiny of the country but for the fatal division created by the preachers of Mahomet.

The most important of these was the great Sabæan migration, which left the Yemen after the rupture of the dikes at Mareb, toward the year 104 of the Christian era. The tribe of the Jifnides established itself in Central Syria, on the confines of the Roman territories, and introduced into these regions its own habits of civilization. The tribe lived on friendly terms with the empire, and founded the kingdom of Ghassan. After becoming Christian, the kings of Ghassan extended their influence as far as the Hauran. Mr. Waddington found at El Hit an inscription of the King Al-Moundhir, dated in the year 578. He bears the Greek title of patrician, testifying to his alliance with the court of Byzantium. Every thing leads us to believe that this dynasty would have been the instrument of the gradual evangelization of the Arabs, had it not been rudely destroyed by the Mussulman invasion.

But it is in the Safa that we find the most numerous traces of the Sabæan tribes.

I have already explained that the Safa is a volcanic spot situated in the Desert, two days' journey east of the Jebel Hauran. I visited it with Mr. Waddington; and the remembrance of the excursion remains with me as perhaps the most curious of all my travelling recollections. Escorted by a troop of fifty Druses on horseback, in all their military splendor, we went from tent to tent, leading the life of the Desert, without the admixture of a single European element; we penetrated farther east than any previous traveller, and were fortunate enough to combine the interest of our archæological researches with the most picturesque scenery, and the most novel details of manners and customs.

The very centre of the Safa is occupied by a low plain, about twelve miles long by three broad, named Er Rohebeh. The water of the winter rains has deposited a layer of tolerably fertile soil; and in the spring the whole plain is covered with a vigorous vegetation, the verdure of which presents a striking contrast with the naked and desolate aspect of the rocky mountains round it. We reached this plain after a difficult journey of four days, under a burning sun, across rugged rocks and lava-slopes. It was an April evening. As far as the eye could reach extended a carpet of verdure, framed, as it were, in the black irregular lines of the lava; great pools of water, not yet absorbed by the sun, spread freshness and life around; the tents of the Arabs speckled the plain with brown spots; we rode through grass which reached to the horses' bellies; and by degrees, as we approached, scenes of pastoral life displayed themselves to our eyes; the sheep came home bleating; the camels disported themselves clumsily round the tents; bands of plunderers returned from a distant *ghazzou*, while long flights of desert partridges filled the air with their shrill cries as they joyfully sought their evening shelter. The calm of Nature and the serenity of these pictures might almost have persuaded us of the pacific occupations of our hosts, had not the sight of arms and military preparations reminded us that the struggle for water has been, since the days of Abraham and Lot, the fatal

condition of desert-life. But we had not come so far simply
to contemplate scenes of Nature; and the next day we set to
work at the archæological monuments in the place. The
most interesting is a ruin which the Arabs call Kharbet-el-
Beïda, or, The White Ruin—though it is entirely constructed of black lava. It is situated on the lowest slopes of a
lava-torrent from a neighboring crater, and overlooks the
whole plain. It is an old castle, surrounded by a square enclosure, with turrets at the angles. Its construction shows
that it never had any military importance, and it was probably nothing more than the spring retreat of some prince of
Ghassan. The style of the ornamentation, quite different
to what we have seen in the Hauran, and marked by a much
more Oriental stamp, goes to strengthen this impression.
The castle, properly so called, is overthrown; but among
the *débris* there are a certain number of sculptured stones;
the entrance-door was richly ornamented; scrolls of flat
foliage and flowers in a very peculiar style encompassing a
frieze of animals, among which may be distinguished lions,
gazelles, an elephant—all prove the southern origin of the
sculptor. Other fragments show details borrowed from the
Byzantine—geometrical combinations and original designs
all leading to a similar conclusion.

Opposite the castle, on the other side of the Ruhbeh, are
the ruins of a little church, built in the style of the Hauran;
the Arabs still call it El Knêse (Ecclesia).

Every thing leads to the belief that we are here face to
face with an example of that Sabæan art, the magnificence
of which ancient authors have vaunted. Strabo and Pliny
describe the temples of stone and brick, ornamented with
precious stone, and inlaid with gold and silver, the luxurious
palaces of the indolent inhabitants of Mareb, Saba, Nedjran.
Their accounts are anterior to the migrations of the Djifnide
Arabs, and several centuries earlier than the construction
of the castle of Safa; nevertheless we may see in this monument a production of Sabæan traditions, modified by the
succession of years, and the employment of different materi-

als. One proof in support of this opinion is drawn from the curious inscriptions which are found, not on the monument itself, but in all the surrounding country. It is one of the most curious traits of the physiognomy of these regions. On certain determined points, as at Sinai, the rocks are covered with inscriptions, rudely traced on the black surface of the lava. These texts are especially found on kinds of *tumuli*, in part natural, in part artificial, formed of an accumulation of rough stones, called Rejm. The use of these *tumuli* to commemorate an event in nomadic life is as old as history itself: the adventures of Jacob, of Joseph, of Absalom, furnish well-known examples. The Hebrews called these mute witnesses of a treaty, a victory, or a murder, *Gal;* but the word *Ridjmah* also existed in their language, where it meant a pile of stones, and belonged more especially to the punishment of lapidation.

I do not know whether the *Rejm* of the Safa have any traditional connection with unknown history of these far-back times, but certainly the inscriptions which they bear do not go back beyond our own era. Although we have only as yet arrived at the making out of a few words, we believe that we may be assured that they belong to the family of Himyaritic inscriptions. The alphabet presents a strong analogy with that of the monuments discovered in the Yemen, of which the British Museum possesses such beautiful examples; but the difficulties of reading are augmented by the coarseness of the execution. Like the inscriptions of Sinai, those of Safa appear to contain nothing but proper names, accompanied by formulæ of souvenirs, or prayers, gross representations of nomadic life, combats, lion-hunts, figures of camels, goats, and women. It is more than probable that these mysterious documents have been traced by Sabæan immigrants, grouped around the chief who built Kharbet-el-Beïda, and before they had lost by their close neighborhood to Syria the use of the dialect and the writing of their mother-country. The principal of these Rejm are the Rejm Marra, R. Kakhoûl, and others whose names have escaped me. We copied more than five hundred texts, but thousands more remain. It is at Rejm Marra that the Safa terminates northward; it marks the limit of the territory occupied by the tribes of Bedouin who inhabit this rocky district. On this account they have on the summit of the hill a kind of observatory, from the top of which they watch the arrival of the bands of the great tribes of the plain, with whom they are in open war. It was in order to pass this point that we were obliged to provide ourselves with an escort capable of resisting one of these unexpected attacks. We wished to reach the Jebel Sès, an isolated mountain, which can be seen on the horizon, and where the traditions of the Arabs announced the existence of important and unexplored ruins.

We set off in the morning with our little troop well armed, without baggage, and after five hours of rapid travelling reached the end of our expedition. The Anezéh showed themselves nowhere, and we had half a day's leisure to examine this interesting spot, hitherto untrodden by the foot of any European.

The Jebel Sès is an extinct volcano; it has externally the form of a cone, which may be 150 to 200 feet in height, and half a mile in diameter. In the interior lies an enormous crater, with a breach to the north, from which an immense jet of lava and ashes has issued, and stretched away as far as the horizon. At the bottom of the crater rise five small secondary cones, uplifted by later eruptions. At the foot of the great cone, and on the eastern side, a great depression in the plain receives the winter rains, and forms a temporary lake. On its banks is excavated a well of permanent water, close to which we were not a little surprised to find the well-preserved ruins of a Roman military establishment.

It is composed of an intrenched camp, a square enclosure, of 100 feet on the side, in good masonry, and with a tower at each angle. In the centre of one of the faces is the entrance-gate, in a semicircular tower of great beauty and well disposed for defence. Under the protection of this fortress were built several houses at present destroyed; and a little farther a bath, properly arranged according to Roman tradition, and affording the soldiers of the garrison the means of continuing their home habits in the midst of the desert. The baths are in Roman bricks, on a sub-basement of cut stone; all the chambers were wagon-vaulted; the great hall is terminated by an oven-like apse; and several stoves are perfectly preserved.

Strangely enough, we found no inscriptions to preserve the memory either of the builders or the temporary inhabitants of this abandoned post.

The camp at Sès formed part of a line of fortified posts, which defended the Hauran against incursions of the Bedouin. It is probable that it was joined at the north with Palmyra, and that it continued to the south in the direction of the strongholds of Moab and Ammon. These posts were placed beside permanent wells, not only on account of the wants of the garrison, but also because the occupation of the wells is the only way to command the respect of the nomadic tribes.

We visited another of these posts, situated at Nemara, at the southern extremity of the Safa, exactly on the other side of Sès. It is much less important than this last; but on account of this it is perhaps still more interesting, since it offers a rare example of a frontier post under the Roman empire.

A small mamelon, commanding the well situated in the valley and a kind of high-road (perhaps a direct route from Palmyra to Bosra), is crowned by a wall of stone. In the centre of this enclosure is a small house, closed by a single stone door, and serving as a lodging for the soldiers; an inscription on the lintel bears the name of Marcus Aurelius; a great number of soldiers have written their names on the walls or on the surrounding rocks, accompanying them by their rank or their native place. We gather from these that the post was commanded by a decurion. It was composed of a certain number of soldiers, chiefly taken from the third Cyrenaic Legion, stationed at Bosra; and to these were joined the inhabitants of the neighboring villages, Egla, Sodala, Tharba, who doubtless came in turn to mount guard —in fact, a sort of local militia, which assisted the regular army in its work of protection. We meet here, too, a *dromedarius*, that is to say, a soldier belonging to one of the *ala dromedariorum*, or squadrons of auxiliaries mounted on dromedaries, which were attached to the armies of Syria and Egypt.

THE SURVEY OF PALESTINE.

BY LIEUTENANT S. ANDERSON, R. E.

"So Joshua sent men to measure the country, and sent with them some geometricians, who could not easily fail of knowing the truth."—JOSEPHUS, *Antiq.* v. 1, § 21.

THE Ordnance Survey of Jerusalem having been successfully accomplished by Captain Wilson, R. E., and a party of the Royal Engineers in the season of 1864–'65, the Palestine Exploration Fund determined upon sending out an expedition to make such a general survey of the country as would enable the Society to fix on particular spots for further investigation. Captain Wilson was appointed to take charge of the party, and he was accompanied by myself and a photographer, Corporal Phillips, of the Royal Engineers. The party left England on the 8th of November, 1865, and arrived at Beyrout on the 22d of the same month; there, with the assistance of Mr. Eldridge, the Consul-General, the requisite number of muleteers and mules were engaged, as well as a dragoman, or interpreter, who provided tents and complete camp equipment.

Space will not admit in the present article of describing the proceedings of the expedition on the journey between Beyrout and Banias (Cæsarea Philippi), the northern limit of Palestine; but it may be interesting to describe, as briefly as possible, the method of conducting the Reconnoissance Survey of the Holy Land which commenced at this point.

The instruments employed were, an eight-inch sextant, the size generally used on board ship, an artificial horizon, a small theodolite for measuring angles, two measuring chains, a pocket prismatic compass, four pocket chronometers or watches, one mercurial and one aneroid barometer. The latitudes and longitudes of the halting-places between Beyrout and Banias were taken, and thus the position of Banias was definitely fixed with reference to Beyrout on the sea-coast.

The first operation in every survey is the measurement of a base-line. The country round Banias was not favorable for the ground measurement of a base-line, nor was it possible for an officer single-handed to accomplish this satisfactorily, hence it was determined to measure one in the Jordan Valley by means of the stars. It is most fortunate that the general direction of the survey of the country is north and south, since by selecting two prominent points lying nearly north and south, and also visible from each other, the latitude can be accurately observed at each place. The difference of latitude in miles is the distance between the stations, a small correction for difference of longitude being applied where the points do not lie exactly north and south of each other. For example, if two pairs of north and south stars are observed with a sextant, the latitude of a place on the earth's surface may be relied upon to be within 100 yards of the truth. In a similar manner, the latitude of the next station would be found within 100 yards, and the average error in the distance between the two points would be within that amount. Such an amount of error would not be appreciable in a reconnoissance survey where a base-line can generally be chosen of at least six miles in length. It was considered sufficient for this purpose that the map should be prepared on the scale of one inch to a mile, this being the scale of the Ordnance Map that is found invaluable in every country house.

The base being decided on, excursions are made to the most prominent points and hill-tops, from which angles are taken by a prismatic compass to the ends of the base-line. In this manner all prominent points are visited, and are referred either directly to the terminals of the original base or to points that have been already so referred, and thus, the more distant points at first, and the nearer points afterward, are all linked together by the method technically called triangulation.

In riding from point to point, care is taken to travel as much as possible at a uniform pace, and the time at which any important point is passed, such as a village or crossing of a stream, is noted, and angles or bearings are taken to any previously-fixed points, by which the position of the new site can then be definitely determined. This is all entered at the time in the sketch-sheet, the angles being laid down on the paper by means of a protractor, and the actual topographical features of the ground marked as they occur. At the same time the reading of a pocket aneroid barometer is noted, and thus a fair approximation is arrived at of the altitude of the different points. By this method contour-lines at any required intervals (such as 25 feet) are obtained, and by inserting them in the reconnoissance-sketch, the eye can recognize at once the prominent features and the varied slopes of the ground.

Peculiar facilities exist for making a survey of Palestine: the country is studded with prominent hill-tops, "the highlands," from which the adjoining country can be seen for long distances. One instance may be quoted. From the top of Safed Hill a round of angles was taken, and all referred to the sun at a known time; one hill to the southward was very distinct, and for want of a name it was entered in the note-book as the "triangular hill." For many weeks, as the expedition moved southward, no trace could be found of this unknown hill, till at last, when examining the Jordan ravines 20 miles to the north of Jerusalem, the triangular hill rising out of the plain of the Jordan Valley burst into view, and was at once recognized. This hill was found to be 52 miles from Safed, where angles were first taken to it, and even at that distance it was perfectly distinct. The atmosphere is very clear, and there are many points from which Mount Hermon, at one extremity of the Holy Land, and the Dead Sea at the other, can be distinctly seen, the view thus extending over a distance of 150 miles. The hill-tops also are all bare, and large trees are so rarely seen that, if a prominent one can be distinguished, it is noted on the sketch. Thus any separate sections of surveying-work undertaken in different parts of the country can be readily and accurately bound together by reference to well-known and prominent points that have been previously fixed.

The great object in the first surveying expedition was to lay down accurately the position of the highlands or western water-shed of the whole country. This being accomplished, the survey could then be extended on the same scale to the seaboard on the west to the plain of Bashan on the east, and the work ought not to cease till this is accomplished. The Biblical student, with his map before him, can trace out at his leisure the great high-roads of old; with the aid of any local description, or perhaps traditionary legends, he can identify many ruined and nameless sites of the old fenced cities, for the map will show what are the sites pointed out by Nature for fortresses, and search may successfully be made for the principal cities of old among the ruined heaps near the precious water-springs of the country.

Nestling under the southwestern spurs of Mount Hermon is a triangular terrace, which rises 500 feet above the plain beneath. At its innermost angle, there issues forth from the rock a spring which rises a full-grown stream. From the earliest times settlers must have been attracted to this highly-favored spot, but its history can only be traced with certainty to the first century, when we read that Herod the Great built a temple at the fountain in honor of Augustus Cæsar, and round this spot the town of Cæsarea Philippi sprung into existence.

Starting from a Mussulman tomb in the mountain-side overlooking the spring a reconnoissance of the valley commenced, with the assistance of an Arab from the village. Our camp is pitched in an olive-grove, between two torrent-beds that are dry at this winter season: on the little plateau between the streams is the modern village of Banias, with the remains of a modern fortification still encircling it, and on the whole of the terrace to the west and southwest of the village are the ruins of the once-famed frontier city Cæsarea Philippi. Here were the villas of the Roman settlers, and in their midst stood the public theatre, where Titus, on his return from the capture of Jerusalem, held a great festival, and compelled the captive Jews to act as gladiators and fight with wild beasts in the public arena.

Three-quarters of an hour's ride from Banias westward, by a path winding through oleanders and shrub-oak, brings us to a curious grassy mound, rising to a height of 25 feet, and overlooking the whole of the plain to the southward. This is Tel el-Kadi, and here was Laish, the site of Dan, the frontier town of the Holy Land. The hill is 300 yards long from north to south, 250 yards from east to west. The eastern and western slopes are very irregular, and toward the northwest it falls away and assumes a bowl-like form. Ascending the hill, and passing along its summit, we see an old tomb in honor of a Mussulman saint, under the shade of a magnificent oak-tree. Standing on the west side of the hill, we hear the sound of a great body of rushing water, and on penetrating through the thick oleander-bushes, and traversing a most rocky slope, we discover a large pool 50 or 60 yards wide, and the water, bubbling out of the ground, rushes away another full-grown stream. The pool is partially filled up, and entirely surrounded by shapeless basaltic stones, and it is evident that all with any architectural detail or with well-dressed faces have been removed long ago for building in other parts of the plain. At the southwest corner of the Tel rises another smaller fountain. The two streams join, and form a large pool 150 yards wide, delta-shaped, and covered with bushes. From the apex of this delta the stream flows away in a southwest course across the plain. This tributary of the Jordan, called by Josephus the Lesser Jordan, is twice as large as the fountain at Banias, and three times as large as the main stream of the Jordan coming from the north. The southern ridge has still traces of the wall which was built there to command the plain toward the south; and a position so well chosen, when fortified, might well be considered secure. Such was the impression of the five Danite spies who came to seek for an inheritance for their tribe; and even now the park-like beauty of the plain, and the surpassing luxuriance of the soil, confirm their report: "We have seen the land, and here is no want of any thing that is in the earth."

Our reconnoissance was extended down the valley to ascertain the exact spot where the principal tributaries unite. The great feature in this part of the valley is the succession of terraces through which the streams pass before reaching the plain. Five of these may be distinctly counted from Tel el-Kadi, forming natural contours at about 25 feet intervals. Following the stream on its right bank, some curious openings are observed in the hill-side, which is composed of a soft limestone; and on closer examination three caverns are discovered, extending 30 feet under the hill, and with a natural roof 10 feet high. The largest cave was tenanted by cattle, and in two or three corners human beings were sharing it with them. Farther on we come to the village of Monsourah, where there is an encampment of Arabs. They live in huts composed of the long babeer-canes that abound in the swamps of the valley, and which grow to a height of 15 feet. The people farm on a small scale, and possess herds of black buffalo-cattle. These animals, with their large backward-turned horns and very short hair, are usually seen contentedly standing in the swamps of the Hûleh, with their heads only out of water, to escape the torments of flies and mosquitoes.

The people of the village were very friendly, and the

lazy ploughmen, only too glad for an excuse to stop work,
left their ploughs to see the "Frank" taking his observations
and making his sketches. The women were all busy, some
weaving camel's-hair, to form one of the most admirable
materials for clothing (it keeps out the heat, cold, and rain),
others weaving mats, others grinding corn between two
stones, others rocking and kneading a goat-skin full of milk,
the Arab process of butter-making, others *minding the ba-
bies*. Here we come upon the Banias waters, which sweep
round so close to the village, and so swiftly, that the ground
under the huts is rapidly being washed away. Half an
hour's journey down the valley brings us to the junction of
the Banias and Tel el-Kadi streams; the latter scarcely rec-
ognizable as it flows in a sluggish stream, having parted
with nearly all its waters in supplying the artificial rivulets
that irrigate the upper part of the plain. A quarter of an
hour's walk brings us to the junction with the main stream;
and on a hillock overlooking the spot observations were
taken for latitude at mid-day. This point is now geographi-
cally determined. The Jordan here is 45 feet wide, of a
dirty-yellow color, and flowing between banks 25 feet below
the general level of the plain, while the united streams flow
in a channel 90 feet wide. From this point southward for
seven miles to Lake Hûleh (the waters of Merom) the whole
of the plain is marshy, and the lower part covered with babeer-canes.

From Tel el-Kadi we take the path westerly over stony
ground, and cross many artificial rivulets for irrigating the
land. One mile and a half from the Tel brings us to the
Jordan gorge running north and south, and 60 feet below is
the stream itself. There is a very stony descent to its bed,
and the river itself is crossed at this place by a bridge of
modern construction, with three pointed arches, the water,
which was only 30 feet wide at this time of the year, flowing through the western arch only. The gorge continues
for a mile to the southward, and then abruptly terminates,
the river issuing on the plain. Continuing our journey to

the northwest, we pass the sites of the old town of Ijor, with its little plain, now called Merj Ayûn, and the site of Beth Abel, now called Abil; and, on the rising ground farther on, we come to the line of water-shed, the great geographical line separating the waters of the Mediterranean from those of the Jordan. It is our special object to trace this western backbone continuously, and with that view we follow the dividing ridge, which is extremely narrow and well defined, to the southward, and at the end of the day's journey come to Hunin, on the summit of the western hills.

Here is the site of a very old and important fortress, which bears the stamp of several successive occupants, Roman, Saracen, Crusader, Turk, and Arab.

It must have been the site of a fenced city even when the tribe of Naphtali occupied this region; for Nature has made the site a fortress, and it commands the mountain-pass through which is the high-road from Acre to Damascus. A part of the ditch of the fortress has been excavated out of the solid rock, and in one place a beautiful geological section has been disclosed. From this place we look down upon the plain of the Jordan, and the undulating hilly ground sloping toward the Mediterranean, and here the depression of the Jordan is very striking, the whole valley looking like a vast fissure with elevated plateau on each side. The Jordan is some 2,000 feet below, and its very waters seem to flow suspiciously, as if they were going on a fruitless journey, never to reach the sea. It seems to linger on its course, and winds about and across the valley, and just below Hunin it overflows nearly the entire valley, converting it into a vast swamp; and again, a few miles below, it resolves itself into a triangular lake, 3 miles broad and 4 miles long, known as Lake Hûleh. Here, having formed a lake walled in on both sides by hills, it seems to make another effort to reach the sea, and we can see it flowing in a narrow channel with precipitous banks; unconscious of the fact that its waters are now at the sea-level. for 9 miles more it rushes onward, till it is again arrested in its course by the formation of a large lake of great beauty, 14 miles long and 6 miles wide—the Sea of Galilee. Then it leaves the lake so stealthily, and by so obscure an outlet, that it can only be detected on visiting the exact spot. Another effort is made to reach the sea; the river rushes on boisterously; but it is too late to accomplish the great object of all other rivers, for its waters are now 600 feet below the level of the ocean.

Our reconnoissance along the water-shed from Hunin embraces a succession of mountain-peaks forming the great western wall of the Jordan. These hills of Naphtali are still well wooded, but the oaks are being rapidly thinned out to supply the Damascus market with charcoal. The great feature of these highlands in the succession of valleys with which the country is intersected, the ridges between them being somewhat of the character of open glades gently sloping toward the sea.

At the last peak, which is nearly opposite the point where the marsh-land of the valley commences, the hill slopes to the southward and overlooks a little plain, 1 mile wide and 2 miles long, lying sheltered and completely enclosed by the hills. This is the plain of Zaanain; and in the middle of its western side is the undoubted site of Kedesh, the northern city of refuge. It is situated on a little tongue of land, projecting into the plain, and from the rising ground that encloses the plain on the east we overlook the Valley of the Jordan, but from a much less elevation than from Hunin. The tongue of land on which this border city stood was regularly fortified with a wall and towers at intervals, as the heaps of rubbish show; but below the town is another tongue of land, stretching out into the plain a quarter of a mile, lower than the first, and rocky. Here are situated some remains of undoubted antiquity. On a large massive platform of masonry stand two or three magnificent sarcophagi, and, curiously enough, one of them is a double one, and made to contain two people under one lid; the stone pillows in each loculus being at alternate ends. On an adjoining hill, Tel Kureibeh, a sarcophagus was discovered with three loculi. A conspicuous hill, Tel Hara, is in full view to the southeast, and on its summit, which had not been previously visited, are the remains of a very old fortress, surrounded by a strong wall, with towers at intervals, and the remains of building could be traced over the whole of the hill. It is thought that this may be the long-lost Hazor, for it answers exactly the description of the Jewish historian, and it overlooks immediately the waters of Merom, and the plain adjoining, where a thousand chariots could be marshalled. There can be no doubt, however, that this plain was the scene of the great battle, when Jabin, King of Hazor, collected the vast host to fight Joshua; and the track of the fugitives is in full view, up the valley, past our first camp at Banias, and into the ravines of the Lebanon, " till none remained."

From Kedesh we continued our journey through very steep and rugged ravines, and after being engulfed in these for several hours we come out upon a plateau and again reach the water-shed at Kefer Birim. The recess in the hills caused by the little plain of Zaanaim pushes the line of water-shed farther west, and we find it gradually extending westward, and leaving larger areas of country to be drained into the Jordan basin. On the highlands are the modern villages of Maroon and Yaroon; the first on a solitary hill-top, without wood or water, the latter on lower ground, and chiefly interesting on account of its ruins of an early Christian church. The similarity of the name has led to this place being recognized as the "Iron" of old, one of Naphtali's fenced cities. Half a mile to the eastward there is a clump of trees and brushwood, where some men were cutting firewood, and on inquiring they said there was nothing to be seen there, but the place looked so like the site of an old town that we went on in spite of them, and found a heap of ruins; and among them, and nearly overgrown with brushwood, a temple built of hard white limestone, almost like marble. These ruins would probably repay closer examination. Farther on to the northward is the modern village of Ainata, supposed to be the Bethanath of Scripture. This was the very centre of the wooded hills of Naphtali, and from the summit of a prominent hill near the village of Khunin the Mediterranean was in full view, the ridge of Cape Carmel extending to the shore-line, and the town of Acre lying in the plain on the sea-shore, a little fortress completely enclosed in its walls. To the north, across some gently undulating ground, could be distinctly seen the crusading castles of Tibneh and Belfort.

At the neighboring village of Shalaboon, on the hill-top, is an immense sarcophagus large enough to contain one of the giants of old. This massive block of limestone was deliberately removed from its bed and turned over. Lower down the hill were two other stone coffins, both partially overturned. The designs sculptured on the sides are very perfect. In the centre is a grotesque figure, supporting on his shoulders a massive wreath, which hung down in a festoon on both sides of him, and the ends are gathered up in a masonry-knot at each angle of the sarcophagus. From the centre of each festoon is suspended a bunch of grapes. At the end are a shield and a pair of short javelins, which marked the rank or dignity of the deceased warrior. This would be a great curiosity to send to England if the roads would admit of its being transported to the sea-coast.

The reconnoissance was continued along the water-shed from Kefer Birim to the southward. On the hill-side, near the village of Sasa, is an old Jewish tomb cut in the rock. A small entrance leads into a chamber 12 feet square, and around this space are the coffin-shaped recesses, or loculi, in which the bodies were placed.

Some of the recesses were very small, as if for infants; the mouth of each loculus had at one time been sealed with a stone. The principal entrance of the tomb is so low that it is necessary to stoop in order to get in. The scene described in St. John (xi. 38) is most vividly realized, after seeing the style and arrangement of these old Jewish tombs.*

---

* See Quarterly Statement II. Captain Wilson's Notes on the Rock-cut Tombs of Palestine.

Following the line of water-shed, we reach the summit of Jebel Jermuk, the culminating summit of Galilee, 4,000 feet above the sea, hitherto an unexplored region. The summit was reached by a woodman's path, which was so overgrown that it was impossible to ride along it without frequently leaning forward on one's horse while he forced his way under the branches. The woodman's path soon came to an end, and there was great difficulty in reaching the summit. Clambering up the wooded ravine, the inhabited village of Jermuk was found on the summit, and the people of the village declined to give any information. In such a remote spot they might well consider themselves secure. Following toward the south the narrow mountain-ridge, the land falls on each side, and the water parting is here defined exactly, and at last it reaches the southern peak of the Jermuk mass, and descends precipitously 2,000 feet into the plain of Rameh; and 1 mile east of the village Rameh, possibly the site of Ramah, one of Naphtali's fenced cities, one small precious spring supplies the village with water, and close to the spring vegetation is most luxuriant, and in marked contrast with the parched land adjoining. Here the people had erected summer-houses of branches on the flat roofs of their mud houses. The mud houses of the village seem to possess so little attraction even to their owners, that they never sit in them in the daytime, but assemble in groups in the different sunny corners of the village, and idle there the whole day.

And now we have reached the southern limit of Naphtali. Its boundary is most difficult to trace, as many of the border towns detailed by Joshua as defining the boundary are not yet identified; but the modern Tel Hazor is probably the site of Enhazor, and the village of Yagoog, in the plain below to the eastward, may possibly be the site of the border town Hukkok. The tribe of Naphtali possessed as much of the northeastern country as they could conquer, and it is probable that their possessions extended as far as Damascus. The peculiarities of their country must have made them a hardy race of mountaineers, and an agricultural people, compelled to clear the land before they could cultivate it, and possessing vast pasture-lands in the Jordan Valley.

Our reconnoissance has now laid down definitely the natural features of this northern region, and I am obliged reluctantly to leave the valleys of Galilee and the shores of its lake, which were all embraced in the survey, and resume the geographical line of travel dividing the eastern and western system of valleys. Here, on entering Zebulon's territory, we find its characteristic features are low ridges of hills enclosing most fertile strips of plain; and at last, as the ridges become less elevated, the plain is still more raised, and we find plain and ridge blended together into a vast plateau ending abruptly near Nazareth, where a range of hills forms the great natural step leading to the great plain. There is something very striking in the position of Nazareth. It is completely shut in by hills, which cluster round it on all sides, and shelter it from the bleak winds. The town is built principally on the slope of the western hills; the houses, constructed of the white limestone of the neighborhood, are of dazzling brightness in the sunlight. At a distance they have a remarkably clear appearance, and it must not be forgotten that this effect is very much increased by the absence of smoke, from which all Eastern towns are free. The streets are very narrow, and the bazaars or shops are quite of a miniature character, mere cupboards or recesses in each side of the street. The largest and most important building is the Latin convent, surrounded by substantial walls, a most hospitable establishment, whose doors are always open to travellers. On Sunday morning the great bell of the convent commenced ringing before the dawn of day, and if this is the *réveille* of the monks, they might have made a little less noise, for they must have roused the whole town long before any one thought of getting up. There is one other place of great interest for us to visit, and that is the well of the town, and the whole water supply is drawn from this one source. There seems to be a large tank constructed in the hill-side, and from a slab of masonry forming one of the sides the water issues through several taps, and collects in a trough below, for horses to drink. When we reached the well we found a great cluster of women, with their pitchers, waiting for their turn to draw water, and not appearing to hurry themselves when it did come. Our horses, being very thirsty, made a rush at the fountain where the women were all collected, and commenced to dance and jump about in a playful way, sending women and pitchers flying in all directions. We suddenly found ourselves left alone at the spring, the frightened crowd having formed a large circle round us. The young drawers of water thought it great fun; the more aged dames scowled at us, and seemed to regard us as wanton intruders. They soon collected their courage again when the horses were quiet, and while our horses were drinking the women came close up to them to draw the water to wash clothes, to wash their hands and feet, all these operations going on simultaneously around us. Just behind us a string of camels had appeared to take their turn at the watering-trough, and these docile animals seemed to have patience enough to wait till dark; indeed, there was such a crowd of women waiting with their pitchers, that the sun must have set before they could all have had their turn at the spring.

The Nazareth hills have for the most part become rocky and barren, and the effect is to make the little town and basin of Nazareth appear more beautiful—a lovely little spot, shut in on all sides by dreary and unprofitable hills. And yet, in spite of the beauty of the place, it had a very mean reputation nineteen hundred years ago. We hear the question put, "Can any good thing come out of Nazareth?" and the very villagers themselves spoke with a rude and uncouth provincialism that marked them at once as Nazarenes. The hills of Nazareth, although at one time under cultivation, are for the most part neglected now. The plan by which the people make the slopes fit for cultivation, is to collect all the loose stones and build rough walls, supporting terraces along the face of the hills, giving the latter the appearance of a series of steps. These little terraces are levelled, and thus strips of land of great fertility are gained, producing grapes and all kinds of fruit. The supporting walls, if neglected, tumble down; the earth on the terraces is then soon washed away by the heavy rains, and the slopes of the hills in time present nothing but barren rocks, a feature now only too common throughout the country.

It is two hours' journey from Nazareth due east to the foot of Mount Tabor, and half an hour's journey to the summit, 800 feet above the plain. Mount Tabor is a very remarkable feature. It has a flat summit, a little less than a quarter of a mile long, and an eighth of a mile wide, and it stands not quite isolated, though on its northwestern side it is joined to the Nazareth hills by a low ridge. There are the remains of a fortress on the summit, and in the midst is a capital piece of pasture, where there is a herd of goats grazing, tended by one of the monks. The Greek Church have obtained possession of this mountain, and have built a church there, and there are one or two small dwellings close to the church. There are now no remains characteristic of great antiquity on the mountain-top, though it must always have been an important site, and probably fortified. The present Saracenic ruins appear to be composed of the old materials.

Our reconnoissance is continued southward from Nazareth, and an hour after leaving the town we descend from the Nazareth hills by a deep gorge without a path, and come at once on the great plain of Esdraelon, apportioned to Issachar, and the scene of most of the great battles in Palestine. The line of water-shed is found entering the plain close to the village of Iksal, the site of the ancient town Chesulloth, one of Issachar's cities. This great plain of Esdraelon, the μέγα πέδιον, extends from the base of the Nazareth hills for about 12 miles to the south and from east to west nearly double that distance. A considerable portion of it is under cultivation, ploughing going on vigorously, even at the end of February, some using a yoke of oxen, some a single horse, and one man had a donkey and an ox yoked together. The plain is not quite a dead level. It is more undulating than level, but we can trace the extent of the plain very clearly, for the mountain-range of Carmel bounds it on the west, the hills of Samaria on the south, Mounts Gilboa and Tabor on the west, and the hills of Nazareth, which we have just descended, on the north.

We have left the mountainous country behind us, and now we see to the southward long monotonous ranges of hills in the distance, without a peak or prominent mark to attract the eye. The small amount of wood that we saw on the hills of Galilee has now disappeared, and in the plain, as well as on the hills to the south, there is not a tree to be seen.

On the first day's journey from Nazareth I came to a village called Fuleh, in the plain, celebrated as the site of Napoleon's battle of Mount Tabor in 1799. General Kleber, with a few thousand men, held his own for several hours against an overwhelming number of Turks till Napoleon himself came to the rescue. An old Arab told me that the French buried the bodies of the Turks by throwing them all into one large tank, which was completely filled with the dead. We reached Zerin, the site of Jezreel, in about half an hour, and were disappointed at finding the old site of the royal city not only an immense heap of rubbish, but covered with modern hovels. The search for Ahab's Palace was quite hopeless above-ground, for there was not a vestige of any old building to be seen. The site of the town is well chosen; it commands a view of nearly the whole of the plain of Esdraelon, and overlooks immediately to the northward a beautiful valley, the vale of Jezreel. Mount Gilboa rises from the plain close to the old city, overlooks the vale, and, in fact, forms its southern boundary. In this valley, and in full view of our tents, was encamped the vast host of the Amalekites and Midianites, that had formed an alliance to invade the land of Israel. Gideon was divinely ordered to repel the invasion, and he assembled 32,000 men of the neighboring tribes just below the village of Jezreel, and at the foot of Mount Gilboa. Here is a beautiful spring, which must have been the scene of the selection of the 300 who proved their courage and calmness by lapping the water from their hands. The attack was made at night; the invaders, in their alarm, fell upon each other and routed themselves. Gideon, it is said, returned from the pursuit with his 300 men, so that not a man of his heroic company perished.

The next invading host we find here was that of the Philistines, who came from the sea-coast, when Saul was king. We can trace exactly the adventurous journey he had the night before his death, from Jezreel, across the vale, in the greatest peril of capture by the Philistines, whose camp he was stealthily avoiding, and round the shoulder of the opposite hill to the village of Endor, at the back of the hill, 6½ miles distant from his palace. Here, in one of the numerous caves which are still inhabited, the witch of Endor lived. The next day, on Gideon's old camping-ground, the Israelites suffered a grievous defeat, and in the battle Saul and his three sons perished. The lamentation of David on this defeat is most touchingly recorded, and refers minutely to the character and scene of the action. The vanquished threw away their shields, leaving themselves utterly defenceless, and proving how closely they were pursued. They fled to the ravines and up the mountain-slopes of Mount Gilboa, southeast of our camp, and there miserably perished.

Here, in the vale and in the immediate neighborhood of Gideon's spring, must have been the site of Naboth's vineyard; and at this spot we read with deepest interest the account of the murder of Naboth, the seizure of his vineyard through the instrumentality of Ahab's queen, and how rapidly the murder was avenged by Jehu, who seized the government, killed Jehoram on the very site of the vineyard at Gideon's spring and advancing to Jezreel caused Jehoram's mother to be thrown out of window. There are now, as at all other villages, crowds of starving dogs ready to devour every particle of refuse, and we vividly realized how, when the men went out in the evening to bury Jezebel, they found no more than the skull, the feet, and the palms of the hands.

While we were encamped at Jezreel, the sheikh of the village complained that a tax-gatherer from the neighboring town of Jenin had just paid them a visit, and had flogged our water-carrier because the latter would not wait upon him. The chief desired Captain Wilson to make a report to the governor at Jenin, and our dragoman was accordingly directed to write a letter in Arabic and submit it for signature. The dragoman's interpretation of his own letter was as follows: " To the Governor of Jenin. The chief of the village of Jezreel, what you send one policeman he come speak bad words and beat near to kill him one man what fetch de water for one English *colonel* I come for see you presently." This was duly signed by Captain Wilson, and, as the chief insisted on a seal being appended to the signature, an old monogram was cut off a sheet of note-paper and affixed to the letter. This was supposed to prove the genuineness of the document, as a man's seal cannot be forged.

From Jezreel an excursion was made to El Lejjun, on the western side of the plain, and we pitched our camps by the waters of the ancient Megiddo. The encampment of the invading host, under Sisera, extended from this point along the edge of the hills southeastward as far as Taanach, which can still be identified. Barak's army was collected on Mount Tabor, 14 miles distant, but in full view of the invader's camp. The advance of the Israelites was at once discovered, and Sisera pushed forward his army till the engaging armies met in the midst of the swamps of the plain. A gale from the northeast blowing over Hermon's snowy peaks drove a blinding hailstorm direct in the faces of Sisera's army. The swamps of the Kishon soon became rushing torrents; the 3,000 chariots, once so formidable, now sank to the axle-trees in the mire. The principal bed of the Kishon, which the Canaanites had at first crossed, is now a foaming torrent in their rear, and on attempting to retreat from the first onslaught of the Israelites they were utterly routed. Sisera fled on foot from the plain, over the Nazareth hills, across Zebulun's territory, and, after travelling 40 miles from the battle-field, reached Heber's encampment at Kadesh, where he was treacherously murdered by Jael, who had for her murderous deed the implements always at hand in a tent, a tent-nail and a tent-mallet.

The whole of the southwestern portion of the plain having now been added to our map, the work was continued eastward down the valley of Jezreel, past the hill of Moreh at the modern village of Kumieh, and to the confluence of the vale with the valley and plain of the Jordan. At this point are the remains of the ancient Bethshan or Scythopolis, one of the cities of the Decapolis. On reaching Beisan, the first thing we remark is a prominent mound, partly natural and partly artificial, the site of the Acropolis. The ruins of the place were hopelessly covered with weeds, in most places 4 feet high. This increased the difficulty of making a survey of the ruins. The remains of two theatres can still be traced, the columns of two temples, two colonnaded streets running through the city, and one-half of the city wall; also the great gate-way at the northwest corner of the city, whence the high-road to Gadara started. The plain of the Jordan stretches away to the southward almost in an unbroken view to Jericho, and the hills to the eastward rise in a long and steep ascent to the elevated plateau, the land of Bashan, 2,000 feet above the valley. At this time the Bedawin Arabs below Beisan were at war with a neighboring tribe. The two hostile tribes had assembled on opposite sides of the Jordan, and had been firing across the river at each other. They were only waiting for the fords to be passable to cross over and have a pitched battle. A fortnight later, on our way to examine the celebrated crossing-place over the Jordan, where Abraham and Jacob passed on their way from the east country to the land of Canaan, we fortunately missed by two hours a band of five hundred horsemen, who had crossed the river, and were robbing all the villages on their march. The tribe that attacked Dr. Beke was very friendly to us, and escorted us to the river and back again to the more frequented line of travel.

The unsettled state of this neighborhood caused a break in our reconnoissance survey, for the line of water-shed, which was traced through the plain of Esdraelon to a minimum elevation of only 400 feet above the sea, was lost after passing the summit of Mount Gilboa, a district which has never been explored by any traveller. Our reconnoissance was continued southward from the plain of Esdraelon, following the great high-road to Jerusalem. The path leaves the plain at the modern village of Jenin (the Engannim, of Issachar), and follows the course of a little valley thickly planted with olive-trees. After a gentle ascent of 2 miles the valley ends in a little plain, having the village of Kubatiyeh at its southwestern corner, built upon the slope of the hill. The locusts were very thick in this plain, and were settling upon the blades of corn, now 6 or 8 inches high. The women and children of the village were distributed over the plain trying to drive away the locusts with sticks and branches. In the course of a month the young locusts would be hatched, and while they are in the crawling stage they devour every trace of vegetation that comes in their way.

In the continuation of this plain, and a little to the westward, is a hill called Dotan, which has been recognized as the site of Dothan, where Joseph's brethren were feeding their flocks when he came from his father's settlement at Hebron to visit them. The numerous rock-hewn cisterns that are found everywhere would furnish a suitable pit, in which they might have thrust him; and as these cisterns are shaped like a bottle, with a narrow mouth, it would be impossible for any one imprisoned within to extricate himself without assistance. These cisterns are now all cracked and useless. They are, however, the most undoubted evidences that exist of the handiwork of the inhabitants in ancient times.

In the course of our day's journey from Esdraelon we passed through a succession of narrow valleys, occasionally relieved by strips of plain, and these are the chief characteristics of the central portion of Manasseh's territory. After seven hours' travelling the path skirts the western shoulder of a very prominent hill, and then descends into the vale of Nablûs.

This spot, the site of the ancient Shechem, the City of Refuge, is unrivalled in Palestine for beauty and luxuriance. There are two mountains parallel to each other, almost meeting at their bases, but one mile and a half apart at their summits. They enclose a beautiful little valley between them, not more than 100 yards wide at the narrowest part, and widening out in both directions. The town of Nablûs is situated at the narrowest part of the vale. The mountain on the north is Ebal, that on the south Gerizim, and the vale lies east and west. The site of the town is admirably chosen, on the water-shed, in the middle of the pass, easy of access to the Jordan country eastward, and to the sea-coast on the west. The whole of Mount Gerizim was thoroughly examined, and the plan of Justinian's church disclosed by excavation. It had been built upon older foundations, probably those of the old Samaritan temple. An excursion was made to the summit of Mount Ebal, 1,200 feet above the vale. The summit is rocky and bare, and there are no ruins on the mountain-top, except a curious square enclosure, with very thick rude walls. Just below the summit there is a break in the regular slope of the hill, and a small but steep valley comes up from the vale below almost to the summit, forming a vast natural amphitheatre, in height equal to that of the mountain. Immediately opposite to this the steep slope of Mount Gerizim is similarly broken by a valley forming a second natural amphitheatre of equal beauty and grandeur. In these two lateral valleys were assembled the twelve tribes of Israel under Joshua, six tribes on Gerizim, and six on Ebal. The Levites and the ark were in the strip of the vale, and the blessings and cursings were read before the whole congregation (Josh. viii. 32 to 35, and compare Deut. xxvii. 11). Nothing is wanting in the natural beauty of the site to add to the solemnity and impressiveness of such a scene. The best view of the town of Nablûs is from Ebal. It seems to repose so snugly in the little vale, and while the houses seem to shrink from the base of the Epal slope, they cling to and attempt to climb the slope of Gerizim, the mountain of blessings. At the edge of the plain of Mukna (Moreh), a mile and a half east of the town, is Jacob's Well, on the piece of ground he purchased from the Shechemites. Not far from the well is the site of Joseph's Tomb. The identity of the well has never been disputed. Christians, Jews, Moslems, and Samaritans, all acknowledge it, and the existence of a well in a place where water-springs are abundant is sufficiently remarkable to give this well a peculiar history.

Some men were set to work to clear out the mouth of the well, which was being rapidly covered up. A chamber had been excavated to the depth of 10 feet, and in the floor of the chamber was the mouth of the well, like the mouth of a bottle, and just wide enough to admit a man's body. We lowered a candle down the well and found the air perfectly good, and, after the usual amount of noise and talking among the workmen and idlers, I was lashed with a good rope round the waist and a loop for my feet, and lowered through the mouth of the well by some trusty Arabs directed by my friend Mr. Falcher, the Protestant missionary. The sensation was novel and disagreeable. The numerous knots in the rope continued to tighten and creak, and after having passed through the narrow mouth I found myself suspended in a cylindrical chamber, in shape and proportion not unlike that of the barrel of a gun. The twisting of the rope caused me to revolve as I was being lowered, which produced giddiness, and there was the additional unpleasantness of vibrating from side to side, and touching the sides of the well. I suddenly heard the people from the top shouting to tell me that I had reached the bottom, so when I began to move I found myself lying on my back at the bottom of the well; looking up at the mouth, the opening seemed like a star. It was fortunate I had been securely lashed to the rope, as I had fainted during the operation of lowering. The well is 75 feet deep, 7 feet 6 inches diameter, and is lined throughout with rough masonry, as it is dug in alluvial soil. The bottom of the well was perfectly dry at this time of the year (the month of May), and covered with loose stones. There was a little pitcher lying at the bottom unbroken, and this was an evidence of there being water in the well at some seasons, as the pitcher would have been broken had it fallen upon the stones. It is probable that the well was very much deeper in ancient times, for in ten years it had decreased 10 feet in depth. Every one visiting the well throws stones down for the satisfaction of hearing them strike the bottom, and in this way, as well as from the *débris* of the ruined church built over the well during the fourth century, it has become filled up to probably more than a half its original depth. I was drawn up without mishap, but was bumped about sadly from side to side in consequence of the Arabs pulling me up by jerks, and at the same time the rope and its burden revolved. My kind friend and host the German missionary was glad to see me up again, and remarked, "*Now* I had fear for you, lest the rope did break." The mouth of the well is close to the high-road from Jerusalem to Galilee.

The gardens in the vale of Shechem were looking very beautiful at this time (May 1st). The fig-trees, the latest of all, were in full leaf, and the people commenced to reap in the plain on this day. It was high time too, for the young locusts were commencing their ravages, and the people seemed really roused to exertion at this critical time.

While we were breaking up our camp and preparing to

start, the lepers of the town gathered round the camp, making their piteous appeals for money. These unfortunate people, both men and women, were ordinarily found sitting on the heaps outside the town wall, close to the wayside. They were most distressing specimens of humanity; most of them without hands, some with no teeth or hair, and shunned by every one.

After leaving Nablûs, the reconnoissance survey was continued to the Jordan Valley, to fix the confluence of the Zerka, the great highway from the east, and it was then necessary to return westward to trace the line of water-shed that we found crossing the vale of Shechem between the town and Jacob's Well. On reaching the western ridge, the country is very broken and intersected by numberless ravines, so narrow and tortuous that it is not safe to trust the eye to mark out their courses, without traversing their entire length. The nature of this part of the country was consequently most unfavorable for rapid reconnoissance, and it was only found practicable to fix the position of the prominent hills near the dividing ridge. On the journey southward several points of great interest were visited and surveyed, and among others the sites of Shiloh and Ai.

The ruined village Seilûn is the site of Shiloh, where the Ark first rested after the capture of Ai and Jericho, and where Joshua divided the newly-conquered land of Canaan among the twelve tribes. The position of Shiloh is accurately defined in the Book of Judges to be on the north of Bethel, on the south of Lebonah, and on the east of the highway that goeth from Bethel to Shechem. There is very little to mark the site now, but there are ruins and a curious excavation in the rock in the side of the hill which might have been the actual spot where the Ark rested, for its custodians would naturally select a place sheltered from the bleak winds that prevail in these highlands. In a little valley about half a mile from the ruins are the spring and well of Shiloh, and this must have been the spot where the daughters of Shiloh came out to dance at their periodical festival. On one of these occasions the survivors of the tribe of Benjamin carried off two hundred of them. There are many rock-hewn tombs in this neighborhood, but they have all been broken into and ransacked. There is a pretty piece of plain adjoining the ruins of Seilûn, which are otherwise shut in by stony and deep valleys, torrent-beds in the winter, and dry during the rest of the year.

Nine miles south of Shiloh is the modern village of Beitin, the site of Bethel. Here there is nothing but a heap of ruins, but on the hill adjoining and east of Bethel are the remains of a fortified Christian church, which was probably built by the early Christians to consecrate the spot where Abraham built his second altar after entering the Promised Land, and where he separated from Lot. The latter, attracted by the apparent fertility of the Jordan Valley lying beneath him, contrasted with the barrenness of the stony ravines and ridges on the westward, chose the country of the Jordan, and journeyed eastward to the shores of the Dead Sea. The site of Ai may be confidently assigned to a ruined hill-top east of the church, called by the Arabs Et Tel, "the heap." This corresponds exactly to the description, when we know the site of Bethel and the site of Abraham's encampment, where he built an altar; for we read that he pitched his camp having Bethel on the west and Hai on the east. There is a valley behind the ruined heap where Joshua placed his ambush. There is a spot opposite, across the intervening valley, where Joshua stood to give the preconcerted signal; and there is a plain or ridge down which the men of Ai hurried in pursuit of the retreating Israelites, so that the men in ambush rose and captured the city, and made it a "heap" (or a "Tel") forever. Mr. George Williams has pointed out that the word which is translated "heap" in our version exactly corresponds to the Arab rendering "Tel." *

In passing through the highlands of the district allotted to Ephraim, the rocky valleys and ridges became more numerous and more sterile. Then, after passing Bethel, we

* See Quarterly Statement IV. Captain Wilson on the site of Ai.

enter upon the land of Benjamin, and find nothing but rocks and stones and ruined heaps; and low ranges of hills without a prominent peak or feature to vary the scene. From Bethel to Jerusalem the great high-road follows the line of watershed; and, on both sides, valleys take their rise, and become at once rocky ravines, descending precipitously on the left hand to the Jordan, and on the right hand more gradually to the Mediterranean. After three and a half hours' weary travelling from Bethel, the last ridge is crowned, and the city of Jerusalem, not half a mile distant, bursts into view.

Our reconnoissance survey has embraced the western highlands down to this point; and the amount of work accomplished compared with what remains to be done is as the seam of a coat to the whole garment. The vast system of valleys east and west of the line we have followed has still to be examined. There is not a hill-top on the ridges between them that does not contain the ruins of some ancient city; and the work that has been commenced should not cease till the topography of the whole of Palestine has been carefully worked out. The length of the Holy Land, from Dan to Beersheba, is only 140 miles, and its breadth 60 miles: and yet this small area, the theatre of the most engrossing portion of the world's history from the earliest times, still remains only partially explored. A knowledge of its topography is indispensable for an accurate comprehension of the varied scenes which are described, and without which the significance of the records must remain more or less obscure. We are unable as yet to trace with precision the course of any one of the boundaries of the twelve tribes as described in the Book of Joshua; and all subsequent topographical accounts will be intelligible if the localities could be accurately determined.

The success which has hitherto crowned the efforts of Dr. Robinson and other explorers in identifying the old sites is sufficient to insure still further discoveries following upon more extended examination. The land is now undergoing changes; the people are dying out or migrating, the old habits and customs are disappearing, and no time should be lost in completing the work before the levelling hand of civilization shall have effaced the relics of the past.

ON THE POTTERY AND GLASS FOUND IN THE EXCAVATIONS.

ALTHOUGH large quantities of pottery have been found in the various excavations carried on by the Palestine Exploration Fund, few objects of very high antiquity, and scarcely any of fine art, have been discovered. The shafts and galleries having been mostly sunk in masses of *débris* and in "made ground," the fictile objects are generally in a fragmentary state; the few exceptions to this rule being those disinterred from passages and tombs. Many of the fragments, moreover, are of such a rude and common description, that it is difficult to fix correctly the date of their manufacture; and this the more so, since the commonest ware of different nations is precisely that which possesses the least distinctive characteristics. It is the object of this Paper to describe some of the more interesting specimens, and to assign them, as nearly as may be, to the period and country to which they belong.

And here, at starting, it must be confessed that no specimen found as yet can be pronounced to be from the workshop of a *Jewish* handicraftsman. Most of the earlier specimens were probably imported from the opposite shores of the Greek Islands, and in some few instances from Italy; a few Phœnician vase-handles and the Christian objects alone possessing sufficient individuality to justify their assignment to manufacturers within the limits of the Holy Land.

The pottery found in the excavations may conveniently be considered in the following order:

I. Phœnician Pottery.
II. Græco-Phœnician Pottery, *i. e.*, Pottery made in Cyprus and elsewhere, where there were Phœnician colonies influenced by Greek culture.
III. Pottery of Roman manufacture.
IV. Christian Pottery.
V. Arabic Pottery.

I. *Phœnician Pottery.*—The very interesting specimens which may safely be referred to this head are six vase-handles, found by Captain Warren on a bed of rich earth, from eight to ten feet in thickness, lying on the rock at the southeastern angle of the Haram Enclosure, at the depth of sixty-three feet from the present surface. Each of these handles bears impressed upon it a more or less well-defined figure, resembling in some degree a Bird, but believed to represent a Winged Sun or Disk, probably the emblem of the Sun-God, and possibly of royal power. On each handle Phœnician letters appear above and below the wings; and

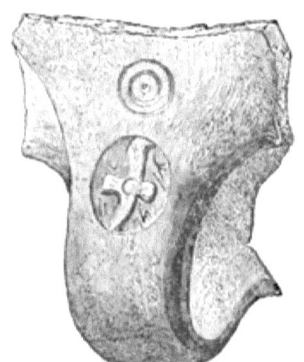 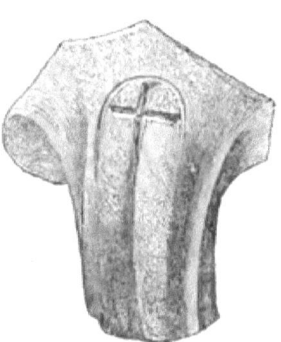

ANCIENT MARKS ON HANDLES OF VASES.

these, in two instances, have been interpreted by Dr. S. Birch, of the British Museum, and imply that the vessels were made for the royal use, or at all events in a royally-privileged manufactory.

A. [See Figure.] LeMeLeK ZePHa.—To or of King Zepha.
B. ———— LeK SHaT.—King Shat.
C. ———— LeK.—The letters which follow are uncertain.
D, E, F. The letters are nearly obliterated on these examples.

Another vase-handle, found in the same place, and apparently of the same ware, bears as a potter's mark a cross within a semicircular mark. This cross, it is needless to remark, has no relation to the sign of salvation.

When the rarity of Phœnician inscriptions of any kind is taken into consideration, the importance of these fragments, which are probably as old as the Moabite Stone, will become apparent, and the practical importance of collecting and preserving even the smallest pieces of pottery is proved. The letters were not discovered until the handles were cleaned, after their transmission to England. It may be hoped that future discoveries may add to our knowledge of the royal personages now for the first time indicated, and that the researches of the Association may be hereafter rewarded by the finding of a fragment of the work of the royal establishment of potters mentioned in 1 Chron. iv. 23, as existing at Jerusalem.

II. *Græco-Phœnician Pottery.*—In the bed of solid earth *upon* which the Phœnician vase-handles were found, several broken lamps occurred. These are of red or brownish ware, with one, two, or three lips, and seem adapted for the burning of fat rather than oil. A specimen of the same period, remarkable as having *four* lips, and in perfect preservation, was found in a cave upon Olivet. Lamps of the same design with the former of these have been found in considerable numbers in the Island of Cyprus (*Chittim*), and also in the semi-Phœnician tombs in the rocks of Ben Gemmi, in Malta. They are considered by Mr. A. W. Franks to be of late date—not earlier, i. e., than the second century

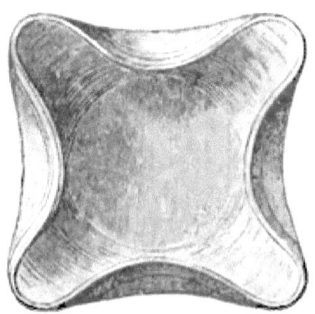

before the Christian era. The position of the broken lamps and other pottery found with them may be accounted for by the supposition that they were thrown down upon the surface of the solid earth, and afterward trodden in before the

ANCIENT JAR.

accumulation of the superincumbent mass of *débris*, or they may have been deposited with the earth itself. Underneath this earth, and at the depth of sixty-three feet from the surface, Captain Warren discovered a small vase [see Figure], placed in a cavity scooped out of the rock, at three feet from the angle of the Haram Wall. This vase is of pale-red ware, and of a common Græco-Phœnician type.[*] The fact that the inscribed Phœnician vase-handles were found *above* the last-named lamps and pottery does not militate against the period to which the latter have been attributed, for they may have been found in some ancient excavation within the wall, and thrown over it *after* the deposition of the solid earth, and *before* that of the looser soil which lies above it. A considerable number of vases, dishes, and pateras, have also been found in various other excavations, and notably in caves about Olivet. Many of these vessels are of exactly the same type as those found in the tombs of Ben Gemmi. They had all, probably, a common place of manufacture in Cyprus or some other of the Greek islands, which, as especially Rhodes, are known to have imported largely to Alexandria. In this last city vase-handles are constantly found bearing the Rose of Rhodes and the names of the Greek potter who made them. One fragment alone bearing a pure

ANCIENT DISH.

Greek inscription was found on Ophel. A dish of brown ware, measuring ten inches in diameter, and found in a cave near Olivet, is remarkable for having its feet perforated like handles, as if for the purpose of suspension when the utensil is not in use.

[*] See Quarterly Statement, 1869, No. I., p. 85.

Two circular disks, each pierced with two holes, and an oblong object, resembling an unengraved stamp, found at Saida, probably belong to this period. Some suppose these objects were used as weights for looms.

Of a different character from the above are a few specimens, less than a score in number, which may be safely asserted to be of the Græco-Phœnician fabric of Cyprus. These are of yellowish color, profusely ornamented with barred and interlaced patterns of dark red. The designs strongly resemble those seen on the pottery of the aboriginal Kabyle Mountaineers of Algeria, and on that of the almost unknown Riff People of the Empire of Marocco. The largest specimen is a portion of a large single-handled jar,

and, from the perforated stoppage in the interior of the neck, like that of an Egyptian "*Gulleh*," was probably used for water. It was found at the depth of nineteen feet in the Muristan, and is here figured in conjunction with a smaller fragment from the same spot. [See Figure.] Large quantities of precisely similar pottery have been found from time to time in Cyprus, and a fine collection has recently been added to the Royal Museum at Turin. Specimens also exist in the British Museum and in the Louvre.

Excavations at the Birket Israil, the Muristan, and on Ophel, have produced six fragments of vases, which, with a perfect specimen obtained by Captain Warren from the French Consul at Saida (Sidon), are among the most curious objects in the possession of the Association. They are here described with very great hesitation as belonging to this division, and considerable doubt exists as to their proper appropriation. Several precisely similar vases exist in the *Egyptian* Collection in the British Museum, one of which was presented by Sir Gardner Wilkinson; but in no instance is the locality of their discovery stated in the Register. Two are figured in the " Antiquités d'Egypte." Vol. V., Plate 76, Nos. 8 and 16; but here, again, strangely enough, though engraved along with specimens of vases from Thebes and Sakkâra, they are simply described as "other vases." These curious vessels are all of an extremely hard, massive, black ware, coated in three instances with a dark-crimson glaze, perhaps produced by cinnabar. Five out of the seven specimens, including the perfect one, are in the shape of the *Thyrsus*, or pine-cone, so often represented on ancient monuments and gems as the symbol of Dionysus.* The neck, in the two instances where it is preserved, is short, and the orifice extremely small. The apex of the cone being downward, it is evident that these vases were not intended to stand upright. [See Figure.] It was diffi-

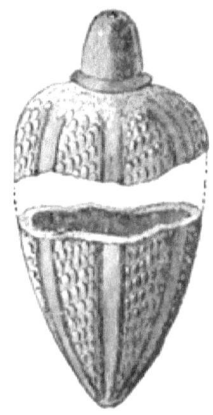

VASE FOUND AT BIRKET ISRAIL.

cult to assign a use to these singular vessels; but the problem has apparently been solved in the following manner: The writer passed a bent quill down the narrow neck, and scraped the inner surface of the perfect vase. By this means pieces were detached of a gray substance, which, on being analyzed by Prof. N. Maskelyn, proved to be small flakes of decomposed beeswax, and among these appeared several small globules of quicksilver in its usual state. It therefore seems almost certain that these vases were designed for the importation or preservation of quicksilver, a use to which their massiveness, weight, and the narrowness of the neck, which would insure easy stopping, would render them peculiarly appropriate. The beeswax was doubtless used for closing the orifice.

* The cone, if such it be, is in each case *fluted*, and may, therefore, represent some other seed or fruit. Three of the British Museum specimens are likewise fluted.

III. *Roman Pottery.*—Considering the great abundance of Roman ware which is commonly found in places of Roman occupation, it is singular that very few specimens have been found in the excavations. A fragment of the so-called "Samian" ware was discovered near Wilson's Arch, in a

passage leading south; another came from Ophel, at the distance of fifty-two feet from the surface, and a third was found elsewhere. This last piece has an interesting potter's mark impressed upon the bottom inside: it is in the shape of a foot, with distinctly-marked and elongated toes, and the letters CANRI.* [See Figure.] To the Roman period, also, belong three or four lamps of late date and poor design; a jar covered with circular horizontal flutings of a type common in Egypt, where it was perhaps made; some earthen-ware water-pipes from the so-called "Bath of Helena," east of Olivet; and the fragments of a large amphora of pale-red ware, stamped with a curious potter's mark. This reads BARNAE, and implies that it was the work or

from the shop of *Barna* or *Barnas*, a very peculiar and unusual name, and one probably of Jewish origin. The two

---

* Mr. W. Chaffers, in his "Marks and Monograms on Pottery and Porcelain," p. 13, figures a very similar mark, and ascribes this ware to *Aretium* (Arezzo).

syllables of the name are arranged above and below a monogram. [See Figure.] This amphora seems to be of late work; it was found by Captain Warren eight feet deep in the mound at Wady Kelt, near Jericho. A small vase with a single handle covered with a shining brown glaze is also probably Roman; it was found near Saida.

III. *Christian Pottery.*—Of pottery which can unhesitatingly be assigned to the Christian period the Association possesses a large series of lamps. Some of these are distinguished by extremely curious inscriptions, and most of them possess a local character which is extremely interesting. Many lamp-types of more Western Christendom, from the Catacombs of Rome, Syracuse, and Carthage, such as the Good Shepherd, the Sacred Monogram ☧, the Dove, the Cock of St. Peter, and the Chalice, are entirely absent; and the same may be said of the disgusting and probably Gnostic device of the Toad associated with the Cross, so often found in the Catacombs of Alexandria and elsewhere in Egypt. The earthen-ware bottles with the effigy of St. Menas, an Egyptian Saint who flourished in the fourth century, and whose name recalls the first Egyptian king, so commonly found with Christian lamps in Egypt, are also absent. The usual symbols of the Jerusalem lamps, which are all of a rude and cheap description, and which give an affecting indication of the poverty of the " Saints " of the early Church of Jerusalem, are the Cross, the very Sign of their Salvation; the Seven-branched Candlestick, which reminded them not only of the dimmed glories of Zion, but of Him who is the Light of the World; and the Palm Branch, which was dear to them not merely for its own exquisite grace and beauty, but by its association with Psalm xcii., with the Gospel narrative, John xii. 13, and with the Apocalyptic Vision, wherein the glorified saints are described as " clothed with white robes and palm-branches in their hands," Rev. vii. 9. These emblems, which the Christians of the " Mother of Churches " used and rejoiced in, in common with their brethren in more Western lands, are all more or less conventionalized in their treatment, and are represented in a distinctive and different manner, occurring in every instance, not as is usual in the West and even in Egypt, in the *centre*, but along the edge and near the outer lips of the lamps, which are pear-shaped, and in no instance round. Uninscribed round lamps of a different description have, nevertheless, been discovered, and probably belong to this period. [See Figure.]

The following inscriptions occur; they are written in barbarous Greek, the words being often mis-spelt, and the letters frequently braced together or turned upside down.

It is noticeable that one form of the **A** which is used, is that which is constantly found upon contemporary work in Egypt, and indeed is frequently employed as a potter's mark for ware made at Alexandria, which seems to have been to Egypt what Stoke and Worcester are to England, and Dresden to Germany.

1. **LVXNΑRIA KALΑ** *A Seven-branched Candlestick, conventionalized.* The first word is not classical Greek, but the inscription seems to signify " Good," or " Beautiful Lamps."

2. **ΦѠC X̅V̅ ΦЄΝΙΠΑCΙΝ.** *A Cross.* This misspelt inscription may be translated, "The Light of Christ shines forth," " or gives light to all." [See Figure.]*

LAMP WITH CHRISTIAN INSCRIPTION.

3. **ΦѠC XV ΦЄΝΠΔCΙΝ**, followed by two letters whose meaning has not been explained. *A conventionalized Seven-branched Candle stick.* There are several specimens of this type.

4. The inscription on this lamp appears to begin with the letters **ΙXΘ**, which may stand for *Ιησους Χριστος Θεος*, or it may possibly allude to our Lord under the well-known

* Compare a lamp in the Museum at Leyden, which bears the inscription **ΦѠC ЄΞ ΦѠTOS**, *Light of Light.*

symbol of the Fish, **IXΘVS**, the letters of which form the initials of the Greek equivalent of "Jesus Christ, the Son of God, the Saviour."

Some other lamps have a running pattern of the conventionalized tendrils, leaves, and fruit of the vine, executed with considerable freedom and elegance; but although they

LAMP.—POOL OF BETHESDA.

exhibit something of Greek freedom of treatment, they may probably be assigned to the Christian period, and the design may have reference to the mystery of the Holy Eucharist. [See Figure.] One of the Jerusalem lamps bears the letters I I, probably for Jesus; and another of somewhat different fabric, besides two palm-branches, exhibits a tree within a circular fence. It may be conjectured that this is intended to represent the Tree of Life. The writer has seen a somewhat similar tree in the mediæval Hebrew map of the Holy Land. The Christian lamps have been found not only in tombs but in numerous other excavations in and about Jerusalem. It is remarkable that none of them bear potter's marks on the under side.

V. *Arabic Pottery.*—Of Arabic pottery scarcely any thing of importance has been discovered. Among the specimens are two or three pots covered with a green glaze, and numerous fragments of domestic use. Perhaps the most interesting object under this head is a small lamp found in an excavation at the Muristan, at a depth of twelve feet. It is colored white, barred with blue and black lines. Though the ancient classical form—which indeed still lingers in the South of Europe, in the East, and, it is said, even in Germany—has to some extent been preserved in this specimen, it may nevertheless be considered a work of Arab art, as the texture, glaze, and patterns, are precisely like those on pieces of undoubted Arabic pottery found by the writer upon the mounds of Musr Ateekeh, or Old Cairo, the ancient Fostat of the Arabian conquerors of Egypt. A few morsels of Cufic inscriptions on green and yellow ware, have been found at Birket Israil and at Ain es Sultan, from which also was obtained a fragment of a blue and white dish representing two birds among foliage.* It should be mentioned here that the Society possesses a few specimens of Arabic wall-tiles, one of which, with a characteristic blue pattern on a pale-green ground, is from the Great Mosque at Damascus, formerly the Church of St. John Baptist.

Glass.—Besides pottery great quantities of fragments of ancient glass have turned up in the various excavations. Most of these, although extremely beautiful from their iridescent colors—the result of decomposition—are of little or no importance. Not even a single portion of such beautiful bottles of opaque and wavy glass as those yielded by the tombs of Saida and its neighborhood, and only two variegated beads, such as those which may still be obtained from the peasant-lads of Tyre, have as yet been discovered. One vase, however, found with Graeco-Phœnician pottery in a sepulchral cave on Olivet, merits attention from its rare and

* This is but one out of many proofs that Mahommedans are by no means so consistent in rejecting forms of animal life as is vulgarly supposed.

peculiar form. It is *double*, with two handles, and a third, now unfortunately broken, originally arched over the top. The color is a pale green, with circular and zigzag lines running over it in relief, of a much darker tint, approach-

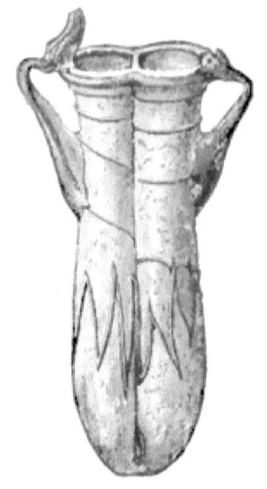

ing to blue. [See Figure.] To the Roman period belong several fragments of glass mosaic of the ordinary type,

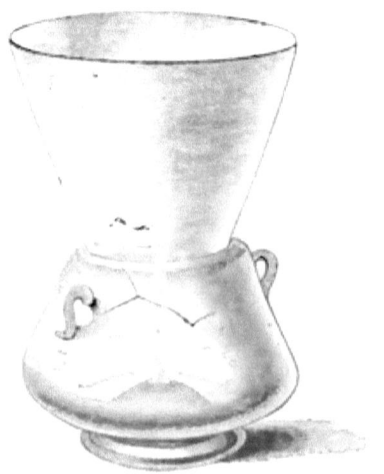

which have been found in various parts of the excavations. Of Arabic glass three lamps are worthy of especial notice. Two of these are of a pale-green color, with three dark-blue rings or handles, by which they were formerly suspended by means of chains, and contain perforated stems designed apparently to hold a wick. [See Figure.]

These lamps may be advantageously compared with the more magnificent and inscribed specimens brought from Cairo, and now in the Slade Collection in the British Museum, and with those purchased by the nation from Dr. Meymar and now at South Kensington. A very few of like form may yet be seen in some of the oldest Coptic *Dayrs*, or Convents, and in the Mosques in the neighborhood and city of Cairo. The present specimens were found by Captain Warren in a rock-cut and vaulted chamber in a passage leading down to the Fountain of the Virgin. The third specimen is of smaller size; it is likewise of a pale-green tint, the three handles being of the same color, and, like the other examples, contains a central stem for the wick.*

Greville J. Chester, B. A., M. R. A. I.

* It is right to state that this paper was written under pressure of other work, as the contributor originally appointed was prevented by sudden illness from undertaking it.

NOTES ON MISCELLANEOUS OBJECTS FOUND IN THE EXCAVATIONS.

BY GREVILLE J. CHESTER.

The following brief notes have been drawn up in the hope that they may aid persons wishing to have their attention drawn to the most interesting objects in the collection of the Palestine Exploration Fund. These, as will be seen, are but few in number, a fact to be accounted for by the narrowness, and by the small area occupied by the shafts and excavations as compared with the vast mass of *débris* in which they have been sunk. The objects have been arranged for the sake of convenience, according to the material of which they are formed.

Objects made of Stone.

1. A shallow trough, 13 inches in diameter, made of limestone. It was found at a depth of 27 feet on Ophel. Another and smaller specimen, 6½ inches in diameter, and formed of hard stone, probably from the Hauran,* was discovered by E. H. Rogers, Esq., late Her Britannic Majesty's Consul at Damascus, in the Mound of Tell Salahiyeh, near that city. These troughs were probably used for pounding grain, and preparing it for food. They are not unfrequently found with Roman remains, but may possibly belong to an early period.

2. Balls of flint and other stone. Several balls of flint were found by Captain Warren, near the pool of Siloam, in the Valley of the Kedron. Another ball of like size is formed of some hard volcanic rock. Similar balls have been found in this and other countries of Europe. Their use is still a problem to antiquaries. Certain American tribes

---

* The volcanic stone of the Hauran is to this day used for mill-stones, which are brought down on the backs of camels to Tyre and other places on the coast for exportation.

use stone balls in the preparation of food, heating them red-hot and then throwing them into skins filled with water, in which flesh has been placed in order to be cooked. The balls have thence been named "pot-boilers." It is possible that some of the present specimens may have been intended to serve this use, although flint, from its liability to crack when heated, would not be the best stone for the purpose. Some of the balls which have been partially worked into facets were probably used as *mullers* for pounding grain. Some *larger* balls, formed of limestone, and found at Jerusalem, are supposed by some to have been used as missiles to be hurled from a *Balista*. This is possible, as Vitruvius mentions one so small as to throw a stone of only two pounds weight.*

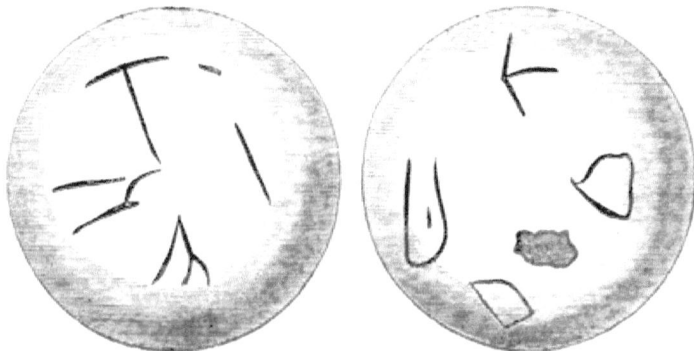

3. Stone weights. A number of these were found in shafts at Ophel, Robinson's Arch, and elsewhere. Their approximate value has been given by Captain Warren in "Quarterly Statement" No. VI., p. 330. One, with supposed Hebrew characters, found at Robinson's Arch, is here figured. [See Figure.] Another weight has upon either side the following mark. It was found in a passage above the Virgin's Fount, and weighs 2,301.8 grains troy.

4. In the same passage was found a round object of soft stone, bearing in its centre a circular mark, surrounded by a much-obliterated inscription in Greek letters. It seems to be a stamp of the Christian period. Somewhat similar stamps were used in making the Eucharistic Bread.

5. Small seal of hard close-grained black stone. This is one of the few *Jewish* objects discovered by the Society. It was found at the southwest angle of the Haram Area. The inscription is in old Hebrew characters arranged in two lines. [See Figure.] It records the name

* Dict. Greek and Roman Antiquities. Art. " *Tormentum.*"

of the owner, *Haggai, son of Shebniah.* Its discovery is narrated above, p. 95.

SEAL OF HAGGAI (FULL SIZE).

6. Head of limestone; Late Roman Period, found in the English cemetery west of the Holy City.

7. Three sepulchral chests of the Christian Period found in the neighborhood of Jerusalem. These are among the most interesting objects found. They are all formed of white or pale-red limestone, and the style of their execution is of considerable elegance. When discovered, they contained human bones and skulls, and it is much to be regretted that the latter were not preserved. Captain Warren states that the skulls and other bones found in these chests are "generally adult." They must therefore have been disinterred for some particular reason and placed in the chests after the decomposition of the bodies. Is it possible that the individuals thus interred were martyrs ignominiously buried at first, and afterward exhumed and honored with more careful interment?*

SARCOPHAGUS.

* In some places at the present time, as in certain Italian convents and at Stanz, Canton Unterwalden, it is customary to dig up the bones or skulls of the dead after they have been buried a certain time, and then to arrange them fantastically or with the names attached in churches or crypts.

MISCELLANEOUS OBJECTS.   387

Chest No. 1. This is formed of reddish limestone, and measures 32 inches in length, by 19½ inches in height, to the top of the rounded lid. It was found in a cave in the Valley of the Convent of the Cross, and contained a skull and a few bones. The front is ornamented by three roundels, containing a kind of star ornament, the central one having a pillar with a large capital upon either side. The whole design is surrounded by well-executed wreaths of leaves, resembling those of the bay or laurel. The front of the lid bears in low relief a series of eight arches upon pillars with a small roundel in the midst of each arch. [See p. 305, and Figure.]

Chest No. 2. This example, which also contained bones, was found in a cave north of the English sanatorium, about a mile from Jerusalem. It measures 20 inches in length, by 19½ inches in height, and stands upon four feet or pedestals at the angles. The material is white limestone. The ornaments are roundels enclosing stars and other designs, with a kind of chevron moulding between; roundels are also found on the lid.

Chest No. 3. This chest is 27 inches long by 13 inches high, and, unlike the other examples, has a perfectly flat and unadorned top

COPPER LAMP-STAND.

The ornaments on the front are two roundels. It was found in a cave near Bethany, and contained a human skull and bones.

Numerous examples of these mortuary chests have been found near Jerusalem.

Objects made of Metal.

1. Dagger of bronze, found with pottery (probably Græco-Phœnician), in a sepulchral cave, east of Olivet. A portion of the wooden handle still adheres to the base.

2. Bronze boss of a shield found at Robinson's Arch at the south end of the Bridge, at a depth of 35 feet. Roman.

3. Copper lamp-stand. Apparently of the Byzantine period. Found in a cavern 160 feet south of the Haram Area.

4. Small head of bronze, apparently a portion of a larger object. Probably Phœnician, or Græco-Phœnician from Cyprus.

6. Small Christian ring of bronze, found outside St. Stephen's Gate, in a cave lined with *loculi*, or shelves for the dead, along with a sepulchral chest. Christian lamps were found in the same cave.

7. Bronze head of the cobra serpent; the breast was formerly enamelled. Pure Egyptian; from the head of a god.

Objects of Shell, Ivory, and Wood.

1. Five objects from the Mound of Tell Salahiyeh, near Damascus. Three are round and one square. They are formed by cutting sections from the shell of a *conus*, or some other species of shell, and were probably part of a rude necklace.

2. Three pieces made of ivory, and belonging to some game. Found at Ophel.

4. Fragments of carved cedar-wood, found with pieces of white marble lattice-work, in a Christian church, discovered about three-quarters of a mile north of Ain es Sultan. (Jericho.)

THE MOABITE STONE.

HARDLY any discovery has ever been made which has excited so widely-extended an interest as the Moabite Stone. Other *graffiti*, such as those of Assyria, are found year by year, which bear more or less directly upon Jewish history, and are published in journals without producing an interest at all proportionate to their real value. The great and immediate excitement produced by this record of King Mesha is due chiefly, of course, to the utterly unexpected nature of the discovery and the publicity given to it. The Assyrian inscriptions have to find their way slowly into public notice. Those few scholars who are interested in them get their information bit by bit as it comes out; and there is no volume generally known, or easily accessible to those who do not follow the discoveries, which gives the results of the deciphering of these monuments. The Moabite Stone, however, has another and a deeper claim upon our interest. It does not merely confirm or illustrate the narrative of the Second Book of Kings; it *adds* to our knowledge. It appears to be the contemporaneous record, from the Moabite point of view, of the rebellion of that King Mesha who, after a struggle whose duration is uncertain, and which is first noticed in a single verse (2 Kings i. 1) by the sacred historian, was finally overcome by the combined armies of Judah and Israel. It commemorates his successes and triumphs; it explains how he wrested towns from his old enemies, and rebuilt the ruined cities of his own country; it shows that his wars were, to a certain extent, religious, that the king believed himself to be under the Divine guidance; and that no expedition was made unless by express direction of the god Chemosh or Chamos. This unexpected record of a nation entirely perished and passed away could not fail to be of the greatest possible interest. Slight as may appear its contributions to history, it has a very real value, if it were only for the human interest it gives to that shadowy king who, brought to bay at last, when all his new-built towns were destroyed, all his cisterns and wells filled up, and all his good land marred, slew his eldest son upon the wall as a burnt-offering to the god Chemosh, by whose advice he was ruled; and, with that supreme act of despair, vanishes forever out of history.

To the unscholarly world, then—that majority of mankind who are unacquainted with Assyrian and Phœnician literature, and care little about the history of alphabets—the historical interest of the stone is its chief interest. It will be shown directly that this is not its only, or, indeed, its most considerable element of importance. Let us first narrate briefly the story of its discovery, and the circumstances which led to its destruction—in which, although the fullest accounts have been published in the Quarterly Statements of the Palestine Exploration Fund, almost all writers have made mistakes.

The circumstances were these:

In August, 1868, the Rev. F. A. Klein, an Anglican clergyman, attached to the Jerusalem Mission Society, was travelling to Jebel Ajloon and the Belka. On the 19th of that month, he arrived at Dibân, the ancient Dibon. Here he was received with friendliness by a tribe of the Beni-Hamideh, encamped near the ruins, and was informed by Zattan, sheikh of the Beni-Sades, who accompanied him, and by the friendly sheikh of the Beni-Hamideh, of the existence of an inscribed stone, which had been seen by no European whatever. It must be remembered that the situation of Dibân, east of the Dead Sea, and a few miles north of the Wady Mojeb (Arnon), renders it peculiarly inaccessible. Very few travellers have ever visited the place, and the ruins in the country of Moab have never been thoroughly examined. The sun was setting as Mr. Klein arrived at the spot where this relic of antiquity was lying. He had no time to do more than take a sketch, with measurements of the stone, and copy a few of the words. He found the stone one mètre thirteen centimètres in height, seventy centimètres in breadth, and thirty-five in thickness. "It was," he says, "*in a perfect state of preservation*, not one single piece being broken off; and it was only from great age and exposure to the rain and sun that certain parts, especially the upper and lower lines, had somewhat suffered."

It is greatly to be regretted that Mr. Klein did not take a squeeze, rubbing, or some kind of copy of the inscription. He formed, instead, the idea of getting the stone to the Museum of Berlin; and communicated, in secret, his discovery to Dr. Petermann, the Prussian Consul, who took measures, through his own Government, to get possession of the stone. The negotiations were intrusted first to one, and then to a second Arab, but without any success—the greediness of the Arabs being an insuperable obstacle. It was at this point that Captain Warren first heard of it, nothing having been told him either by Mr. Klein or Dr. Petermann. Captain Warren, however, hearing from Mr. Klein at the same time that the Prussians were moving in the matter, thought it best, on all accounts, to abstain from any action which might rouse the cupidity and jealousy of the Arabs. Nor was it till the spring of 1869 that he felt himself at liberty to mention the subject; when, on hearing an account of it from the Rev. Dr. Barclay, who told him and M. Clermont Ganneau what was being done, he wrote to England on the matter. By the next mail, however, he wrote again, stating that the Prussian Consul had obtained a firman for the stone; and that, consequently, information on the subject must be got from Berlin before anything more could be done. All this time, it must be remembered, no squeeze or copy of the inscription had been taken; its real value was quite unknown, and, in consequence of the protracted negotiations, the jealousy and greed of the Arabs were being roused thereby more and more.

In July, 1869, Captain Warren left Jerusalem for the Lebanon, and did not return till November. On the road, half-way up from Jaffa, on his return, an Adwan met him, with the story of the destruction of the stone. Captain Warren instantly sent him off with squeeze-paper to take an impression of what was left; for M. Ganneau had, early in November, sent down an Arab with instructions to obtain, if possible, authority to take a squeeze of the inscription. This was granted after some difficulty; but while the squeeze was still wet, a quarrel arose among the Beni-Hamideh, blows were exchanged, and M. Ganneau's messenger, tearing off the wet impression, had only time to spring upon his horse and escape by flight, bringing with him the squeeze in rags, and receiving a spear-wound in the leg. After this the Arabs lit a fire under the stone, and, throwing cold water upon it, broke it into fragments. Little could be done with the impression—the only one, such as it is, that remains of the complete stone.

Captain Warren's Arab, however, returning with good squeezes of the two large fragments yet remaining, M. Ganneau at the same time succeeding in getting two squeezes of the same, and, certain smaller fragments of the stone finding their way to Jerusalem, a first attempt was made by M. Ganneau at deciphering the inscription.

By the same mail there arrived in Europe M. Ganneau's first translation and Captain Warren's tracings of his squeezes. The former was published immediately by the Count de Vogüé; the latter was referred by the Committee of the Palestine Exploration Fund to Mr. Deutsch.

The history of the stone is nearly ended at this point. Another and a more perfect squeeze was got by Captain Warren; further emendations were furnished by M. Ganneau. The tracings sent home by Captain Warren were

photographed and published. The large fragments were
brought up by M. Ganneau, and small fragments by Captain Warren; and, as the matter at present stands, out of
one thousand letters, which at first were cut upon the stone,
the number actually preserved amounts to six hundred and
sixty-nine,* or nearly seven-tenths of the whole. There is
reason to hope that by degrees every fragment of the stone
will find its way to Europe, and this invaluable inscription
wholly put together again. Until this is either done, or
till it becomes quite clear that it cannot be done, all attempts at translation must be premature, and can only lead
to controversy and dispute. On this point, viz., the expediency of waiting till the materials for as complete a translation as possible should arrive in England, Mr. Deutsch, in
three separate letters to the "Times," dwelt with great emphasis. And while he pointed out the gains to palæography
and Semitic science, he abstained from enlarging on its historical importance. "It will be well," he urged, "if both
the learned and the public at large hold their hand for a
brief space yet. At this moment there is but one thing
certain: that, whether we ever recover the whole of the
stone—the fate of which is still uncertain—or must remain
satisfied with but half-intelligible fragments, the gain to palæography and Semitic science is already enormous. It is,
unquestionably, whatever the precise date of this King
Mesha, the very oldest Semitic lapidary record of importance as yet discovered. And, apart from certain geographical and other data given in it which are already incontestable, it illustrates to a hitherto unheard-of degree the history
of our own writing—I mean that which we all use at this
hour. Nearly the whole of the Greek alphabet is found
here; not merely *similar* to the 'Phœnician' shape, but as
identical with it as can well be. Not merely such letters
as the *Δ, P, M, N, Σ, E, O, Q* (Koppa), etc., but even the
Ξ—one of the letters supposed to have been added during
the Trojan War by Palamedes, because not extant in the

---

* Of these letters M. Ganneau obtained 613, and Captain Warren 56.

original 'Cadmean' alphabet—is of constant occurrence here (as *Samech*). Further, will the knotty digamma question receive a new contribution, by the shape of the *vau* in this monument, which is distinctly the Greek Υ—another letter of supposed recent origin. . . . And another thing will become clear, viz., that the more primitive the characters, the simpler they become; not, as often supposed, the more complicated, as more in accordance with some pictorial prototype."

The advice of Mr. Deutsch has not been followed. Treatise after treatise has been issued from the English, German, and French press. These are necessarily all based on the imperfect materials at present in Europe, and all, consequently, obliged to resort to conjecture. To show the judicious nature of Mr. Deutsch's recommendation, the first and last translations, between which is an interval of five months, by M. Clermont Ganneau, are subjoined; and, to illustrate the discrepancies caused by conjecture, the translation of Prof. Schlottmann, dated March 15, 1870, is printed side by side with the latest rendering of M. Ganneau.

I.

(Date, January 16, 1870.)

1. I am Mesa, son of Chamos [nadab?] King . . . .
2. . . . [My father reigned over Moab . . . and I have . . . .
3. reigned after my father. [And I have constructed this *high place* (sanctuary) with its platform (?) for Chamos . . . .
4. [I call myself] *Mesa*, because he (Chamos) has saved me from all the . . . . . . to both the (?)
5. . . . of the King of Israel . . . and he oppressed Moab . . . Chamos was angry . . . .
6. . . . . . [and he changed it . . . . I will oppress (I have oppressed ?) Moab. [In my days I have (he has?) said . . .
7. . . . and I saw him, him and his house (his temple?). [And Israel was dispersed, dispersed forever, and Omri gained possession of
8. Medeba (?) and remained there . . . he constructed forty . . .
9. When Chamos is (reigning) in my days (to-day). [And I built Baal Moon, and I sacrificed there [and I built . . . .

10. Qiriathaim | And . . . took the land . . . . . formerly; and built
11. the King of Israel the (city of) . . . . | And I fought at Qir (or, I made the siege) and I took it | and I killed all the . . .
12. . . . . (sacrificed ?) for Chamos and for Moab | . . .
13. . . . . before the face of Chamos, at Qerioth | and I there made prisoners the (old ?) men and the . . .
14. of the youth (morning). | And Chamos said to me . . Go! have dominion over Israel. |
15. I went by night, and I fought with him from the . . . of the dawn to mid-day, | and I . . . .
16. . . . . entirely . . .
17. . . . who is for Astar Chamos . . . .
18. . . . Jahveh (Jehovah?) . . . . before the face of Chamos. | And the King of Israel [came to]
19. Yahas, and dwelt there (until ?) my combat with him. | And Chamos drove him from . . .
20. I took of Moab two hundred men in all, | and I made them go up to Yahaz, and I . . .
21. . . . on Dibon. | It is I who built the esplanade (?), the walls of Yearim (?), and the walls of . . . .
22. . . . . And it is I who have built its gates, and it is I who have built its fortress, | and it is
23. I who have built Bet-Moloch, | and it is I who have made the two . . .
24. . . . Qir | and there were no wells in the interior of Qir on its esplanade. And I said to all the people,
25. "Make every man a well in his house." | It is I who have offered the holocaust on the esplanade (?) in
26. . . . Israel. | It is I who have built Aroër (?) and it is I who have made the road of Arnon.
27. It is I who have built Bet-Bamoth, which was destroyed (?) | It is I who have built Bosor, which . . .
28. . . . . Dibon, of the military chiefs, because all Dibon was subject, | and I have
29. . . . with the cities which I have added to the earth, | and it is I who have built . . .
30. . . . . Bet Diblathaim | and Bet Baal Meon, and I have erected there the . . ——
31. . . . the land. | And Horonaim, where resided . . .
32. . . . Chamos said to me . . "Fight at Horonaim." | And I
33. . . . Chamos . . . on . . ——
34. . . . .

Subjoined are, side by side, the version of Prof. Schlottmann, and the latest (June 15th), published by the Count
de Vogüé, received from M. Clermont Ganneau.

M. Clermont Ganneau.	*Prof. Schlottmann.*
I am Mesa, son of Chamosgad, King of Moab, the Dibonite. ∣ My father reigned over Moab thirty years, and I have reigned after my father. ∣ And I have built this sanctuary for Chamos in Qarha [sanctuary of salvation], for he has saved me from all aggressors, and has made me look upon all my enemies with contempt. ∣	I Mesa, son of Chamos-nadab, the King of Moab [son of] Yabni. My father ruled over Moab [. . years], and I ruled after my father. And I made this high place of sacrifice to Chamos in Korcha, a high place of deliverance, for he saved me from all [who fought against Moab.]
Omri was King of Israel, and oppressed Moab during many days, and Chamos was irritated at his aggressions. ∣ And his son succeeded him, and he said, he also, "I will oppress Moab." ∣ In my days, I said "I will . . . him . . . . . and I will visit him and his house." ∣ And Israel was ruined, ruined forever. Omri gained possession of the land of Me-deba. ∣ And he dwelt there . . . . [Ahab] his son lived forty years, and Chamos made him [perish] in my time. ∣	Omri, King of Israel, allied himself with all his (Moab's) haters, and they oppressed Moab [many days]: then Chamos was irritated [against him and against] his land, and let it go over [into the hand of his haters], and they oppressed Moab very sore. In my days spoke Ch(amos), I will therefore look upon him and his house, and Israel shall perish in eternal ruin. And Omri took possession of the town of Medeba, and sat therein [and they oppressed Moab, he and] his son, forty years. [Then] Chamos looked upon Moab in my days.
Then I built Baal Meon and constructed Qiriathaïm. ∣ And the men of Gad dwelt in the country of [Ataro]th from ancient times, and the King of Israel had built the city of Ataroth. ∣ I attacked the city and I took it, ∣ and I killed all the people of the city, a spectacle to Chamos and to	And I built Baal Meon, and made therein walls and mounds. And I went to take the town of Kirjathaim, and the men of Gad [lived] in the district [of Kirja-thaim] from days of their grand-fathers, and the King of Israel built Kirjathaim. And I fought against the town, and took it, and

Moab, | and I carried away from there the . . . and I dragged it on the ground before the face of Chamos at Qerioth, | and I brought there the men of Saron (or of Chofen) and the men of Maharouth (?).

I strangled all the people that were in the city [as a sacrifice] to Chamos, the God of Moab.

(Here follows a lacuna: at the end of it the words " before the face of Chamos in Kirjathaim." Probably stood here, just as in lines 17-18, a notice of the change of an Israelitish to a Moabite sanctuary.)

And I destroyed the High Place of Jehovah, and dedicated it before the face of Chamos in Kirjathaim. And I allowed to dwell therein the men of . . . . and the men of . . . .

And Chamos said to me, "Go; take Nebah from Israel." | I went by night, and I fought against the city from the dawn to mid-day, | and I took it: and I killed all, seven thousand [men, and I carried away with me] the women and the young girls; for to Astar Chamos belongs the consecration of women; | and I brought from there the vessels of Jehovah, and I dragged them on the ground before the face of Chamos. |

And Chamos said to me, "Go up. Take [the town of] Nebo against Israel . . ." and I went up during the night, and fought against it from the dawn to midday, and I took it . . . and I saw it quite . . .

(In the rest of this part—more than two lines—there are, besides isolated letters, only legible through the gaps the names of God separated from each other),

to Astar Chamos . . . Jehovah . . . . before the face of Chamos.

(It may safely be presumed, that mention was made here of the restoration of Heathen in the room of the Israelitish worship.)

And the King of Israel had built Yahas, and resided there during his war with me. | And Chamos drove him from before my face: I took from Moab two hundred men in all; I made them go up to Yahas, and I took it to annex it to Dibon. |

And the King of Israel built Jahaz, and sat therein, while he fought against me, and Chamos drove him before my sight. And I took from Moab two hundred men, fully told. And I beleaguered Jahaz and took it, in addition to Dibon.

it is I who have built Qarha, the Wall of the Forests and the Wall of the Hill. | I have built its gates, and I have built its towers. | I have built the palace of the king, and have constructed the prisons of the . . . in the midst of the city.

And there were no wells in the interior of the city in Qarha: and I said to all the people, "Make you every man a well in his house," | and I dug cisterns for Qarna for . . . of Israel. |

I built Korcha, the wall toward the forest, and the wall . . . and I built her gates, and I built her towers, and I built the king's house; and I made store-places for the mountain water in the midst of the town. And there were no cisterns within the town, in Korcha, and I said to all the people, "Make (you) every man a cistern in his house."

(Here follows a sentence with difficult expressions at the beginning, and a gap in the middle. The following is conjectural:)

And I hung up the prohibition for Korcha [against association with the] people of Israel.

It is I who have built Aroer, and made the road of Arnon. |
It is I who have built Beth Bamoth, which was destroyed. | It is I who have built Bosor which (is powerful) . . . Dibon of the military chiefs, for all Dibon was submissive. | And I have filled . . . with the cities which I have added to the land (of Moab. |

I built Aroër, and I made the streets in Arnon. I built Beth Bamoth, for [it was destroyed]. I built Bezer, for men of Dibon compelled it, fifty of them, for all Dibon was subject; and I filled [with inhabitants] Bikrân, which I added to the land. And I built . . . the Temple of Diblathaim, and the Temple of Baal Meon, and brought thither Ch[amos].

And it is I who have built . Beth Diblathain, and Beth Baal Meon, and I have raised there the . . . the land. | And Horonaim, he resided there with . . . | And Chamos said to me, "Go down and fight against Horonaim." | . . . Chamos, in my day . . . the year . . . .

(After a hiatus are the words:)
. . the land . . And Horonaim . . dwelt therein . . .

(Probably there followed the name of an Edomite parent tribe, or clan. Then again after a gap:)

Chamos said to me, "Come. Fight against Horonaim and [take it]."

In the last gap, out of more than two lines it is only possible, besides separated letters, to read the word of

Chamos. Without doubt it was here related how the king, by the help of Chemosh, took the town.

Prof. Schlottmann divides the inscription into three parts; the first to the sixth section, inclusive, of the victories of Mesa over Israel; the second, sections seven and eight, of the buildings and erections of the king; and the third, of a battle in the south, toward Edom.

It will be seen that there is no doubt at all as to the general tenor of the translation; and the discrepancies may appear such as mainly to interest scholars. But, when all that M. Ganneau has is safe in Paris, when the fragments obtained by Captain Warren are fitted in their places by means of M. Ganneau's imperfect squeeze, and the monument restored as nearly as can be hoped, a good many of these *Lacunæ*, these conjectural readings, will, it may be confidently expected, disappear. We can never hope to have a complete restoration; but, for what we have, we may be thankful to M. Ganneau's energy in recovering the fragments, and Captain Warren's forbearance and prompt action at the right moments. To use the words of Captain Warren himself, "Whether the stone gets to Berlin, London, or Paris, appears to me to be a small matter, compared with the rescuing of the inscription from oblivion." And it must be remembered that the Committee of the Fund carefully abstained from entering into any competition for the stone or its fragments, either with the Prussians or with M. Clermont Ganneau. It is not intended here to give more than the mere story of the stone. The learned writer who was to have enriched this volume with a treatise worthy of the subject has been prevented by sickness from fulfilling his intention. What has to be said, therefore, in place of what would have been said, is necessarily brief and incomplete. But a few words may be added in illustration of the interest of the stone, apart from its purely scriptural bearing. In the seventeenth line occur the words "Astar

Chamos." Prof. Schlottmann, in his learned treatise, calls
attention to this name. It is found, he explains, here for
the first time on Canaanitish soil. It is the male name, corresponding to the female form Astarté; it is identical with
the Athtár, or Athtór, found on a well-known Himyaritic
inscription, and probably also with the Estar of the Ninevitish cuneiform writings. The etymology of the word is
stated by the learned professor to have nothing whatever to
do with the Hebrew name Esther, which is borrowed from
an Indo-Germanic source ($ἀστήρ$), but must be referred to a
root signifying "to close together: to form an alliance with
one another;" the significance of which appears from the
fact that in Astar and Astarté was placed the power which
binds creatures to one another, and the world to the God-
head; and, in alliance with this, the productive strength of
Nature. He endeavors to establish a connection between
Ares and Astar, Aphrodité and Astarté, Baal and Chamos.
"It is strange," says Prof. Schlottmann, "that this bare
name, on the monument of a small nation of herdsfolk long
forgotten, should have even for classical archæology a many-
sided interest. It is the Canaanitish original, now first
found, of the Aphroditos mentioned in Aristophanes, of the
name for Venus Amathusia, represented as bearded, 'eadem
mas et fœmina.' . . . The name Chamos has reference to
his taming, compelling power. He is the fearful god who
is appeased by human sacrifice, especially the sacrifice of
children. . . . Any one, not otherwise acquainted with the
characteristics of Chamos, might suppose from our inscription that he was only nominally different from Jehovah. . .
Chamos is angry with his people; he delivers them into the
hands of their enemies; he again looks mercifully on them;
he drives Mesa's enemies from before his face; he speaks in
the same manner as Jehovah. But the wrath of Chamos
was like his mercy, blind and fitful; not like the wrath of
Jehovah, a symbol of that true Divine energy by which an
eternal moral order is preserved." To conclude: the nature
of this monument was summed up by Mr. Deutsch in a

recent speech at Oxford. "It was," he said, "the monument of a Moabite king—Mesha—who, after a brief record of himself and his father, tells of certain deeds of war, from which he issued victorious. Further the names of Israel, Omri, Chamos, and a number of well-known Moabite cities, occurred up and down: . . . but, *so long as there was any hope of the recovery of one single scrap of material, so long must the final investigations remain in abeyance.*"

NOTE 1.—*Extract from Report of Mr. Deutsch's Speech at Oxford on the Moabite Stone*

Mr. Deutsch next alluded to the number of decipherments and translations, hypotheses and suggestions, to which this stone had already given rise, and dwelt upon the fact that, apart from the precise date of this King Mesha, which indeed was still a moot point, very little was doubtful of that which really existed on or of the stone. The chief difficulty and the variance of opinion arose from the questionable letters, the gaps and lacunæ, though even these could scarcely affect the general gist of the monument. Its language was easy and translucent even to a beginner, though, will-o'-the-wisp-like, words suddenly appeared which, either from false transcription or some other cause, not merely interrupted, but seemed to subvert the whole meaning and structure. He had from the very outset, and for very good reasons, ventured to beg the world at large, as well as the learned, not to be hasty. The great fact of this intensely important find was clear at first sight; also that the monument was that of a Moabite king—Mesha—who, after a brief record of himself and his father, tells of certain deeds of war from which he issued victorious; further, that the names Israel, Omri, Chemosh, and a number of well-known Moabite cities, occurred up and down; and that indeed the greater part of the last half of the stone was a record of the king's [re]buildings of and improvements in these cities, while the very defective end seemed once more to speak of war. If he had lifted up his warning voice then, he, notwithstanding all that had come between—emendations, chips, squeezes, dissertations, pamphlets, etc.—would still beg for a little patience before a final and definitive conclusion could be arrived at on all points—if ever that could be the case, inasmuch as there were some more materials extant, which had not as yet been taken into consideration. There was, e.g. (besides M. Ganneau's not yet published corrections), a certain chip acquired by Captain Warren some time before his "squeezes," which did not figure in any of the known texts, and which seemed to belong to the right-hand corner—a matter on which a decision could only be arrived at when the other pieces have been brought home. Besides this, he would draw the attention of his hearers to certain fragmentary lines of Mr. Klein, which also appear in none of the materials extant, and which, if accurately copied, would be of some considerable import. Thus one line seems to exhibit the word "*Ratzim*" (Runners, military Executioners, "footmen," in O. T.) in a connection which seems to point to some sanguinary work after a battle, while another distinctly read "*Tamar* to [*Je*]*richo*." There was no need to think of Tadmor. Tamar was the place mentioned by Ezekiel as the southwestern limit of Palestine, and the juxtaposition of the two cities in question would be rather significant. But, Mr. Deutsch said it was to be hoped that these lines had survived in the original, and were among the recently-acquired new fragments, so that full opportunity might be given for further examination. He had mentioned these facts to show that every thing was not settled yet, and, as long as there was any hope of the recovery of one single scrap of material, so long must the *final* investigations remain in abeyance.

NOTE II.—The following are some of the most important places in the Bible where reference is made to the people and country of Moab: Numbers xxi. 26, xxii., and xxiii.; Deut. ii. 9; Judges iii. 17, xi. 15, *et seq.*; 1 Sam. xiv. 47; 2 Sam. viii. 2; 2 Kings i. 1, iii. 4–27, xiii. 20, xxiv. 2; 2 Chron. xx.; Isaiah xv., xvi.; Jer. xlviii.; Dan. xi. 41; Amos ii. 1, 2.

NOTE III.—The reader may also be referred to the Article "Moab," by Mr. Grove, in the Dictionary of the Bible, to Mr. Deutsch's Letters in the Quarterly Statement, Nos. V. and VI., of the Palestine Exploration Fund, and to the Essays on the stone by M. Ganneau, Prof. Rawlinson (in the Contemporary Review), Prof. Schlottmann, and Prof. Nöldeke.

EXPLORATIONS IN THE PENINSULA OF SINAI.

BY THE REV. F. W. HOLLAND.

At last, the obscurity which has so long hung over the Peninsula of Sinai, with regard to the possible determination of the route of the Israelites through the desert, has been removed. Almost the whole of the country has now been explored; and that portion of it which possesses the greatest interest for us has been most carefully mapped, by an expedition sent out under the auspices of the Director-General of our Ordnance Survey. Until lately no one traveller had traversed more than two of the routes of the desert. Hence no just comparison could be instituted between the facilities, or the difficulties, which attended them all. Each traveller also had yielded more or less to the temptation to make the Israelites follow his own track; and critics at home have consequently striven in vain to reconcile conflicting descriptions of the country, and to find in them some definite traces of those sacred events which have rendered the Peninsula of Sinai a land of such intense interest to us.

Now, however, we have had gathered up by professional men, the well-known accuracy of whose work places their report and maps beyond suspicion, all the materials that the desert affords for setting at rest the important topographical questions which have been at issue.

It was my privilege to form one of the exploring party; having been requested, in consequence of my knowledge of the country, and personal acquaintance with the Arabs, gained during three previous visits in 1861, 1865, and 1867, to accompany the expedition in the capacity of guide. In the following pages I shall endeavor to give an account of the results which have been obtained, rather than a history of the proceedings of the expedition itself; and I shall only add such details of our work as seem to illustrate those results, and explain the manner by which they were arrived at. I may state, however, that the opinions here expressed with regard to the position of the true Mount Sinai, and the route followed by the children of Israel, are those held unanimously by all the members of the expedition.

Our exploring party consisted of Captains Wilson and Palmer, of the Royal Engineers (the former of whom is so well known for his admirable survey of Jerusalem); Mr. E. H. Palmer, Fellow of St. John's College, Cambridge, whose knowledge of Arabic, and rare power of distinguishing between those letters in the language which are so puzzling to European ears, rendered his services of infinite value in many ways, and especially in collecting the traditions and ascertaining the correct nomenclature of the country; Mr. Wyatt, whose occupation was the collection of specimens of natural history; myself; and four non-commissioned officers of the Royal Engineers, all of whom were specially selected for the work from the staff of the Ordnance Survey, one of them, Sergeant-Major MacDonald, being an experienced photographer.

Our mode of travelling, after Mount Sinai had once been reached, was generally on foot; our baggage, tents, and other necessaries being carried on camels. For ordinary purposes of travelling the camel is invaluable in a desert country; but he unfortunately possesses so strong a will of his own, and his swinging gait is so prejudicial to the taking of notes or compass-bearings, that he is by no means a satisfactory animal to ride, when accurate observations are required; and for this reason I regard it as a matter of no small moment that we were enabled to perform the greater part of the work on foot.

We started from Suez on November 11, 1868, with a caravan of forty-four camels, attended by nearly forty Arab drivers from different parts of the Peninsula. Having to carry with us all the necessaries of life, including even water, we were unable at first to travel with a smaller number; but there was one advantage in this, viz., that we secured additional evidence respecting the names of the various localities which we passed on our journey to Jebel Mûsa, and, by questioning independently one Arab after another as we went along, Mr. Palmer succeeded in obtaining the correct name of every spot, and the history of whatever traditions were connected with it.

Those only who have made the experiment know how difficult it is to obtain reliable information from a Bedouin Arab. Suspicious by nature of all strangers, and unable to estimate the real objects which a traveller has in view in making inquiries respecting his country, a Bedouin systematically endeavors to deceive the inquirer; and, fearing lest he may entertain some sinister designs upon his territory, he invents false names, and frequently raises difficulties where none really exist. It is only by patient examination, and comparison of names, that the truth can be arrived at.

It was arranged that we should make our way at once to Jebel Mûsa, and establish under the care of the monks in the convent of St. Catharine, which stands at the foot of that mountain, a depot for our stores.

Jebel Mûsa is situated almost in the centre of the Peninsula, and, being easily accessible from all points, forms an admirable position for the headquarters of an exploring expedition. There was some little discussion as to the route which we should take to this point, but we finally settled to follow the northern route by Serâbit-el-Khâdim and Wady Berah, as being not only the most direct, but also the best adapted for a continuous line of observations to connect Jebel Mûsa to Suez.

We arrived at the convent after a journey of ten days, having made, as we went along, a rough sketch of our route, and taken a chain of bearings from point to point, in addition to laying down by astronomical observations the exact position of each of our camping-places.

My old friends the monks, with whom I had lived for some weeks during the previous winter, gladly received us, and at once placed a room at our disposal for keeping our stores. They pressed us much to take up our abode under their roof, but we preferred the freedom of tent-life, and pitched our camp at the bottom of the valley in which the convent stands.

A special survey of Jebel Mûsa, and the surrounding mountains and valleys, on a scale of six inches to the mile, was to form a portion of our work, and this we immediately commenced. A base was chosen in the plain of Er Râhah; every prominent peak was scaled, with no little risk sometimes to limbs and instruments, and their relative positions and altitudes were determined by triangulation.

This special survey contained an area of upward of seventeen square miles, and included the mountains of Jebel Mûsa and Jebel et Deir, the Ras Sufsâfeh, the plain of er Râhah, Jebel Sona, the convent valley, Wady Leja, and the lower portion of Wady Sebaiyeh. When the triangulation was completed, while the non-commissioned officers were engaged in the levelling and hill-sketching, excursions were made to different places of interest in the neighborhood, and the general reconnoissance survey was extended.

Toward the end of December it grew so cold, and occasional snow-storms interfered so much with the progress of the survey, that we moved to the lower ground of Wady Feiran, and, pitching our tents near the mouth of Wady Aleyat, which runs down from the central peak of Jebel Serbâl, we commenced the special survey of that mountain and its northern valleys. This survey took in an area of

Wilderness of the Wandering
ET TIH

GULF OF SUEZ

Ras Mohammed

Scale 25 Miles

J. Catherine 8537 ft   J. Serbal   6735 ft
J. Umm Shaumer 8450 ft   J. Hummum 1567 ft
J. Musa   7375 ft

nearly the same extent as that of Jebel Mûsa, and was also made on a scale of six inches to the mile. Here, again, as soon as the ground for the special survey was triangulated, the general survey was continued in the surrounding districts, and excursions were made to Wady Mokatteb, the mines and ruins of Wady Mughârah, Serâbit-el-Khâdim, and other places.

When the weather became less severe, the camp was again removed to Jebel Mûsa and the survey there completed. Other expeditions were also made, and, before the exploring party finally withdrew to the Peninsula at the beginning of April, the special surveys of Jebel Mûsa and Jebel Serbal were completed, and seven hundred miles of route survey had been made, laying down accurately the course of the principal valleys, and giving with the reconnoissance a survey of about 4,000 square miles of country, including almost the whole of the region bounded on the north by the ranges of Jebel er Râhah and Jebel et Tih; on the south by a line drawn from the seaport of Tor to Jebel Abou Masûd; on the east by a line drawn northward from the latter mountain to Jebel Ojmeh, and on the west by the Gulf of Suez—that being the portion of the Peninsula through which the Israelites must have marched on their way from Egypt to Mount Sinai, if either Jebel Mûsa, or Jebel Serbal, or indeed any mountain to the south of the Tih range, be the true Mount Sinai.

But it may be asked, Is there any proof that the true Mount Sinai was situated here, or that the country which we now call the Peninsula of Sinai is that through which the children of Israel marched? More than one author has attempted to prove that Mount Sinai was far away eastward in the Peninsula of Arabia, and that the Gulf of Akaba was the Red Sea of the Bible. What is there to prove that they are not right?

A careful comparison of the geographical features of the Peninsula of Sinai with the history of the Exodus appears to afford abundant evidence that, whatever may be the general value of the traditions attaching to that region, they are at least right in pointing it out as the scene of that history. It is now pretty generally agreed that the portion of the land of Egypt occupied by the children of Israel must have lain to the northeast of that country, and that the land of Goshen probably comprised the district called El Wady, the fertile valley on the edge of the desert, through which now flows the fresh-water canal leading from the Nile to Ismailia. The starting-point of the Israelites cannot have been very far from the latter place.

It appears from the history of the Exodus that the Red Sea was only three days' journey from that point, a distance which exactly agrees with that to the head of the Gulf of Suez, but which does not agree at all with the distance to the head of the Gulf of Akaba, which lies more than 150 miles eastward. This seems to prove that the Gulf of Suez alone can possibly be the Red Sea of the Bible.

Again, we know that when the children of Israel had crossed the Red Sea they kept down its shore, for, in Numbers xxxiii. 10, we read of their "encamping by the Red Sea" after five days' journey; far too short a time for them to have reached the Gulf of Akaba, if, after crossing the Gulf of Suez, they had marched in that direction. A glance at the map shows that, if this point be once established, Mount Sinai must have been situated to the south of the long range of Jebel et Tih, which forms a barrier, stretching across the whole breadth of the Peninsula from the head of one gulf to that of the other.

Having thus fixed the situation of Mount Sinai within certain limits, our next business is to decide which of the mountains within that area best answers to the Mount of the Law as described in the book of Exodus. It is true that the account which we have of it is but scanty. Yet still there are certain points in connection with it which appear to be indisputable. *First.* It must have been a mountain easy of approach, and having before it an open space sufficiently large for the whole congregation of the children of Israel to have been assembled there to receive the Law. Although it is not necessary to suppose that the whole host pitched their tents before the mount, their camp being probably spread over an area of many miles, still they were all at certain times assembled before the mount at the command of Moses.

Secondly. Mount Sinai was evidently a prominent mountain, rising up abruptly from the plain before it; for, in Deut. iv. 11, the people are said to have come near, and "stood under the mountain," and it is described in Exodus xix. 12, 17, as a mountain that could be touched, and "at the nether part" of which the people stood. It seems also to have been separated by valleys from the surrounding mountains, since bounds were ordered to be placed around it.

Thirdly. Its immediate neighborhood must have afforded a plentiful supply of water and pasturage.

Of all the mountains within the area designated, two only, viz., Jebel Serbal and Jebel Mûsa, have been generally considered to satisfy these requirements. And, now that the neighborhood of Jebel Serbal has been carefully surveyed, it will be seen at once from the maps, or, still better, from the excellent model which was made of the ground on the spot, that that mountain neither has before it any open space for a large assembly to gather in, nor is any one peak of it separated from the rest, so that it could be enclosed by bounds. In massive ruggedness, and in boldness of feature and outline, Jebel Serbal unquestionably presents an aspect unequalled by any other mountain in the Peninsula; and, though far from being the highest above the level of the sea, being only about 6,300 feet in height, rising as it does from a lower level, it has a greater command than almost any other mountain over the surrounding country, and looks more imposing from the valleys beneath. But unfortunately there is not a single point in the valleys near its base which affords a comprehensive view of it; and, it is only by ascending some of the neighboring hills that the whole range of its magnificent peaks can be seen at once.

28

Two valleys, Wadys Aleyat and Ajelah, each from three to four miles in length, run from its base to Wady Feiran; but each is a wilderness of bowlders and torrent-beds, which render it most unsuitable for a large encampment. From certain points in these two valleys, and from a few spots also in Wady Feiran, imperfect views of Serbal may be had; but from Wady Ajelah the highest peak is never seen. One of the chief advocates in favor of Serbal being the true Mount Sinai has placed the camp of the Israelites between these two valleys, having been led to suppose that there was a plain there; such, however, is not the case: the space between the two valleys is a chaos of rugged mountains, rising to as many as 2,500 feet above Wady Feiran, and intersected by deep ravines. In fact, when engaged in fixing the trigonometrical stations for this portion of the survey, we found that the mountain-climbing here was almost more severe than at any other spot. The members of the Survey Expedition, after a careful examination of the ground during a stay of several weeks, came to the unanimous conclusion that Jebel Serbal could not possibly be the mountain from which the Law was given.

Let us now see how far Jebel Mûsa meets the necessary requirements. Under this name I include also the peaks of Ras Sufsâfeh, which have been wrongly described by some travellers as an independent mountain. The Ras Sufsâfeh does, in fact, form the northern portion of Jebel Mûsa. Its two peaks rise up precipitously from the bottom of the plain of er Râhah to a height of about 2,000 feet, being distinctly visible from every part of that plain, and they are well described by the Dean of Westminster as "standing out in lonely grandeur against the sky like a huge altar." A central elevated basin, encircled by a ring of higher peaks, is a common feature of the granitic mountains in the Peninsula of Sinai, and such, more or less, is the character of Jebel Mûsa, which is about two miles long from north to south, and one mile in breadth. The southern peak, on which stand a little chapel and the ruins of a mosque, is its highest point; and, although the name of Jebel Mûsa is used for the whole mountain, it is more especially applied to this one peak.

On the east of the mountain runs Wady ed Deir, "the Valley of the Convent," so called from the convent of St. Catharine, which is situated near its head. On the west of it runs Wady Shuraich, a very steep and rocky valley, containing old monastic gardens and a copious spring. This valley, again, is separated by the narrow ridge of Jebel Fara from Wady Leja, a valley lying farther westward.

Thus, on the north, east, and west, Jebel Mûsa is separated from the surrounding mountains; on the south two smaller valleys—one flowing eastward into Wady Sebaiyeh, and the other westward into Wady Leja—separate it also from the range of mountains which lies between the Wady Sebaiyeh and Jebel Catharine. And so, being isolated by valleys from the mountains on every side, it would be by no means difficult to set bounds round about it, while, at the same time, its northern cliffs rise so precipitously from the plain beneath that it might well be described as "a mountain that could be touched," and at the nether part of which the people could stand. It is easily seen on the spot that the Wady Sebaiyeh could not have been the place where the Israelites were assembled to receive the Law. That valley does not lie immediately below the mountain; and its character, position, and extent, all appear to render such a view extremely improbable. On the other hand, no place could be conceived more suitable than the plain of er Râhah for the assembling together of many thousands of people, both to witness " the thunders and lightning, and the thick cloud upon the mount," and to hear the voice of the Lord, when He spake unto them.

The plain itself is upward of two miles long, and half a mile broad, and slopes gradually down from the water-shed on the north to the foot of Ras Sufsâfeh. About 300 yards from the actual base of the mountain there runs across the plain a low, semicircular mound, which forms a kind of natural theatre, while farther distant on either side of the plain the slopes of the enclosing mountains would afford seats to an almost unlimited number of spectators. The members of our expedition were as unanimous in their conviction that the Law was given from Ras Sufsâfeh to the Israelites assembled in the plain of er Râhah, as they had been unanimous in rejecting Serbal as the mount of the giving of the Law.

As I have before said, it appears to be quite unnecessary to suppose that all the tents of the Israelites were pitched before the Mount; but I may mention that there is near the mouth of Wady Leja an extensive recess, about a mile and a half long, by three-quarters of a mile broad, which would add largely to the available camping-ground so situated. With regard to the water supply, there is no other spot in the whole Peninsula which is nearly so well supplied as the neighborhood of Jebel Mûsa. Four streams of running water are found there: one in Wady Leja; a second in Wady et T'lah, which waters a succession of gardens extending more than three miles in length, and forms pools in which I have often had a swim; a third stream rises to the north of the water-shed of the plain of er Râhah, and runs westward into the Wady et T'lah; and a fourth is formed by the drainage from the mountains of Umm Alawy, to the east of Wady Sebaiyeh, and finds its way into that valley by a narrow ravine opposite Jebel ed Deir. In addition to these streams there are numerous wells and springs, affording excellent water. Throughout the whole of the granitic district I have seldom found it necessary to carry water when making a mountain excursion; and the immediate neighborhood of Jebel Mûsa would, I think, bear comparison with many mountain districts in Scotland with regard to its supply of water. There is also no other district in the Peninsula which affords such excellent pasturage.

Having, for the above-named reasons, fixed upon Jebel Mûsa as the true Mount Sinai, and the Gulf of Suez as the Red Sea of the Exodus, we have next to trace out the prob-

able route of the children of Israel, in their march from the
one point to the other.

The exact spot of the passage through the Red Sea will
never probably be identified. It is difficult even to determine
how great a change the lapse of 3,500 years may have
made in the condition of the gulf. Its head has evidently
been silted up to some extent, but the ruins of an ancient
town at Suez seem to point to the fact that the level of its
shores has not materially altered. The passage of the Israelites
is generally supposed to have taken place in the immediate
neighborhood of Suez, and a careful examination
of the isthmus and head of the gulf has led me fully to concur
in this opinion. On leaving Egypt the Israelites had
probably intended to cross over into the Wilderness of
Etham, or Shur, by the higher ridge of land which separates
the head of the Gulf of Suez from the Bitter Lakes on the
north. This was the natural road to have taken on the way
to Sinai, but God commanded Moses to alter their intended
course: He bade them turn and encamp before Pihahiroth,
between Migdol and the sea—that is, probably in the desert
which lies between the range of Jebel Attâkah and
Suez. Pharaoh coming up in pursuit of them, and seeing
that they had missed the road leading round the head of the
gulf, would naturally exclaim, "The wilderness hath shut
them in!" The sea was on their left, a high range of desert
mountains on their right, beyond them a narrow road
along the shore, leading only to a yet more barren desert.
Escape was impossible unless God had opened a way for
them through the sea. Ayoûn Mûsa—the "Wells of
Moses"—formed probably their first halting-place after the
passage. Here, about eight miles south of Suez, are several
springs or pools, most of which have been artificially formed
by digging a few feet down in the sand. The water is
brackish, but quite drinkable, and the wells are now surrounded
by groves of palm-trees and flourishing gardens,
which supply Suez with vegetables. Leaving this small
oasis, and travelling on southward, the desert becomes

more and more dreary. Some twelve or fifteen miles from the coast, and parallel to it, runs Jebel er Râhah, appearing in the distance as a long, flat-headed range of white cliffs, which forms as it were a wall enclosing the desert on the north. Hence, probably, arose the name of the "Wilderness of Shur;" for the meaning of the name Shur is "a wall."

We read that the children of Israel, on entering the wilderness of Shur, "went three days in the wilderness and found no water." With such a host, encumbered as they were with women and children, and flocks and herds, the distance of a day's march cannot have averaged more than from twelve to fifteen miles. How striking to find that even now a journey of about thirty-five miles has to be made before water is reached, and then that the water is bitter and unwholesome, as were the waters of Marah!

The want of pasturage for the flocks of the Israelites, especially at this point in their journey, has always appeared to be one of the great difficulties in connection with their march. Travellers have generally described this wilderness of Shur as a hard, barren plain, with here and there a few shrubs, but utterly incapable of supplying any herbage. Such is the character of the higher portion of the plain across which the road usually followed leads; but, on approaching the sea, and keeping near the shore, a broad tract of alluvial deposit is found, which affords extensive pasturage, and forms a favorite feeding-ground for the young camels of the Terabein Arabs. To the south of this more fertile tract are the wells of Abu Suweirah, mere holes dug in the bed of a water-course, and yielding a very limited supply of water, though doubtless other wells might easily be sunk in the neighborhood with equal prospects of finding water. About this point the country becomes more broken, and the road usually followed turns farther inland. After passing over some low hills, which glitter brightly with the gypsum of which they are largely composed, the head of Wady Amârah is reached. Here, on a raised platform, is

situated the well-known 'Ain Howârah, which has generally
been identified with Marah. It is but a small water-hole,
capable of affording a very limited supply of brackish
water; but it is surrounded by a thick calcareous deposit,
which seems to prove that the water which flowed from it
was at one time more abundant than it is at present. I
have found that the quality of the water varies much in different years. I have known it at one time quite drinkable,
and at another so bitter that the taste of it was exceedingly
nauseous. Camels are frequently watered there, and it
forms one of the usual camping-places of the Arabs on their
way to and from the Peninsula; but they never drink the
water, if it can be avoided. A small group of desert palm-
trees stands near the spring, the first that the traveller
meets with after leaving the wells of Moses. Five miles
farther south the road descends to Wady Gharundel, a broad
valley enclosed on either side by steep banks, running down
from the Tih plateau. Just below the point where the road
crosses it several water-holes are found, which have been
frequently described. But it is not generally known how
large a supply of water is to be found about two miles lower
down the wady. A stream here gradually oozes out from
the bed of the wady, and soon forms considerable pools of
water, which are overgrown with rushes, and afford a favorite resort for wild-ducks and many other birds. An abundant supply of water is to be found here during the whole
year. The banks of the stream and dry pools, from which
the water has evaporated, are often covered with a white
deposit of natron, and the standing water is brackish and
unwholesome; but, when running briskly, and freshly drawn,
it is very drinkable, and the traveller's water-skins are generally filled here on his way to and from the south. The
lower portions of Wady Gharundel are well clothed with
tamarisks and palms, and a few tents of the Terabein Arabs
are generally to be found here. It has been supposed by
some to mark the site of Marah, by others that of Elim.
However that may be, it can hardly have failed to have pro-

vided the children of Israel with water on their march; for, wherever we may place those stations, their road must have crossed the wady. Before my last visit to the Peninsula, I was under the impression that the high ground on the north of Wady Gharundel, near the sea, would have afforded a very convenient spot for a large encampment; but on closer examination I discovered that it was intersected in every direction by deep ravines, which would render such a supposition impossible. The yet more broken ground at the base of Jebel Hummam Faroun would render an encampment on the opposite side of the wady equally impracticable; so that, if one of the stations of the children of Israel was situated here, the camping-ground must have been confined to the bed of the wady, and the small plain at its mouth.

The precipitous bluff of Jebel Hummam, thrusting its white cliffs down to the very water's edge, obliges the traveller at this point to turn inland and seek a road round the back of that range. Wady Gharundel affords the best road up from the coast; Wady Useit, which is situated a little farther to the south, being so steep and narrow that laden camels can scarcely climb it.

On joining the road which leads from 'Ain Howârah, and mounting the southern bank of Wady Gharundel, a raised and undulating plain of considerable extent is reached; this plain is drained by Wady Useit, and contains a few water-holes and scattered palm-trees. The high range of Jebel Hummam completely shuts out the view of the sea; and the glaring whiteness of the limestone is unrelieved by vegetation.

The station of Elim is generally thought to have been situated in this plain, and, in spite of its present barrenness, it is quite possible that the ancient inhabitants, by sinking wells and utilizing the water thus obtained, may have rendered it a pleasant spot for an encampment.

The marvellous effect that water has in producing vegetation in the most barren desert is exemplified a few miles farther northward, where a small natural basin receives the drainage of the surrounding ground, and produces a luxuriant crop of grass and other herbs. It is called by the Arabs Engí el fúl, " the bean-field."

It is, therefore, by no means improbable that these few water-holes, and groups of palm-trees, may mark the site of the "twelve wells of water, and threescore and ten palm-trees" which the children of Israel found at Elim. At all events, up to this point there can, I think, be no doubt as to the route which they followed, however uncertain the exact position of their several encampments may be.

But now the road divides, one branch running down to the sea again by Wady Tayibeh, "the good wady," so called from its stream of water and accompanying vegetation; the other turning northward by Wady Hamr to Wady Nasb and Serábit-el-Khádim.

The arguments in favor of the latter road having been that followed by the children of Israel are, first, its being the most direct road to Jebel Músa; and, secondly, its containing an extensive plain at the foot of the range of Jebel et Tih, which would appear to correspond better in some respects with the apparent character of the Wilderness of Sin than the plain of El Murkhahon the southern road. It is not so level, consisting rather of a succession of shallow basins separated by low hills than of one extent of plain, but its geological character—sandstone resting upon a bed of gneiss—makes its vegetation extremely abundant after rain, and the water collects in the hollows and forms considerable pools. I visited it once shortly after a heavy storm, and found many Arabs encamped there with their flocks for the sake of its water and pasturage. A few days had made an almost miraculous change in its aspect. The wilderness had literally been " turned into a standing water, and dry ground into water-springs."

If the northern route by Serábit-el-Khádim were that taken by the children of Israel, it probably differed slightly from the road now usually followed by the Arabs. Instead of keeping along the confined wadys of Khamileh and Bark, which are ill-suited for the march of a large multitude encumbered by wagons and much cattle, they would have kept farther to the north in the more open ground under the Tih range until they reached Wady Keneh, which would bring them down to the head of Wady Berah, and so into the Wady es Sheikh. This route would have been suitable enough, and, as I have already mentioned, the open ground under the Tih range would answer admirably in position to the Wilderness of Sin. But there appears to be one fatal objection to such a supposition—it would seem to necessitate taking the children of Israel down Wady Tayibeh to their encampment by the sea at its mouth, and then making them retrace their steps up the same wady until they reached Wady Hamr, a most useless and improbable proceeding. The mention, in Numbers xxxiii. 10, of the encampment by the Red Sea seems therefore to compel us to adopt the southern route by Wady Feiran as that described in the history of the Exodus.

Let us now see how this route agrees with the details of that history. At the mouth of Wady Tayibeh is found a considerable plain, which would afford an admirable position for a temporary camp. To the south the mountains approach nearer to the sea, but sufficient space is left for a road along the shore for several miles until the mountains again recede and the plain of El Murkhah is reached. There can, I think, be little doubt that this plain marks the site of the Wilderness of Sin, where the children of Israel made a long halt, and where God gave them bread from heaven, and they were fed with manna and quails, Exodus xvi. 1-15. This plain extends as far south as Wady Feiran, a distance of about twenty-five miles. Like most of the coast plains, it is somewhat barren now; still, it is not without some vegetation, and probably in former days, when the rainfall was larger, and the drainage from the mountains descended gradually, instead of sweeping every thing before it by a flood as at the present time, it would have afforded excellent pasturage.

BATTLE OF REPHIDIM.   419

The usual road from this plain to Jebel Músa is that by the Pass of Badera and Wady Mokatteb into Wady Feiran. This pass would hardly allow of the passage of wagons, and it would also lead the children of Israel past the mines of Wady Mughárah, which, as some tablets of hieroglyphics still existing there describe, formed at that time a strong Egyptian military position. It may naturally be supposed that Moses would avoid taking so disorganized and encumbered a body as the Israelites then were into the presence of an armed force of their old enemies, and hence would avoid passing near the mines; and this, too, is an argument against their having followed the northern route by Serábit-el-Khádim, which was also at that time an Egyptian settlement. The circumstances of the case, therefore, and the character of the ground, both lead to the opinion that their course lay down the whole length of the plain of Murkhah, and then up Wady Feiran. This wady presents a level bed up which wagons might be driven without the slightest difficulty. It is somewhat confined in parts by the surrounding mountains, but opens out here and there so as to present admirable positions for encampments. It is impossible to identify in any way the stations of Dophkah and Alush, which are merely mentioned by name in the Bible. There are no existing names in the Peninsula which correspond with them; but they may be placed somewhere in Wady Feiran, or Wady es Sheikh, up which the children of Israel must have marched to Mount Sinai.

Rephidim, the spot where the battle with the Amalekites was fought, presents more definite prospects of identification, for, although we have no description given of it, we may yet gather from the history of the battle certain features connected with it. The position of this spot is, however, the only point in connection with the route of the children of Israel on which there was any division of opinion among the members of the survey expedition. We were all thoroughly agreed as to the route followed, and were also so far agreed with regard to the position of Rephidim, that we were convinced that the battle must have been fought at one of *two* places; either in Wady Feiran, a short distance below the spot where Wady Aleyat runs into it from Jebel Serbal, or at the narrow pass of El Watiyeh in Wady es Sheikh. I myself held to the latter opinion; the other members of the expedition were in favor of the former.

My reasons for arriving at the conclusion that the pass of El Watiyeh marks the site of the battle of Rephidim are, first, its nearness to Jebel Músa, from which it is distant only about twelve miles, and the Bible apparently speaks of Rephidim as within a day's journey of Mount Sinai, Exodus xix. 2, Numbers xxxiii. 15; secondly, my belief that all the requirements of the battle are to be found there. The pass consists of a narrow defile about three hundred yards in length, and from forty to sixty yards in breadth, with a level bed, but enclosed on either side by lofty perpendicular rocks.

A very remarkable line of precipitous granite mountains stretches across the centre of the Peninsula from the head of Wady Hibran, and presents an imposing barrier to an invading force. In this line of mountains are found only three passes, the most eastern being that of El Watiyeh, which affords an easy road, while the two western passes of Nukb Howa and Wady T'lah are too narrow and rugged to allow even a laden camel to pass without great difficulty. They are altogether out of the question for wagons, which evidently were used by the Israelites, since they formed a portion of the offering of the princes at the dedication of the tabernacle (Numbers vii. 3). This natural barrier defends on the north the high and well-watered central group of mountains which includes Jebel Músa, and the holding of the passes by the Amalekites would then secure to them the most fertile portion of the whole Peninsula.

It appears to me that the Amalekites, having heard of the miraculous passage of the Israelites through the Red Sea, and of the death of Pharaoh and his host, would be anxious to avoid, if possible, a collision with these invaders of their country, and would therefore act on the defensive rather than go forth to attack them. This being the case, they would probably intrench themselves behind some strong position, and await their approach. The mountain-barrier which I have described presents a most suitable line of defence, and behind this I believe that the Amalekites assembled; those who inhabited Jebel Serbal, and other more northerly districts, retiring thither with their flocks. They may have hoped that Moses would not lead his people so far south; but, if he did, they occupied the position which of all others could most easily be held against an overwhelming force, for the battle would necessarily be confined almost entirely to the pass, and, if conquered, the eastern valleys would afford a safe way of retreat.

The features of the ground at El Watiyeh agree well with the short account which is given us of the battle of Rephidim. There is a large plain destitute of water for the encampment of the Israelites; a conspicuous hill on the north side of the defile commanding the battle-ground and presenting a bare cliff, such as we may suppose the rock to have been which Moses struck; and another large open tract of country on the south of the pass for the encampment of the Amalekites, with abundance of water within easy reach. Curiously enough, at this very spot at the foot of the hill on which Moses sat, if this be Rephidim, the Arabs point out a rock which they call "the seat of the prophet Moses." I do not attach much importance to either Arab or monastic traditions, but it is singular to find such a tradition at this spot.

Captain Wilson states his reasons for placing the site of Rephidim in Wady Feiran to be as follows: 1. He does not consider it necessary to place Rephidim within one day's march of Mount Sinai, since he thinks that, in Exodus xix. 2, there is an indication of a break in the march of the Israelites, the operations of "pitching in the wilderness" and "encamping before the mount" being separate and distinct.

2. Believing that the Amalekites would probably come out to oppose the march of the invaders of their country, he holds that the position in Wady Feiran would for military reasons be more naturally selected as the point of attack. 3. Mr. Palmer has succeeded in bringing to light an Arab tradition, which places the rock, from which Moses brought water in Wady Feiran, at a spot called Hesy el Khattatin, not far below the position assigned by the earliest Christian tradition to Rephidim.

Captain Wilson and the other members of the expedition consider Jebel Tahûnah, which is situated opposite the mouth of Wady Aleyat, to be the hill on which Moses sat while Aaron and Hur supported his arms as he overlooked the battle. The churches and chapels on the summit and sides of this hill evidently mark it as a very sacred spot in the eyes of the old inhabitants of the city of Paran; and I have little doubt that this was believed to be the site of Rephidim, when Serbal, as was once certainly the case, was held to be the traditional Mount Sinai; but its distance from Jebel Mûsa, about twenty-five miles even by the most direct road, seems to me to prove that the site of the battle must be looked for at a nearer point to that mountain. I may add, that Captain Wilson and Captain Palmer both acknowledge the value of the pass of El Watiyeh as a strong military position that could be held with ease against a large force, and would certainly place the site of Rephidim there, if not at Wady Feiran. As I have before stated, we are all quite agreed with regard to the route followed by the children of Israel in the march to Sinai, and this is the only point on which we differ.

A more southerly route than that by Wady Feiran has been proposed by some travellers. It has been said that the children of Israel might have continued down the coast plains until they reached Wady Hibran. Having, however, several times followed that route, I can pronounce it most improbable, if not actually impossible. It would involve a considerable circuit by which nothing could be gained; and the pass at the head of Wady Hibran is a very rocky and difficult one for a large and much-encumbered body of people.

My readers will have gathered, from the description which I have given of the various routes through the Peninsula, how mountainous and rugged a country it is. Few countries present to the view so wild an aspect. The mountains appear heaped together in utter confusion, and they are intersected in every direction by deep valleys, which in the lapse of ages have been cut out by the winter torrents.

Were the country less mountainous, it would be impossible to speak of the roads with such precision, or to attempt to lay down any one as the most probable line of march of the children of Israel. But, being such as it is, there are absolutely no other roads leading down from Suez to Jebel Mûsa besides those which I have mentioned; for the roads can only run along the wadys and the coast.

The mountains are chiefly composed of granitic limestone, and sandstone rocks. Speaking roughly, the granite may be said to form the nucleus of the whole Peninsula; Jebel Mûsa and all the central mountains, including Jebel Serbal, being composed of different varieties of it. The limestone is chiefly confined to the Tih range and plateau, but it also occurs at Jebel Humnam and the neighboring district, and large masses of nummulitic limestone are found on the north of Jebel Serbal. The sandstone extends across the Peninsula south of Jebel Tih, separating the limestone from the granite rocks. It is remarkable for the extensive turquois-mines which were worked by the ancient Egyptians in the neighborhood of Wady Mughârah and Serâbit-el-Khâdim. Hæmatite iron, manganese, and copper ores, also appear to have been worked in the sandstone district; but the largest workings for copper I discovered in the granite near Wady Senned, about eight miles northeast of Jebel Mûsa. Here a vein of ore, which crops up to the surface, has been worked almost continuously for a distance of nearly two miles. I have found traces of the smelting of copper in Wady Shellâl, Wady Nusb, Wady Mughârah, Wady Senned, and on the coast of the Gulf of Akaba, about thirty miles north of Sherm. Iron-ore was perhaps worked at Jebel Hadid, " the Iron Mountain," about ten miles southeast of Jebel Mûsa. In Wady Gharundel also the slag from copper-smelting works has been found. Thus mining operations must have been carried on over a large area of the Peninsula; and, since the smelting of the ore must have required a great amount of fuel, it is very probable that the fertility of the country has been much decreased by the destruction of the trees for this purpose.

There are evident traces that there has been, owing to various reasons, a very considerable decrease in the amount of vegetation in the Peninsula; although even now the country is not so barren as it has generally been described. The observations of travellers on this point have been chiefly confined to a few of the main valleys and principal mountains; but it is not till one has wandered off the beaten tracks, and explored the slopes of the lower mountains and the less frequented wadys, that one can really arrive at a just estimate of the supply of water, and capabilities of the country for affording pasturage.

Long before the children of Israel marched through the wilderness, the mines were worked by the Egyptians, and the destruction of the trees was probably going on. It is hardly likely that the Israelites themselves would have passed a year in an enemy's country, knowing that they were to march onward, without adding largely to this destruction. Their need of fuel must have been great, and they would not hesitate to cut down the trees, and lay waste the gardens; and thus before they journeyed onward from Mount Sinai they may have caused a complete change in the face of the surrounding country.

It is a well-known fact that the rainfall of a country depends in a great measure upon the abundance of its trees. The destruction of the trees in Sinai has no doubt greatly diminished the rainfall, which has also been gradually lessened by the advance of the desert and decrease of cultivation on the north and northwest, whereby a large rain-making area has gradually been removed.

In consequence, too, of the mountainous character of the Peninsula of Sinai, the destruction of the trees would have a much more serious effect than would be the case in most countries. Formerly, when the mountain-sides were terraced, when garden-walls extended across the wadys, and the roots of trees retained the moisture and broke the force of the water, the terrible floods that now occur, and sweep every thing before them, were impossible.

In the winter of 1867 I witnessed one of the greatest floods that has ever been known in the Peninsula. I was encamped in Wady Feiran, near the base of Jebel Serbal, when a tremendous thunder-storm burst upon us. After little more than an hour's rain, the water rose so rapidly in the previously dry wady that I had to run for my life, and with great difficulty succeeded in saving my tent and goods; my boots, which I had not time to pick up, being washed away. In less than two hours a dry desert wady, upward of 300 yards broad, was turned into a foaming torrent from 8 to 10 feet deep, roaring and tearing down, and bearing every thing before it—tangled masses of tamarisks, hundreds of beautiful palm-trees, scores of sheep and goats, camels and donkeys, and even men, women, and children; for a whole encampment of Arabs was washed away a few miles above me. The storm commenced at five o'clock in the evening; at half-past nine the waters were rapidly subsiding, and it was evident that the flood had spent its force. In the morning a gently-flowing stream, but a few yards broad, and a few inches deep, was all that remained of it. But the whole bed of the valley was changed. Here, great heaps of bowlders were piled up, where hollows had been the day before; there, holes had taken the place of banks covered with trees. Two miles of tamarisk-wood, which was situated above the palm-groves, had been completely washed away, and upward of a thousand palm-trees swept down to the sea. The change was so great that I could not have believed it possible in so short a time, had I not witnessed it with my own eyes.

The fact is, that, in consequence of the barrenness of the mountains, the water, when a heavy storm of rain falls, runs down from their rocky sides just as it does in this country from the roofs of our houses. There is nothing in the valleys to check it, and so it gathers force almost instantaneously, and sweeps every thing before it. The monks used formerly to build walls across the gullies leading down from the mountains; they planted the wadys with fruit-trees, and made terraces for their gardens, and these checked the drainage, and let it down by degrees, so that the storms in their days must have been comparatively harmless. The Amalekites, and former inhabitants of the Peninsula, adopted probably the same means for increasing the fertility of their country.

It is interesting to find even now some traces of the ancient inhabitants. The country abounds with ruins of the old monastic times. The walls of the old cathedral of Paran are still standing. Ruined chapels and monasteries are frequently met with, and hermits seem to have established their cells far and wide over the central mountains. The tradition that a population of seven or eight thousand monks once inhabited the Peninsula is quite confirmed by these remains of their occupation. But during my wanderings in 1867 I found that there were other ruins of a much older date: houses similar in form to the "bothan," or beehive houses in Scotland, built of rough and massive stones, about 5 feet high, and 40 or 50 feet in circumference, with no windows, and one small door about 20 inches high. In the walls each successive course of stones is made to project slightly inward beyond the one below it, and so a dome is produced, the top being formed of one large slab of stone. These houses are generally found in groups, and near them are often seen the ruins of tombs—circles of massive stones

—similar to those which in England and Scotland are called Druids' circles.

Of course, it is impossible to say with certainty that these are Amalekite ruins; but they agree exactly with what we should expect to find of the buildings of such a people. They are of the oldest form of architecture which is known to us; and they evidently were made by a large and powerful people who inhabited the Peninsula at a very early period. The Amalekites are the only nation of antiquity of whose existence in that country we have any record. Their buildings, then, we believe them to be; and, if we are right in doing so, they go far to prove this interesting fact, that the Amalekites were to some extent an agricultural as well as a pastoral people, for in two or three spots I have found evident traces of gardens in connection with these ruins.

It is even possible that some of the circles of stones, many of which are fifteen, thirty, and even more than one hundred yards in diameter, may mark the spots where the children of Israel buried their dead. The ruins of an Egyptian temple remain, and tablets of hieroglyphics, which the kings of Egypt caused to be inscribed upon the rocks to mark the progress of their mining operations long before the time of the Exodus, are still almost as perfect as the day on which they were made. Why, then, should not some relics of the march of the Israelites be found? If any heaps of stones or burial-enclosures were made by them, they surely must remain, unless the storms have swept them away. There is, however, no mark by which to recognize such relics of the past. There is nothing to tell the history of many a huge stone, which has certainly stood there for thousands of years, but whether raised by an Israelite or an Amalekite, or even some more ancient race, remains unknown. One can but look, and wonder.

Traditions of the passage of the children of Israel through the country are common enough. Many, no doubt, are merely of monkish origin, yet some appear to have been handed down from far earlier times. But these traditions are extremely vague. They seem, indeed, to prove that the country is the wilderness of Sinai, but they prove nothing more. It is to the natural features of the desert that we must alone look for any help in following the steps of the chosen people. Even the ancient names, which generally cling so long and closely to a country, appear to have been lost here. There is not a single name of any one of the roads to Mount Sinai that bears any resemblance to the names of the encampments as recorded in the Pentateuch, unless it be " Wady el Esh, ' the valley ' of the nest ; " which seems, after all, not a very probable corruption of Alush.

The Sinaitic inscriptions have been supposed by some to have actually been the work of the children of Israel during their wanderings in the desert. The fact, however, that bilingual inscriptions, Greek and Sinaitic, are found, is alone sufficient to prove the fallacy of such a theory. But, by the help of these bilingual inscriptions, Mr. Palmer has been able to read with ease and certainty the Sinaitic character, and he has found that the inscriptions consist mainly of detached sentences, for the most part proper names, with such introductory formulæ as Oriental people have from time immemorial been accustomed to prefix to their composition, such as " Peace be with him," or, " May he be remembered." Christian signs and symbols are also frequently connected with the Sinaitic inscriptions; and there appear to be good reasons for believing that the greater number of them were made about the second or third centuries of our era, and that the date of the very earliest cannot be prior to the second century before Christ. If, however, some interesting theories and statements of former travellers have been upset by the more careful and accurate examination which has been made of the Peninsula of Sinai by the Ordnance Survey, this at least has been firmly established—that the physical conditions of the country are such as to render it quite possible that the events recorded in the book of Exodus occurred there ; a fact which has been denied by more than one writer. It is wonderful how apparent difficulties melt away as one's acquaintance with the country increases.

The route of the Israelites has not indeed been laid down with absolute certainty, but much light has undoubtedly been thrown upon it by the explorations that have been made; and I may add, that not a single member of the expedition returned home without feeling more firmly convinced than ever of the truth of that sacred history which he found illustrated and confirmed by the natural features of the desert. The mountains and valleys, the very rocks, barren and sun-scorched as they now are, seem to furnish evidences, which none who behold them can gainsay, that this was that "great and terrible wilderness" through which Moses, under God's direction, led His people.

INDEX.

Abd al-Malek, 244.
Abel, or Abil, 348.
Abu Zany, 267.
Acra, 185, 210, 237.
Adullam, 177.
Ai, 365.
Aiha Temple, 308.
Ain. *See* Fountain.
Ain Hershah Temple, 308.
Altar of burnt-offerings, 161, 247.
Amûd, Wady, 274.
Anselm, 154.
Antonia. *See* Tower.
Antoninus, 268, 298.
Aqueducts and canals, 8, 11, 14, 15, 18-20, 23, 69, 72, 80, 96, 100, 128, 133, 139, 140, 176, 182, 199.
Arak el Emir, 304, 313, 315.
Arbela (Irbid), 277.
Architectural styles, 312-318.
Arculf, 22, 251, 280, 298.
Armenian convent, 8.
Arub, Wady, 19.
Asneric, 216.
Asiatic Venus, 328.
Auranitis, 323.
Ayûn, 348.

Baalbec, 304.
Baal Samin, 327.
Banias, 341.

Baris, 236.
Basalt of the Sea of Galilee, 266.
Bashan, 322.
Bathaniyeh, or Batanæa, 323.
Batihah, 264, 284.
Beitin, or Bethel, 365.
Benjamin of Tudela, 251.
Beth Mokad, 161, 257.
Bethshan, or Beisan, 350.
Bethesda. *See* Pools.
Bethsaida, 153, 267, 285, 292.
Bethzatha, 9.
Bezetha, 9.
Bir. *See* Wells.
Birket. *See* Pools.
Boaheddin, 273.
Bordeaux Pilgrim, 153, 154, 236, 250.
Bosra, Kings of, 324.
Bridge, supposed, near S. E. Angle, 117.
Brocardus, 154, 251.
Burj Laklah, 125.
Byar, Wady, 19, 289.

Candlestick, seven-branched, 268.
Capernaum, 265, 266, 292.
Cartography, 22.
Castle of Antonia, 235. *See also* Tower.
Cavern in front of Triple Gate, 121, 230, 233.
Cemetery, excavation at British, 218.
Chel, 247.

Chorazin, 270, 292.
Church of the Holy Sepulchre, 9, 22, 209.
Church of the Resurrection, or Anastasis, 8.
Church, English, 209.
Church of St. Etienne, 216.
Church of St. Anne, 9, 10, 22, 150, 151, 153.
Church of the tomb of the Virgin, 125.
Cisterns and tanks, 7, 13, 15, 16, 18, 21, 24, 70, 75, 78, 81, 89, 143, 159, 182.
Citadel or Tower of David, 8, 22, 23, 209.
Constantine, 8.
Coracinus, 275, 293, 294.

Dan, Laish, or Tel el-Kadi, 345.
David, 69, 236, 245.
Débris, character of, 44.
Deir-el-Ashayir, 309.
Dothan, or Dotan, 360.
Drains, 79, 88, 138, 143, 145, 172, 231.
Drainage, 22, 73.

Ebal, 361.
Ecce Homo Arch, 153.
Endor, 357.
En Rogel, 239.
Eusebius, 153, 287, 298.
Epiphanius, 268, 298.
Er Rohebeh, 335.
Esdraelon, 355.
Et-Tel, 284, 365.

Fik, 265, 288.
Florus, 243.
Fountains and springs:
  Ain Ayshch, 267.
  Ain Barideh, 279.
  Ain el Luz'h, or Fountain of the Almond, 201.
  Ain Etan, 19.
  Ain et-Tin, 272, 293.
  Ain et-Tabigah, 271, 293.

Fountains and springs—*continued*.
  Ain Mudawarah, or round Fountain, 271, 293.
  Ain Zany, 267.
  At the Church of the Flagellation, 154.
  Fons Sion, 23.
  Saracenic Fountains, 19.
  Sealed Fountain, 19, 184.
  Fountain of the Virgin, or Ain Umm ed-Deraj, 12, 15, 17, 20, 58, 186, 187, 239.
Fresco, 137.

Gadara, 289.
Galilee, Sea of, 263.
Gamala, 265, 288.
Gates of city:
  Damascus, 6, 150, 216.
  Dung, 7, 73, 96, 227.
  Jaffa, 6, 8, 17, 20, 72.
  Sion, 7.
  Bab az-Zahiré, or Herod's Gate, 7, 130, 132.
  St. Stephen's or Bab Sitti Miriam, 7, 9, 23, 125, 126, 133–139, 150, 153.
Gates of the Haram, or Sanctuary:
  Single, 7, 93, 103, 176.
  Passage under Single, 102.
  Double or Huldah, 7, 13, 91, 179, 231, 249.
  Triple, 7, 91, 103, 176.
  Golden Gate, 7, 10, 18, 119, 144.
  Column in front of Golden Gate, 121.
  Barclay's Gate of Mahomet, or Prophet's Gate, 12, 24, 79, 83, 84, 86, 252.
  Bab el-Magháribe or Moor's Gate, 12, 86.
  Bab el-Mathara, or Gate of the Bath, 13, 89.
  Bab es-Silsileh, or Gate of the Chain, 17.
  Bab el-Hytta, 152, 163.

Gates of the Haram, or Sanctuary—
    continued.
    Bab en-Nazir, or Gate of the In-
        spector, 175.
    Bab el-Aten, 152.
    Gates into the Parbar, or Suburb,
        60, 86.
Gate Gennath, 9, 213.
Gate Tadi, 160, 161, 242, 247, 257.
Gate Nitsots, 160, 247, 257.
Gate-way in Secret Passage, 72.
Gaulanitis, 321.
Gennesareth, 264, 271.
Gergesa, 264, 269, 287.
Gerizim, 361.
Ghassan, 334.
Ghuweir, 264, 274, 293.
Gilboa, 357, 360.
Glass, 381.

Haman, Wady, 274.
Hamman-esh Shefa. See Well.
Hamrath, 326.
Haram esh-Shereef, or Noble Sanc-
    tuary, 7, 9, 11, 19, 86.
    Character of masonry of the walls,
        303.
    North side, 147.
    South wall, 91.
    East wall, 12, 105.
    West wall, 58, 89.
    N. E. Angle, 10, 124, 132, 140, 142,
        143.
    Passage under N. E. Angle, 126.
    S. E. Angle, 11, 12, 107, 117.
    Jars found at S. E. Angle, 109, 119.
    S. W. Angle, 12.
    N. W. Angle, 10.
    Great course of stones, 92, 97.
    Kubbet es-Sakhra, or Dome of the
        Rock, sometimes called improp-
        erly the Mosque of Omar, 7,
        11, 14, 22, 146, 170, 172, 174,
        242, 244.
    Platform of ditto, 130, 150.

Haram esh-Shereef—continued.
    Phœnician characters (supposed)
        on walls, 108, 111, 113, 115,
        119, 130, 143, 247.
    Bir el-Arwah, 12, 160, 174.
    Dome of the Roll, 161, 247.
    Dome of St. George, 174.
    The cup, 246.
    Stoa Basilica, great Southern Por-
        tico, or Royal Cloisters, 7, 13,
        73, 104, 179, 252.
    Solomon's Stables, 12, 176, 234,
        251.
    Cradle of our Lord Jesus, 178, 181.
    Mosque of el-Aksa, 7, 18, 22, 167.
    Tomb of Aaron's sons, 168.
    Standing-place of Elias, 168.
    Robinson's Arch, 13, 15, 60, 72,
        96, 242.
    Mosque of El-Burak, 12, 86.
    Wailing-place, 60, 87, 89, 98, 131,
        140, 142, 247.
    Wilson's Arch and Viaduct, 14,
        19, 23, 58, 63, 65, 85, 96.
    Masonic Hall, 66.
    Secret Passage, 70.
Harat ad-Dawayeh, 234.
Harat esh-Sharaf, 209.
Hattin, 264, 265, 278.
Hauran, 319.
    Architecture of Hauran, 329.
Hazor or Hara, 350.
Hazor or Enhazor, 352.
Hebron, 29, 304.
Hermon, 263, 344.
Herod, 7, 69, 84, 91, 131, 176, 179,
    222, 236, 241–254, 323, 324, 327.
Herod Agrippa, 134, 324, 327.
Hesban, 33.
Hezekiah, 23, 176, 185, 236
    Pool of. See Pools.
Hibbariyeh, 308.
Hinnom, 5, 6, 15, 239.
Hippicus, 6, 8.
Hosh Bezbizi, 154.

House of Baptism, 156, 257.
Huleh, or Waters of Merom, 348.
Hukkok, 352.
Hunin, 348.
Husn Niha, 307.

Idumean Princes, 324.
Iturea, 323.

Jacob's Well, 362.
Jebel Sès, 338.
Jebel Yermuk, 352.
Jerash, 310.
Jerusalem:
    Ordnance Survey, 3.
    Description of the site, 5.
    Walls and gates, 6.
    "Mezzeh" and "melekeh" limestone, 7.
    Haram esh-Sherif, Mosque el-Aksa, Kubbet es-Sakhra, 7.
    Various theories as to the site of the Temple, 7.
    Tower of David, 8.
    Church of the Holy Sepulchre, 8.
    Gate Gennath, 9.
    Bezetha, 9.
    Description of the Haram, 10.
    Water supply, 14.
    Rainfall, 20.
    Sanitary condition, 21.
    Drainage, 22.
    Cartography, 22.
Jordan, 347.
Jotham, 222.

Kadesh, or Kedes, 349.
Kakûn, 74.
Kalet Husn, 288.
Kalat Jalûd, 8, 235.
Kalat Ibn Ma'an, 275.
Kalybeh, 332.
Kedron, 6, 9, 10, 14, 15, 22, 105, 199, 239.
Kerazeh, 270.
Kharbet-el-Beida, 336.

Khureibeh, 273.
Khureitun, 177.
Khan Minyeh, 263, 271, 273, 293.
Khersa, 264, 286.
Kureibeh, 349.
Kurn Hattin, 278.

Ledja, 321.
Lifta, 50, 206, 238.
Lightfoot, 170, 239, 257.
Lubieh, 265, 278.

Machpelah, 31.
Manasseh, 222.
Manna, Pot of, 269.
Marinus Sanutus, 23.
Mariamne, 6.
Maundeville, 173.
Mezzeh, 7.
Melekeh, 7.
Megiddo, 358.
Mejir ed Din, 69, 161, 175, 251.
Moriah, 6, 7, 11, 237, 245.
Mejdel, or Magdala, 264, 275.
Merom. See Huleh.
Moabite Stone, 389.
    Discovery of, 390.
    First translation, 394.
    Latest ditto, 396.
    Prof. Schlottmann on the, 396.
    Mr. Deutsch on the, 401.
Muristan, 209, 213.

Nabathæan Princes, 324.
Nablûs, or Shechem, 362.
Nazareth, 353.
Nehemiah, 185, 218, 236.
Nemara, 359.
Nitsots. See Gate.

Objects, miscellaneous, found in excavations, 384.
Olivet, 238.
Ophel, 222, 237.
Ophel wall, 116, 224, 232.
    Extra tower on ditto, 228.
Oulam, 327.

Palace of Solomon, 84, 91, 222, 249.
Palace of Hezekiah, 236.
Palmyra, 305.
Paschal Lamb sculptured, 268.
Passargadae, 303.
Pavements, 77, 94, 98.
Persepolis, 310.
Phasaelus, 6, 8.
Pompey, 237, 242, 247.
Pontius Pilate, 19, 183.
Pools:
  Siloam, 17, 18, 185, 239.
  Near Tombs of the Kings, 17, 18.
  Of Hezekiah, 17, 18.
  Bethseda, or Birket Israil, 9, 10, 17, 18, 124, 127, 129, 130, 132, 134, 139, 147, 150–156.
  Near Jaffa Gate, 17.
  Near Gate of the Chain, 17.
  Near Church of St. Anne, 10, 17.
  Of El-Burak, 13, 17, 58, 64.
  Of Solomon, at Urtas, 14, 19, 174, 182.
  Birket Mamilla, 17, 18, 184, 185.
  Birket es-Sultan, 17, 19, 185.
  Birket Sitti Miriam, 17, 125.
  Gihon, 184, 185.
  Pool of the Bath, 209.
  Bath of the Sultan, 219.
Porch of Solomon, 237, 247.
Pottery, 109, 119, 368.
  Phœnician, 369.
  Greco-Phœnician, 370.
  Roman, 376.
  Christian, 377.
  Arabic, 381.
Psephinus, 8.

Qanatha, 324.
Qennawât, 326.

Rainfall, 20.
Ramah and Ramch, 352.
Rejm and Ridjmah, 357.
Rephaim, Plain of, 20, 23, 184.

Roofs, 85.
Rubudiyeh, Wady, 274.

Sæwulf, 154, 251.
Safa, 321, 335.
Saida, 135.
Sarcophagus, 237, 386.
Sculptured slab, 234.
Seal of Haggai, 95, 98, 386.
Scilûn, or Shiloh, 364.
Semakh, 265, 286.
Serai, 150.
Sês, 338.
Sewer, 73, 148.
Shahbeh, 329.
Sheebem. *See* Nablûs.
Siah, 326, 328.
Siloam, 6, 16, 20.
Sinai, 403.
  Mode of travelling, 404.
  Survey of, 407.
  Position of, 408, 412.
  Wilderness of Sin, 418.
  Battle of Rephidim, 420.
  Former fertility, 424.
  Ancient inhabitants, 426.
  Old traditions, 427.
Sion, or Zion, 185, 237.
Sisters of Sion, 9, 11, 21, 25, 151, 175
Solomon, 84, 119.
Soueidah, 325, 328.
Springs. *See* Fountains.
Strato's Tower, 156.
Streets of David, 63, 69.
  Bab Hytta, 124.
  Tarik Bab Sitti Miriam, 152.
  Via Dolorosa, 150, 152, 156.
  El Wad, or the Valley, 209, 219.
  Christian Street, 210.
  of the Bazaar, 210.
Suwaineh, 74.

Tabigah, 269, 271.
Tabor, 355.
Tacitus, 174.
Tudi. *See* Gate.

INDEX. 435

Takeyeh, 209.
Tanks. *See* Cisterns.
Tarichew, 282.
Tel Hum, 267.
Tel Lareyné, 273.
Temple (*see* also Haram), 7, 24, 84, 91, 94, 160, 172, 173, 176, 241-254.
Templar's Cross, 217.
Tesseræ, 145.
Theatre of Hadrian, 231.
Thelthatha, 307.
Tiberias (Tabariyeh), 265, 280.
Titus, 83, 176, 242, 283.
Tombs, 119, 135, 312-316, 325, 326.
Tower at N. E. Angle, 130, 137.
Tower of Antonia, 130, 152, 156, 172, 176, 236, 341-354.
Tower of David. *See* Citadel.
Tower, supposed, at S. E. Angle, 117.
Tower of Hananeel, 126.
Tower of Meah, 126.
Tower of Maidens, 216.
Trachonitis, 323.
Tyropœon, 6, 8, 11, 13, 15, 92, 94, 97.

Umm Keis, or Gadara, 289.
Umm Ez-Zeitûn, 332.

Upper City, 6, 8, 240.
Urtas, Wady. *See* Pools of Solomon.

Valley of Doves, 264.
Vespasian, 281.
Via Dolorosa, 150, 152. *See* Streets.

Walls, 8, 237-254.
  Second Wall, 212.
Wells :
  Bir el-Arwah, or Well of the Souls.
    See under Haram.
  Bir Eyûb, or Well of Joab, 6, 15, 16, 20, 200.
  Well of the Steps, 200.
  Hamman esh-Shefa, 15, 20, 58.
  Of the Leaf, 162, 167, 169.
William of Tyre, 251.
Willibald, 299.

Xystus, 249.

Zaanain, 349.
Zion. *See* Sion.
Zehwele, 239.
Zoheleth, 239.
Zerin, or Jezreel, 158.

THE END.

www.ingramcontent.com/pod-product-compliance
Lightning Source LLC
Chambersburg PA
CBHW020836020526
44114CB00040B/801